AMERICAN LAUGHTER

AMERICAN LAUGHTER

Immigrants, Ethnicity, and 1930s Hollywood Film Comedy

MARK WINOKUR

St. Martin's Press
New York

AMERICAN LAUGHTER
Copyright © 1996 by Mark Winokur

ISBN 0-312-12342-6

Library of Congress Cataloging-in-Publication Data

Winokur, Mark.
    American laughter: immigrants, ethnicity, and 1930s Hollywood
film comedy / Mark Winokur.
        p. cm.
    Includes bibliographical references and index.
    ISBN 0-312-12342-6
    1. Comedy films—United States—History and criticism.
2. Minorities in motion pictures. 3. Popular culture—United
States. 4. Minorities in the motion picture industry. I. Title.
PN1995.9.C55W52 1995
791.43'617—dc20   95-12030
                                                    CIP

Book Design by Acme Art, Inc.

First Edition: February 1996
10 9 8 7 6 5 4 3 2 1

PERMISSIONS

The portrait stills of Fatty Arbuckle, Adolph Menjou, the Marx Brothers with Minnie Marx, and Myrna Loy are reproduced with the permission of Culver Pictures. Picasso's "Head of a Bull," Leger's "Chaplin," Icart's "Le Cocktail," and Paul Colin's "Josephine Baker" are reprinted with the permission of the Artists Rights Society (ARS) New York / Paris. The photograph of Louis B. Mayer is reproduced by the permission of *The Los Angeles Times Syndicate*. The Yiddish Art Theatre still is reproduced with the permission of The Billy Rose Theatre Collection of The New York Public Library for the Performing Arts, Astor, Lenox and Tilden Foundations. The Massaguer drawing of Chaplin is reproduced with the permission of *The New Yorker*. "Chaplin and Hitler" is reproduced with the permission of the Münchner Stadtmuseum. "A Study in Contrasts" and "Chaplin at Play and at Work" are reproduced with the permission of Scribner's. The latter two illustrations, and the rest of the Chaplin stills, are reproduced with the kind permission of the Roy Export Company Establishment. All stills related to the production of *Duck Soup*, the extended excerpt from *Duck Soup*, and the still from *Cleopatra* are reproduced with the permission of Universal City Studios and MCA, Inc. The photograph of the Hollywood party is reproduced with the permission of *Life Magazine* and Bert Granet. The *Ambassador Bill* still is reproduced with permission of Twentieth Century Fox Film Corporation. *The Bohemian Girl* still is reproduced with permission of Larry Harmon Pictures Corporation, Hollywood, CA 90028 USA. The illustration of the hobbleskirt is reprinted with the kind permission of the Fashion Research Centre, and Museum of Costume, Bath. "Salome" is reprinted with permission of the Städtische Galerie im Lenbachhaus, München. Stills from *Ham and Eggs at the Front*, *Crimson City*, *A Connecticut Yankee*, and *The Thin Man* are reproduced with the permission of the Turner Entertainment Co. The Myrna Loy article is reproduced with the very kind permission of *The Boston Herald*. A portion of chapter 4 appeared in earlier form as "Improbable Ethnic Hero: William Powell and the Transformation of Ethnic Hollywood," *Cinema Journal* 27, no. 1 (5-22), and appears in this volume by permission of the University of Texas Press.

This book is dedicated to
Katherine Eggert and Anne Buccheri Winokur,
daughters of old and new immigrants.

CONTENTS

Acknowledgments ix

Introduction: Theorizing Ethnicity and Immigration 1

1. Connections between American Literary Humor
   and Film Comedy 23

2. Charles Chaplin and the Comedy of Transformation 75

3. The Marx Brothers and the Search for the Landsman 125

4. Unlikely Ethnic Heroes: William Powell, Myrna Loy,
   and the Fantasy of Assimilation 179

5. Conclusion 235

Notes 239

Index 297

ACKNOWLEDGMENTS

I would like to thank first and foremost Katherine Eggert, a scholar without whose inspiration, material help, and moral support this book might never have been finished. I would also like to thank those scholars whose input over the years has been invaluable: Micahel Rogin, Lester Friedman, Richard Hutson, Abdul JanMohamed, David Lloyd, David Desser, William Nestrick, Ernest Callenbach, and Merle Bachman. A special thanks to Richard Onorato for getting me into this fine mess. I would like to thank James Welsh and James Palmer for encouraging me to publish my first faltering pieces in *Literature/Film Quarterly*. Thanks to Kurt Eggert, Paul Eggert, Clare Pastore, and Stacey Byrnes, who provided material comfort during several research trips to Los Angeles. Many thanks for the courtesy of the following people at various archives, libraries, studios, newspapers, and similar institutions: Jill Frisch, Rebecca Herrera, Nancy Cushing-Jones, Andrew F. Costello, Richard Rynes, Annie Auerbach, Elizabeth M. Weisberg, Janet Lorenz, Dr. Travitsky, Briggitte Kueppers, Cathy Lendech, and especially Mrs. Pamela Paumier, whose kindness is both casual and occult. I would like to thank the National Endowment for the Humanities, Rhodes College, and Dickinson College for their institutional support, and especially Dean Marshall McMahon of Rhodes College.

—◆—

INTRODUCTION
THEORIZING ETHNICITY AND IMMIGRATION

GENERAL CRITICISM AND THEORY

In 1940, near the end of the era with which this book is concerned, Foster Rhea Dulles asserted in *America Learns to Play* that at the end of the nineteenth century Americans began to experience recreation in a new way as the puritan work ethic was supplanted by the new machine age, whose human face was that of the recently arrived Eastern and Southern European new immigrants. (Dulles was not very interested in trans-Pacific migration.)[1] Dulles revised the traditional notion of the melting pot to create a somewhat more active cultural role for the immigrant. In perfectly hegemonic fashion, he had both discovered and circumscribed the contributions immigrants had made to American culture. These included the development of the "lower" pastimes—spectator sports, the movies, vaudeville[2]—that were not invented by these immigrants but invented *for* them, to render endurable the machine for which they provided the fuel.[3] At best, immigrants were viewed as having contributed the idea of leisure to a culture obsessed with work.

Dulles's insistence on America as an essentially binary system in which a dominant culture is opposed (or complemented) by a tardy, subordinate upstart was typical of the cultural analysis of this era. Puritan-derived, male, white, Anglo-Saxon Protestantism had become more than even the cultural arbiter that contemporary Frankfurt School criticism asked of any hegemony (more, even, than the "arbiter elegantium" the Frankfurt School believed itself to be): it became the omphalos, the central *mythomoteur,* the originary culture out of which all other cultures arose and to which they returned. Various ethnic minorities were infantilized as mere special interest groups seeking to assert their importance in a culture already characterized as stable and monolithic. Dulles described an Anglo-Puritan culture that offered itself as the reality principle to all other cultures while maintaining its oppositional stance against all comers.[4] The immediate predecessors of Dulles were sociologists such as Robert Parks, who documented the assimilation and amalgamation of immigrants into the mainstream in the first quarter of the century; but this bipolar vision had its origins in an Enlightenment-era British version of imperialism and assimilation (second-class citizenship and "orientalizing"), which was itself in part modeled on the extension of classical Roman citizenship to the provinces.[5]

Cultural theorizing after Dulles and until the 1980s has been more insidious in that it avoids defining Puritan-derived culture as the superior ethnic category. Rather, it considers Anglo-Puritan culture the founding half of a binary opposition the other side of which is every other reactive cultural influence. Dulles's argument had at least the merit of acknowledging that Anglo-Puritan culture, though eternal, grudgingly accommodated itself to changed circumstances. In most subsequent criticism, however, Anglo-Puritan culture not only has a moral imperative, it becomes the very ground against which any other influence is perceived or measured. The classic Marxist critique of cultural "hegemonies," some of whose features I shall modify and use in this book, still employs this binary opposition even more insidiously through its assertion of an important half-truth: that minority groups are complicit in their own oppression.[6] Such an assertion does not offer much room for maneuvering by minorities, except through "critiques," "resistances," and "subversions," whose effects are often difficult to detect. This critique of hegemony is as binary as Dulles's interpretation: there is the possibility for some change, but all "constituting" of culture is on one side; immigrants and ethnics revise rather than compose culture.[7] Wayne Franklin is worth quoting at length as an early critic of this line of thinking:

> I cannot support the arguments of various recent writers who would see the Pilgrim and Puritan plots (both announced and endured) as the definitive, or even predominant, means by which American identity and nationhood were achieved. This kind of argument is the latest in a chain of mythologizing efforts. . . . It attempts to unify American life by locating *the* beginning point of a single converging action, and then by interpreting subsequent experience (or rather those parts of it which may be made to fit the assumed plot) in light of that presumably central action. . . . We traditionally leave out far too much in asserting our own schemes over

the past. People and events that depart from the center (or never were there in the first place) are made to seem less important by our exclusionary rhetoric.[8]

The theoretical dismissal or neglect of the constitutive quality of immigrant/ethnic culture, so at odds with the historical record, thus supports the group that has become defined as the dominant culture. This is the standard exercise of any cultural hegemony. The group that sets cultural standards at the same moment demonstrates and conceals that power by denying alternate identities in other groups and by denying that such a denial is anything other than a natural function of society. Defining differences through antagonism between ethnic groups is rather standard practice in sociology and ethnology.[9] As cultural critique, however, this unself-conscious dichotomization is questionable practice. As Barbara Christian asserts, "Many of us have never conceived of ourselves only as somebody's *other*."[10]

Some contemporary cultural theory has attempted to collapse this bipolarity by asserting that it resulted from a one-sided representation of history: the Virgilian account of Rome as descended from Troy; the Renaissance representation of London as New Troy. One strain of this criticism has been a kind of archaeology of the unrepresentable. Cultural theoreticians from Louis Althusser to Fredric Jameson treat the question of the specific relation of the cultural artifact to the historical truth:[11] how can one account for the disparity between history and its representation—or *lack* of representation—by hegemonic groups that have a stake in maintaining an "official story"? At a certain moment in his career, Fredric Jameson stated the general problem—and the necessity of addressing it—in its most accessible form: "It is in detecting the traces of that uninterrupted narrative, in restoring to the surface of the text the repressed and buried reality of this fundamental history, that the doctrine of a political unconscious finds its function and its necessity."[12] Terry Eagleton converts Jameson's perception of a "repressed and buried reality" into a critical mandate. Criticism's task, he writes, "is to show the text as it cannot know itself, to manifest those conditions of its making . . . about which it is necessarily silent. . . . [I]ts very self-knowledge is the construction of a self-oblivion."[13]

Noting the difficulty in American culture of representing the ethnic, historians have derived a number of possible, practical consequences from the problematics of political nonrepresentability. For some writers, the absence of ethnic or subculture representation is lamentable but correctable (for example, Lary May in *Screening out the Past;* Orlando Patterson in *Slavery and Social Death*).[14] For others, depending on the critic's particular allegiance or ethnic neurosis, the absence of subculture representation is proof of either the sterility of the mainstream culture (for example, Michel Foucault in, say, *The History of Sexuality*[15]), or the impotence and sterility of ethnic cultures (for example, John Murray Cuddihy in *The Ordeal of Civility*[16]).

For film scholars, the issue becomes this: how do the events on the film screen explicate, and how are they explicated by, events on the larger, cultural stage, when both arenas are defined as much by omission as by praxis? How does one relate (filmic) representation to its referent(s), in this case the new-immigrant[17] *ethnie*? My first assumption will be that the absence of the immigrant and ethnic as fully fleshed characters and lead players in the American film industry, and the substitution instead of various stereotypes, new and old, about ethnicity, should interest any "reader" of culture who takes into account that the film medium is and has been to a great extent dominated by immigrants and children of immigrants. Elite culture's great blindness to film culture has had the same effect as its blindness to other popular culture forms: it has left a "space" for determining the meaning of a new technology that would in turn determine the meaning of its host culture.

My second assumption concerning this ethnic and immigrant absence in film representation is a standard psychoanalytic borrowing that determines the negotiations within this space: the absence of naturalistic immigrant themes constitutes a repression by and of the immigrant and the ethnic that results in a displacement of ethnic tensions onto other issues that allow these tensions to emerge in disguised form. In different ways, critics such as Louis Althusser, Terry Eagleton, Pierre Macherey, and Fredric Jameson also seek a hermeneutic that discovers value or a "privileged content in rifts and discontinuities within the work."[18] However, unlike various schools of poststructuralism that choose to elevate discontinuities as obscurely meaningful in themselves, or in their meaninglessness, the present work makes the small leap from the knowledge that films were produced by immigrants and ethnics to the assumption that the nonrepresentation of immigrants motivates the discontinuities and rifts in narrative. As in Jameson, and contrary to traditional Derridean notions of text, the assertion of the present work is that such rifts are motivated by a culturally unrepresentable experience rather than that they display the text not only to be devoid of manifest content, but also to be assigned to the illusory status of the category "meaning."[19] In short, I am asserting both that nonrepresentation is significant, and that, as the *ethnie* are repressed into nonexistence, ethnic and immigrant representation seeps through anywhere and everywhere. This will lead me, for example, to read Charles Chaplin and his tramp not as emigrés but as immigrants (chapter 2) and to read two standard representatives of

Anglo culture as ethnic protagonists (chapter 4). Like Jameson's (and Althusser's) Marxism, ethnicity and immigration serve a "mediatory" function, breaking down borders across the disciplines. Like other critics, I acknowledge the existence of hegemonic culture. However, while they insist on a preexisting culture against which subordinate cultures must resist, I am suggesting that minority groups create the particular cultural forms of that repression; the warping of both the ethnic and hegemonic cultures is always already their own. The present text is then an attempt at a hermeneutic of ethnicity and immigration and an attempt both to read the significance of these phenomena and, more importantly, to use them as tools for reading. The notion of subordinating a Marxist to an ethnic critique should make even more sense in the context of Althusser's sense of history as absent cause. Along with gender, ethnicity is one defining category of that history.

The immigrant experience has been nonrepresentable not because experience is nonrepresentable in its infinite particularity, though this may also be true. We may not, for instance, assert that because ethnics were key participants in the creation and development of a particular medium, that that medium directly reflects the experience of those ethnic filmmakers in all its particularity. (Even very conventional scholars like Neal Gabler, Lee Lourdeaux, and John Russell Taylor, while discussing the determinative Jewish, Catholic, and German Hollywood, respectively, are not generally guilty of this particular heresy.)[20] The present work is not a "celebration" of the ability of the ethnic/immigrant successfully to adapt and prosper in his/her receptive host culture. In an official culture that trusts only immigrants who can repress the visible characteristics of ethnicity, economically and socially successful immigrants will tend to be uninterested in portraying a way of being that they must repudiate, at least in their public lives. Denial of ethnicity becomes a piece of the fabric of success, of how one achieves status and recognition in American culture, and probably in all Western cultures.[21] The assimilated Irving Thalberg is unambiguously successful, while the unassimilable Louis B. Mayer, Harry Cohn, *et al.* appear ridiculous. As a result, ethnic and immigrant filmmakers of the 1920s and 1930s were encouraged to repress representations of ethnicity on the screen as in life. Such discourse as proceeds from such a source will be, in Abdul JanMohamed's and David Lloyd's phrase, the "product of damage."[22]

I will not be asserting, however, that ethnic representation is merely representation. Such assertions are trivializing and dangerous because they allow no room in discussions of hegemonic cultures for ethnic praxis. In other words, that line of cultural studies that pretends to a kind of liberation through the realization of universal appropriation (already critiqued in the observation that such liberation is impossible because also appropriated), is, despite its Marxist lineaments, probably the true inheritor of the mantle of genteel reform. My argument assumes that it matters who originates representation; it attempts to constitute ourselves "as subjects as well as objects of history . . . the makers of history and not just the objects of those who have made history until now."[23]

As a result of this emphasis on the subject, the present work is in part a psycho-analytic study of ethnicity that avoids the dualism implicit in choosing between Irving Thalberg's self-identification with the modern, industrial state on the one hand, and the popular identification of Louis B. Mayer with some more "primitive" or "atavistic" sense of tribe on the other. I am asserting that American culture has always been not ethnicity's patron but its palette. The host culture that believes itself to be making inscriptions on a tabula rasa is itself treated as a palimpsest, its own inscriptions erased and rewritten, the erasures (of previous ethnic groups) barely visible beneath the new text but accessible to analysis. Ethnicity mediates between identification with tribe and identification with technology and job because, in an urban environment, it is—almost of necessity—composed of subgroups living in close proximity at work and at home. Ethnicity acts as a kind of group ego, mediating between the old, increasingly repressed sense of tribal identification with a nation and the newer sense of identification with an increasingly repressive technological environment.[24] When immigrants arrive in the new land, they are forced to adopt a new stance in relation to their own ethnic identity, their own ego: a split identity implying a new self-irony. But, like Freud's Rome, the culture into which the old ethnicity disappears is itself profoundly defaced, erased, and rewritten. The Augustan arch now propping up a renaissance palazzo, the whole surrounded by nineteenth-century government buildings and hotels, constitute a new meaning, ontologically other than anything imagined in Heidegger's temple.

This book is more and less than a rerepresentation of the experience of immigration. I am not really interested in reproducing in any anecdotal or generalizing way the trauma of new immigration, a program so excellently accomplished by writers such as Oscar Handlin in *The Uprooted*.[25] Subscribing to Jameson's notion that formulating a collective historical experience is difficult except by detecting its traces in cultural texts, this book examines some of the most typical texts of popular culture: comedy films. This work examines some of the strategies open to the American immigrant for gaining a submerged voice with which it can de-express and de-realize itself, a non-voice that allows the immigrant an entry into the discourse about itself in mainstream culture. The survival mechanisms traced here—exclusion, assimilation, amalgamation, and acculturation—are by no means universal or exhaustive categories meant to stand for assimilation as a whole—or exclusion as a principle—among *all* ethnic groups. Moreover, the present text maintains that in the furtherance of the possibility of a benevolently pluralistic culture, universalizing the immigrant experience is undesirable. Still, one cannot avoid a generalizing tendency when going from the particular cultural artifact to general statements about immigrant experience and sensibility.[26] Some excellent books on both film and ethnology have done just this.[27] While being careful not, in the time-honored American nativist tradition, to lump the various ethnic groups together under any single syncretically biological or cultural rubric, one may assert that most immigrants have at least two experiences in common: the trauma of departing from the parent country and the trauma of adjusting to the host country. My first chapter fashions from these two experiences a tentative model, a dialectic of acclimation if not adjustment or assimilation, within which most ethnic groups may recognize some relevant dynamics.

It will be objected that though this work is "ethnological," it does not, as in the ethnological sciences, differentiate among ethnic groups or discuss one paradigmatic group. A four-fold response is possible. First, as stated, some dynamics are constant. For example, all new-immigrant groups are diaspora communities. A first generation travels to a new land, and subsequent generations must cope with the consequences of that move. There are the traumas of travel, of leaving the parent culture, and of encountering a host culture. Second, the present work does not characterize the behavior of ethnic groups as constant under all conditions: chapters 2 through 4, though not exhaustive, treat three possible responses to ascribed and self-ascribed ethnicity and immigration. Third, even sociology and ethnology texts such as Robert C. Christopher's *Crashing the Gates* are also thematized by the immigrant experience in general, rather than through any single group.[28]

The final possible response to any accusation of over-universalization is probably most historically pertinent. The present text studies the effect of ethnicity in a country and in a time when the manifestations of ethnicity were discouraged. New immigrants were encouraged to believe that relinquishing a publicly ethnic identity was the price of success. Yet even though the postwar incorporation of larger numbers of African Americans into the American middle classes was different from the incorporation of new immigrants in the 1920s and 1930s, very recent African-American criticism is beginning to take a similar line to the present work in explicating the role of African America in cinema. Thomas Cripps, in *Making Movies Black*, asserts that "movies should be seen as a pliant medium emerging from a corporate setting that was itself rent by fissures through which . . . minorities . . . have been able to exploit cultural politics at those points where momentarily shared goals invite cooperation rather than conflict. . . . [I]ts ability to 'engineer' a mentality has remained so feckless as to only 'half create the environment [it is] half created by.' "[29] Though this book is not feckless enough to attempt demonstrating this "half-creation" for all ethnic and immigrant groups, I assume that a plural population will necessitate a reciprocity in cultural influences. This reciprocity results in a nation that whatever its official culture can be only a network of heterogeneous influences, resulting, not in a center or periphery, but in Bakhtinian "dialogism."[30] As with the life of the psyche, when those influences are unconscious their importance is further enhanced.[31]

My work takes up where the ethnologist's leaves off. I wish to examine the point at which ethnicity is left behind, either by choice or through coercion, and discover the isotopic trace elements this action leaves in the hegemonic culture and the way in which the (ill-named) host culture mutates as a result.[32] In examining the point at which the characteristics of ethnicity disappear into the host culture, where difference from the host culture is erased and ethnicity appropriated, I am necessarily examining the point at which the culture is structurally implicated and so itself transformed. Like several recent books on American ethnology, such as Christopher's *Crashing the Gates,* the present work posits the move away from the Anglo-Saxon domination of American culture by immigrants and ethnics, but my argument implies about Christopher's metaphor not so much that ethnics have crashed the gates but that they designed them, built them, and are buried under them.

While this work in part locates the vanishing point of ethnicity, it also delineates the horizon of mainstream culture. In America, "dominant" or "mainstream" culture can mean only the amalgam of insecure influences that stands as if at the center of an (anthropologically defined) whole culture, as if arbiter and yardstick. The mainstream merely *includes* Anglo-American culture as another voice attempting to be heard. This mainstream is in part Roland Barthes's system of mythologies,[33] in part Ernest Gellner's "high culture,"[34] in part the official national culture, and in part Alan Trachtenberg's Anglo-American middle-culture establishment, or "middle-class paradise," at the end of the nineteenth and beginning of the twentieth century:

> Founded on a newly fashioned creed of art and learning in the service of
> Protestant virtue, it came to represent an official American version of

reality. And although that outlook crystallized in almost direct response to the turmoil and impassable gulfs accompanying industrial incorporation—the new immigrant work force, the doom of the countryside and the rise of the city . . . it sealed itself off from these realities. . . . Stock notions of the "other half" were implanted in the evolving middle-class consensus, *notions which served the negative purpose of proclaiming what the true America was not, what it must exclude or eradicate in order to preserve itself.*[35] (my emphasis)

Finally, mainstream culture is the disseminator of the kind of insecure gentility about which Trachtenberg speaks. This culture defines itself, mythologizes its derivation, in many ways. Initially, it seems the inheritor of Puritan culture. But as the inheritor of American Transcendentalism, it also inherits what it perceives as the greatest reaction against Puritanism. A culture less than four hundred years old, confronted on the one side by a preexistent culture (more authentically "native American") and on the other by a continuing influx of people with no prior relation to the "first" ethnic group, can only problematically constitute itself as dominant. It is an hegemony, a web of power relations, seeking its own survival at any cost (to competing cultures). This assertion is really a variant of Gellner's ambivalent views about a nation's tendency to construct a culture for the sake of homogeneity rather than of plural representation: "The cultures it claims to defend and revive are often its own inventions, or are modified out of all recognition."[36] I admit, however, to being only incidentally interested in any but the most recent writings on nationalism by historians and political scientists such as John Armstrong and Anthony Smith, for whom nationalism is more than merely an adjunct of Enlightenment thinking;[37] for many scholars, the notion of nationalism must by definition subordinate the question of ethnicity to itself.[38]

My most important assertion is not really about film at all, but is rather an actualization of a traditional ethnological realization: the ethnic representation—or nonrepresentation—of the experience of ethnicity determines the structure of mainstream culture as much as, say, the representation of gender, in a way that is neither acknowledged nor even, except very speculatively, discussed.[39] The "archetypal" American (and even thinking in terms of archetypes is a capitulation to American hegemony, not only because of its link, through Jung, to a dangerous habit of totalizing, but because of the inevitable association with Puritan theology) and the "archetypal" situations represented as American are informed by the immigrant experience. All of American culture reflects, in disguised form, the dilemmas of ethnicity and immigration. The literary and filmic representation of behavior described as archetypally American—brashness, confidence, the ability "naturally" to cross class boundaries—is the result not only of a strain of Puritan democracy or transcendentalism, as Stanley Cavell brilliantly contends in *Pursuits of Happiness*,[40] but is as much—perhaps more— informed by responses to the experience of immigration. The "formula" in American film is at least a repressive response to the fact of an extremely heterogeneous culture that cannot be satisfied by representing the experience of individual ethnic groups. The disappearance of the *ethnie* leaves in its wake a culture that repudiates its own ontology.

In short, while seeming to retain the very suspect notion that America does in fact contain a mainstream culture, I will assert that this mainstream is at all times constituted, rather than contributed to, by immigrant and ethnic cultures. This assertion is only a step further than Werner Sollors's thesis that ethnicity is merely a construct; I am merely asserting that it is the defining construct. The very choice between Westernization and ethniciza- tion is false because it does not recognize the fact that Western modes of industrial and postindustrial behavior have not all been determined by the customs of the elite of two or three industrialized countries. The export of culture as hegemony is matched by the import, from the earliest times, of either the goods or the individuals of the peoples whom they are attempting to Westernize. These populations have already had a real, if too often unconscious and unacknowledged (and so warping), effect on the culture that is seeking to find ways of consciously appropriating them. Industrial culture already "belongs" to the populations to which Western culture would bequeath it. Or, to substitute a psychological trope for a sociological assertion in a way that may (mistakenly) irritate: hegemonic culture belongs to those oppressed by it as the unconscious belongs to the individual, who can only infer its existence through dreams and neurotic behavior.

Ultimately, an enormous number of Americans pass as some version of Anglo-American. But the very attempt to pass by an enormous number of people both changes the image of the Anglo-American and calls into question the constitution of the mainstream by Anglo-America. Finally, it calls into question the possibility of an Anglo-American culture at all, except by very broad ascription. There is a vast difference between a people who at least believe themselves legitimately entitled to a unified identity and a culture that is being dictated by people pretending to an identity. Finally, it is not possible to speak of a *center* of mainstream culture, against which other influences are measured; we can speak only of a culture of Americans passing as American.

SOME RELEVANT FILM CRITICISM

In contrast to cultural critics and ethnologists such as Wayne Franklin, Alan Trachtenberg, and Werner Sollors, film critics and historians of new immigration are oddly self-effacing in their insistence on the primacy of outlining immigrant and ethnic "contributions" to politics, the arts, and sciences.[41] Dulles's bipolarity permeates most ethnic film criticism in a way that makes the present work more necessary than a similar critique of literary criticism. The program of highlighting ethnic contributions, though excellent in itself and something that will happen as a matter of course in this text, has been treated more fully elsewhere, particularly in African-American studies,[42] and studies of Jewish assimilation.[43] But again, the very program of writing the history of minority representation in the industry assumes the existence of a monolithic mainstream culture utterly other than the minority culture. Histories about the film industry's minority subcultures thus ironically ghettoize their subjects. When addressing the mass of films that are not overtly ethnic, such histories make the underlying historical assumption that "ethnic pluralism in America had limited the range of the moviemakers. They were primarily capitalist, not social activists or apologists for special groups."[44] And the consensus about audiences generally recapitulates the traditionally genteel line: "It is generally agreed that many members of the working-class audience sought, albeit unconsciously, to pick up and reinforce American values."[45] There is no real sense among critics of the tension between capitalist and ethnic or a sense that this tension might be represented on screen. This stance, as I shall argue, is as much Marxist as it is traditional historical-critical. Of course, the equal and opposite assumption—that ethnic filmmakers have controlled their own representation—must seem equally well-intentioned but misleading to anyone with a sense of the complexity of American hegemonic culture.[46]

The implicit assumptions of histories aside, the filmic representation of immigration and ethnicity is still waiting to be theorized.[47] Most recent general works on the film industry still do not as a general rule treat ethnicity seriously. Writers such as John Izod, Leo Handel, Michael Wood, Brian Neve, and Gorham Kindem[48] still believe it possible to speak of the industry without also treating in some extensive way its ethnic and immigrant components.[49] Part of the reason for not pointing out the ethnic origins of one's subject is a fear of accusations of racism. But in avoiding conversation we become guilty of a more discreet racism in which the influence of subcultures is only implicitly acknowledged, rather than granted whatever distinction scholarly dialogue can confer.

This lack of interest in ethnicity derives partly from a crypto-reactionary mania for revisinng the scholarship primarily of the 1970s and early 1980s of scholars such as Garth Jowett and Lester Friedman, who find some value in ethnicity.[50] For example, the tendency in recent film criticism has been to push back the time at which the American middle class became interested in film; two seminal works in this direction are Robert C. Allen's essay "Motion Picture Exhibition in Manhattan, 1906-1912"[51] and Thomas Elsaesser's and Adam Barker's anthology, *Early Cinema: Space, Frame, Narrative.*[52] But the most significant work along this line is by Charles Musser, who merits an extended mention. Under the guise of revisionist history, both of Musser's recent works—*Before the Nickelodeon* and *High-Class Moving Pictures*[53]—are in large part concerned with establishing the importance of middle-class audiences and genteel filmmakers at the beginning of the history of American film, despite his own assertion elsewhere that "the ethnic diversity of this [pre-1910] group should not be minimized."[54] While several critics in the last five years who have begun to concentrate on the earliest years of film—the 1880s to the 1900s—have perhaps inadvertently given primacy of place to white, male, middle-class Anglo-America in determining film practices, Musser's work shows a real contempt—disguised as *erlebte rede* (the narrator speaking in the voice of his subject)—for immigrant classes. In one instance he asserts that one exhibitor's wares, "less ambiguous in its educational aspirations, catered to people with a more fastidious temperament."[55] In speaking of urban venues, however, he asserts that "nickelodeons multiplied like cockroaches."[56] His criticism reflects both the point of view of the affluent audience of 1905 and its modern, reformist descendants.

While such criticism should be acknowledged as adding to our sense of early film, its less savory implications ought also to be acknowledged. These include the increasingly visible and reactionary notion that American film (and film critics) should be somewhat embarrassed by its nickelodeon, immigrant roots and should consequently attempt to explain those roots away. As a result, increased attention is paid to the role of white, male, middle-class Americans such as Edwin S. Porter and Thomas Edison in originating contemporary film practices or even in providing alterity in such practices. Further, such "recuperations" seem even more grotesque when one considers that they are done under the aegis of new historicism and cultural studies, the presumed promoters of multiplicity and heterogeneity. The thrust of these accounts is marvelously reactionary: to limit the amount of significance an alternative voice may have in delineating the culture of the nation. If the important moment of American film is set between 1895 and

1905, then the influence of later Irish and German actors and Jewish furriers who made films, and their immigrant audiences, is negligible, except, of course, as historical victims.[57] The archival work that was supposed to serve as an antidote to "institutional forgetting" thus becomes the means by which such forgetting is perpetuated.[58]

Though attempting to valorize film pioneers such as Edwin S. Porter and Lyman H. Howe, Musser is also careful to assert at several points that he is not positing a contest between high- and low-class sensibilities. For example, he attempts to create a triangle of influences and viewers consisting of the genteel, the religious, and the popular (middle class). But this is not a triangularity supported by the bulk of his argument, which really posits a dualism between "new" and "old" folk (like Dulles's Puritans and "urban dwellers"), in which religion and gentility have more in common with each other than with the popular.

Unlike ethnic studies in film, comedy film criticism in the last twenty years has attained a high degree of critical rigor. The initial task of cataloguing and defining subgenres of film comedy has been adequately launched in various ways; comedies have been categorized within subgenres (as in Ted Sennett's *Lunatics and Lovers*) and by comic types (as in Penelope Gilliatt's *Unholy Fools*). Specific theories have been applied to specific categories of films, as in Steve Seidman's *Comedian Comedy*. The most comprehensive earlier critical histories—Raymond Durgnat's *The Crazy Mirror* and Gerald Mast's *The Comic Mind*—include explications of virtually all categories of American film comedy. Later texts, such as Gerald Weales's *Canned Goods as Caviar,* refine this classifying tendency by choosing one decade or one kind of comedy to subdivide further.[59]

One of the most important limitations of this body of criticism is endemic to most humanities disciplines: the correspondence of the universal with the particular, or the problem of constructing a single paradigm or theoretical construct that will adequately account for most works in a genre. Seidman, while semiologically rigorous, errs on the side of particularity, explicating only those films that contain instances of self-referential acting. Mast and Durgnat, while comprehensive, are extremely eclectic in their use of theories to explicate various subgenres of film comedy. Mast, for instance, speaks of Mack Sennett's Bergsonian physicality, Charlie Chaplin's Brechtian twists, and Ernst Lubitsch's and Woody Allen's Freudian overtones. Theoretically picaresque, Mast intelligently reveals the relevance of the major comic theories to film comedy but fails to subsume or synthesize these theories under a comprehensive comic film aesthetic.

Another problem with criticism of the 1960s through the mid-1980s is that despite a bow in the direction of social causality, it tends toward (a largely unacknowledged) classical, formal analysis. None of these critics is particularly interested in immigration or ethnicity, though most refer to them in one way or another. For example, though most early theorists of film comedy were concerned with the anxiety about the exclusion of the individual from society,[60] the kind and range of exclusion practiced remain matters for dispute. Recent critics rely on Plato, who believed that audiences should minimize their exposure to comedy in order to shield noble behavior from ignoble influence; on Freud, for whom comedy is founded on involuntary masculine sexual rejection; and on George Meredith, Henri Bergson, and other theorists, for whom humor is more explicitly a social corrective, a reversible exclusion of the undesirable individual from society. Film critics as otherwise diverse as Thomas Schatz, Charles Higham, Stanley Cavell, and Steve Seidman all assume that a movie protagonist's exclusion reflects the audience's fear of exclusion from a diffusedly exclusive society.[61] A considerable number of films and at least one whole genre—screwball comedy—justify this partial generalization. But, in the fashion of the classically steeped Northrop Frye, these critics are not equipped to ask: whose exclusion? Whose anxiety? What society? One of Weales's chapters in *Canned Goods as Caviar,* for example, explicates *Duck Soup,* without once touching on race, immigration, or ethnicity. In *Comedian Comedy,* one of the smartest of the above-mentioned critical texts, Seidman discusses the way in which resolutions are necessarily "happy" in comedies and how the outsider becomes reincluded into the world of the Jungian trickster.[62] But identifying archetypes and explicating themes does not *necessarily* explain the nature of, or the necessity for, film comedy. Identifying the necessity for the comic ending is not the same as identifying the social need for laughter. *The Odyssey* is a comedy in the sense that it ends with a satisfactory social reintegration. But this more cosmic sense of the comic is not an explanation of the need or desire for laughter. The present work, though employing a variety of critical models, always keeps at the forefront a sense of those psychological and physical straits whose repressive qualities produce comedy as a disguised ethnicity.

Unlike the film criticism of the previous two decades, and with some exceptions (most notably Stanley Cavell, whom I shall treat in a later chapter), very recent general film criticism, tending as it does to exist in the spotlight of cultural studies, tends explicitly to address social theorizing in comedy. Some excellent recent criticism on early cinema has, in the wake of Marxist and cultural studies critics such as Kristen Thompson, David

Bordwell, and Janet Staiger, concentrated on class issues.[63] However, this approach is problematic: Marxist criticism tends, like more traditionally conservative formalist criticisms, to view ethnicity as an issue subordinate to itself. The best example is Henry Jenkins's *What Made Pistachio Nuts?* Though disclaiming universality, Jenkins successfully describes early sound comedy as a transition from vaudeville, thus contextualizing film comedy with perhaps the greatest degree of historical specificity yet attained. Derived from such critics as Mary Anne Doane and Roland Barthes, Jenkins's theoretical parentage is spotless. But, with one conspicuous exception, he ignores the ethnic and immigrant culture of the performers themselves, concentrating instead on class issues. Though his discussion includes Eddie Cantor, the Marx Brothers, Harry Rapf, George Burns and Gracie Allen, George M. Cohan, Jimmy Durante, Skeets Gallagher, Sam Goldwyn, and Jerry Lewis, his discussion of ethnicity is largely relegated to twelve pages on Eddie Cantor, an analysis of the reduction of overt ethnic representation from his early to his late films.[64] In summing up his sense of the origins of early sound comedy at the end of his book, Jenkins does not once mention the ethnicity of the performers, an incredible omission.[65] Recent books by David Marc, Stephen Neale and Frank Krutnick, and Andrew S. Horton, equally concerned with the evolution of studios and star systems, are equally unconcerned with larger questions like ethnicity and nationalism.[66]

Critics seem to believe that filmmakers consciously understand their own texts as Marxist critiques of capitalist modes of representation. But it seems to me far less likely that the filmmakers' critique will come from a reasoned attack at capitalist substructures than that it emerges as an (un)conscious, Bakhtinian comment by the ethnic outsider on established forms of representation.[67] While disparaging the "Mast-Agee tradition" of identifying a "golden age of screen comedy," Jenkins makes the same error, merely placing the end of that golden age ten years later, by assuming a consciously political anarchy without accounting for the consciousness.[68]

The limited criticism in film and vaudeville comedy that registers ethnicity and immigration still, in its insistence on a particular conversation about class dialectics, tends, like Dulles's commentary, to see American culture as polarized and to see the ethnic and immigrant as hapless victims or manipulated tools. Robert C. Allen's tour de force, *A Horrible Prettiness: Burlesque and American Culture,* details the struggle for survival—and ultimate extinction—of the lower-class burlesque form in the last decades of the nineteenth and first decades of the twentieth century.[69] Though occasionally mentioning the ethnicity of a performer or the role, that ethnicity is of only incidental interest.[70] What is interesting about Allen's text is its well-expressed ambivalence (typical of such criticism) toward the explicit sexism of burlesque and its explicit repression by genteel America. It is as if he is no longer able to speak with Dulles's false neutrality but must start taking sides; like Jenkins (and all the "golden-age-of-comedy" critics Jenkins deplores), he begins to be saddened by the passing of an era and its types.

Similarly, Charles Musser, who at least acknowledges the presence of roleplaying and ethnicity in film, views that ethnicity as victimization, a rather traditional argument. The problem with Musser's argument is that he sees one part of the dynamic, the half in which the immigrant is victimized, as assimilated, but not the half in which he or she is dictating culture: "Immigrants could only fully embrace American individualism by freeing themselves of ethnic traits, by constructing a new identity. Assimilation was thus closely linked to American individualism."[71] This strategy of viewing the new immigrant as victim can be, as critics in African-American Studies and Women's studies have explained, a particularly insidious form of help, akin to the help of the turn-of-the-century reformers themselves.

Finally, and again, the argument of most such criticism is really derived from Foster Rhea Dulles. *America Learns to Play* makes the argument of most of these critics that there is some negotiation between genteel work culture and the new amusements. The reason most critics do not acknowledge Dulles is that his thesis is classically liberal: generous in its acknowledgment of class and ethnic contributions to culture, racist in its virtually genetic separation of the races. To take a page from more recent work on ethnic (Chicano) representation that refuses to yoke ethnicity and victimization, the present work will assume "the political centrality of humor," that it exists at the "border" as a "heterogeneous space of . . . cultural creativity."[72]

THE PLAN OF THE BOOK

The plan of this book is simple. Chapter 1 provides a historical context through an analogy to literary humor. Because the logic of my argument is not causal, however, it does not, unlike Robert Stam's *Reflexivity in Film and Literature*, expand on antecedent and contemporary literary models.[73] Because it avoids the almost inevitable reference to Puritan culture as either the prime mover of American culture or the prime culture against which all oppositional cultures must measure themselves, this homological explanation allows a space for outlining an immigrant aesthetic more fully described in the later chapters. This first chapter intentionally excludes causal explanations of American humor, not only because such explanations would not be true but also because they would help establish an ideological tyranny over explanations valorizing other cultural influences. The rhetorical logic used in explaining (literary) history determines the kind of history being told. Argument by analogy, in contrast, can account for the fact that wave after huge wave of significantly unrelated groups arrived on an alien shore, having in common only brutal living conditions in the originary culture, an inhumane journey, a hostile reception, and an immediate and pressing need to survive. It allows for a comparison of generally incomparable groups: eighteenth-century Scotch-Irish settlers and "new-immigrant" Italians, for example.

Though it may seem odd to begin a film book with a chapter on American popular comic literature, the logic of my argument—that American popular culture is constituted by a series of immigrations with no central culture—demands some small look at seventeenth-, eighteenth-, and nineteenth-century culture. (Because of the enormous debt that cultural studies owes to the historicisms of Stephen Greenblatt and Michel Foucault, among others, it is truly odd that most cultural criticism of the twentieth century does not begin in the seventeenth or eighteenth century.[74]) I chose popular literary comedy (with significant reference to oil painting and book illustrations) and vaudeville because of the ease with which one may indicate some thematic unity between these works and later cinematic comedy.

As a direct result of the attempt to recast traditional arguments about film and culture, some of the information in and deriving from the first chapter will not be new, but rather purposeful revisions of previous critics on vaudeville and film.[75] For example, I will recast Gerald Mast's sense of Chaplin's comedy as transformative, seeing the transformations as part of the immigrant requirement of re-viewing the objects of a new culture. Some of my arguments about the Marx Brothers will also be much-needed revisions of Jenkins's and Musser's work.

The last three chapters group American film comedy under three social headings that reflect different audience responses to ethnicity and immigration: "transformative," "antic," and "screwball" comedy. Their order is made in part with an eye toward chronology, but also with a sense (unintentionally following Northrop Frye) of decreasing degrees of humorousness and increasing degrees of irony. Briefly, transformative comedy is about physical inclusion into a physically dangerous world; antic comedy is about inclusion into a socially restrictive world; and screwball comedy is about inclusion into a social or physical world that seems deceptively safe. All three types are instances of immigrant humor, which treats the anxiety inherent in not belonging to the culture of which one is at least an economic part. Each kind of comedy embodies a different fantasy of resolving the cultural tensions of immigration and/or ethnicity. Each fantasy comes in some way to define American culture.

Each of the last three chapters contains one or more presiding theorists to be considered along with a particular comic type. For Chaplin (chapter 2) it is Henri Bergson and Elaine Scarry; for the Marx Brothers (chapter 3), Jacques Lacan; and for screwball comedy (chapter 4), Leopold Sacher-Masoch (and, by extension, Gilles Deleuze). But my assumption that immigrants and ethnics originate as well as subject themselves to cultural theorizing leads me to allow comics and commentators to read each other in a critical daisy chain. So, for example, I do not use Bergson, as comedy theorists normatively do, to explicate silent humor. Rather, I understand Chaplinesque comedy as a radical critique of Bergson, reconfiguring value in Bergson's normalizing comedy so that the lone comedian rather than his society contains the positive valence. In other words, in reducing the primacy of the critic, my methodology is itself a model for the relationship of the immigrant and ethnic to his or her culture.

In regard to Chaplin, the term "transformative comedy" seems preferable to "slapstick" or "silent comedy" because it immediately identifies the silent clown's humor as a visual activity very like the social requirement placed on the immigrant. The transformation the immigrant is supposed to render in him/herself is projected onto a conveniently prosthetic technology composed of airplanes, Model T's, lampshades: the bricolage of a partially comprehended environment. Transformative comedy emphasizes the difficulty of functioning in the new, mystifyingly industrial world. The Keystone Kops, for example, live in a perilously technological world. Chaplin lives in a world in which the purpose of things is trivial or indeterminate; he must reinvent sometimes familiar artifacts as tools of survival. This filmic world reflects the anxiety of an immigrant population inhabiting a society more interested in a self-serving, self-perpetuating technology than in the (spiritual) values implicit in such increasingly antiquated activities as working the land or crafting a product. The performers themselves, if not all immigrants (though the preeminent figure—Chaplin—is), are interested in the portrayals of transients and misfits: Chaplin's tramp, Buster Keaton's bantamweight milquetoast, W. C. Fields's alcoholic, Harry Langdon's juvenile adult. These personae do not inhabit a world of benevolent possibility; they are the products of a hostile, frightening, physically assaultive environment.

Antic comedy includes comedy teams. Though teams like Our Gang and Laurel and Hardy existed in the silent era, they were more successful in the sound era because they have an intrinsic motive for conversation that the lone silent comedian does not. Because teams form a community, their conversations are about power relations between individuals whose professions and environments vary from film to film but whose relation to each other is always the same. The team ethic allows the individual members to remain themselves in any environment because their identities are defined by the group, not by the nation. Groucho Marx, Oliver Hardy, and Bud Abbott are almost always the articulate, powerful figures in their respective teams, while Harpo Marx and Stan Laurel are politically powerless eirons (comic deflators) whose strength lies in their lack of pretension. These definitions and relations remain stable whether the group is out west, at the circus, at the races, or at the opera. Even actors whose reputations were made as solo performers during the silent era—Thelma Todd and Zasu Pitts, for example—were often paired during the sound era. Because of its concern with the group, antic comedy includes all those comedians who are external to any romantic interest in their film or whose films have no romantic interest at all. The Marx Brothers are the best exemplars of this tendency; their story runs parallel to the romantic plot, and marriage or other normative conventions of social inclusion are rarely options for them.

Alternatively, screwball comedy is obsessed with legitimization through marriage, a trope that describes anxiety about endogamy, exclusion from the place from which one came and in which one has a stake. Paradoxically, screwball comedy involves a nostalgia for the place in which one is already situated. It tells the story of a misfit who belongs to an (essentially conservative) society but who needs a marriage or other conventional social contract to sanction his or her membership. Screwball contains a subordinate humor about exclusion, an ironic or sarcastic character humor that reflects not an anxiety about one's own exclusion but the fear of intrusion by others into one's own society. (In their treatment of the social-climbing fiancé, the most extreme exemplars of this desire to exclude may be C. K. Dexter Haven and Tracy Lord in *The Philadelphia Story*.) For Stanley Cavell, the screwball heroes and heroines both do and do not belong to the society they inhabit: this society desires the individual, but without the idiosyncrasies the individual brings to it. Marriage becomes the occasion for reinclusion of the protagonist into a society that acknowledges her or his difference.[76] But this explanation, if one replaced the word "marriage" with, say, the phrase "upward mobility," would sound precisely like a fantasy account of immigrant assimilation. I retain the traditional appellation "screwball" rather than Cavell's "comedy of remarriage" because, though, like Cavell, I view marriage in the genre as a trope, I do not finally view it as comprehensively normalizing but rather as one of several sites of obsession and neurosis.

Because they describe audience fears and anxieties as much as they do subgenres, these three kinds of comedy can be found in various combinations within individual films. At some level they collapse into each other as readily as any Fryean category—and all the more so as Hollywood traditionally mixes its genres. *The Tramp* is more purely visual than *Modern Times,* and Laurel and Hardy films contain the best of antic and visual comedy.[77]

Along with the normative "cultural studies" sources (such as the biographies of Chaplin in chapter 2), this work has the advantage of containing a range of reference not usually presented as a part of scholarship on American film. Chapter 1 includes a brief excurse on American comic literature and the landscape; the last chapter is in part about Balkan politics. Because the book ultimately insists on the formative influence of ethnicity on culture as on film, it may occasionally sound, as Mark Twain remarks about another text concerned with ethnic difference, as if the various voices are trying to talk alike and failing. Because the strategy of each film persona is different, the logic of the explanations is different as well. The Chaplin chapter is about acclimating to an alien and hostile environment, the Marx Brothers chapter about forcing that environment to assimilate itself to oneself, and the screwball chapter about disguising the fact of difference. The Chaplin chapter is more traditionally biographical/historical; the Marx Brothers chapter, in its use of Lacan, is more explicitly introspective and psychoanalytic; the screwball chapter, in its absorption with "passing," is more traditionally a "cultural study."

There are some structural constants across the last three chapters. While referring to a plethora of other filmmakers, the last three chapters of this text are primarily readings of three films and three film personae: *Modern Times* and Charles Chaplin's tramp, *Duck Soup* and the Marx Brothers' tricksters, and *The Thin Man* and the Loy-Powell screwball romance. Star personae will constitute the largest object of this study. As Richard Dyer asserts, "Star images have histories, and histories that outlive the star's own lifetime."[78] Still, I will not merely be asserting, as Dyer (arguing from Hume and Diderot in a rather refreshing accidental genealogy of deconstructive criticism) does about Marilyn Monroe and Paul Robeson, that these images are essentially insubstantial, constructs of an always-appropriating capitalism.[79] Rather, I will argue that the immigrant and ethnic experience results in a desire for insubstantiality that underlies the apparent desire for substance. If capitalism incorporates and changes the ethnic, it has itself learned to wish for change and appropriation from its object. A further difference from Dyer in the present work is that his "neutral" Marxist critique reveals itself at key moments as Anglocentric, as when he asserts that the star system originates in a change in the Shakespearean actor's relation to his role,[80] while I will alternatively suggest in chapter 3 that the star system is in part patterned after ethnic responses to ethnic theater.

On the other hand, because it is easy to confuse persona criticism with the public adulation of the star it is critiquing, I should probably assert that this text is a reading not of the actor's intentions but of the use by the Hollywood studio system of the actor's persona. As such, my readings of the Nick Charles persona grant to William Powell the same status that a reading of Art Deco in set design would assign the ziggurat.[81] The Chaplin and Marx Brothers personae are palpably constant from film to film, making the reading of one film convincingly representative for the rest. But this persona integrity also characterizes lead players in screwball comedy. Post–method acting criticism until the 1980s tended to excoriate Cary Grant or Katharine Hepburn for always being Cary Grant or Katharine Hepburn, no matter what the film or role. One might as well lament the inability of the early sound actors not to have been born twenty years later than they were. The real questions are: what is the purpose of maintaining a recognizable film persona? Why vary its formula? Why would an audience, many of whom are enmeshed in a problem of personal identity, in a country with a large identity problem, expect its stars always to "be themselves"?

While Henry Jenkins and others are correct in wanting to plug the current cultural-studies interest in alternative texts into the study of film comedy, and to valorize alternative film practices, a large part of this book is devoted to demonstrating that what we think of as normative film and genre practice does not derive, as we think it does, from Anglo-Puritan culture. Not including canonical texts, however, would be a bit like making a radical assertion about English Renaissance dramatic texts while excluding Shakespeare from the formulation. It is not to say that the Marx Brothers are better comics (whatever that would mean) than the Ritz Brothers but that they have become a familiar touchstone for criticism. Any argument about "New Humor" will have to consider them.

Though I will make frequent reference to the 1920s in all chapters, I am not treating films made much earlier because I am not particularly interested in the play of ethnic stereotypes in the early part of the century.[82] I am only incidentally interested in the assertion, made in different ways by different critics, and probably true, that ethnic stereotyping is generally followed either by muted versions of that stereotyping or by a disappearance of that particular ethnic from the mainstream screen.[83] I am "reading" the 1930s because I am interested in the twilight of new immigration and the representation of its penumbra, the moment of disappearance in film and society and its simultaneous influence. I am not, however, reading films of the 1940s or after, not because I believe the war to be a watershed—this fact is "abjectly true"—but because postwar culture presents a slightly different set of problems for the filmic representation of ethnicity: the death of independent black cinema, the relationship between the second and third generations of immigrants, the "rediscovery" of ethnicity, the new black cinema, and so on.

That I begin with late-seventeenth-century American humor does not make this any less a film book, just as André Bazin's assertion that the "total cinema" is a primal wish, Irwin Panofsky's assertion that film begins in the Renaissance, and Jean-Louis Baudry's assertion that film begins with Plato do not make these critics's observations about film less relevant to film studies.[84] My lesser claim is that if one wishes to understand American film, one must understand something about movement, immigration, and ethnicity. In order to understand these in a way that makes them determinative— not merely constituent—elements in film, one must understand *how* they are determinative elements of American culture. My largest claim is that the history of film is an index for the history of American culture: the repeated irony of a culture defining itself as definitive, yet time and again failing to recognize important cultural moments on its own horizon and, as a result, being redefined by its "subordinate subcultures." The whole of this argument will take volumes to prove. I begin with a small corner of that culture: American comedy.

1

—◆—

CONNECTIONS BETWEEN AMERICAN LITERARY HUMOR AND FILM COMEDY

A BRIEF CHRONOGRAPHY OF AMERICAN COMIC LITERATURE

Though their accounts of where and when vary, Americanists return again and again to the time at which the New World reconfigures our sense of geographical space. For Jose Rabasa it happens in the fifteenth and sixteenth centuries, with the Spanish rediscovery of the New World. For Clive Bush, it is a product of eighteenth-century Enlightenment thinking. For most earlier commentators—F. J. Turner, Richard Slotkin, Leo Marx, and others—it happens later, with either the early-nineteenth-century frontier literature, the American Renaissance, or American realism. For Benedict Anderson, it happens "between 1500 and 1800 [during] an accumulation of technological innovations" that becomes responsible for "a sense of parallelism."[1] This specifically spatial parallelism is seen in the linguistic "new-ness" of the New World: "New York, Nueva Leon, Nouvelle Orleans, Nova Lisboa,"[2] and so on, which, rather like crosscutting, juxtaposes worlds that cannot in reality coexist. All assign a moment in which, as Rabasa asserts about the Renaissance, "The . . . invention of America sees a reduction of the notion of a New World into a geographic concept denoting and naming a new region of space."[3] Ultimately, "space" comes to have the widest possible allegorical application, from Marxist critiques of "reified space" to psychoanalytic critiques of the space of the unconscious, or, in popular psychology parlance, the geographic/psychic "space" needed to preserve identity.

The present chapter will discuss with somewhat greater specificity this new notion of a new space and define the metaphorical implications of the changed perspectival relation of immigrant and environment. Though not yet about film, this chapter presupposes that space—and, consequently, film—to be a significantly ethnic phenomenon, and further asserts that film and a certain literary strain derive from the same ethnic-cultural source. As a result, this space is less a product of a particular moment than a recurring dynamic—a *longue durée* of movement and alienation.[4]

Thinking of history in this way discourages a vision of history as "mechanically causal," a "billiard-ball model of cause and effect."[5] Instead of considering American history as derived in lineal fashion from a prime cause—the landing of the Puritans, for example—this first section provides a provisional answer to a question almost never, until the last decade, asked in American and cultural studies: how would a history of American literature read if it did not derive from a tension created between Puritan culture and all subsequent cultures? This history would be a fairy tale, but no more so than the more normative histories created by scholars intent on retaining a particular vision of America as an idea organized around one particular ethnic sensibility, often coincidentally that of the historian.[6] This alternative history might begin, not with Puritan America as the ancien régime,[7] but with the other traditions the Puritans were at pains to erase. It might culminate, if at all, in such popular culture forms as the classical Hollywood film. The present text provides an alternative traditional rhetoric, an escape from what an Irish immigrant to the European continent referred to as the "nightmare of history." It postulates an America that might be not about mission and religion but about deceit, desire, and revenge; not about the settlement of the West but the unsettlement of the eastern seaboard by the west, or the collapse of distinctions between the two; an alternative fairy tale: the story of an American literary scene in which Puritan culture is part of the atonalities and harmonies of competing ethnic groups. Telling such a story is difficult because hegemonic cultures are at pains to erase whatever is not hegemonic or appropriable, especially alternative versions of its own history.[8] So, let us recount, not a history, but a recurring theme.[9] Let us pretend that a film history can begin, like other recent histories, with a Spanish sailor's descriptions of the scenery, or a Native American creation narrative, not with a Puritan captivity narrative. Let us assume that literature of the Americas begins not in a northern city on a hill, but in a swamp, not with Native Americans as spiritual enemies, but with the most ubiquitous of American literary predators. Not with God but with the mosquito.

— ◆ —

Until the discovery of the Americas, Europe had for centuries imagined ideal landscapes—from Arcadia to Atlantis to El Dorado—one of whose underlying similarities was the advanced degree to which each was a desirably civilized departure from the overcrowded, unsanitary, politically unstable cities of a Europe about to feel the repressive move toward nationalism. For a moment after the discovery of the American continents this ideal was projected onto the New World, in works of fiction and drama (*The Tempest*), in narrations of "fact" (Captain Smith's narratives), in poetry,[10] and in historical speculation (theories, for instance, about the American aborigines as descendants of the ten lost tribes of Israel).[11] However, despite the fact that the landscape continued to be a powerful metaphor for the alien, and an arena for utopian projects of various kinds, the disastrous early experiences of the Jamestown colony and other New World catastrophes brought into question the viability of establishing a golden age in North America.

When the dream of finding or creating an ideal, Arcadian home was confronted by a landscape that negated it, four overlapping kinds of praxis could follow.[12] First, the contradiction could be ignored, in the belief that the ideal was real but as yet undiscovered (the Hudson River School, the search for El Dorado, American corporate capitalism). Second, an attempt at creating an ideal under conditions that were at least new, if not themselves ideal, could be hazarded (the Puritan "City on the Hill" and such utopian successors and derivatives as Brook Farm, suburbia, and edge city). Third, and more interestingly, the landscape could be seen as debased in some fashion that was always a projection of the fears of the gentry settling the land—a sort of orientalizing of the forest, different from the first projections because more ambivalent. The landscape could be variously defined as either harboring or being the person one most feared. Various critics of the landscape have seen that person in various guises. For Richard Slotkin, it is the Native American; for Annette Kolodny, it is the feminine; for Jenny Franchot it is Roman Catholicism.[13]

Finally, attempts were made to embrace the new reality, at first by adapting to the new surroundings and then by repudiating previous notions of the new environment. Inappropriately labelled "going native" (it was as much determined by Western culture as by any other), this reaction was characterized by the antinomian tendency to disappear into the landscape, to become part of the background, or to reconfigure background as foreground. Its avatars ranged from the mild to the wild: from Roger Williams's antinomianism to stories of the wild man or the feral child.[14] Becoming what we now ironically call the "literature of dissent," this embrace of the landscape was most feared by the Puritans, who attempted to suppress such inclinations in their own ranks.[15] Ironically, both the Puritan and antinomian responses embody a kind of orientalizing tendency (the projecting of one's own fears onto an objectified "other") best documented by writers like Marianna Torgovnick.[16] Slandering this nativizing tendency remained for a long time a part of the American literary and political tradition. J. Hector St. John Crèvecoeur and Thomas Jefferson, for instance, both perceived the first settlers as necessary but transient and barbarous.[17] This suppression of any identification with the landscape was also, not coincidentally, the suppression of comedy, which then reemerged with a vengeance against the Puritans in, for example, the person of Thomas Morton, a neighbor of the Puritans whom the latter perceived as unserious.[18]

In one version of the literature of dissent, anachronistic landscape ideals could be remembered in such a way that the recollector's present behavior was dictated by a desire to contradict those older, European notions of the landscape as conventionally Edenic or postlapsarian. This tendency to nativize, this visceral embrace of the landscape when coupled with a memory of the incorrectly formulated ideals of the landscape, became early American comedy. In other words, the socio-psychic origin of American comedy is located in the self-conscious recollection of error committed in a past prediction of the present.[19] From its earliest colonial avatars, American literary comedy involved that recollection, that memory. New World comedy began as the historical account of the mistaken projections of the ideal into a practically unimaginable future, recorded by that future as present. It was the future's revenge on the past on which it was otherwise so dependent for continuity. Or, if "revenge" seems over-dramatic, then an insistence on a reversal of the axes of cultural value, an insistence that the failure of the new landscape to live up to imaginative expectations, was really the failure on the part of these imaginations to envision the representational potentialities of the new environment.

Popular culture gradually appropriated this motive for—and implied mechanism of—comedy in the eighteenth and nineteenth centuries through a population uncertain of its relation to its new surroundings on one side and its parent culture on the other.

Thomas Morton's New English Canaan (1637) is probably the first extended comic attempt to explode various myths about the New World as idyllic refuge;[20] Joseph Hall's Mundus Alter et Idem is one of the most elaborate new-world hoaxes (whose nations—Moronia, Crapulia, and so on—sound like coinages from Duck Soup);[21] and the anonymous "An Invitation to Lubberland" is one of the earliest works to refer to immigrant hoaxes.[22] But Ebenezer Cooke's "The Sotweed Factor" (1708) is probably the best starting point for a theory of American comedy. "The Sotweed Factor" is one of a small genre of satires that repudiate all cultural ideals imposed on the new

Figure 1.1 "Hey for Lubberland." "Lubberland" was the seventeenth-century English pejorative for the New World, a fool's paradise of plenty and idleness.

landscape.[23] Understanding these cultural ideals as ideological hoaxes imposed on a gullible public, the poet narrates the misadventures of an English emigrant to Maryland who tries to establish himself as a trader ("factor") in tobacco ("sotweed"). After a series of disastrous encounters with the climate, the fauna, the food, and the gentry of the New World, Cooke ends his sojourn:

> Raging with grief, full speed I ran,
> To join the fleet at Kickatan,

returning from there to England.

The narrative is replete with mythological, classical, and biblical allusions. Cooke applies them in an ironic fashion to the new land and its inhabitants: the Native Americans are descendants of either the Chinese or the Phoenicians (Cooke compares them to the Picts); the food is like the diet of the infant Orson. Cooke frequently and disturbingly uses the language of pastoral poetry to undercut the pastoral ideal with a comically cacaphonic reality:

> But as I there a-musing stood
> And quite benighted in the wood,
> A female voice pierced through my ears,

> Crying, "You rogue drive home the steers":
> I listened that attractive sound,
> And straight a herd of cattle found.

Choosing to reverse allusions to the Americas as an Eden, Cooke alludes instead to a malevolently classical or biblical world, most obviously to Pandora's box, Balaam's ass, Cain's Land of Nod, and Egypt's plagues. (Several historians have observed that propaganda about the bounty of the New World was a corporate and civic fact from the earliest days of settlement, continuing as long as immigration remained a necessary precondition for industrial expansion.)[24]

Cooke's narrative is different from those of the often humorous journal-keepers and observers of roughly the same period (Sarah Kemble Knight and William Byrd)[25] in the exaggerated quality of Cooke's catastrophes. In one passage of twenty lines, Cooke is driven to look outdoors for a comfortable place to sleep because of the pandemonium in his host's home. He is persecuted in a series of catastrophes reminiscent of the Mosaic plagues: a horde of frogs and snakes, an uncomfortable perch in a tree, and, finally, the "cursed mosquitoes," which keep him awake "'[t]il rising morn, and blushing day." Cooke thus repudiates the application of imaginative and ideal alternative worlds to the new landscape:

> I think it fit I open lay
> My entertainment by the way,
> That strangers well may be aware on
> What homely diet they must fare on.[26]

Though prior to most major works treated in histories of the humor of this country, "The Sotweed Factor" embodies most of the important issues about assimilation into, and alienation from, the landscape that will be treated in later periods.[27] It is about hoaxes and travel to and repudiation of a new land experienced as a demystification of that land. It is about loss of identity, humiliation as rite of passage, and predators—both animal and human. Like the more familiar later frontier heroes described by critics from Constance Rourke to Jesse Bier, the New World characters Cooke encounters are uncouth and equivocally dishonest, predecessors in rough of the Yankee and the frontiersman. They are not gentlemen.

Because the poem proceeds smoothly from Cooke's trials with the land through his trials with food to his trials with the inhabitants, one may infer that these inhabitants have become a slightly luxuriant outgrowth of the land, themselves a part of the landscape. (Even near the beginning of the seventeenth century, Europeans were still trying to determine what in the New World was human; whether, for example, pygmies existed and whether they were not really apes.)[28] Bestiaries of the New World included such animals as the "Su" that, "like the manticore and other mythological beasts (and like the 'half man, half alligator' of a later century), were odd products of a presumed zoophilia."[29] The form of the poem suggests a hierarchy of natural predators. Beginning with forms of wildlife inimical to human life, the poem ends with human predators: the trickster who steals Cooke's boots, the swindler who absconds with his goods, and, finally, the corrupt judiciary that legitimizes the swindle as an instance of the law of the wilderness. The wilderness and its writers recognize no difference between attribute and essence, between "predatory" and "predator." Getting from Cooke's predatory rascals to Mike Fink's "half horse, half alligator" requires the realization of a metaphor through a sympathy with the object metaphorized, and a benign confusion between a metaphorization of the wilderness's inhabitants and a demystification of the wilderness itself.

Despite thematic interests different from those of his literary successors, Cooke shares with later writers more than an interest in repudiating a naive ideal; like them, he is absorbed with the particularities of the landscape. Cooke demonizes the landscape as much as later writers will romanticize it. His sotweed factor is constantly moving to evade the assaults of snakes, mosquitoes, trees, and other predators. Finally moving out of the landscape completely, he returns to England, bereft of goods and clothing. Oddly, the only static, safe element of the landscape, which Cooke at first does not realize to be so, is a lone Native American, whom one would expect to be one of the greater threats.[30]

Cooke differs most from later literary humorists (but is like later film comics) in his inability to harbor sympathy for the wilderness landscape and its denizens. While later humorists will find a more or less happy sympathy between humanity and the environment, Cooke observes the inhabitants' moral sense evaporating into the new air. Cooke represents a departure from English humorists in his self-conscious recognitions of the failure of utopia and his consequent defeat by the landscape. He is caught between a disbelief in old cultural ideals and a distaste for the new cultural pragmatism. By the end of the poem he has in common with later American writers a knowledge of, and respect for, the immensity, danger, and mystery of the landscape but no mechanism through which he can ally himself to it. For Cooke, the character who can successfully live in the new wilderness is as dangerous as his surroundings.

Just as British chapbooks and jestbooks never became as popular in the New World as in England,[31] so satires repudiating European ideals of the landscape quickly disappear as a dominant motif in American letters (although it does remain as submotif: in Mark Twain's travel journals, *Gentlemen Prefer Blondes, Lolita,* and *Gravity's Rainbow,* for example). Repudiation becomes less necessary as the hostility of the new landscape and its inhabitants to another culture's imposition of pastoral ideals becomes more explicit.[32] The sheer fact of the gradual change in the status of many of the inhabitants of the New World from immigrant—aware of the discrepancy between the ideal and the reality—to citizen, with fewer resources for comparison, is partly responsible for this attitudinal change. The replacement of the uninformed seventeenth- and eighteenth-century European ideals of the habitability of the wilderness by the merely somewhat better informed ideals of such American writers as Crèvecoeur, Franklin, and Jefferson is also responsible.[33]

After Cooke, American comedy adopts several modes that use this pastoral danger in several ways, all of which have to do with its absurd magnification. At a time when the colonies become unproblematically habitable, the wilderness still represents a magnified barbarity. And even though the colonists were at pains to distinguish themselves from the landscape, the audience—the more established Atlantic seaboard as well as England—came to identify them with it. The colonists—and then-colonial and post-colonial writers—subsequently revenged themselves on this audience first by magnifying the strangeness of the country and then by implicitly finding this strangeness to be mundane, a new prosaicness that encompassed the exotic. In two anecdotes related to Mrs. Trollope, the urbane author of *Domestic Manners of Americans,* the English tourist, visibly contemptuous of Jacksonian-era mores among the easily offended citizens of the new democracy, is sufficiently gullible to relate as factual one story about a crocodile who devours an entire family and another about a drunken bear who placidly canoes into New Orleans.[34]

Early American humor tended to be characterized by the degree to which it was visual and improbable. The specificity of setting and person differentiated an American joke from its English incarnation.[35] Even regional dialect worked to establish an *image* of the American: the slow speech, the loudness, and the quaint diction all characterized the untutored but wily, lanky Yankee. And the quaintness of speech more often than not included images and metaphors striking in their ability to evoke a simultaneously realistic and grotesque version of the landscape ("The tinder box in my cabin would no more ketch fire than a sunk raft at the bottom of the sea").[36] The more the European insisted that the American was a savage, the more the American reveled in his literary barbarity.[37]

Coming hard on the heels of a century that learned to repress ethnicity, or any unofficial differences, for the sake of the new notion of nationalism, Jacksonian America contained a final development in early American humor of this "barbaric" revel: humorists aligned their heroes more closely with the strangeness of the landscape by magnifying their feats and peculiarities.[38] Tall-tale heroes were a final refinement: the establishment of a moral and intellectual superiority of the upstart official culture over the more traditional official culture. Not coincidentally, the Jacksonian era was also the beginning of the "old" antebellum immigration movement, a moment at which, in the rise of the periodical literature of the early to middle nineteenth century, journals and newspapers became the Bakhtinian testing ground for competing voices in the liveliness of the dialogue between editors and contributors, and between magazines.[39] From these periodicals emerged the heroes of tall tales: Mike Fink, who was wilier and stronger than any of the representatives of established authority he encountered, and Davy Crockett, who was more eloquent, more morally upright, and nobler than his adversaries, as well as stronger and larger. Though their ethnicity was played down in the legends, the historical Crockett as well as Daniel Boone were Scotch-Irish in deriva- tion.[40] While becoming one of the most important symbols for Jacksonian (imperial) democracy, the Scotch-Irish tales were also the model for a counter- culturalism with which the newer old immigrants could identify, as if the discontents of the previous generation were able to speak to the cultural burden of the next. It is no coincidence that the publishers of the new popular literature were from the same ethnic group. The Scotch-Irish published stories that magnified the exploits of one of them, changing and defining the new nation- alism, but they did so at the necessary expense of the ethnic group.

The newer culture and the newer publishing industry, each with the need to situate itself as different but visible, made a virtue of the exaggerated qualities the older culture found repugnant. The most articulate early de- fender of the American ideal was the character Sam Slick, in *The Clockmaker* (written by a Canadian, T. C. Haliburton). Like other tale-tellers who are the heroes of their own tales he inverts the scales of cultural value. For instance, he quotes a judge addressing a group of miscreant Yankees:

> Bring up them culprits, said he, and when they were brought up he told 'em it was scandalous, and only fit for English and ignorant foreigners that sit on the outer porch of darkness, and not high-minded, intelligent Americans.[41]

The tall tale and the trickster tale were at this time beginning to be identified as "native" American literature. The three decades in which the tall and trickster tales reached fruition fell between William H. Gardiner's 1822 call for an indigenous literature (in his review of Cooper's *The Spy*), and the 1850 publication of *The Scarlet Letter* (often seen as the response to that call).[42] William Lenz has observed that "oral tales began to appear in local newspapers in the 1820s as humorous filler contributed by amateur writers."[43] The most famous disseminator of tall tales—the New York *Spirit of the Times*—began publication in 1831, and continued throughout the 1850s. *The Lion of the West*, a stage play based very loosely on the life of Davy Crockett, was produced in 1830, while the Crockett almanacs began publication in 1835, and the *Life of Colonel Crockett* was first published in 1833. In point of fact, Gardiner's 1822 call was rather tardy. As Walter Blair observes in discussing the same period:

> [W]riters noticed that both serious and comic tensions could be exploited by moving a character from one region to another. Cooper's Harvey Birch in *The Spy*, Dr. Obed Bat in his *The Prairie*, and Melville's cast of characters in *The Confidence-Man* represent relatively serious applications of the formula; *but comic migrations seemed felicitous years before those books appeared.* Rural Yankees—Joe Strickland, Enoch Timbertoes, Jack Downing, and Sam Slick—wandered into towns and cities, gawking and mystified, then reported back to the home folks the wondrous and peculiar ways of city residents.[44]

The early frontier tales contain two kinds of hero: the physically large and the morally small—Mike Fink and Davy Crockett on the one hand, Sut Lovingood and Simon Suggs on the other. Fink and Crockett are as largely generous as they are generously large while, in illustrations of the day, Lovingood and Suggs are physically as well as morally slim.[45] While not always Gargantuesque in physical dimensions, frontier heroes are out of proportion to the mass of humanity. But in being socially ill-proportioned they are in proportion with the nature that surrounds them. They are equal to the task of adjusting to the landscape through an aesthetic that dictates that anything out of scale with realistic depictions of settled life must be in proportion with a nature antagonistic to that life. The Comte de Buffon's accusation that new-world flora and fauna (including humanity) are stunted becomes, on the one hand, countered by the Enlightenment assertion that the new American aristocracy is equal to the European. On the other hand, Buffon's accusations become the occasion for celebration in New World comedy.[46]

Our laughter at the tall tale or the trickster tale is complex: it resides in our sense that humanity is precariously out of scale with nature and in our recognition that the tale serves as an allegorical procrustean bed. We laugh in part at exaggeration alone: the exaggeration of the mysteriousness of the landscape and the frontier character's stature within that landscape. We also laugh at the realistic character's insufficiencies in coping with that landscape. But our most complex laughter is at the creation of an exaggerated character sufficient to an exaggerated landscape, the creation of an ideal champion for an ideal fear. The creation of an implausible hero elicits a belief that our fears, equally implausible, evaporate. Our laughter is probably all the more, not less, because we know that the hero is probably a lie.[47]

Another cause for laughter in the exaggeration of the landscape and the people who inhabit it is the release of an anxiety that humanity may have already achieved its full potential for transformation and adaptation. The only way the imagination in these stories can conceive of human transformation is in degree, not in kind. Larger and smaller are options; different is not. This limited flexibility is both a consolation and a disappointment: consolation in the possibility that humanity can find itself valuable (the tall-tale landscape is neither larger nor smaller than its inhabitants); disappointment in the belief that transformation is possible only in the physical realm, because only the physical realm exists as an arena for confrontation between humanity and nature. Most of the *spirituelle* of the landscape, as inscribed upon it by Rousseau and other early mythmakers who see in it the possibility of moral regeneration, disappears at the same time that comedy rejects any romantic notions about the landscape.

One fundamental cultural aim of early American society—to distinguish itself from the wilderness landscape that surrounds it—is therefore opposed with an oral and written literary culture that closely identifies humanity with its wilderness and surroundings. Jeffersonian, Franklinian, and Crèvecoeurian ideals, however unrealized and different from each other, were still cultural virtues embraced because they were paradigms establishing a special superiority of humanity over the land and of landed humanity over landless humanity. From Crèvecoeur: "This formerly rude soil has been converted by my father into a pleasant farm, and in return it has established all our rights; on it is founded our rank, our freedom, our power as citizens, our importance as inhabitants of such a district."[48] And from Jefferson: "Those who labor in the earth are the chosen people of God, if ever He had a chosen people, whose breasts He has made his peculiar deposit for substantial and genuine virtue. . . . Corruption of morals in the mass of cultivators is a phenomenon of which no age nor nation has furnished an example."[49]

Figure 1.2 "Davy Crockett," by John Gadsby Chapman, 1834. Courtesy of Art Collection, Harry Ransom Humanities Research Center, The University of Texas at Austin.

Figure 1.3 "Sut's Backside." *Sut Lovingood: Yarns* (1867). "Davy Crockett" and "Sut's Backside" are obverse sides of the same impulse to see the frontiersman as out of scale with the rest of humanity: either heroic or absurd.

For pastoral idealists, humanity may transform the wilderness into rural community, but in American comedy, the land physically transforms the human, making it larger or smaller, while humanity preserves and demonstrates in itself the amorality of the landscape. Historically, society "conquers" its surroundings, but in the tales nature prevails over history. Even while it is constantly being shoved back in fact, the wilderness proceeds to the foreground of the literary landscape, making Jacksonian comedy sound rather like Ronald Reagan's "morning in America." This return of the repressed is a return of the endangered or extinct. Boone and Crockett communicate with the animals they are extinguishing, and they are in several respects like the Native Americans they are decimating. Recall, to take only one instance, the raccoon that Crockett does not kill because it acknowledges him master: "I stoops down and pats him on the head, and sez I, 'I hope I may be shot myself before I hurt a hair of your head, for I never had sich a compliment in my life.'"[50]

Lying to the reader will reach a kind of apotheosis in such Mark Twain stories as "The Petrified Man," in which, while recounting the story of a hoax to the reader he is perpetrating another one *on* the reader, or in *Life on the Mississippi,* which is a tissue of lies about famous liars written by a consummate liar. But such lying has an explicitly political face: the tall tale is a Jacksonian-era device for winning elections. Crockett tales were invented to enlarge the hero into Congress, while slurs about other candidates were explicitly obscene.[51] The political hoax also had racial implications: antebellum Democrats, posing as Republicans, distributed an "anonymous" pamphlet "advocating political and social equality, and specifically the mixture of black and white."[52]

To recapitulate: the original impetus for American comedy is spatialized as a sense of direction and a sense of scale. It becomes defined as the immigrant's desire to overcome both the internal sense of physical inadequacy the individual feels in the face of the mysterious wilderness of the Western frontier and the external cultural inadequacy imposed on the frontier community by the traditional cultures of the East. (In time, this more traditional culture will include New England as well as Britain and the Continent.) The most sophisticated comic response to this dilemma is one in which the comic protagonist identifies himself with the landscape, increasing or decreasing himself in proportion to what the land requires of him and establishing this new human scale as the norm against which more traditional cultures are ridiculed. As Simon Suggs has it, "It is good to be shifty in a new country." The most obvious exaggerations are the tall tales of Mike Fink and Davy Crockett, but the trickster tales, in which figures of less than human stature overcome traditional figures, are equally appropriate examples. The aspects of the landscape that were feared become celebrated as exempla of the obstacles overcome by the gentry telling the story. The greater the obstacle, the greater the magnification of the heroism necessary to overcome that obstacle. This initially individual, antisocial allegiance of the exaggerated frontier protagonist to the landscape is ultimately identified as a national trait, so that the tall-tale protagonists become national symbols and cultural heroes. (Incongruously, even the originally Canadian Paul Bunyan is adopted as a belated member of the American pantheon at the end of the nineteenth century.) The asocial protagonist thus becomes a typical member of the communities of larger-than-life heroes who ultimately become identified as frontiersmen, keelboatmen, or, more especially, Yankees.[53]

As a reaction and cultural revenge against the more traditional cultures that initially repudiate this community as inferior, American humor's identification of the community with the landscape is effective in three ways. First, it creates a viable alternative community to the normative Eastern culture. Second, this alternative community claims a superiority by virtue of the fact that it succeeds—morally and intellectually as well as physically—in a setting in which the other has failed. The third, and most proficient, revenge is the imposition onto the older culture of belief in the exaggerated quality of this world. An example of this imposition is the hoax. Beginning with tales told by the first travelers to the New World, through the tales recounted to such gullible tourists as Mrs. Trollope, through the impositions of Mark Twain on a gullible East Coast, the hoax, by presenting the East with even more monstrous versions of reality than the East could have itself imagined, is a response to the Eastern impulse to create a western frontier more monstrous than reality. In actuality, the fabulous stories exported toward high and normative culture are often all the same: elaborated, garnished, and validated by circumstantial description told to forewarn against the frontier. The revenge is biblically appropriate: a lie for a lie, a truth for a truth.

HISTORICAL HOMOLOGIES BETWEEN FILM AND LITERATURE

> The discovery of the New World had an impact on the European imagination which it is now difficult to understand. It was as if the wilder reaches of contemporary science fiction were discovered to have an immediate and actual reality.[54]

As his use of science fiction suggests, Clive Bush's description of the explorers of the fifteenth through seventeenth centuries is equally applicable to the new immigrants of the late nineteenth and early twentieth centuries. The visual and literary representations of these experiences are also analogous. More specifically, the genesis and development of American film comedy are homologous to the genesis and development of literary comedy because they mature at historically analogous moments: during a sudden and rapid influx of immigrants into an alien and alienating landscape. Though, of course, the differences between these two cultures are profound, it is not true that they are incomparable. The same sociologist who asserts that the colonial settlers "came not as migrants entering an alien society, forced to acquire a new national identity, but as a colonial vanguard that would create a new England" ignores the historical realities of both the culture the colonists tried to displace (that of the Native Americans) and the new-immigrant desire to maintain the old culture in the new neighborhood.[55]

Bush describes the ideological changes in regarding the landscape in spatial tropes: "In the 1840s views of the city diverge in two complementary directions. On the one hand the point of view gets closer to individual people and on the other there is a striking development of panoramas which show the whole city imagined from an increasingly aerial perspective. As the city got bigger the sense of the individual and small groups could only be retained by a close-up view."[56] At this point in his final chapter, Bush finally makes some connection to film, discussing Eisenstein on D. W. Griffith and urban alienation. Like Eisenstein, Bush is utterly uninterested in race and ethnicity (not a trivial omission, given that Griffith is the subject). But he does make a necessary assertion for the present argument: that, in the eighteenth and mid-nineteenth centuries, "the relation of the American individual to a newly emerging sociogeographical space" was different from previous, European envisionings.[57] Building on this claim, I am further asserting that this new space is constantly changing its boundaries (even before the eighteenth and after the nineteenth centuries), and thus, like the tall-tale hero's, the perspective of the subject is likewise constantly changing, because both are defined by recurring ethnic and immigrant encounters with an unknown landscape.

Social Homologies

In discussing another ethnically problematic form, minstrelsy, Alexander Saxton asserts: "Underlying the sociological congruency between city and frontier was a psychological similarity between traveling to the city and traveling west. Each was a difficult journey involving a traumatic break with a previous life. In minstrelsy . . . the journey became the central theme. It stood in contrast to the celebration of urban opportunity and permissiveness as a lament for what had been left behind and lost."[58] This historical similarity yields stylistically and thematically similar features in popular culture. The messages of both film and nineteenth-century literature are also homologous: both deliver fantasy strategies for fitting into an alien landscape. These strategies for assimilation—which become mythic and permanent in American culture because the need to expand the size and expertise of the American labor force with imported labor recurs cyclically—are based on the sublimation of older ethnic identities to newer ones ostensibly more "American." But "America" is a site obsessed with arrival, escape, inclusion, and exclusion. In both literature and film, identity is finally determined as *Anglo*-American, but in both cases this appropriation disguises the profound effect of non-Anglo culture. Examining the immediate history of filmmakers and their audience reveals a low-culture medium absorbed with foregrounding a people and a landscape, part real, part imaginative, that resist classification by a genteel audience.

The now-standard reading of this homology on both the left and the right is that the new immigrants are appropriated into a preexistent ideology that identifies them with archetypal stories and characters that support that ideology's praxis. For example, Chip Rhodes chooses a moment—the exchange between an immigrant and a college dean—in Anzia Yezierska's 1925 novel, *Bread Givers,* to reveal the workings of progressive ideology: "All pioneers have to get hard to survive. . . . My grandmother came to the wilderness in an ox cart and with a gun on her lap. She had to chop down trees to build a shelter for herself and her children. . . . [Y]ou, child—your place is with the pioneers." Rhodes condemns the equation between the early pioneers and the new immigrants as "not simply a falsification of reality. It implies that different phases of capitalism are legitimated by different means."[59] But, in condemning the progressives' self-interested appropriation of historical and mythic representations, Rhodes dismisses more authentic connections—the problem of creating a new culture in a new land, for example—as "falsification."[60]

American film began at a time when the social climate shared two important historico/geopolitical attributes with the earliest period of American letters: the exodus of a heterogeneous, multiethnic population from the economically and socially hostile European and Asian landscapes, and the entry of that population into the radically unfamiliar landscape of the New World.[61] In 1910, for instance, foreign-born citizens and natives of foreign or mixed parentage comprised 35 percent of the total U.S. population.[62] This immigration was monolithic: an "extraordinary population movement—the largest in recorded history."[63] The New World these "new immigrants" confronted was new in more than a geographical sense. The new-immigrant populations came from largely Eastern and Southern European countries, areas that tended to be much less industrialized than Western Europe: "Many of the Italian peasants lived in houses of straw or even in rock caves and abandoned Greek tombs. Often, one-room shacks housed people and livestock together. An agricultural laborer earned from 8 to 32 cents a day in Sicily but rarely found enough work during the year."[64] Because the political climate in most of Eastern Europe was more or less feudal, the classes to which these immigrants had belonged were even more economically polarized than those of their Western European counterparts. And, because of these disparities, lower-class immigrants had had almost no access in Europe to whatever industrial technologies did exist. The products of industry and the mechanics of the new technology were as mysterious and largely unknown for a large portion of this new population as maize had been for the Anglo-Saxon immigrant group. (In fact, the original landscape can almost be characterized as a new technology.)

Consequently, as the earlier immigrants had been ridiculed by English tourists, so the new-immigrant population was ridiculed by the established American culture for its strange dress and speech. Overt nativist tendencies were supplemented by the more genteel racism of the educated:

> Genteel writers chastised immigrants for an inability to absorb Anglo-Saxon traditions. The "new immigrants," they insisted, could never learn the ways of the town meeting, the quintessential democratic assembly so characteristic of America. . . . [P]articipatory democracy could be practiced only by the most advanced race. . . . Charles Eliot Norton, professor at Harvard, pointed to immigrant emulation of American rootlessness, while Henry Adams, noting that Hebrew peddlers mimed Vanderbilt and Rockefeller, equated "Jew" with grasping capitalists.[65]

Woodrow Wilson, a future promoter of *Birth of a Nation,* described the new immigration as a travesty, "as if the countries of the south of Europe were disburdening themselves of the more sordid and hapless elements of their population."[66]

Like the earlier settlers, the newcomers were ambivalent about remaining in the New World. The two immigrant groups shared a privation, misery, and rejection that belied the promise of affluence. (Bernard Bailyn describes the horrors of the mortality rate in the early Chesapeake community, including the fact that "half of the children born in these disease-ridden colonies in the seventeenth century died before the age of twenty. . . .[M]ost immigrants to the Chesapeake who survived to the age of twenty died before reaching forty.")[67] As Glenn C. Altschuler observes, "For every one hundred southern and Eastern Europeans that arrived between 1908-1910, forty-four made the return trip."[68] The fairy-tale assertion that the distinguishing feature of the Puritans as immigrants was their arrival by choice, while later immigrants were forced by economic circumstance, is the partial statement of a larger truth. For these immigrants, the choice between the old country and America was not the choice between "Joyless Street" and streets of gold but, in many cases, a Hobson's choice between preindustrial and industrial poverty.[69] Not all the immigrants who remained in the United States fared well. The statistics for disease and infant mortality in the ghettos at the turn of the century were more staggering even than they are today.

Further, in both the seventeenth and early twentieth centuries, corporations and states allowed immigration for the purpose of increasing the labor force, using immigrants as pawns in immense speculation schemes that promoted economic expansion. For prerevolutionary settlers, expansion took the horizontal form of land speculation: migrants were encouraged to settle on relatively large grants of land farther and farther west.[70] In contrast, the new immigrants contributed to the vertical expansion of industry and the city. When the need for cheap labor was filled, or countered by a more pressing greed, immigration was discouraged. British immigration was restricted, for instance, when it was discovered that the British labor force was being depleted.[71]

Finally, in both populations, corporate speculation was accompanied by a trickery and fraud that would inform the narratives of each audience. New World entrepreneurs presented the unknown continent to both original and new immigrants in similar fashion. Though initially attracted by the large tracts of midwestern land, most new immigrants were ultimately expected to become part of the East Coast industrial machine.[72] While still in the old country, the prospective immigrant was lured by corporate America's promises of acres of land or gold in the streets. Myths about access to wealth as strong as the earlier myths of El Dorado or the "City on the Hill" were disseminated as propaganda among the poorer classes of Europe:

> The wonderful Couza . . . returned to [his] home town dressed in frock coat and silk hat, bringing gifts of razors, pen holders, and music boxes, donating 125 francs to the *shul* (synagogue), and telling everyone "there were many ways of getting rich in America. . . . (Later it turned out that poor Couza, with frock coat and silk hat, lived in a tenement on Attorney Street, and his wife too, on piecework.) Steamship agents, spreading Yiddish leaflets, were shameless in their deceptions. Little brochures in Yiddish and Hebrew tempted the Jews with stories of riches and freedom.[73]

The newer hoaxes, then, like earlier avatars observed by writers like Ebenezer Cooke, were invented for a desperately poor and crowded European audience willing to believe in the possibility of affluence. The American corporations that would exploit their labor imposed a false sense of destination on the immigrants even *before* they ventured from home. This false impression became a part of their way of thinking about the New World, so that a radical economic and social disillusionment had to be a part of the experience of arrival. The fantasy of instantaneous wealth quickly dissipated in sweatshops and tenements. Only the fortunate few could realize that fantasy in the only way possible, by accepting an ideological framework that insisted on the possibility and even normality of magical transformations that collapsed time and probability. Transformation became disguised as quotidian by the ascription of success to "hard work" (Andrew Carnegie and the Horatio Alger myth) or to some medieval combination of luck and fate (the miners of the Comstock Lode, who embodied a mythology Chaplin would exploit and explode in the transformative fairy tale, *The Gold Rush*). Statistics notwithstanding, the culture perceived the proletarian immigrant who died in obscurity as the exception to the rule of magical transformation. The Old-World fairy tale of transformation was itself transformed into a fairy tale of modern capitalism. The only real difference was that this fairy tale was endowed with the lineaments of historical truth. The generic peasant ("Clever Hans" or "the third son") who married the princess and won the kingdom, reigning wisely and justly forever, had, in a democracy, achieved a name. Clever Hans had become Andrew Carnegie; his realm was U.S. Steel, his sword the "Gospel of Wealth." A completed immigration involved the exchanging of names: Zeleznick to Selznick, Goldfish to Goldwyn. The child received its adult name; the other name became secret, part of the "childish prattle" of a foreign language. (We shall see the fantasy implications of renaming/re-ascription in chapter 3.) The myth of upward mobility, *always* a myth for most, became part of a belief system that encouraged an individual and social amnesia about one's previous family and allegiance: those who had become downwardly mobile, or who had disappeared altogether. Worshipping individuality, America sacrificed the history of individuals at its altar.[74]

Media Homologies

American film as a popular culture was adopted, as was book printing, by Scotch-Irish immigrants in the eighteenth century, when genteel America had for the most part allowed its control of the medium to lapse. Though we acknowledge that the emergence of the print medium was largely responsible for the shift in Europe in favor of the Protestant Reformation, it is more difficult for our culture to assert that the film medium has had the same magnitude of effect on American culture.

Still (and despite the version told by Hollywood in *The Wizard of Oz* and *A Star is Born* in which the Kansas farm girl saves a golden city), the consensus among most historians of American film, from Terry Ramsaye to Lewis Jacobs to Lary May, is that the number of "new immigrants"—and their children, America's new ethnics—who work in Hollywood in creative, technical, and economic capacities has been, and continues to be, extremely disproportionate to the population at large.[75] But to respond to the most recent revisions that conflate ethnic desire for assimilation with gentility, the following elaboration may be necessary.[76] Of the thirteen founders of the "Big Eight" studios, for example, eleven were born outside the United States. The other two, Harry Cohn and Jesse Lasky, were the son and grandson, respectively, of immigrants.[77] The early audience for film was working class,[78] and significantly ethnic and immigrant. Add to this the fact that by 1930 immigrants and their children numbered about 40 million, or about one-third of the entire U.S. population, and it becomes more significant than antagonistic to any argument about ethnicity in American cinema to note that until the 1950s overt representation of ethnicity on the screen was limited, with some notable exceptions, to stock characters and stereotypes.[79] These demographic factors helped to transform the medium into an organ of a population with otherwise little voice in the cultural mainstream. Along with vaudeville and the foreign-language newspaper, American film became an alternative to a high culture that was economically, geographically, and linguistically prohibitive for immigrants and ethnics. A disproportionate number of key figures in the film industry came from this immigrant class because few mainstream businessmen believed that film had more than a passing appeal to a vulgar lumpenproletariat.

Like both eighteenth- and nineteenth-century literary comedy, film comedy began as an expression of bewilderment in the face of a new landscape and a hostile middle and high culture. As the expression of a group otherwise largely unrepresented in the arts, film comedy, like early literary comedy, became preoccupied with the "historical real" in a mutated fashion that reflected both the repressiveness of dominant culture and a sense of the way the historical real might be experienced by those who lived it but did not write about it. Early film and literary humor in America originated in the suppression of ethnicity, which reemerged as comic eccentricity. This eccentricity was still predicated on a number of immigrant-like concerns, the most important of which was an obsession with the relation of the individual to the landscape. In this regard, early filmic and literary humor were alike in several ways: both were visual and improbable; both exaggerated the plastic qualities of the visible. Both established the superiority of the upstart culture over the preexistent culture, each medium realizing that characters out of proportion with real life were in harmony with the environment controlling that life. Both assumed that humanity was out of scale with nature, though, in each medium, comedy existed in the procrustean fit of an absurd hero with an absurd nature. Both kinds of humor derived in part from the fact that while society historically conquered its surroundings, the environment in this case prevailed over society by making over the individual in its own image. In both media, a strange landscape was made less frightening through its identification with an eccentric self. Both media tended to create an alternative community of social outcasts,[80] and both mystified their respective environments. The exaggeration of the real did more than pay tribute to burgeoning technologies; it both paraded and denied a fear that the miracle of technology was controlled by a very few magically endowed individuals, whether robber barons, film moguls, tall-tale heroes, or silent clowns. Landscape, which remained passively in the background in European comedy literature and film, thus moved actively to the foreground in America. The differences in the way the landscape was exaggerated in the two genres, though not insignificant, was as much due to the abrupt acceleration of technology at the turn of the twentieth century as to any more gradual changes in cultural sensibility: where exaggerations in the eighteenth and nineteenth centuries had to do with mass—exaggeration, most often, of size—the exaggerations of the early American cinema were more often exaggerations of size *and* motion—fast, slow, and reverse motion techniques.[81]

The similarities in portrayal of the landscape determine a similarity in the portrayal of characters who must assimilate into that landscape. Early American film and literary comedy both portray a series of rogues who successfully usurp established seats of power in sometimes sadistic fashion. (Even the early Chaplin is often more sadistic in the persecution of his persecutors than he is loveable [in, for example, *Tillie's Punctured Romance*].) At the turn of both the nineteenth and the twentieth centuries, a potentially nightmarish environment was habitually opposed by the protagonist, and in both cases the protagonist's success or failure depended more on the character's moral imperative than on his or her actual aptitude for adjustment to the environment. And, like much early frontier humor, very early arcade films were, as John Izod coyly asserts, "somewhat too salacious for the taste of large sections of the Victorian audience."[82]

Both media critiqued science as a hegemonic tool. Though the tall tale developed a sense of historicity, most noticeably in the works of Mark Twain (*Huckleberry Finn* and *Life on the Mississippi*) and William Faulkner (*As I Lay Dying* and *Absalom, Absalom*), it began as zoology and botany. Daniel Boorstin speaks of the difference between the science pursued in the United States and that pursued in Britain as "the difference between natural history and the physical sciences."[83] In opposition to the more theoretical British, Americans pursued a science that required only a recording of the landscape: that landscape provided even the casual observer with remarkable natural discoveries. Boorstin recounts a seventeenth-century American anecdote about a merman as an example of radically imaginative biological reportage; the story is remarkably similar to Walter Blair's examples of the same kind of anecdote as joke.[84] As naturalist, the humorist wrote about a world that might be improbable but was possible. Mrs. Trollope believed, with some skepticism, the stories of the man-eating crocodile and the drunken bear. This world demanded the kind of half-belief that science demands today in impossible marvels based on existing marvels. Early American humor professed to explicate to humanity a world external to itself, a fantastically plausible (or plausibly fantastic) world. That the explication is spurious, a part of the joke, was unimportant. All that mattered was momentary belief in the joke.

Early film humor is like its earlier literary incarnation in being perceived as based on the physically and biologically possible. Artists like Sennett *did* employ trick photography to gain the impossible effects they wished; they used mannequins in long shots of heroes going over cliffs in automobiles, for example. But the scenes we remember and call to mind about the Sennett films are not the instances of trick photography, but the audacity that informed his exaggerated use of familiar objects: the limit to which he pushed the airplane, the car, the baked good, the human body. If the person in the car was not real, the car itself was. Even his choice of human faces reflected this exaggeration of the real. Sennett did not opt for the clown makeup of the Continent; instead, he often picked for his biggest stars faces that were already exaggerated natural statements—one need only think of Ben Turpin's crossed eyes, Fatty Arbuckle's phenomenal obesity and his even more phenomenal grace, or Harry Langdon's baby face.

The clown personae were inscribed on the body of the performers, not painted on (as, for instance, in *commedia dell'arte*) so that they carried a degree of unselfconscious plausibility and integrity not otherwise possible. The films were not perceived as tricks: like Fellini, the earlier dir ctors identified truth with the grotesque.

But in early film this world of biology and technology was—except for the earliest film experiments by Edward Marey and Eadweard Muybridge—anthropomorphized and urbanized: it invented history as well as portrayed specific historical events. Early film comedy depended on an anthropomorphized world, a world dependent on human technology that reflects only ourselves at every turn. (Bela Balazs early and benignly indicates this anthropomorphism when he asserts that the human face organizes everything else

Figure 1.4 Exaggerations of scale: Fatty Arbuckle's phenomenal obesity matched by an even more phenomenal grace. Reproduced by permission of Culver Pictures.

within the filmic frame.)[85] The film world contained dangerous appliances, speeding cars, and mass-produced flotsam that we created, and which then alienated us from ourselves. This world took on a life of its own and in so doing became a source of mystification. Technology was an emblem for a mass divided consciousness, a consciousness that required rediscovery. In film comedy, the signal for this rediscovery lay in the comedian's ability to find new uses for created objects. These uses were often harmless—the lampshade as disguise—but they were often dangerous: the skyscraper as Mt. Everest. The most dangerous uses of a mysterious technology indicated the simplest level at which film comedy rediscovered humanity. The comic figure discovered herself or himself capable of triumphing over the physical dangers of technology by discovering even more dangerous potentials and overcoming them: again, a triumph over landscape. Like early literary comedy, then, early film comedy involves the triumph of the individual over the ridiculously and impossibly dangerous. Both comedies believe in the ability of the specific, the technological, and the visible to expose the invisible and the ideal as impositions on consciousness. Finally, because both early literary and filmic comedy expose the insults that culture imposes on the *body,* they both also expose the falsity of investing belief in the tyranny of the mind over the body, the tyranny of duality. (Physical comedy, as I shall assert at greater length in the next chapter, is about thinking bodies.)

Early American comedy's emphasis on the visual as collapsing the distinction between the physical and intellectual led to a reliance on slapstick, which tended to render as parallel and simultaneous anxieties the inclusion of the individual into an alien landscape, and the inclusion of the individual into a strange or hostile society he or she did not completely understand. Both American literature and film relied heavily on slapstick at a time when their European counterparts were relying on it less and less. (Mack Sennett made films at about the same time as Max Linder.) Slapstick was appropriate, however, to a culture whose most important encounters were with physical danger because such comedy was *about* physical danger—from either the city or the country—and about fantasy methods for evading that danger. In slapstick the individual or group is always either actually in peril, in the act of creating danger, or in peril of having danger thrust upon him or her by another individual or group. No one is irrevocably hurt. Death is banished, but the expectation of death informs the audience tension on which slapstick humor depends. Slapstick, which centers on the destruction of objects, appeals to an audience who fears the denial of its humanity by those objects, who live in a world where objects (or authority, which became objectified) threaten the physical margin of movement in any human direction. In denying historical determinism, slapstick transforms the exigencies of the marketplace into acts of volition. As we shall see in chapter 2, the assembly line became a playground. American comedy thus began by reading the activities forced on its audience as instinctual activities ambiguously accessible to all, turning a technological, economic, or social exigency into a volitional virtue.

Though its motive was the destruction of a threatening world, slapstick also betrays the audience's absorption and fascination with that world. That the same audience wishing the destruction of things wishes to see those things at all is a marvel; these are objects that the audience wishes to have as well as to destroy. Fear of inadequacy motivates the fantasy of super-adequacy. The fascination with objects reflects the ambivalence of the have-nots toward the haves, the confidence of the cartoon character who has run past the precipice and momentarily walks on air because his eyes are on the object of desire, not the ethereal means onto which that object has led him.

The comedy of the great silent comedians who descended directly from Sennett and "primitive" slapstick comedy—Arbuckle, Semon, Chaplin, Turpin, Lloyd, Keaton—deviated from Sennett not through an abandonment of slapstick but through its apotheosis. They were less concerned with destroying objects (or this is not so much how we remember them, unless they do it in an absolutely ironized fashion, the way Keaton destroys the boxcar in *The General* [1926]) and more interested in *transforming* them. They even transformed themselves *into* objects in an attempt to reinvent themselves (as when Chaplin turns himself into a lamp in *The Adventurer* [1916]). This impulse toward reinvention—and the impulse to find it comic—has a complex, overdetermined source to be elaborated on in chapter 2. But part of its motive was the audience's ambivalence toward artifacts, which the audience wanted, and their manufacture, in which most of the audience was forcibly engaged. The transformation of objects could be a fantasy of effortlessly creating artifacts using the materials of quotidian existence—the illusion supporting Picasso's "Head of a Bull" as well as Chaplin's "Dance of the Oceania Rolls" in *The Gold Rush* (1924). Picasso and Chaplin respectively transform mundane technologies (bicycle, fork, and roll) into modernist animated spectacles.

It could be a fantasy about creating artifacts valuable for their unique utility (the pie), or creating them in an artistic (unmachinelike) way (such as "Our Gang" imitations of the necessities of adult life). Transformation could even reflect a fantasy about becoming the artifact created: Chaplin as part of the statue at the beginning of *City Lights* (1931) or, in a nice visual pun, Chaplin becoming one of the nuts he is tightening at the beginning of *Modern Times* (1936).

The comic absorption with technology was reflected not only in the comic object but also in the comic manner. Think of what it means to refer to the "timing" of a joke. The sense that there is a perfect moment during comic "business" in which to deliver a "punch" line, that its maximum effect depends on a sense not of pages or minutes but of seconds, is a very industrial sense of humor. It reflects a world of machines and assembly lines. "Timing" suggests not only the origins of film technology itself in Muybridge's stop-motion experiments, but also the Frank Gilbreth efficiency studies in the saving of industrial time. This is the way Sennett and subsequent artists thought of placing jokes on the screen. But timing is important only to a society that has come to feel the pressure of time as an assembly-line phenomenon, where one production activity should follow another not only in correct sequence, not only in an efficient amount of time, but in a *standardized* amount of time. The double take must always be done at the same speed by the same actor; the *slow burn* must be so slow. The comedian—say Edgar Kennedy in *Duck Soup*—turns an assembly-line trope into an instinctual response. The immigrant change in perception is as much a part of the modernist response to the new urbanity as are Gertrude Stein's and Ernest Hemingway's revisions of the plain style of speaking; its impulse to brevity permeates the language over time so much so that the entries of the latest revision of Bartlett's tend to be briefer than in earlier editions.[86]

IMMIGRANT/ETHNIC MOGULS AND AUDIENCES

Anti-immigration legislation virtually ended the new-immigrant wave in 1924. Sound film became a commercial reality in 1926. This conjunction seems to me as fortuitous in its own way as that of the expulsion of the Jews from Spain and the Spanish landing in the "New World" in 1492. The first feature-length film with an extended soundtrack—*Don Juan* (1926) was a period piece about virility co-starring Myrna Loy, set in a foreign land (Spain) of long ago. The second—*The Jazz Singer* (1927) featured a Jewish performer in blackface who would not shut up, and who played an American Jew torn between amalgamationist and cultural-pluralist versions of ethnic inclusion.

Sixteenth- and seventeenth-century Europe saw the loss of Latin as the language of choice for educated people of all disciplines and ranks and the rise of the vernacular. But Latin did not cease to function in the culture as a result. Rather, it became a language nostalgized, whose knowledge became somewhat more arcane but whose use brought a certain virtuosity to vernacular use. The common argument in Renaissance studies is no longer that

Figure 1.5 Picasso's "Head of a Bull." © 1996 Artists Rights Society (ARS), New York / SPADEM, Paris

Shakespeare knew little Latin and less Greek, but that his Latin was a perfectly adequate tool that, in the midst of a vernacular culture, allowed him to highlight the ambiguities and resonances of Renaissance English. At the turn of the twentieth century, African-American, Irish, and Jewish composers in Tin Pan Alley and elsewhere were changing the way in which Americans felt rhythm, in part because of a similar clash of languages and cultures. (I will provide a more detailed account of this clash in chapter 3.)

The rise of the vernacular during the Renaissance resulted in part from a new technology: the printing press, which gave the vernacular a voice in a manner that had complicated nationalist implications.[87] It helped create the preconditions for the modern nation while it helped demolish the traditional rule by right—the first best-selling author as such was Martin Luther.[88] The rise of film sound technology was equally overdetermined. On the one hand, it is easy to imagine that sound was supposed to homogenize the population further, in a simple formula equating one language with one nation. The classical Hollywood style's tendency toward synchronous sound thematizes

Figure 1.6 "Mechanical reproduction of art changes the reaction of the masses toward art. The reactionary attitude toward a Picasso painting changes into the progressive reaction toward a Chaplin movie" —Walter Benjamin, "The Work of Art in the Age of Mechanical Reproduction." Chaplin's "Dance of the Oceania Rolls" © Roy Export Company Establishment. Courtesy of the Academy of Motion Picture Arts and Sciences.

this uniformity as structure—sound is to picture as people are to nation: adjunct, reflecting rather than originating meaning. On the other hand, as the first two feature-length sound films indicate, this reduction disguises the tension between the structure and the content: the presence of the speaking ethnic is a source of ambivalence in the structure itself of American film. Technological ambiguity reflects audience ambivalence. The story that Al

Jolson ad libbed when he was only supposed to sing, thus introducing speech to the feature film, is compelling in part because the ethnic voice in which he speaks suggests the spontaneous eruption of the ethnic at a historical moment when the more refined diction and accent of John Barrymore as Don Juan might have been thought a more appropriate first utterance.

To analogize once more: Gilles Deleuze and Fèlix Guattari, in an essay on Kafka, define minority literature as a re- or de-territorialization, a subverting of the dominant language in its use by minorities who must adopt that language.[89] How much more significant will this re-territorializing be when practiced in a new medium, when the possibility exists for the (unconscious) structuring of the medium according to one's own sensibility and background? I would in fact extend their argument, observing not only that the language changes but that the main theme within any such dynamic is going to be ambivalence about definitions of culture that marginalize the writer: host/guest (or at least *gastarbeiter*), minor/major, center/periphery, center/margin, and so on. In other words, immigrant and ethnic intervention in culture makes—or keeps—that culture modern. Having accepted the notion that immigrant/ethnic ambivalence structures American film, one may more easily understand some traditionally opaque filmic dynamics: for example, the tendency for the classical Hollywood style to maintain its distance from traditionally modernist techniques, as its audience and producers attempt to define their relation to traditional culture before taking on modernism. Our culture's countertendency, in spite of this reluctance, to define cinema as modern, because it is technologically so, is the tendency of cultures newer to the idea of industrial technology. More important, certain central themes can be recast as immigrant/ethnic: the tendency toward ambivalence, from the general—*Cahiers du cinema*'s sense of American cinema as subversive within its conservatism[90]—to the specific—the sense, for example, that the musical remystifies what it pretends to demystify.

The very originality and technical expertise called upon to entertain American society also and continually recreated American society. In appropriating the immigrant and the ethnic, society brought about the transformation of the same "American" identities the mainstream culture was attempting to preserve. These cultural identities—these myths—were filtered through immigrant and ethnic sensibilities that restructured these identities, reshaping the myths. The dominant American identities—the cowboy, the businessman, the playboy—though losing the quality of ethnic pluralism, retained the sense of eccentricity, what Americans uniformly call "individuality." As Werner Sollors asserts, "In America, casting oneself as an outsider may in fact be considered a dominant cultural trait."[91]

Moguls and the First Generation

From about 1908 to 1925 the sociology of film changed in several ways. Film distribution moved out of the ghetto: production moved from New York to California, and the Edison trusts finally lost to the new Hollywood culture. That each move contains an immigrant/ethnic dimension should be fairly obvious. The irony, of course, is that as ethnics gained greater control over the product, ethnicity disappeared from it. Even the early ethnic owners did not approve of the origin of cinema's popularity with the working class, as they were forced to reject their own origins in order to succeed.[92]

During the transition from the "primitive" to the "classical" era of filmmaking, early filmmakers, for causes impossible to distinguish as either merely economic or social, desired to remove the new medium from the site of its first success. (A "classier" clientele meant a better-paying and a wider audience.) The earliest Hollywood filmmaking was motivated in part by the wish to efface its own economic and social origins for a middle-class respectability its own shapers desired for themselves. It may seem paradoxical that the new ethnics replaced many of the genteel inventors—the Edisons, the Porters, and the Lathams—at about the same time that cinema itself was leaving the ghetto. But these movements were parallel: new immigrants were leaving the Eastern ghettos, one way or another, at roughly the same time as was the industry in which they were investing more time and money.[93]

Differences between the plights of the film mogul and the seventeenth-century immigrant stemmed from the fact that the mogul lived in the midst of an established, hostile culture that had for a long time predicated its own existence on decimating any significant difference in other, guest cultures. Whatever else, American culture was, by the time of the new immigration, firmly hegemonic; its survival depended on the genius and labor of larger and larger populations that it could not afford to reward, since to do so would require acknowledging this dependence and delegitimizing an economic and cultural elite. The new populations, unlike the Native Americans, were too large and too necessary to destroy. But their ethnicity, their difference, might be neutralized.

A spurious struggle over ethnic identity resulted, a struggle between self-identity and definition assigned by popular culture, spurious because both sides of the struggle meant a loss of overt ethnic identity. The treatment of the new film moguls serves as a good example. They were satirized by the press because on the one hand, as new ethnics, they did not have the gentility that powerful American men were supposed to have; nor, on the other hand,

Figure 1.7 Newspaper photograph of Louis B. Mayer. © L.A. *Daily News* photo/Reprinted by
permission from the *Los Angeles Times Syndicate*. Courtesy of the Academy of Motion Picture Arts
and Sciences.

could they possess insight into the mass tastes they claimed to have. But their
megalomania in claiming to reflect public taste was the new manifestation of
the impulse in the earlier literature to make the illiterate backwoodsman a
culture hero. Like Davy Crockett, the larger-than-life figure was comic in his

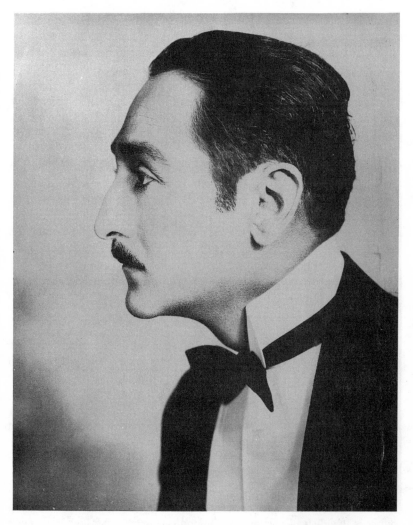

Figure 1.8 Studio portrait of Adolph Menjou: the media representation of the mogul, and the studio's vision. Reproduced by permission of Culver Pictures. Courtesy of the Academy of Motion Picture Arts and Sciences.

boorishness and social ineptitude. (The treatment of Louis B. Mayer is perhaps the best model, but Harry Cohn, Mack Sennett, and others also became famous for their often apocryphal gaffes and their egotism. Of the early famous producers in the generation after Edison and Porter, only D. W. Griffith had a legitimate claim to middle-class gentility, and, as a Southerner, he had his own cultural cross to bear.) In both eras, the producer was admired for his power and expertise in his chosen field but also condemned as an idiot savant. In each case the figure has an alter ego, either fictional or real. The Davy Crockett we know is fictional and the Louis B. Mayer we know is real (marginally), but the first has his living correlative and the second his fictional—even mythic—self. The studios themselves represented the studio heads as apotheoses of "class." If, on the screen, they were sometimes not very bright, they were at least elegant and mid-Atlantic: Adolph Menjou in *Goldwyn Follies* (1938) and in *A Star is Born* (1937), Ralph Bellamy in *Boy Meets Girl* (1938). Even the dunderhead who heads Monumental Pictures in *Singin' in the Rain* (1952) is tall and articulate, with no distinctive ethnic characteristics.[94] (Interestingly, the most salient feature of this dunderhead is his indecisiveness, one of the few unattractive qualities *not* often attributed to the moguls.) The type even made it to stage productions never destined for film. In *Hollywood Pinafore* (1945), Joseph Porter (Victor Moore) discusses in operettic style his rise to the chief position in the studio: "So all shlemiels, whoever you may be, / If you want to rise to the top of the tree . . . /Just turn your back 'neath the mistletoe, / And you all may be rulers of the studio."

Essentially agreeing with the mainstream culture's judgment that the public display of ethnicity by a ruling elite was undesirable, but unable to gain access to Anglo respectability, the immigrant filmmaker participated in his own suppression by effacing his ethnic identity and replacing it with a fantasy of auto-genesis. The industry must have seemed designed expressly for the unconscious purpose of acting out a self-creation not merely within one's own private, fictional world but also in a community at large that was itself clamoring for more film fantasy. The mogul's flattering self-portrait, in being ethnically self-effacing, was also becoming America's picture of itself. (See chapter 4 for the elaboration of this dynamic.) The fantastic degree to which the moguls identified their own tastes with those of the movie-going public is already well-documented and indicates a fantasy of control that was true only within the confines of a limiting dialectic that they neither recognized nor controlled.

The moguls went further than merely representing themselves on film as American. Filmmakers also created their own cities in the desert— Hollywood and Los Angeles—after their own alter-ego images. They erected a fantasy city dependent on, but removed from, traditional culture, in order to create a new landscape that could accommodate the moguls' personae. As Richard Maltby illustrates, their economy allowed eccentricity to appear normal, perhaps conservative, but above all desirable: "[The moguls] more or less deliberately set out to create in Hollywood a separate, enclosed world, whose image to the rest of America was as important an ingredient in the product they sold as were the stars or plots of individual films. More than anything else, it was this construction of 'Hollywood' that constituted the key to their autonomy from East Coast control."[95] In the same essay, Maltby explains the relationship between production and investment: even the underlying economy of Hollywood during the studio era opposed the creative West and the controlling East. Like the original pattern of American settlement, movies expanded from east to west, from New Jersey and New York to California. This move, in recapitulating westward expansion, was an attempt to repeat the liberation of identity from Eastern values and strictures. However, as in the earlier representation of the wilderness, the more Hollywood came to appear *sui generis,* as Eastern interests played an increasing economic role in Hollywood, the moguls responded with an ever greater regimentation, a tightening of the studio system in a fiefdom/assembly line that, like Chinese communism, was both medieval and high-capitalist.

The moguls were not the only immigrants forced to abnegate responsibility for representing their backgrounds in the art they controlled. They were merely illustrative of this impulse in the highest reaches of the industry hierarchy, at a level that dictated formal policy for the rest of the industry. Historians such as Leonard Dinnerstein, Roger L. Nichols, and David M. Reimers notice that a disproportionate number of immigrants and newer ethnics became actors and technicians as well as businessmen.[96] The Hollywood system offered a modern analogue to the early literary system because immigrants in both eras had access to a medium spurned by representatives of higher culture. Immigrant insecurity at not belonging to mainstream culture led in both cases to the reconstitution of culture in their own image. The "central theme" of this culture was the attempt to efface regional, national, ethnic identity in favor of an American norm as established in such vehicles as the star system. The irony of the attempt to repress ethnicity in America was a return of the repressed as a series of industrial repressions: the Hollywood star, genre, and classical photographic system provided a universal norm to regulate human behavior far beyond the desires of Henri Bergson. While attributing the fall of the studio system in the 1950s and 1960s to television, baby-boom apathy, Eisenhower, etc., no one has yet charted the relation between the decline of Hollywood and the increasing centrality of the struggle for civil rights, and the concomitant collapse in the belief in traditional genres and character types.

Audiences to the 1930s and the "New-World Plot"

Understanding that ethnicity and immigration inform the ethos of filmmaking helps us to read the structure of films. In considering, for example, the problem of the representation of affluence we often find deceptive, even hypocritical, the plot dynamic within which protagonists choose mates so often in spite of the fact that those mates are wealthy (*My Man Godfrey* [1936], *It Happened One Night* [1934], or *You Can't Take it With You* [1938], for example). The explanation for this tortuous, counter-Marxist and counter-capitalist logic is often equally tortuous: Stanley Cavell, for example, ascribes such economic reluctance to American transcendentalism, which respects money in a way that capitalism does not.[97] It seems to me easier to assign this indifference to wealth to an equally traditional immigrant tension between Old-World values and New-World behavior modification, in which a reward is promised to behavior that supports high capitalism more immediately than to Old-World rituals not easily appropriated for the new regime. Films in all genres are interested in accommodation and resistance to a variously defined community in what we might call the "New-World plot."

One might equally argue that the New World plot, though possibly existing in the nickelodeon era (during which the first ethnic and immigrant moguls were finding their way to film), would by the 1930s be anachronistic. Film in the 1930s, one might argue, is not going to be influenced by an immigrant wave that ended in the previous decade. After the 1920s, the United States itself, not Europe or Asia, provided the United States with the largest source of lower- and working-class ethnicity.[98] The immigrants in the largest wave at the beginning of the century had long been somewhat acclimated to the United States. They spoke English and had settled into those employments and into those areas of the country they would in many cases inhabit for several generations. But immigration restriction intensifies the alienation and ambivalence that characterizes the "structure of feeling" of the immigrant. Restriction not only meant a loss of immigrants to the United States, but also further alienated second- and third-generation ethnics from their origins, leaving them ambivalent about their status as Americans. The problem of severing the connection with the parents was familiar to both the first and the second generations; assimilation, acculturation, and amalgamation were as much generational problems for the native-born children as for their immigrant parents: if the parents were not greenhorns, "I'd be accepted."[99] Both generations felt the tension of renouncing ethnic identity for one more successful in the New World. In both sets of generational conflict the child feels scapegoated by the family, either by the parent who

Figure 1.9 The visual pathos of the Old World in the New. © The Billy Rose Theatre collection, The New York Public Library for the Performing Arts, Astor, Lenox and Tilden Foundations.

remains in the old country or by the first-generation parent who objects to the assimilated child. The paradox of assimilation is that, in conforming to mainstream culture, the immigrant/ethnic rebels against his own home. Movement toward the host culture is, in ethnic terms, oedipal rebellion: "Jacob Gordin's drama *The Jewish King Lear* showed a pious Jewish father abused and neglected by heartless daughters, a theme close enough to reality to bring tears to the eyes of foreign-born parents less than satisfied with the behavior of their Americanized children."[100]

The revision of a Shakespearean text as a New-World plot would have implications for film representation, in which the tension between appropriation and critique is especially marked. But in rejecting the primary family, the second generation rejected much of itself. Richard Sennett asserts that even when the native-born ethnic attains to a position of respectability he still feels passive, insecure, and inferior to those with better or more traditional education. "[One subject] takes personal responsibility for his social position, and the result is that he makes himself feel inadequate no matter which way he turns in attempting to deal with success."[101] Assimilation for the second-generation "marginal man"[102] also meant rebellion against the immigrant parents, but the perceived reward was an affluence based on conformity and characterized as status, prestige, and acceptance, rather than as merely survival. Assimilation subverted the ethnic self and family in proportion as it seemed socially the opposite. The more genteel (the more pseudo-Anglo), the more differentiated from the parents and the first generation. Because assimilation and upward mobility felt like rebellion for a significant portion of the population, American mass culture tended to confuse conformity with individualism: it conflated individuality and individuation from the parent. Rebellion from the family was almost inevitably identification with the New World and its ways. Being less Italian meant being more American, so that being more American was both extremely satisfying and fraught with ambivalence.

Conversely, the more ethnics chose to identify with their origins or their parents, the more they had the air of being *socially* subversive. Despite the official story, the more Jewish, Italian, Catholic, or Irish one remained, the less "American" one was. Even the representatives of the official culture upheld this dichotomy in no uncertain terms. Barbara Miller Solomon observes: "Boston became the center of the advance-guard movement for the restriction of immigration and lent her influence to spreading the idea that the capacity for democratic citizenship was an inherited characteristic, which could not be developed equally in all races. Repudiation of a free America for all was the last step in the Brahmin deviation from the ideals of the New

England Flowering.[103] The Myrna Loy and William Powell personae, for example, developing by the 1930s from ethnic villains to models of mainstream social behavior, had to spurn their ethnic associations. The Marx Brothers, always categorized as at least relatively subversive, maintained an ambiguously ethnic public identity.

Assimilationist guilt helps explain the peculiar amatory choices in the New-World plot. In canonical Western narratives the traditional choice between the wealthy and the simpatico suitor is not particularly vexed. The suitor is either appropriate despite his or her economic or social status, or inappropriate because of it. Petruchio chooses Katherina, and Ivanhoe does not choose the "Jewess," each from a sense of his lover's rank. Nearly everyone in the eighteenth-century novel marries according to his rank, or rues the day. The Miller's Alisoun pointedly chooses Hende Nicholas (a "povre scoler") over Absalon, and Emma Bovary pointedly chooses Leon Dupuis ("a clerk at Maitre Guilleumin, the notary"), despite their poverty. Courtly and cavalier lovers from Ovid to Shakespeare demonstrate the correctness of their love, despite their lack of means. Or, more correctly, their lack of means implies a kind of spirituality that the more well-heeled suitors presumably cannot cultivate in their counting houses or their busy estates. But the New-World plot, often borrowing from European folk and fairy-tale traditions more than from the realist or naturalist novel, sets about to prove that the rich suitor and the poor suitor are the same person. American film comedy, in a complex assimilative dynamic engendered by a complex ethnic industry and audience, refashions our perception of the attractive man or woman as unorthodox while underpinning that unorthodox behavior with an ultra-orthodox code of conduct, an orthodox voice: Cary Grant's weirdly mid-Atlantic accent beneath the nonconformist in Holiday; Katharine Hepburn's Vassar accent beneath Sylvia Scarlett in male drag.

Because Hollywood's claim that in America one may choose wealth is spurious, America's contaminated claim to newness is often perceived as hollow. Film critics tend to see the paradoxical pairing of familial rebellion and social conformity as falsely dichotomous. The choice presented to the hero or heroine is unreal; opinion can side only with the favored suitor. The American film hero in all his avatars is seen as instinctually right for the heroine, and vice versa, even if the couple are from opposite sides of the railroad tracks, even if the hero or heroine is perfunctorily presented as in some ways undesirable. But the immigrant structure of feeling that informs that representation of wealth is genuine. The social and economic choices— so correctly criticized as non-choices—in the films of the 1920s and 1930s feel volitional because they suggest a series of submerged problems that are real for a segment of the population that cannot itself represent the reality of those problems. Critics see this screwball dynamic (by no means limited to the screwball comedy) as an apologia for industrial capitalism, in which the promise of a democratic society is subverted by the reality of much wealth in close proximity to so much more poverty. But the choice of a partner different from oneself, though a fiction of a capitalism whose reality, for the most part, still insists that like remains with like, represents a necessary rebellion for those ethnics who do achieve any success within mainstream culture.

The choices that film personae made in the 1920s and 1930s were not, for the most part, genuinely premeditated. To consider the dilemma of assimilation—even transformed versions of it—was to be defeated by it, for few publicly ethnic avenues allow for economic affluence and social success. Stars in formula films make choices that they do not examine too closely but rather take on faith. The cultivation of instinctual "coolness"—beginning in the 1920s with the flapper and the sheik—was a hegemonic strategy for making cultural exigencies appear to be personal choices. Part of the mystique of cool is that its dicta not be too carefully examined.

The price of assimilation is the individual's renunciation of his old family and the conscious and so necessarily incomplete identification with a new family whose signs of communality are based on affluence rather than on shared historical referents. For those born wealthy, affluence is a shared culture, and success is a return to the parents. For the wealthy, success allows for oedipal individuation, in which one may be like the parents without having precisely what they have. For those born poor and ethnic, success is traumatic, a renunciation of the consensual reality one knew in favor of an alternative, alienating reality that nevertheless must be life sustaining. The New-World plot, in which success may be chosen without consequences, is a fantasy of an acculturation that has already taken place without its concomitant identity-suicide.

VAUDEVILLE AND FILM: A HOMOLOGY

Two points establish a line, three points a screen. Vaudeville provides a traditional last reference point to show how ethnicity has its inevitable effect in constituting the structure of popular culture, and so the structure of American self-identification.[104] One could use several possible media of *fin-de-siecle* popular expression to demonstrate the unconscious presence of the ethnic: opera, newspaper illustrations, dime novels, strip cartoons, animated film, and so on.[105] But the vaudeville stage has been cited as an especially self-evident space for ethnic contention, a place that used spectacle to test various theories of ethnic accommodation—not just in the use of stereotypes, but in the relations between actor and owner, labor and management, and spectator and spectacle. Vaudeville is not merely the site at which ethnics learn English manners and language, as some critics continue to suggest.[106] It was, in fact, a Bakhtinian testing ground on which a radically changing culture was reflected and founded.[107] The understanding that a whole world was being satirized is the only feasible way an ethnic audience could laugh at the particular slurs against its own group.[108] For example, not just the Irish, but the world scheme within which the Irish were seen as lazy and drunk, was the object of satire.

Notes on Origins

Like the rise of early film, the rise of American vaudeville coincides approximately with a mass immigrant movement: the movement of people from Western and Northern Europe to the United States. Its roots, more particularly, are in the post–Civil War immigration of Germans, Scandinavians, and English.[109] American vaudeville grows out of the German beer garden and the English music hall at least as much as from the American legitimate stage, the variety hall, and the saloon.

However, since vaudeville varied according to the class, ethnicity, and gender of the audience and performers, it was significantly different from its European avatars, especially from the English music hall.[110] Despite claims about the rowdiness of its patrons, the British music hall was regulated in a number of ways that even B. F. Keith did not conceive. First, theater in England had existed under an onus since before Cromwell. As a consequence, laws regulating the format of the stage—from the Drury Lane patent allowing women into the acting profession in the 1660s[111] to the 1892 parliamentary committee recommendation that variety theaters "be licensed to perform sketches if not over forty minutes long"[112]—were commonplace. Extra-legal restrictions existed as well, such as the "chairman, who sat in a limbo between stage and audience, announcing the turns and rapping for order when the public grew too obstreperous."[113] The music hall had a greater tendency toward political conservatism and xenophobia (especially during the Crimean and Boer conflicts) than the vaudeville stage could afford (at least until World War I).[114] Further, vaudeville and film slapstick had its influence on European culture, from the famously documented love the surrealists bore for the medium to the lesser known, even quirky, influences

on, say, German Expressionism.[115] While any claim that vaudeville was an
uncensored medium would be absurd, so too is the normative claim that the
medium is derived essentially from the British music hall tradition or that
their liberties and repressions are alike. The music hall could provide only
one of several analogies or voices, others of which would be the contemporaneous cabaret scenes of Paris and Berlin, the Yiddish stage, African-
American music, and so on.[116]

Every serious critic of American vaudeville has remarked that vaudeville reaches maturity through at least two different and simultaneous ethnic
phenomena: legitimate ethnic theater and ethnic vaudeville. As Leonard
Dinnerstein and his co-authors observe:

> The Swedes, Poles, and Czechs had an ethnic theater, as did the
> Germans, whose earliest performances were staged in local taverns
> without props. . . . The Yiddish (Jewish) theater, the most famous of
> the ethnic drama groups, originated in the 1880s in New York City
> and lasted for more than half a century. . . . The Yiddish theater
> eventually spawned a large number of actors, writers, and directors
> who achieved fame in New York's commercial theater as well as in the
> motion picture industry in Hollywood.[117]

Different largely in its more manifest intensity, ethnic theater, like
vaudeville, was absorbed with ethnic accommodation. (In this regard, ethnic
theater is to vaudeville as vaudeville is to film.) As Maxine Schwartz Seller
describes it:

> One of the most popular subjects for comedy on European immigrant
> stages was the new arrival, the "green one," who made ridiculous mistakes
> and was victimized by his own countrymen as well as by native-born
> Americans. These comedies allowed immigrants to measure themselves
> against the "green one" on the stage and to rejoice in how far they had
> come. These and other comedies also provided opportunities to satirize
> the ethnic community—the boarding-house proprietor, the saloon-
> keeper, the clergyman, the self-serving politician, the social climber—and
> to criticize the hypocrisy and corruption in mainstream American life.[118]

Critics provide hints of the interrelatedness of ethnic theater and more
mainstream entertainments; Seller, for example, discusses the occasional
forays of ethnic actors onto the legitimate stage and the translations of the
major plays of one country into the language of particular ethnic theaters.

Such critics are beginning to review the larger political impact of the ethnic theater on the culture when they discuss the attempt to improve ethnic images in the larger society and the cohesive quality of ethnic theater.[119] But these analyses remain relatively undeveloped;[120] critical attempts to correlate influences between contemporary media that must have had a largely overlapping audience are still, because of the current historical moment, very subordinate to the impulse to define the boundaries and qualities of ethnic theater.

If ethnic theater is difficult to define, the variety hall is even more so, except to say that acts were lower-class and bawdy and that performances were staged for a predominantly male audience. Extant studies are otherwise comparatively sketchy. (I take this relative critical indifference to indicate more about the critic and historian than the audience or performer.) The literature does not contain much that characterizes the acts as ethnic except, of course, in the case of minstrelsy, which was quickly appropriated by white performers; it does assert that the German Americans patronized the beer halls they imported from their native country and that the various ethnic theaters attracted primarily patrons of the same ethnicity. (They even attracted the appreciation of a wider audience at times.)[121] But scholars of the genre, such as John Dimeglio, Robert C. Allen, Douglas Gilbert, Albert McLean, Henry Jenkins, and Shirley Staples, do not document the specific ethnicity of the variety hall performers and patrons, asserting only that performers tended to be poor and working-class men.[122]

Just as films were first mass-projected in large, unadorned nickelodeons that were dirty, masculine, and unsavory, so one predecessor of vaudeville was held in the "variety saloons." As with early film, one of the main appeals was sex. But according to Robert C. Allen, sexuality was not relegated only to the stage in the early "concert rooms," "music halls," and taverns of the 1850s and 1860s: the audience space was a part of the spectacle as well. "The young ladies were waitresses, virtually the only females in what were almost exclusively male haunts. The enticing young ladies coupled with the often risque nature of parts of the stage entertainment gave these establishments dubious reputations."[123] Douglas Gilbert describes a typical opening skit in the variety house as much more overtly sexual than high vaudeville would be.[124] He recounts rituals of public sexuality and the conflation of stage, audience, and backstage in a spectacle of excess, the ghost of which can be seen in the 1930s, in the pre–Hayes Production Code musicals and the spectacular excesses vis-à-vis stage and sexuality of the Marx Brothers and other groups.[125] The overt stage sexuality enabled a neo-Brechtian space that would carry over into film, a realism in relation to desire that would draw "no clear line between the stage and the street, between sexy performances and sexual acts, between the theatre and the disorderly house."[126] As we shall later see, the ambivalent collapse between "real" and "play" space becomes one vehicle for ethnic self-expression in the films of the Marx Brothers.

Related to a sexuality spilling over the stage is a peculiar exoticism, again favored by film in the 1920s and 1930s.[127] While it is not possible to assert that the majority of chorines of the variety stage were ethnic, the sexuality of the vaudeville stage was often orientalized, from the British invasion of actresses around the turn of the century to the inclusion of "exotic" dancers and performers on the variety bill: Raquel Meller, Lydia Lopokova, Fritzi Scheff, and Vesta Tilley, for example. The effect of this exotically sexualized space was to create even obviously homespun products as foreign. The Hammerstein Victoria and Pastor's house both featured exotic newspaper headliners of the day, such as Hammerstein's Evelyn Nesbit, the woman for whom Stanford White was murdered.[128] Helen Morgan at one point anagrammatizes her name to the more exotic Neleh Nagrom. Vaudeville thus became the experimental ground for reinventing American culture as exotically sexual, which is to say it became one stage version of ethnic. (The sexual exotic will be further explored in chapter 4.) This orientalized stage is, however, always ironized, assumed to be at some level false: "Gaby Deslys, who made her reputation by losing it, is the feature of the new *Revue of the Revues* at the Winter Garden. . . . Personally, I doubt whether Mlle. Deslys would know the former King of Portugal if she passed him in the street, but her supposed share in the downfall of his dynasty has been advertised sufficiently to give her much of the vogue once enjoyed in this country by the late lamented Lola Montez."[129] In other words, if the immigrant is lured and repulsed by the host culture, his stage avatar is at the same time luring and repulsing its audience. This sensibility is, as I will show, the same one the Marx Brothers and other film comedy teams will employ in researching the origin of the *untermensch* (the submerged ethnic).

Vaudeville Analogies

We can discuss with the greatest specificity the structure of the spectacle that was high vaudeville (1880s-1910s) because by this time vaudeville had become characterized, first through the efforts of a few canny entrepreneurs and subsequently by critics and historians, as a respectably middle-class entertainment whose less savory aspects had been sloughed off onto the burlesque revue. Like film, vaudeville attracted immigrants and ethnics in its origin, its management, and its talent, picking up such acts as minstrelsy, clog dancing, and ethnic humor. Ethnic performers were gleaned not only from the United States, but from other nations. Visiting performers received acclaim—or ignominy—here and then returned to their homes. Gilbert's chapter "The Foreign Invasion" invokes a wide array of visiting dignitaries, among whom were comics Harry Lauder, Albert Chevalier, and Vesta Victoria, some of the most famous names in the business.[130]

Further, though vaudeville, like early film, tended to portray a middle-class ideal, vaudeville houses and vaudeville distribution in the major cities were designed with ethnic differentiation in mind: "There was a vaudeville house for practically every kind of New Yorker. Middle-class women out shopping could seek a refined Keith-Albee theater. Working-class Jewish immigrants on the Lower East Side found vaudeville at Loew's theaters. . . . Vaudeville reached people from different classes and ethnic groups because for each of them it appeared in familiar surroundings."[131]

Vaudeville, like film, had its small coterie of moguls—B. F. Keith, F. F. Proctor and E. F. Albee—who dictated the tastes of the rest of the industry and who were as sure that they themselves reflected the tastes of the American mass audience as Harry Cohn, Sam Goldwyn, and Mack Sennett were sure that they, too, were reflections of mass taste. (If Sennett did not laugh at a gag himself, he threw it out.) Many of the most prominent names in vaudeville management made their way into the early history of film, including Harry Cohn, William Fox, Marcus Loew, and Jesse Lasky, to name only a few. Many of the businessmen individually responsible for the character of vaudeville were ethnic or immigrant: Tony Pastor was of Italian extraction and devoutly Roman Catholic, Martin Beck was of German extraction. Like the later film moguls, the vaudeville managers were insecure about their status as genteel but nouveau riche; they often came from the same lower-class or immigrant background as the film moguls.[132] Oddly, though they believed themselves to reflect public opinion in part because they were from that public, they also wished to differentiate themselves from theater patrons and, more especially, from the performers. As a consequence of the moguls' desire for American success, the structure of this American entertainment is as much informed by the desire to mediate between various definitions of ethnicity as was that of film.

The moguls brought into vaudeville countless stars who later entered film, including Mae West, W.C. Fields, and Danny Kaye. But, as in the case of the film bosses, the vaudeville moguls brought not only personalities but a system: the vaudeville prototype of the star system, replete with issues about top billing and about the amount of money a famous name could attract (like film and until vaudeville's decline, always on the increase, always increasingly phenomenal for its day). The business mechanics and star system of the vaudeville industry provide further analogies to film. The early movie industry was divided into three strata: theater chains, distributors, and studios. As the industry grew, the largest studios and distributors attempted a vertical assimilation of the industry, trying to appropriate two or even all three of these strata. Most film scholars know the history of block-booking, under which producers and distributors gained access to the theaters by assuring that desirable films would be released only to theaters affiliated with the distributors, and then only under very restrictive conditions. The vaudeville industry was more localized but essentially analogous: it was divided into theater chains (or, more properly, "circuits"), booking agents, and acts. Robert C. Allen puts forth the economic and structural parallel neatly, if tentatively: "It is, perhaps, tempting to see a more direct parallel between the development of the picture palace and that of high-class vaudeville. We might speculate that just as Keith, Proctor, and Pastor, by putting middle-class morality on the vaudeville stage and the stage into luxurious surroundings, had lifted vaudeville from its lowly saloon origins, so the Marks, Rothapfel, and others effected the transition in motion picture exhibition from the proletariat-oriented nickelodeon to the middle-class institution of the picture palace."[133] Allen also quotes Frederick Snyder as asserting that "[i]n the machinery of big-time vaudeville and its system of production organization were the embryonic concepts for the programming and circulation of popular entertainment on a mammoth scale, tested by time and proved successful at the box office."[134] Along with the octopus of vertical and horizontal expansion, vaudeville, like film, had problems with performers who wanted a larger share in the running of the medium: the White Rats strike of 1901, and the various later retaliations of the managers, including the use of film as a strikebreaker, parallels the ongoing problem of suppressing actors' attempts in Hollywood to make inroads on the hegemony of the producer, distributor, and exhibitor. Like their Hollywood counterparts, the vaudeville moguls nearly always won. Because actors were also disproportionately ethnic, this class antagonism was also inter- and intra-ethnic rivalry.[135] So for the moguls, the impulse toward ethnic and exotic inclusion was always and paradoxically coupled with economic repression—the industry became an expression of partial self-denial.

Vaudeville Humor: Analogies

Though it had its melodramas and sentimental songs, the "essence of American vaudeville" was, as one contemporary critic observed, comedy.[136] For Henry Jenkins as for Albert McLean, that comedy is iconoclastic "new humor."[137] It is almost too simplistic to point out that vaudeville comedy is closer than comic literature to film comedy in many ways, as much because of temporal proximity as because of their similarity as visual media. But a common theme having to do with anxiety about inclusion into mainstream culture is common to all three. The various treatments of this anxiety across media, though radically different in so many ways, have in common a tendency to gentrify the medium, signaling both a greater degree of inclusion of the implicated audience/participants and a more subtle kind of discrimination against them.

Like filmic and early literary humor, vaudeville humor reflected the American theatrical tendency to transform anxiety about inclusion into a celebration of difference. This fantasy celebration becomes more hysterical and extreme as possibilities for ethnic inclusion are denied. Albert McLean, the most archetypally inclined critic, makes an analogous assertion: "That humor should take this course toward compression and frenzy says much about the nature of the audience and their lives. The impulse toward hysteria was rising closer to the surface and, given the protective cover of the vaudeville ritual and its sympathetic audience, needed relatively fewer incitements to be released."[138] Vaudeville humor, like its American counterparts in early literature and early film, is a response to an essentially hostile, alien, and alienating landscape. It is a fantasy inclusion of the self, into a landscape that rejects it, by recreating that self as superior to that landscape through the very qualities—modified or exaggerated—responsible for the rejection. This time the landscape is the city rather than the wilderness, but it is still alienating. McLean claims for vaudeville the kind of ethnic cultural concern that also characterizes film: "[V]audeville, as a ritual of a New Folk, was one means by which Americans came to terms with a crisis in culture. . . . Vaudeville was one means—a primary one—by which the disruptive experience of migration and acclimatization was objectified and accepted. In its symbolism lies the psychic profile of the American mass man in the moment of his greatest trial.[139] Vaudeville, like early American comic literature and early film, is a response to a society that only equivocally initiates its neophytes.

Even more than the older comic literature or the coming film, vaudeville relied on spectacle in Bakhtinian fashion as a significant portion of its appeal, celebrating an inverted version of mainstream culture as freakish: from actually designated "freaks" and "rarities" like Little Alice, "the smallest baby ever born live,"[140] to personalities notable for attributes not connected to any performative ability at all (Jim Corbett, Annette Kellerman, and Carrie Nation). The ethnic hence became allied to the freakish and the spectacular. This inversion was created to evade the blue laws of an earlier century and the decrepit enlightenment notions of public edification that informed them, notions that bored even those who subscribed to them, and were senseless to the new ethnics. Like film, vaudeville confounded genteel notions of education, instead offering a medium that redefined the educational public spectacle as entertainment. According to Allen, for example, vaudeville houses begin as unconscious burlesques of the eighteenth-century notion of the museum.[141] Allen sees the variety bill, with its deemphasis of narration and "continuous performance," as another incidental blow at decorous Brahmin narrativity, aimed not so much at East Coast culture as at a class of patron for whom such culture had become, perhaps always was, irrelevant.[142]

Like film, vaudeville repackaged older, bawdier shows for an increasingly middle-class audience. Like film, it went through a process of increasing gentrification at the hands of businessmen (Pastor, Keith, and so on) whose motives were always immediately economic. The rise of vaudeville is thus part of a recurring motif in American mass entertainment: the movement of a medium from a local to a more general appeal means a greater degree of assimilation and gentility—assimilation because the medium mirrors a similar movement in its original, lower-class, ethnic patrons; gentility because its owners recognize that they can make larger sums of money from the patronage of the preexisting American middle class. Like film and early American comic literature, vaudeville chooses less risque settings and subjects over time in order to attract a wider, more genteel audience. The humorous anecdote tends to move from its oral avatar to the newspaper story, from the almanac tale to the collection to the novel, and from its regional and local appeal as an off-color kind of humor children might read surreptitiously to a less lurid brand of humor that children *ought* to read.[143] Most American media, initially gaining a kind of prominence because they represent some cultural extreme, whether highbrow or low, ultimately assure their own permanence by revising their method and aims to suit a more mainstream audience.

Still, despite the requirements of an ever greater gentility, vaudeville, like early film, continued to depend on comedy genres for its success: rube comedy, nut comedy, dialect, blackface, parody, impersonation, burlesque, "bone crunching comedy," "facials," "knockabouts," animal acts, and sketch-team comedy.[144] Even in the middle of the previous century, Mose, the Bowery Boy, was ambiguously both heroic and comic. (Increasing the ambiguity with an increase in ethnic layering, the bowery also produced a black, minstrel Mose.[145]) A large percentage of these genres exploited ethnic stereotypes; Gilbert maintains that vaudeville comedy, like its filmic counterpart, depended in large part on ethnic humor: "Irish acts predominated, blackface ran a close second, and Dutch, or German, dialect made an important third."[146] Vaudeville, like film later on, included versions of those routines that would be parodic at the same time they were supposed to appeal to the implicated ethnic audience:

> Whenever possible, enterprising performers would no doubt have it both ways. Irish and German patrons enjoyed hearing familiar accents and loving references to "the ould green sod" or "Vaterland"; simultaneously, native patrons could laugh with superiority at the tortured English and funny un-American clothes. And although these airs frequently mentioned ills and complaints about the immigrant's treatment in America, such songs almost always expressed the immigrant's realization that America was now his home and his desire to be accepted.[147]

That "desire to be accepted" was probably more vexed for most immigrants; in vaudeville, as in very early film, much of the comedy was directed against not only the actual "greenhorn," but against the vestigial greenhorn in the more assimilated among the audience. One dialect comedian recounts his experiences in a paddy wagon:

> The other day I got me arrested and I vent to de jail in de Black Maria. Von feller in the carriage says to another feller, "Hello there, Cockeye Mulligan? How long you got dis time?" "Vell," Cockeye says, "two years an' six months." "For why?" says the feller. "For nothin'," says Cockeye. "De judge ees a stiff." I say to Cockeye, "For nothing you get two years an' six months?" He says, "Yes, I stuck a knife in a dago's heart."[148]

The ethnic stereotype succeeded for so many years not despite but in part because of the ethnic component in the audience: they felt that to laugh at this version of themselves was to reject any "greenhorn" part of themselves not yet Americanized. But the more assimilated the audiences became, the more pained and uncomfortable the laughter must have been, as the earlier laughter at Sut Lovingood must have been more ambivalent in a newly genteel Southern population. As immigrants achieved middle-class status, they "did not care to see the scullery side of metropolitan life portrayed; they did not want to be reminded of their parents' early poverty and social ostracism. Immigrants who espoused middle-class values were tiring of harsh satirical pictures of themselves in putty noses and outlandish clothes; they preferred softer portrayals."[149] Vaudeville thus pretended to a greater gentility to attract not only the genteel (which it apparently had little success in doing) but also those who aspired toward gentility. Conspicuous consumption equaled gentility in the gilded and Edwardian eras even more so than in others; to be surrounded by an ostentatious display of opulence meant that an audience could claim a middle-class gentility that it could otherwise claim only by virtue of education or economic reality. The vaudeville houses were often great mirrors of this desire for opulence in a way that foreshadowed the huge movie theaters built in the 1920s. Staples discusses B. F. Keith's ploy to make his theater's basement as much an attraction as his stage with such rococo touches as an expensive rug in the coal bin.[150] The most famous house—to which all vaudevillians aspired—was called, without any irony, the "Palace." (Not surprisingly, the later opulent movie houses were also called "movie palaces.") Even the name "vaudeville" was a step up from the old nomenclature of "variety hall." The exaggerated opulence and "class" of many of the vaudeville houses were a response to an audience need for reassurance that in fact they had the same taste and discrimination as the wealthier, more educated classes. The opulence of the houses was about the economics of insecurity, in which conspicuous expenditure—or the appearance thereof—was paradoxically an equalizer of humanity. For a couple of hours the lower class allowed itself the illusion that it was cared for in a culture that similarly cradled a Rockefeller or a DuPont. A poor man was treated like a rich man; he was surrounded with the "same" luxurious appointments. And because vaudeville was available in regions less accessible to legitimate theater—as, later on, silent film (which, like Griffith's *Birth of a Nation,* sometimes traveled on circuits) would become available in places vaudeville could not reach—vaudeville could therefore bring its sense of opulence to places that had no other standard for measuring the tasteful expenditure of wealth, places in which vaudeville was the sole standard of taste and refinement.[151]

This temporary illusion of wealth conveyed by the vaudeville house must have been fraught with ambivalence: the working-class patron received a kind of respect and service from a class of people (ushers, for example) from which that poor patron had himself derived. It is hard to imagine that the relation of the working person to the service people in the theater could have been the same as the relation of the more affluent theater patron to his or her ushers. And by inference, it is hard to imagine that the relation of the working-class audience to the vaudeville performers was not untinged with a sense of the degree of *work* that went into a performance.

The customer was certainly not in absolute possession of the sensibility he or she pretended to on entering the theater. The garishness of the house, though perhaps not really outdoing the garishness of the parlors and halls of the wealthy in the gilded and Edwardian ages, was of at least a different kind: the colors were more extreme, the appointments called more attention to themselves. The stylistic largesse was, if not more, at least different. But vaudeville moguls purveyed it for an audience that did not appreciate the difference, for whom that lack of appreciation was one of the givens of the decor. The assumption was that the decor must be an exaggeration of "real class" so that the patron would recognize in some way his or her alliance and debt to such class. The same sensibility applied to the stage as to the decor: a desire to see an exaggerated version of the enjoyments of the wealthy. Hence the thirty-minute versions of legitimate stage plays, including Shakespeare. Hence the eager consumption of such legitimate stage actors and actresses as Sarah Bernhardt and Lillie Langtry and the attempts by vaudeville actors to imitate the plays and acting of the legitimate stage. This desire to appear among the settings and the amusements of the wealthy was ironized because the class of people least likely to attend these performances was of course the upper classes, who could sample more refined enjoyments. (If they did attend, they did so in a ritual called "slumming," in which the audience became a part of the show, "all misfits, puttin' on the Ritz.") The acts reflected not only the audience's sense of the wealthy, but the vaudeville industry's sense of the audience's sense of the rich man's sense of fun. The show was in a way an elaborate second-guessing on the part of all concerned.

In celebrating the triumph of fantasy over economic reality, and in being aware of the tensions that gave rise to that fantasy, the vaudeville show was like both earlier American humor and film humor. The fiction of wealth, the portrayal of the ethnic, and the speed of the acts and their style were all fantasy recreations of the audience relationship to the urban environment in which they lived. These recreations amounted to an aesthetic that would have a determinative influence on American culture. For example, the postmodern aesthetic of "pastiche" finds itself an audience in the post–World War II era because the notion of mixing heterogeneous elements is already present in the vaudeville ethos. Of course, the vaudeville aesthetic unconsciously acknowledges its price much more than the postmodern. As Albert McLean implies, and as we shall further indicate with reference to film, this recreation celebrates the American myth of success, but it is a celebration that acknowledges the price of that success—a celebration that is aware of how much the myth is a fantasy, a contradiction of political and economic realities.

2

— ◆ —

CHARLES CHAPLIN AND THE
COMEDY OF TRANSFORMATION

INTRODUCTION

Though early reviews of Chaplin's work centered on its "knockabout" quality,[1] Chaplin critics from James Agee[2] to Gerald Mast[3] to Charles J. Maland[4] have observed that what distinguishes Chaplinesque comedy is a certain transformative ability: whether the ability to transform objects into other objects, himself into an object, pathos into comedy (and vice versa) or the tramp into a gentleman. Most critics have been satisfied merely to record its existence; some few have attributed it to the rigors of childhood and/or poverty. Though I shall also discuss the other hallmarks of the Chaplin style—baggy pants and the mixture of pathos and comedy—this chapter focuses on that transformative ability, explaining it as an immigrant phenomenon derived from the need for transforming both the old and new cultures to which one belongs. As physical comedy, such transformation is part of the immigrant and ethnic redefinition of space put forth in the last chapter. Its intellectual rigor amounts to an attack on nineteenth-century positivism (though such rigor has little to do with whether Chaplin is himself—as he has been accused—a lightweight thinker).

In *American Vaudeville as Ritual*, Albert McLean writes about the way that vaudeville, in its routines and its atmosphere, acts out the motions of a cultural success in which the audience wishes to participate.[5] A similar but more ambiguous dynamic holds true for Chaplin's audiences (and those of most silent film comics). The tramp is not a vision of success. But the audience's knowledge of Chaplin's visibility and wealth informs their sense of his screen presence. As most critics acknowledge, Chaplin is in the unique position of gaining fabulous success by playing a character who is almost by definition congenitally unsuccessful.[6] In fact, most critics have also noticed the dichotomy between the Chaplin persona and the tramp persona: the victimized little fellow and the wealthy filmmaker, the political radical and the miser, the courtly gentleman tramp and the purplish roué constantly embroiled in offscreen scandals. And some critics have remarked on the parallels between Chaplin's early poverty and the tramp's. But the relationship between the two is infinitely more complex than either the similarities or differences between the actor and his role. Part of Chaplin's phenomenal success resides in the difficulty in resolving the relationship between private life and screen character. The dichotomies are matched by equally powerful affinities between the two personae: both are represented as artistic, self-determining dandies and as kindly, sadistic lovers attracted to young, helpless women. Among the yoked opposites are the new immigrant and the newly rich, or the newly arrived and the arriviste. So although Chaplin is only one of many silent comics to use transformation, he is the only one whose life thematically connects physical transformation and the fairy-tale transformation of immigrant into American. Chaplin succeeds so phenomenally because the transformation of objects and bodies that characterizes the "business" of most silent comedy stars belongs also to the "evolution" of Chaplin's "star image," Chaplin's self-image, and the ontology of the Chaplin screen persona.

Chaplin's screen persona seems more immigrant than Chaplin does, and audiences are allowed to identify with the reality of the tramp's failures because those failures are neutralized by the success Chaplin achieved in his offscreen life. Though ambivalent about the phenomenal salaries Hollywood stars earn, audiences still admire their success.

The first section of this chapter, then, will elaborate Chaplin's immigrant status. The second will relate that status to his screen persona. The third will discuss the way in which one central comic technique—transformation—has an ideological value. The last will be a practical, close viewing of one film, *Modern Times.*

WHEN IMMIGRANTS READ DICKENS

America represented opportunity for the comedian, a promised land not unlike the dream world his cinema tramp was often searching for at the end of the road. . . . Stan Laurel, Chaplin's understudy for the first American tour, has stated that as their ship approached shore, Chaplin ran to the rail and shouted, "America, I am coming to conquer you. Every man, woman and child shall have my name on their lips."[7]

with your one foot in Guerrero and the other in Texas
to speak the same to a Chinaman as to an Amazonian
a Russian, a black: to become the one and only, among us all
without words, or filters
or opals
that vast city within you, unknown to us.[8]

Charlie est un peu usurpateur. Venu au début du cinéma, il l'accapare. On demande en classe: "Tom, qui est-ce qui a inventé le cinéma?" Réponse: "Charlot."[9]

Although Chaplin is—along with Alfred Hitchcock, Orson Welles, and D. W. Griffith—the most psychoanalyzed of filmmakers, and perhaps the filmmaker whose private life has been most often carefully combed for information that might elaborate his films, and although Chaplin's public presentation in relation to ethnicity and immigration is marvelously ambiguous, virtually no critic or biographer finds much aesthetic significance in the fact that Chaplin is an immigrant. However, the connection between his ambiguous background and his status as nouveau riche is scarcely submerged in caricature (figure 2.1).

Commentators only become interested in his national status largely at the *end* of his career, when he is deported.[10] That he may or may not belong to an ethnic minority is at best a minor footnote, despite his own ambiguous denial.[11] In fact, Reginald R. Chaplin, in "Charlie Chaplin's Ancestors," repudiates the imputation that Chaplin's forebears might have been Jewish as a misreading of some accidentally Old Testament names on the family tree.[12]

Even ignoring for a moment the various bivouacs of his childhood (when his peripatetic tendency began—according to his own account—because of a need to support a mother too ill to support her children), one notices immediately that Chaplin's life and death are almost surreally international. His removal from England was motivated by the same impulses that forced most immigrants to the United States: escape from poverty and mediocrity, and an ambivalent disaffection with the "old country." Derived from what a more euphemistic era called "doubtful ancestry," Chaplin characterized his child-

Figure 2.1 Chaplin represented as urban Jew: a 1925 cartoon. Drawing by Massaguer; © 1925, 1953. *The New Yorker Magazine*.

hood, in Dickensian fashion, as poverty-ridden and one of neglect; he grew up without his father (an alcoholic, he was estranged from his family), and devoted his time to caring for his mother, who went insane after her means of support disappeared. He appeared on the American stage in order to gain a livelihood rather than for pleasure. As other critics observe, his first autobiography is a compendium of interesting clichés from *Oliver Twist*.[13] He describes his refuge in a checkered, youthful stage career. His first trip to the United States was, in more or less mythic immigrant fashion, disastrous and poverty-ridden.[14] Like Odysseus, he had to return home a second time in order to be happily discovered for his vocation. When he began working for the movies, he moved with the rest of the film industry to California, going the furthest west (the direction in which the European immigrant travels, the horizontal, spatial corollary of upward mobility) he could on the continent. Born in England, trained in a comic tradition "derived from the Italian mime that reached its zenith with the Comèdie Italienne in France," Chaplin completed his international travels by retiring to Switzerland.[15]

As a result of his movements, Chaplin's national status has never been clear. Chaplin never obtained U.S. citizenship, but insisted that he was an American.[16] This led to his expulsion from the United States in 1952 as a political undesirable after an FBI surveillance begun in the 1920s. He settled in Switzerland rather than return to England, despite the fact that the English still revered him as a local hero while the United States reviled him as a communist. He even continued to move after his death—his body was kidnapped in 1978 and not returned for about two weeks.

Seven years into his film career Chaplin revisited England, a successful, Americanized nabob, meeting an idolatrous audience. Chaplin reflected on the reception he received:

> Thousands are outside. This also thrills me. Everything is beyond my expectations. I revel in it secretly. They all stop to applaud as I come to the gate. Some of them say:
> "Well done, Charlie." I wonder if they mean my present stunt between the bobbies. It is too much for me.[17]

The "well done" refers not to any particular sleight-of-hand Chaplin performed, but to the conjury of appearing in front of that crowd rich, famous, respected: visible. England perceived him as the prodigal son returned. While he identified himself as American, the English identified him as one of them. Chaplin recognized this sufficiently to change his account of the return from *My Trip Abroad* to *My Wonderful Visit* for British release.

As hybrid British-American, he was transformed from poor cockney to international icon. In the first flush of Chaplin's success, one did not have to be English to claim him as a native son. In a footnote for *Charlie Chaplin's Own Story*, Harry M. Geduld notices that "As [Chaplin's] fame grew, various other cities and countries were quick to claim him for their own and Charlie did little or nothing to deny the rumors. Thus Leslie Goodwins observed: it has been variously asserted that Chaplin is a Parisian, a Spaniard, a Mexican, and even an Argentine."[18] The internationalism of the tramp was of a particular kind: knowing that Chaplin was American, at least to the extent that he had to work in America, citizens of different nations understood him as an international icon of Americanness. As private corporations used ethnic representatives to proselytize in their native countries, so Chaplin became a visible advertisement of the success of the American system, long after maintenance of cultural hegemony had replaced the recruitment of foreign labor as the crucial motivating factor in foreign policy. Chaplin was the immigrant who returned to visit as a version of the success story that post–World War I Europeans increasingly perceived as the American drama of their relatives. He symbolically resolved the problem of work by transforming it into a fantasy of comic private success and comic screen failure. This was, however, a fantasy solution, as we may note in the hysteria with which Chaplin, one of the first international modern mass media phenomena, was embraced.

As a media icon, Chaplin had to be extremely careful about his self-representation, which, as a consequence, contained the kinds of contradictions that repressions and elisions always do. These contradictions mirrored the mixed reception of the immigrant. Chaplin biographies, though somewhat fictional, could not be conventional immigrant biographies, like Abraham Cahan's The Rise of David Levinsky or Anzia Yezierska's Bread Givers.[19] For example, Chaplin's Englishness is only ambiguously attractive. On the one hand, it makes him a conventionally desirable immigrant, almost non-ethnic in the eyes of the host culture. Further, though he is a cockney Englishman, we don't hear this lower-class accent on the silent screen; he can be identified as a universal figure in any way audiences find attractive. His Englishness makes it easier for the press to elide (except as innuendo) the fact that he may be Jewish. Further, the actual misery of his childhood is aestheticized in a neo-Dickensian narrative. The alcoholism of his father and insanity of his mother are deleted from the early Chaplin narratives. Finally, the cockney youth is buried under an intellectualism that takes place in mid-Atlantic or Oxbridgean tones. So though he is an immigrant, in the United States to seek his fortune, Chaplin's self-presentation does not match the portrait of the Ellis Island immigrant painted by the contemporary popular culture (no pais, no pigtails). Because he was English and close in ethnic self-ascription to the dominant cultural group in the United States, he was able to gain success and acceptance very quickly (in contrast to the actual social and economic progress of the immigrant in the United States). No physical characteristics branded him as a cultural, intellectual, or physical inferior. He arrived with a highly prized skill that was almost immediately recognized in the United States. Chaplin's immigrant experience was more easily transformed into a culturally acceptable artifact than that of most other immigrants, in part because his experience, and that of his compatriots, was easier than for those of other (especially Eastern and Southern European) countries.[20] Chaplin's experience was, in its particulars, the cultural opposite of the experience of most immigrants who landed at Ellis Island. As such, he was the perfect immigrant, a paradigm for assimilation.

On the other hand, however, if the American press did not want its icon to be a Jew, it also did not, except at moments, have much desire to

identify Chaplin as English. In a contradictory manner that perfectly mirrored cultural ambivalence toward the immigrant, the press also subordinated Chaplin's Englishness to his identity as immigrant,[21] choosing instead
to see Chaplin "in the typical rags-to-riches category so central to the
American success myth."[22] And Chaplin's self-identification was ambiguous;
he often had little desire to insist on his Englishness (if we can trust his own
account, which would be weighted heavily in a particular direction as a
defense against his political detractors). For instance, he never joined the
Hollywood "English colony" that attracted Errol Flynn, David Niven, and
other major film stars. He did not retire to England, even after being forced
out of the United States. Nor did he use Hollywood, as Laurence Olivier did,
as a conduit for tapping American dollars for British theatrical projects.

  Setting aside any immigrant's rancor at the old country,[23] one reason
for this rejection of Englishness is that Chaplin wanted to leave behind the
poverty and concomitant lack of formal education that he shared with the
Ellis Island immigrant, as well as the same problems with accent and
assimilation. Though we see him out of costume as dapper and devastatingly
handsome, he grew up, after all, a street urchin: "We have seen that Charlie's
cockney accent was so pronounced that he was hardly comprehensible in
Ashton-under-Lyme. . . . Even after his arrival in Hollywood, interviewers
occasionally referred in passing to his 'cockney' accent."[24] Toward the end
of his life, while writing his autobiography, "Chaplin also complained . . .
that his secretary was forever trying to improve his English."[25] But trying to
reject the paradigm—Englishness—that defined him as lower class could be
at best an ambiguous failure. Though he insisted that he preferred his own
idiosyncrasies to correct English, he tended in his later sound films to speak
in a defensively terse, short prose. His spoken parts are often limited either
to monologues declaimed in British high "theatre dialect," as in the final
speeches in *Monsieur Verdoux* (1947) and *The Great Dictator* (1940), or to
nonsense speech, as in the song at the end of *Modern Times* (1936) and the
nonsense "German" of Adenoid Hynkel. The fear of speech that plagued
immigrants and silent stars was operative for him as an aesthetic category;
he could transform a tangible fear into a creative choice. The fear of being
heard is the fear of the *arriviste,* the fear of detection as a member of a lower
class at odds with the present private persona. Not only would childhood
experiences require revisioning, but the effects of it, such as a lower-class
accent, would also have to be repudiated: either by adopting stage English
or by dismissing all language as essentially nonsensical.

  Chaplin's fear of presenting his lower-class accent to the film world
indicates that his own immigrant experience would not be acceptable in the

marketplace, not because unfiltered personal experience is "aesthetically unpleasing" but because the unmediated representation of the immigrant is unacceptable in an "English-only" culture. John Gilbert's high-pitched voice and Pola Negri's foreign accent were rejected because they did not seem to fit an era that more and more rejected extreme histrionics, which is to say in part alternative ethnic behaviors. Chaplin sensibly feared that either a cockney accent or a stage accent would be equally inappropriate to the tramp. In fact, the declamatory style of British stagecraft would be, after some experimentation, either rejected or radically modified in the American sound film, in part because it was perceived as hiding something—generally a cockney or Bronx accent. An accent drawn from history rather than from the stage would remind the immigrant audience first of the culture repudiated and second of the pain of the transition from Europe to America. To display the reality of the immigrant experience in the United States would also be to provoke the less than savory nativist impulses of a population that needed but feared immigrants. The contradictions in the nativist impulses would come to the fore: the same sensibility that reviled the immigrant as lazy also feared that immigrants would steal all the available jobs by working more for less money. The same natives that reviled the Catholic intolerance for other, less orthodox religions at the same moment revealed its own intolerance for Catholicism. Finally, the natives, "who would not associate with the immigrants in any case, then assailed them for their clannishness."[26]

Myths more acceptable to the mechanics of the dominant ideology thus replace the more authentic representations of immigrant experience. Chaplin's own immigrant experience—beginning with his youthful poverty in England—is unrepresentable except in its unthreatening secondary characteristics (to be reviewed in the next section) or in ways that redeem that experience in art as it was never redeemed in life (depicting himself as a Dickensian waif or allowing "The Kid" to recover his rich, famous performer-mother). So, though both Chaplin and the press cover his background extensively, that background is safely aestheticized.

The rewriting of Chaplin as a necessary component of his acceptance by both an immigrant public and a culture hostile to the immigrant is accomplished in part in the representation of the tramp; the character creates its creator. But the interplay between the tramp and the Chaplin personae is only the most dramatic instance in a media industry that thrived on reading the relationship between public and private in its object. One can find an immigrant-motivated mixture of pathos and comedy even in Mack Sennett and certainly in Chaplin's main rivals: Mabel Normand, Buster Keaton, Harold Lloyd, and Harry Langdon. There is pathos in the sheer presence of

Fatty Arbuckle.[27] All these comics use the transformative comedy I shall cite as an important component of Chaplin's comedy.[28] For several of these comics, that mixture of pathos and comedy spills over into the representation of their lives. Both Normand, who was referred to as "the little Irish tad,"[29] and Keaton, with his checkered vaudeville background, had private personae as interestingly at odds with her or his own public presence as Chaplin. Like Chaplin, all are as much at pains to obscure their private lives as the press is to unveil them. If there is any significant difference, it is that Chaplin thematized the conflation of on- and offscreen personae, making both about movement, magical transformation, and self-obscuration.[30]

We shall discuss the tramp persona later, except to assert here that one of his most important qualities for an audience ambivalently concerned with assimilation or some other reinscription of its origins, is the way in which his origin is obscured by an itinerant present. Like most American comic characters, the tramp has no past. (In *The Immigrant* [1917] we meet him on the boat to America.) This obscurantism makes him, at best, easily identifiable to an audience; one can plug in any past one wishes. But he is completely unidentifiable as anyone in particular. One of the tramp's most salient features is his biographical opacity; what one does not know is unknowable.[31]

Chaplin's life served audiences as an elaboration of the artist's work at about the time modern literary criticism began explaining an author's work through his life. Audiences knew Chaplin first, after the films themselves, through tabloid descriptions (which did not necessarily reflect the way he wished to be known) and through such semi-authorized accounts as *Charlie Chaplin's Own Story,* the first of several biographies and autobiographies, which appeared within two years after his entry into film. The most interesting feature of the autobiography is the similarity between the young Chaplin and the tramp. The obvious inference to be drawn is that audiences wished to see a nascent tramp in the young Chaplin because a direct and causal connection could be made between history and fiction as a result. The tramp could therefore transform and redeem not only his own poverty but also the poverty of the artist and, by implication, the poverty (physical and spiritual) of the audience.

The possessive adjective "own" of *Charlie Chaplin's Own Story* implicitly refers not only to the story's ambiguous authorship, but also to a claim that this autobiography is a private story, a diary. But this diary would be paradoxically recognizable to people who saw themselves in the tramp who, from "humble beginnings," rose to a position of wealth through the devotion of people who chose to identify with him. As in a Dickensian narrative, the story's privacy makes the narrator seem more approachable,

Figure 2.2 "A Study in Contrasts."
Reproduced by permission of
Scribner's Magazine Vol. 86,
no. 3. © Roy Export Company
Establishment. Courtesy of the
Academy of Motion Picture Arts
and Sciences.

Figure 2.3 "Charles Chaplin at Play and Work." These portraits reflect the press's tendency simultaneously to connect and distinguish between Chaplin and the tramp. Reproduced by permission of *Scribner's Magazine* Vol. 86, no. 3. © Roy Export Company Establishment. Courtesy of the Academy of Motion Picture Arts and Sciences.

more human. In a culture built on the distinction between the public and the private selves, the public's desire for identification with the celebrity is a desire for a sense, however deceptive, of sharing in his public success.[32]

In *Charlie Chaplin's Own Story* the celebrity and his audience take advantage of his status to collaborate in rewriting his origins (or, even better, to have them rewritten by a "literary person") as literature rather than as lived life, to have the events of his life written as leading up to a perfect moment that makes that lifetime worthwhile, even valuable. The tramp persona and Chaplin's childhood are thus both inspired misreadings of Chaplin's life.[33] As with the tramp, Chaplin reenvisions his own life as a series of literary conventions that will make sense both to himself and to his audience.[34]

The elder Chaplin offers up a young Chaplin who, in his wanderlust, his victimization, his callowness, and his resilience (his constant reiterations that he "hated to be pitied"[35] implies the contrary), suggests a nascent tramp. Twice as a young child he finds himself on the road alone—once while escaping a "wicked" clog-dancing master, the second time while trying to earn a living after his father has died, his mother is committed, and his older brother Sydney is away at sea. The specific descriptions of the child look forward as biography and backward as literature to the tramp films: "At last I found an overturned barrel with a little damp straw in it in an alley, and I curled up in it and lay there hearing the raindrops muffled, hollow, beating above me."[36] (This is the beginning of, among other films, *A Dog's Life* [1918].) Or, "I imagined myself rich and famous, bowing before cheering audiences, wearing a tall silk hat and a cane, and buying my mother a silk dress."[37] (Recall the fantasy sequences in *Sunnyside* [1919], *The Kid* [1921], and *The Idle Class* [1921].) Or, "'I can look out for myself,' I said. I put my hands in my pockets and whistled to show her I needed no pity, and went out into the street."[38] All that is missing from this description of the tramp at the end of several films, from *The Tramp* (1915) to *The Idle Class* to *Modern Times,* is the characteristic kicking of something away from himself, the repudiation of the things of this world.

The Chaplin of *Charlie Chaplin's Own Story* is constantly on the move, either as a tramp or as a performer. (Two of Chaplin's four authorized autobiographies are about his trips abroad.) In fact, the two roles often become inflated, as when he becomes a clog dancer. He finds himself poverty-stricken and alone at least three times between stints of work. (I shall later discuss this vacillation as a thematizing strategy of *Modern Times.*) As in his films, he constantly discusses food in the book; from cream tarts to a farmer's large breakfast, the autobiography is a lexicon of unsatisfied, or supersatisfied, appetite:

I set out to hunt for a job.

I found one that afternoon. It was hard work, rolling heavy casks from one end of a warehouse to the other and helping to load them on vans. I was about fifteen at the time and slight, but some way I managed to do the work. . . . I held the place almost a week before the foreman lost patience with me and found someone else to take my place.

I had made friends with several of the men, and one of them got me a place as driver for a milk company. . . . I breakfasted and lunched on buns and stolen milk. . . .

Then one morning the loss of the stolen milk was discovered. I had been unusually hungry and drunk too much of it. The boss swore at me furiously, and again I was out of a job. I was wandering up the street wondering what I could do next when I saw a great crowd about the door of a glass factory. It was still early, about four o'clock in the morning, but hundreds of men and boys were massed there waiting. I pushed my way into the crowd and asked what had happened.[39]

He gets the job but gets hurt the same day, ending up in the hospital. This narrative could be an original version of a screenplay for *Modern Times*, especially the sequence in which the factory reopens and the tramp hurls himself through the gate in identical fashion. As in most of his short films, and right up to *Limelight* (1952) and *A King in New York* (1957), Chaplin conceives of his life as a nearly unbroken succession of jobs that he cannot hold, though these failures are mitigated by the fact that they precede, and so magnify, the later screen success. The tramp too is almost never an unalloyed success except when performing on stage, as in *The Circus* (1928). *Modern Times* will end a cycle of jobs from which the tramp gets ejected with the famous nonsense song; he is heard for the first time while performing.

The wrong primary conclusion to reach would be that the tramp is latent in the young Chaplin, or that the older Chaplin is drawing from early childhood experiences to construct tramp scenarios. Though perhaps true, these assertions are not as provocative as another, more manifest conclusion: Chaplin, or those interested in the Chaplin persona, reconstructs his life to make its parallels with the tramp's life more manifest to an audience that ambivalently desires to remember, rewrite, and obfuscate its own origins. Whether he is doing this consciously or not is finally less important, except as a footnote to decide how acutely aware he (or his ghostwriter) was of his life as a public relations device.[40]

Charlie Chaplin's Own Story attempts to recreate Chaplin's past as his present in miniature. It reflects a desire to discover the origin of the tramp by allowing an obfuscation between the identity of the tramp and Chaplin's self. Though, as said earlier, his biographies paint a conventional portrait of childhood misery, this conventionalization sanitizes any extreme behavior in the environment of the child—a mother's madness, for example—in order to account for the present success of a public favorite. The public gains a sense of continuity, while the celebrity gains the more desirable childhood, and so the more integrated, if deceptive, identity. Even the extremity of the poverty and misery painted denies any mundanity in its subject. The story of the clog dancers and Mr. Hawkins, for instance, in which Hawkins plays Oliver Twist's beadle with his scanty meals for the children and his promises of canings and beatings, is an apparent exaggeration of the reality of the situation of a kindly man most of whose own children were members of the infamous Lancashire Eight. Chaplin even gets the names wrong. But the more incorrect the memory (the greater the erasure), the more we have a sense of having stumbled on something important.

Chaplin transformed his childhood experience in ways that flattered the poor and immigrant, while not scaring the native. He attempts what we have become accustomed to film autobiographers doing: transforming a mundane life into something as interesting as the life portrayed on the screen, the miraculous transformation of the valueless into the valued. One can imagine that the experience of reading such an autobiography, or similar tabloid accounts of the lives of the screen heroes, would for the middle class have been to experience poverty and pain as romance. Surely anyone who grew up with such disadvantages would almost inevitably become rich and famous. For the poor, who might not even have been able to afford books and magazines and might not have had the skill to read them if they had, reading or hearing Chaplin's story would have been to reinforce belief in the American dream.

If we are to postulate that Chaplin's success is due to his identification of a particular audience in a particular way, we must recognize that changes in that audience will yield changes in the tramp persona. When Chaplin's popularity begins, a significant proportion of the cinema audience is still composed of the lower and immigrant classes. Part of his change to the less refractory (or the better-rationalized refractory, as we shall see in *Modern Times*) reflects a change in the audience from lower class to more genteel. This middle-class population still enjoys the slapstick but in a less amoral character. The later tramp is less susceptible to the antic maliciousness of his early and middle career (acts like his completely arbitrary destruction of the alarm clock in *The Pawnshop* [1915]). Partly because of the often radically different cultural norms of the country from which they derived their own value systems, and partly because of the amorality of the poverty by which they were surrounded in this country, the earlier immigrant audience did not possess the same Puritan fervor that spurred American temperance and imperialist movements around the turn of the century. The members of the various organizations who agitated for film censorship did not tend, for the most part, to be either poor or immigrant, at least not first-generation immigrant.[41] When Chaplin's audience changed, the tramp's persona reflected that change in taste (despite the complaints of the critics who wanted Chaplin to remain as he was). He did not lose much of his violent nature, but he began to include in it an element of pathos, of sentiment.

Along with Chaplin's and his audience's changed social and economic circumstances, and as a gloss on the increasing pathos of the tramp, came a change in his relationship with his audience, which Chaplin came to view as parental. Sometimes he envisioned the public as ungrateful offspring: "The public is like a child; it gets tired of its toys and throws them away. When that happens I shall do something else, and still be satisfied."[42] At other times the child becomes a nightmare, a fantasy of dependence on a castrated object, or a projection of self-castration, as in this exchange from *Limelight*:

> *Calvero:* I want to forget the public.
> *Terry:* Never! You love them too much.
> *Calvero:* I'm not so sure. Maybe I love them, but I don't admire them.
> *Terry:* I think you do.
> *Calvero:* As individuals—yes. There's greatness in everyone. But as a crowd they're like a monster without a head that never knows which way it's going to turn.

Chaplin's own career is infused with the role of the parent. He chooses the tramp persona to highlight a pantomimic skill that he claims to have inherited from his mother. But he spends his career playing a version of the father: drunk, dissolute, peripatetic. The older he gets, the more comfortable he becomes with the role until by *Limelight* Calvero is his father: an aging, alcoholic, gregariously unsuccessful Edwardian performer. (A nice twist on this occurred in 1992, when Chaplin's daughter Geraldine played his mother in his last biography, the film *Chaplin*.) The structure of Chaplin comedy—pantomime—is maternal, while the role itself is paternal. Silent film was a perfect vehicle because Chaplin was able to circumvent the talent that supported both parents: singing.

The relation of the audience to Chaplin is a bit like the fulfillment of a wish for a bipolar parent who is accessible, kind, feisty, and personally charismatic but who is socially a figure of power and respect with whom one can safely identify. The American audience's ambivalence about Chaplin can be most easily seen in the extremes of the immediate and universal acceptance and the equally summary rejection to which they treated him. They revered the loveable volition of the tramp while deploring Chaplin's private exercise of political belief.

THE TRAMP

> The ethnic group in American society became not a survival from the age of mass immigration but a new social form.[43]

As Chaplin obscures his own origins by claiming birth in half a dozen locations and by transforming an already moribund childhood into a Dickensian fable, so the tramp is obscurantist. Conveying something of the physics of poverty, and a sentimentalism that high culture was beginning to repudiate except in its most sacred cows (opera, ballet), the tramp's ability to kick his heels at the end of the short films provides the model for "a certain tendency" in American cinema to take back at the end the indictment contained in the rest of the narrative, directed at a hegemony that can stand only the most rudimentary "ethnic notions." On their own side, the immigrant audience must discover transformed representations of its own experience because too accurate a representation would be counter to the perceived needs of the culture. (When an audience asserts that hegemonic culture does not censor their desire, they are correct only in the sense that the audience has internalized this censorship, becoming "good Jews" in a panopticon society that makes them their own best custodians.)

This section shall discuss the tramp as a mechanism for repressing ethnicity's primary characteristics for an audience ambivalently resentful at this suppression of difference. Like all manifestations of repressed impulses, the tramp is *secondarily* revelatory, secondarily immigrant. This section shall indicate some of the ways in which, despite this, the tramp retains some vestiges of his immigrant status. The tramp's ambiguity has a physical, visual dimension: repression and its products are spatialized.

—◆—

It is rather easy to associate Chaplin with a particular ethnic type: the comic Irishman. A late-Victorian East-End cockney, he would have without doubt have been exposed to the influx of Irish immigrants to London that began in the first third of the last century and whose place in the city should sound extremely familiar to fans of the tramp: "[T]hey were channeled into the bottom ranks of the capital's social and economic hierarchy, a position that forced a constant scramble for survival and severely limited their prospects for improvement."[44] Chaplin shares qualities with various stages of the comic Irishman, from the *omadhawn,* who, like the immigrants we shall shortly discuss, "doesn't understand how . . . to use any mechanical device";[45] to the rogue figure or *rapparee,* who, like the tramp, is both genteel and criminal, a "genteel robber";[46] to the stage Irishman who, again like the tramp, combines the elements of "farce and melodrama";[47] both drink and both are braggarts. Even the most compelling difference between the stage Irishman and the tramp—the former's facility with language and the latter's silence— are obverse sides of the same critical stance toward English. In England, in the theater of Dion Boucicault, Bernard Shaw, and Samuel Beckett, Chaplin would continue signifying only the stage Irishman, the "anti-self upon whom [the Englishman] projects repressed instincts and desires or in whom he sees tendencies that he fears in himself."[48] By contrasting the handsome, well-dressed British director to his colonialized subject on the other side of the camera, one could then, depending on one's allegiance, construct an argument that makes the tramp either a Gaelophobic representation, or an ambiguous defender of the faith, like the creations of J. M. Synge, Sean O'Casey, and Samuel Beckett.

But though it would be a mistake to ascribe to him a superficial sense of the political, it is also a mistake to associate Chaplin with any single political or ethnic point of view, no matter how deeply felt.[49] His tramp becomes culturally attractive because of the contradictions he contains: he is simultaneously hard-working and lazy, gallant and lecherous, generous and greedy. These contradictions help define the tramp as an epistemological contradiction: he contains the hegemonic representation of the assimilated, as well as various immigrant versions of accommodation. Chaplin finds in the tramp a way of expressing his own contradictory experience as an immigrant to various audiences that can identify certain important features of his transformed experience as a version of their own contradictory discriminations.

The cultural ideal and mechanism specifically created for the treatment of the immigrant by American society has traditionally been *facelessness:* the melting pot and its successors.[50] Leonard Dinnerstein generalizes about the attitudes of even the more liberal thinkers: "[Americans] expected recent arrivals to relinquish their old ways and values. And 'until they have become morally acclimated to our institutions,' Horace Mann, the Boston educator, declared, they were simply unfit for participation in American society."[51] Despite this, the immigrant impulse to maintain an identification with the older nationality remains strong, if it varies in degree of ambivalence. The number of strategies immigrants have evolved for reconciling the external social pressure to repudiate the parent country and the internal psychological pressure to retain some part of one's original identity is even greater than the number of nationalities that have come to the United States.[52] But prominent among these is the hegemonic requirement that the immigrant submerge ethnic identity in public while allowing it freer rein in the home: the bilingual immigrant speaks English in the marketplace, for example, and his native language at home. The ethnic is submerged as much as possible without being erased.[53]

The variable direction and speed of ethnic change implies as much transformation in the host culture as in the immigrant. But even those changes rung in the immigrant become themselves conduits for cultural change. Secondary immigrant characteristics—foreign social values, skills, and dress, or degree of acclimatization to urban life—become more prominent when such primary distinguishing features as language and religious affiliation are submerged. These characteristics are often contradictory, not only because the revenge of repression is confusion, but also because these characteristics are both ascribed and self-ascribed. Many are assigned by the hegemonic culture, for whom these characteristics do not threaten the absolute stability of the standard icons of Americanness. But some characteristics also enable ethnic and immigrant identifications outside normative cultural definitions. For instance, the immigrant can take on both a green-horn sensibility and a new urban wisdom—"street smarts"—both of which become exaggerated in an urban landscape. What is most important, though, is that these characteristics be detachable from their ethnic background so that even the most obvious ethnic typing disappear by name, though their characteristics remain.

So, although the tramp should be immediately recognizable as a stage Irishman, no critic so identifies him. The Irish *omadhawn* and *rapparee* are repressed, and the tramp becomes a visualization of these secondary immigrant characteristics that are never recognized as such. The baggy and oversized clothes, the shabby derby—all accouterments of the stage Irishman—become universal signifiers. Appealing to a number of audiences, this Keystone performer is both a sociological "key symbol" and a hegemonic construct; he represents a host of unconscious immigrant self-identifications and a series of reactionary clichés about the behavior of the proletariat. The tramp embodies, in other words, a lexicon of contradictory secondary immigrant characteristics existing between about 1914 and 1930, an arena of contesting meanings in which "the process of ethnic change, set in tow by a radical shift in the social situation in which people act, is a dialectical one."[54] This contestation constitutes the representation of a complex psychology.[55]

It is possible to list briefly those qualities that used to belong to the comic Irishman and which, in being repressed, now define a visible secondary response to the poverty and alienation that characterizes the immigrant classes more generally:

- Perhaps most important, the tramp perceives mundane objects in exotic ways, either because he does not know how to use them or because he understands them better than anyone else, like the immigrants who are variously portrayed either as not understanding urban technology or, because implicated in its production, understanding it better than its inventors do. He is confused by things, customs, and people's intentions. In *The Immigrant* he clings to his hat in a restaurant, causing a scene because he is not familiar with the custom of doffing one's cap; in *The Fireman* (1916) he mistakes the lunch bell for the fire bell. He is often uncouth and unkempt, with no manners or the slightest knowledge of the uses and benefits of modern plumbing.[56] But the tramp also uses things better than anyone else: watches, brooms, buckets, chairs—the invisible world of mundane artifacts—become visible and other.

- The tramp is criminal, cruel, and amoral, not above stealing, lying, or gambling. But he is also honest and sentimental. In *The Tramp*, the little fellow steals and then returns money to the girl whom he saves from other tramps.

- The tramp is both victim and victimizer. In *The Great Dictator*, for example, Chaplin is both the barber/tramp/Jew and the dictator (see figure 2.4).

- The tramp's code of behavior is inappropriate for his surroundings: a vaguely European politeness and fastidiousness of manner in a paddy wagon, coarseness in polite society. He constantly tries to keep his hands clean in an unsanitary environment or to avoid unpleasant odors in the urban-industrial atmosphere that is by definition offensive to the nose. His manners are pretentious or vulgar, upward-climbing or downward-looking, indicating a fastidiousness or coarseness not appropriate to his status.

- The tramp is excluded from middle-class establishments, spending much of his life being kicked out of stores, parlors, and restaurants. Even before he acts, he is looked upon with suspicion by proprietors of shops and restaurants and representatives of the law. But the tramp is also constantly invited into the precincts of wealth: at a coming-out party he is a count (*The Count* [1915]); fired from a job he returns in drag to seduce his boss (*The Masquerader* [1914]).
- The tramp is usually identified with a particular urban landscape (despite the occasionally rustic film like *The Tramp*), but he is also essentially rootless.
- The tramp is poor, but his manners are (again) those of the wealthy. Further, when Chaplin does not play a tramp, he plays someone at the other end of the economic spectrum (in, for example, *One AM* [1916], *A Night at the Show* [1915], *The Rounders* [1914], *The Masquerader,* and, most conspicuously, *The Great Dictator, Monsieur Verdoux,* and *A King in New York*).
- The tramp has a limitless number of adventures, but he has no past. His origins, useless to him in a perpetual present, are lost to him and to us.
- The tramp is always the tramp. But he is also janitor, drunken gentleman, woman, or actor. Always himself, the tramp always employs disguise.

Other tensions and contradictions overarch the tramp: the celebrated combination of pathos and slapstick noted by virtually every Chaplin critic, for example. The very fact of contradiction is itself a defining quality of the immigrant, who is himself a floating signifier. As a space that allows the existence of a tension between meanings assigned by the hegemony and by the immigrant, the tramp becomes a new meaning.

These characteristics—reperceptiveness, industry, mannerliness, mobility, rootlessness, and criminality—are fantasy elements of the tramp persona. First, they render the picture of the dispossessed in American culture attractive to a middle class whose guilt in relation to the poor is thereby assuaged. (The assertion of one critic—that in Chaplin films "an intolerable situation is treated as if it were normal"—is of course the response of the middle class to the poor, then as now.)[57] Second, they are ways of perceiving the self that are flattering to an immigrant sensibility: ways of rendering odd behavior as above rather than below the cultural norm. These

Figure 2.4 "Chaplin und Hitler." The tramp is both victim and victimizer. © Münchner Stadtmuseum.

attributes are the filmic version of the fantasy immigrant that Chaplin lives out for immigrants, and for the poor at large. They are personal characteristics not immediately tangible and certainly not immediately valorized in a society in which the machine (and the repetition of single motion without thought that machinery requires of its human components) is the predominant symbol of early twentieth-century technology. We have already discussed to some extent the tramp's rootlessness, and we shall discuss reperceptiveness in a later section. (Criminality and ethnic representation will be more fully covered in chapter 4.)[58] But it is worth examining the tramp's work ethic, rootlessness, and origins a bit more here.

The working tramp is self-ascriptive. Chaplin's tramp is sometimes lumpenproletariat, but most often a member of the working class. As Robert Sklar, among others, has observed, he is one of the hardest workers in films.[59] Even the titles of the films reveal their absorption with the issue of work. They may name the tramp in a particular role: *The Property Man* (1914), *The New Janitor* (1914), *His Musical Career* (1914), *The Champion* (1915), *The Floorwalker* (1916), *The Fireman*. Or they may be more generic in naming their absorption: *Making a Living* (1914), *His New Profession* (1914), *Work* (1915), *His New Job* (1915), *Pay Day* (1922). Or they may name the site of work: *The Pawnshop* (1915), *The Circus* (1928). The tramp exploits the close identification that exists between the lower economic classes and ethnic minority populations. Both groups are disenfranchised by definition: one by the inability to buy into the middle-class culture because of lack of means and time, the other by the inability to understand the cultural values into which they are supposed to buy. Of course, the ties between the two populations are even more intimate; the two intersect at many places because the ethnically unpossessed are also the economically dispossessed.

On the eastern seaboard, where many of the people who were to influence the early history of film landed or grew up, both the domestic and immigrant poor moved to major cities at the end of the nineteenth century and beginning of the twentieth. The tramp appeared in 1914. Until at least 1915 the American working force had been drawn from the increasing number of immigrants landing at Ellis Island. In large measure, the poorer, blue-collar factory workers and day laborers were immigrants or children of immigrants.[60] That Chaplin's films should be thematically about work and methodologically invested in pathos makes perfect sense. Such pathos is only partially connected to the love interest; it is finally related to the ability or inability to keep up with the industrial machine.[61]

The rootlessness of the tramp is an ascribed definition of the immigrant. The identification of the tramp image as allied to immigrant concerns is reinforced by the fact that, like the immigrant, the tramp was, especially in the nineteenth century, a figure of xenophobic fear. Alan Trachtenberg, in his discussion of America's image of the hobo, notes that the appearance of the tramp "marked a degeneration of virtue, a loss of those character traits of industry, regularity, and respect for order essential to the republic. . . . The perception spread that America was in the grip of alien forces."[62] For the most part Chaplin did not refer to the character as "the tramp" but rather as "the little fellow," as if to defuse the threatening aspect of the tramp by emphasizing his gentleness, childishness, and helplessness. In at least one film—The Tramp—Chaplin repudiates and confirms any identification of the little fellow with other images of the hobo by featuring his triumph over the negative, culturally acceptable version of the murderous, thieving tramp.

While one symbol of a previous century's rootlessness—Davy Crockett—is unambivalently revered for his individuality, his consummate skill, his independence, and most importantly, an inherent nobility, the frontier folk he presumably represented—often ethnic—were disliked and feared as uncouth, unstable, and partially savage. The cultural impulses that Chaplin's tramp represented were even more ambiguous. While the tramp persona was popular, tramps themselves were deplored as the tangible symbol of a faceless mass that American democracy feared itself to be. The forefather as new immigrant is not precisely an ideal national image, especially in the way American culture has created that image. The new immigrant thus had to be exorcised from the national consciousness in order that the other image of the father—Daniel Boone, Davy Crockett, and so on—might be enshrined without competition.

Ascribed and self-ascribed, nobility of manner helps render the tramp's origins ambiguous. It is just as possible to imagine that the tramp has fallen from a state of economic grace as that he is attempting to become upwardly mobile. Monsieur Verdoux is perhaps the original identity of the tramp rather than his final avatar. The tramp is thus at once a nightmare of middle-class instability and a wish-fulfillment of an immigrant class hoping to see its present poverty as "reduced circumstances." The individuals in this latter class often perceived themselves as living in an inappropriate time and place unappreciative of the fineness of soul better received in the old country. The tramp's alienation and inappropriate behavior are thus justified as the results of an unappreciative culture.

The tramp can thus, in one respect, be seen as an insider out, an ex-member of the bourgeoisie. We can take as evidence of this the tramp's genuinely refined upper-class manners, and the clothes—bowler, vest, cane—are his own, remnants of a fatter, sleeker prosperity. On the other hand, the tramp can be seen as an outsider in, a social climber. We can take as evidence of this moments in which his excellent imitation of refined manners is undercut by a certain awkwardness (for example, the cane scene in *Sunnyside*). The plots of some films suggest that he is a fraud (*The Rink, The Count, The Masquerader*). His clothes are handed down from the petit bourgeois, but he can never truly enter that class because he is lazy, naive, and drunken: too much a Boudeau.

Both explanations of the tramp's attributes are equally possible and equally contradictory: some films seem to suggest the former and others the latter (though the earlier films seem to suggest more the obnoxious social climber, the later films the impoverished but noble gentleman: the *omadhawn* versus the *rapparee*). In a predominantly visual medium, does one determine the truth of a character's psychology from his actions or from his apparel, mise-en-scène or movement? Any critical attempt to reconcile the conflicting meanings is a deviation from the more interesting observation that Chaplin is equating the obscuring of immigrant origins with the revelation of questions about the origin of meaning in cinematic texts.

The tramp's lack of origin derives in part from his evolution in the comic "short," where there is no time to establish a history for the comic character so that greater reliance is placed on situation. However, though the tramp's origin is lost—and with it the primary feature of the immigrant—his new universality of identification indirectly supports the special claim of the immigrant as formulator of culture. If the tramp is allied with the immigrant in American culture, the tramp's universality confers a new, higher status on the immigrant experience. An audience, part of which has no real identification with the immigrant at all, will identify their experiences with some elements of the now universalized, if disguised, immigrant experience. The valorization of Chaplin—and of other comics about whom we shall speak— is as significant for the immigrant as the valorization of Davy Crockett is for the frontiersman. The myth of the immigrant becomes part of the national identity as surely as does that of the cowboy.

THE TRAMP AND TRANSFORMATIONAL
COMEDY, OR, THE LAMPSHADE AS DISGUISE

Mais la réalité fait vite retomber Charly sur ses pieds. Alors, à force de se batter, d'tre battu, de donner la vie aux objets, de vérifier la quatrième dimension, d'animer la matière morte, de créer la génération spontanée avec un balai, un policeman, des fleurs, un banc, une brique, une Ford,

Dulcinée, un téléphone, en bon israélite il est parti pour Jérusalem! Il y recontra une petite juive allemande et M. William Shakspeare. Un juif rend comique toute tragédie prise au sérieux.[63]

Chaplin Reading Bergson

Since Gerald Mast's citation of him,[64] most contemporary critics use Henri Bergson—either implicitly or explicitly—in accounting for the popularity of slapstick comedy.[65] Mast himself remarks on the degree to which Bergson's theory of the inelastic mind works perfectly for the fallible slapstick comedian. The present section is about the limits of that use, about how Chaplin theorizes the limitation of Bergson's argument. In essence, Chaplin reads Bergson better than Bergson reads Chaplin.

Bergson's *Laughter* is about the way technology mediates between people and their environments. He speaks to a twentieth-century audience dependent on an industrial technology that mocks its efforts to control it, showing that instead the manipulator is the technology itself: "The attitudes, gestures and movements of the human body are laughable in exact proportion as that body reminds us of a mere machine."[66] Though Bergson uses Molière's idiosyncratic characters as ideally comic figures, his paradigm is also invoked to explain early silent comedy in its use of caricature, slapstick, and other physical humor. Bergson classifies machinelike behavior under three categories, all present in American slapstick comedy: a rigidity of body, as seen in Ben Turpin's face (or Chaplin's body in the disappearing cabin scene in *The Gold Rush* [1925]); rigidity of mind, a mind unable to change in the presence of altered circumstances, as seen in *The General* (1927) (the northern general's decision to send the train over the burning bridge). Finally, in Erich Von Stroheim's *Foolish Wives* (1921), Mrs. Hughes's anachronistic romanticizing of the villainous Count Karamzin despite all evidence of his villainy (including a description of their relationship in a book she is reading called *Foolish Wives,* by Von Stroheim), reflects a comic rigidity of character, or really a cultural rigidity that continued to romanticize foreign titles.

Bergson attempts to account for the appeal of comedy despite the fact that comedy is often unpleasant through his celebrated notion of a "momentary anesthesia of the heart,"[67] in which we learn not to care about the character undergoing the pain because it is justly inflicted. The term slapstick is itself composed of two words that speak to the exigencies of the body during this humor: one either slaps it or sticks something into it. When comics fight, fall off buildings, fall into water, fall off cars, and get hit by bricks, we laugh at the pain because it is a social corrective administered to prevent too much individual deviation and eccentricity. We laugh also because it is stage pain; we understand that the actor is not really hurt.[68]

Bergson's theory also seems appropriately applied to silent comedy because much of silent comedy is about the mediation between people and landscape by technology. A concern with new technology is one way of expressing a more general comedic absorption with the immediate, the topical. As in tall tales, people defy natural laws if not with native wit, then with the machines that increasingly compose the landscape. It is almost a cliché to observe that at the same time films become commercial entertainment, near the turn of the century, the most visible technology is the automobile, which, as Mast notes, consequently becomes the vehicle for much of the comedy of early slapstick (*Lizzies of the Field* [1924], and *Two Tars* [1928], for example).[69] *The General* puts this concern into historical perspective by considering an earlier fascination with earlier technologies: scenes of a new bicycle, a train, a cannon going off accidentally. More generally, comedies use up speeding cars and trains, guns, pianos, and the bric-a-brac one might find in a shop, parlor, or kitchen (see especially *The Pawnshop* and *The Adventurer* [1917]): the products and mechanisms of the mass production within which the mass of immigrants works.

But using Bergson to justify the social anarchy of slapstick is rather like using libertarianism to justify everyone's right to health care. Though Bergson dislikes the machine, seeing it as essentially opposed to flexible social intercourse, and so in our eyes seems rather progressive, his assertions are socially conservative, even totalitarian.[70] When people behave eccentrically, they act like machines: antisocially. His idealist, neo-Platonic essentialism postulates a central, implicitly correct way of behaving. Comic exaggerations and caricatures imply idealized, uncaricaturizable faces. Eccentric behavior is tangential to more central, organic, normative kinds of behavior. It should be exorcised—not celebrated—through laughter.[71] Comic behavior is unattractive behavior: our laughter is always directed at the person acting comically or on whom comedy is perpetrated. Comic behavior is predicated on an "absentmindedness" on the part of the character, on his lack of self-knowledge.

Bergson's reading of comedy obviously dovetails nicely with genteel notions of film as an instrument for educating the immigrant in behaving in normative, "American" fashion. As earlier asserted, many immigrants moved from extremely primitive conditions to a land of electricity, telephones, ready-made clothes, and automobiles. The assault must have been of the most grossly physical kind. In the overpopulated ghettos immigrants encountered an overwhelming density of humanity. Electricity could kill without being seen and without a moment's notice. An automobile could kill almost as fast, and the ideal of speed it implied in America would be as dangerously alien as the more tangible danger of being run over. Even the exigencies of a presumably desirable upward mobility would be oppressive; the demand to dress differently than one had one's whole life would be a physical insult. As a people failing to understand the kind of physical world they inhabited, immigrants were the perfect objects for Bergson's comedy of social correction.

Tramp comedy also seems in several ways accessible to a Bergsonian reading, and so on the side of a genteel reading of film as a "civilizing" influence on the immigrant. The tramp often falls victim to an absentmindedness or singlemindedness of character that renders him a victim of circumstance. We laugh at him when he leans on a wall and falls into the water, when he closes a door and gets hit on the head by a door-prop, when he sits on a chair while it sinks into a rickety floor, or when he sits on a table that then breaks. But these instances are only a part of Chaplin's physical comedy. While Bergson sees the imposition of the machine on the individual as antisocial, Chaplin sees this imposition as the quintessential function of society, which forces people to work in the machine in a uniform manner in order to survive (figure 2.5). Only the heads of society—the captains of industry—do not have to work; in *Modern Times* only they can read the comics, do jigsaw puzzles, and go to the movies. So far from envisioning the actor as deserving victim, tramp comedy leaves the subject either an undeserving victim or an urban hero.

The tramp does not act in a machinelike manner, but his comedy is a metaphysics of the machine. Any random display of Chaplin sequences will display a spontaneity that attacks the machine as comic. At the most important level of significance the machine itself, in being physically represented, is attacked thematically as a life-denying social force that literally ingests its victims (figure 2.6). The tramp films are made at a time when another landscape has threatened to overcome the individual sensibility. Though not the forest, the new cityscape is more alien for being self-created. Technology, the prosthesis created to outwit one environment, has itself outwitted its inventor by becoming larger than either its creators or the forest.

Chaplin's technique of transformation is very much in one tradition of American humor, the traditional fantasy of reperceiving and reordering an environment in order to make it accessible (see chapter 1). The environment being reordered in this case, however, is not the wild landscape of the eighteenth-century frontier but rather the equally wild cityscape of urban-industrial America to which the vast majority of immigrants gravitated and which was as alien to the immigrants who traveled here at the turn of the

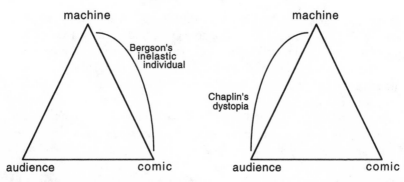

Figure 2.5 Triangles of identification. For Bergson, the individual comic and the machine are closely identified; for Chaplin, society and the machine.

twentieth century as was the forest to the earlier travelers. Like the tall- and trickster-tale tellers of the previous century, and like most other silent comics, Chaplin paints his (urban) landscape bleak and dangerous, itself a character whose treacherous encircling the tramp keeps recreating as an embrace. Like Sut Lovingood and Davy Crockett, the tramp, once recognizing the danger in his surroundings, overcomes them by reconceiving the landscape as the source of salvation from itself. This idea of metamorphosis, crucial to most informed theories of comedy from Kant to Bergson to Eastman, becomes particularly central to any account of Chaplin's humor.

The structure of the paradigmatic Chaplin gag is extremely simple: the tramp converts an often mundane object into something with a different, more exotic use.[72] For example, in the beginning sequence of *The Pawnshop,* the tramp walks into the back office bouncing his cane as if it were a rubber ball, then places it in a tuba as if the tuba were an umbrella stand. He takes a feather duster out of a suitcase as if the suitcase were a cupboard and dusts off the cane, a birdcage, and his hat as if they were furniture. After putting the hat in the birdcage as if the hat were a bird or the cage a hatbox, he dusts himself off, reaching between his legs for his buttocks as if *he* were furniture. Finally, after dusting off his coworker, he makes snow by combining the duster with a fan. Then, with metonymic aptness, he places the defunct featherduster into the birdcage. Chaplin transforms an alien, technological, industrial, politically amorphous world that governs the individual into a world that he administers. This joke structure amounts to the expression of an audience fantasy that they can influence this astonishingly alien, uncontrollable, and incomprehensible environment. (The only object over which he has little or no control is the feminine Other.)

Figure 2.6 In *Modern Times* the transformed machine ingests its acolytes. © Roy Export Company Establishment. Courtesy of the Academy of Motion Picture Arts and Sciences.

The tramp's reperceptive sensibility takes several practical forms, depending on the situation in which he finds himself. These categories reflect different perceptions of ego (especially the body as ego) in relation to the world and to an increasing interiority.[73] This increasing interiority is also chronological: he uses his body more rather than less later in his career, while the props, though sometimes more elaborate, become less important over time. (Certainly he uses more props per minute in *One AM, The Pawnshop*, and *The Adventurer* than in *City Lights* [1931]. For Chaplin, more body in pantomime means greater depth of psychology.)

The focus of transformative comedy is the body or the objects that surround it. All transformations are changes in the material world of either the body of the performer, the artifacts that surround him, or the body of an other, usually an antagonist. Tramp comedy then has the same focus as slapstick comedy—the objectification of the body. But this objectification is not the same as the diffused hostility to the body of slapstick, in which someone is merely punched, prodded, or pushed. Slapstick insists on perpetuating into the realm of fantasy the insult to the body that occurs in the world. Transformative comedy, on the other hand, insists on the intelligence of the body in *avoiding* insult (successfully or otherwise). The body becomes other than itself in order to evade punishment by some authority. Like jokes for Freud, transformative comedy is the expression of a fantasy triumph over anxiety.[74] The anxiety does not, however, exist in a form disguised from the bearer of the joke: the tramp knows he is being chased. Rather, the anxiety is the disguised expression of *audience* anxiety about the insult to the body from a new industrial world. The artifacts that Chaplin transforms, or into which he transforms himself, are generally mundane objects: bird cages, feather dusters, suitcases, lamps, shoes, clocks, brooms. They are almost always popular artifacts, objects mass produced with the technology that produces jobs, without which urban society could not live, but which is instrumental in producing the physical discomfort and claustrophobia of the individuals dependent on it.

When Chaplin turns an artifact into something else, he reproduces technology at an individual level. The form that the fantasy of personal power takes is the desire to locate in one's body the ability to reproduce the processes of technology. This industrialization of the body is more than the fantasy of a poor man wanting to become rich: it is the fantasy of the helpless individual wishing to reproduce the mechanisms of a society that exerts power over him. In opposition to Bergson, who believes that the human is least in control of himself when acting like a machine (again, true only of pure slapstick comedy), the tramp is asserting his humanity only when he internalizes the modes of production. In *Modern Times* and other films, Chaplin deplores the machine. But this dislike is mirrored and undercut by an incorporation of the dynamic of the machine, which while itself magically and mysteriously turning raw goods into finished products, alienates the body of the worker from its owner. Transformational comedy is a fantasy of escape from Marxian reification: it is the fantasy that one's body controls the means of production, that one's body is the primary means of production of all artifacts, the primary product, and the primary owner. This incorporation of all categories of production within one body is achieved through magic, not industry, a magic that, working through material culture, denies that culture any authentic existence.

The use or perception of an object outside its normal functions or setting implies one of two states of mind in the perceiver: either he is extremely aware of the function of the object in such a way that he can play outside the conventional use, or he is completely unaware of its use in a way that still liberates him from conventional use. Though the tramp seems wise to convention, he often acts through ignorance of the different values of otherwise analogous objects (as when he tries to "put on the ritz" in *Sunnyside* with the stick-cane-lighter).

Insofar as the tramp is unaware of the intended use of artifacts, he is a construct of a mainstream inventing an appropriable work force. Insofar as the tramp is a knowledgeable misuser of things, he gives back to an insecure immigrant audience a vision of itself as intelligently knowledgeable. In response to the smug truism that American cinema was instrumental in teaching the enormous wave of immigrants how to behave like Americans, one may assert that the immigrant as often as not arrived with values and skills highly respected, needed, and often unknown to the native populace. And because a disproportionately large number of cinema people were themselves immigrants, one can with equal or greater justice assert that the American populace was taught by new immigrants. Leonard Dinnerstein quotes Carl Wittke, a historian of German-American immigrants, who says that some of the immigrants

> ridiculed such American habits as rocking in chairs, chewing and spitting tobacco, standing up to a bar to down a drink, getting "eye-openers" each morning, wearing hats crooked, and sticking feet on tables and window sills. They were not impressed by the "anarchical noise" of Fourth of July or firemen's parades, or by the muddy streets, the corrupt shirt-sleeve, tobacco-cud politics of the cities, and the "human bullfighting" known as pugilism. They preferred sausage and sauerkraut to pie and pork and

beans. They were shocked to find slavery firmly established and nativism rampant in a free republic. They hated American sabbatarianism, blue laws, and "the temperance swindle," and the more radical ridiculed what they called the religious superstitions of the American people. They were determined to preserve their language and customs and to resist assimilation to an inferior culture.[75]

It is equally true that the cinema probably taught the general populace that its mistakes in relation to modern industrial society were understandable and forgivable because that society was insanely fast and confusing. The films were always an indictment of a society gone insane with its own industry. They tended to provide a (terribly fallible) response to that insanity that consisted of retaining one's sense of autonomy—a pride in one's difference—through a slight rebellion. This rebellion consisted in making one's different perception of the world visible by using society and its artifacts in novel ways. Chaplin was probably beloved because he allowed the mystified audience to feel that its mystification was redeemable as individuality.

An Alternative to Bergson: Elaine Scarry and the Comic in Pain

Though examining Bergson leads us better to define the comedy of transformation, Bergson's model does not work well for all slapstick comedy in part because it is socially conservative and in part because Bergson's argument, despite his implicit or explicit use by standard critics, was not finally directed at slapstick but rather toward the tradition of French stage comedy, principally Moliére. Slapstick figures early in his argument as a rather simple example of later, more complex models. Another, more recent French theoretical model offers a different account for the attraction of slapstick, though it is not about comedy at all. "Body criticism" can further elaborate both slapstick and transformational comedy, especially the latter's tendency to use silence in giving expression to the repressed freedoms of the body. It is, in a way, not surprising that body criticism in relation to comedy has been so scant, even though slapstick and pantomime are the two dramatic disciplines most interested in the deployment of the body and in deploying their techniques on the body.[76]

The first modern critical commentator of the body was Michel Foucault. For Foucault, in texts like *Discipline and Punish, Madness and Civilization,* and *The History of Sexuality,* the most important component in the making of history, and the one most neglected, is the physical body.[77] This body is less a "signified," a thing-in-itself, and more like a web of signifiers and significations: a "text" on which various ideologies are inscribed. It is interesting as a discourse, and for the way ideologies operate in the defining and consequent limiting of the body. So, for example, modern medicine has defined as pathologies some forms of behavior that, in evading definition, were historically allowed a greater range of expressions: homosexuality and insanity, for example. Since Foucault, the conversation about the body has been most audible in various sectors of gender studies, either in feminist criticism, to demonstrate how ideology imposes a tyranny of definition on the female body (Hélène Cixous, for example), or by queer studies, to discuss the oppressions and repressions of gay consciousness (conspicuously Eve Kosofsky Sedgwick).[78]

But at least one body critic discourses on a sexually undifferentiated body. In *The Body in Pain* Elaine Scarry borrows a page from the corpus of Foucault's work (perhaps principally *Discipline and Punish*) as well as from Marxian theory and biblical exegesis in order to create a hermeneutics of the rigors of the body under torture and in war.[79] Her fundamental assertions are that pain—as torture—takes away the voice of the sufferer (as a cultural power as much as a physical attribute) and that torture thus "unmakes" the world and its artifacts. Her work is interesting because she expounds on a number of elements we have been discussing as attributes of transformational comedy and, to a somewhat lesser degree, slapstick more generally: the punishment of the body; the projection of the human into artifacts and their subsequent transformation; the near sentience of the inanimate world; the transformation of tools into weapons; the transformation of the body, language, and silence; the relation between imagination and work; the absorption of the body of the worker by the machine. At one moment she even discusses the Western suspicion of the non-Western embrace of technology.[80]

Viewing slapstick and tramp comedy through the prism of body criticism allows us to examine further the immigrant's pain at being part of a society exercising a broad spectrum of repressions. Scarry's assertions about the mundanity and quotidian nature of torture, about the way in which it takes place with and among everyday objects, sound oddly like a now pedestrian assertion about slapstick. In torture, all the world is a weapon: "The appearance of these common domestic objects in torture reports of the 1970s is no more gratuitous and accidental than the fact that so much of our awareness of Germany in the 1940s is attached to the words 'ovens,' 'showers,' 'lampshades,' and 'soap.'"[81] "Made to participate in the annihilation of the prisoners, made to demonstrate that everything is a weapon, the objects themselves, and with them the fact of civilization, are annihilated: there is no wall, no window, no door, no bathtub, no refrigerator, no chair, no bed."[82] This emphasis on mundane objects as weapons sounds like a perverse echo of virtually every commentator on silent slapstick, beginning with James Agee on Mack Sennett: "[H]e gave inanimate objects a mischievous life of their own, broke every law of nature. . . . [S]ometimes what seemed like a whole city, an entire civilization, were hauled along head over heels in the wake of that energy like dry leaves following an express train."[83] Both Agee and Scarry are interested in the transformation of the everyday into weaponry, and in the anarchic nature of this transformation. For Scarry objects remake the body, rendering "sentience itself an artifact."[84] For the tramp, sentience originates in things; for Chaplin, as for Scarry, people endow things with life.

Setting aside any scruples about whether slapstick in fact represents torture (so far from absolving the audience of responsibility for the comic's pain, Bergson's assertion that we feel an "anesthesia of the heart" in relation to comic pain merely attributes to the audience a torturer's sensibility), we recognize that Chaplin and his numerous alazons are placed in positions of suffering. On the one hand, the photography and blocking of slapstick suggest otherwise; the quick cuts, exaggerated facial expressions and slapstick situations, and the rapidly occurring events all militate against our taking the characters' pain seriously. More important, the slapstick moment seems to differ from the moment of torture in its raison d'être: we understand that the purpose of torture is interrogation. But in fact, as Scarry points out again and again, torture has historically been more useful as an assertion of power than as an instrument for deriving information. Of course, slapstick is also at all times about the assertion of power. But where in Punch and Judy slapstick is about power within relationships, principally between husband and wife or father and daughter, in silent comedy slapstick abuse is about power over all relationships, principally over the physical world.[85] Further, the perception of pain is not always visible, although the infliction of pain (and its motives) is. And, of course, we are often shown the reception of pain, humiliation, and embarrassment, if only for a fleeting moment.

Chaplin's theorizing also parallels Scarry's in its account of pain and torture: though each would repudiate the label, both are in effect neo-Marxists who also critique Marx. Scarry moves from a conversation about things to a conversation about the workplace and the value of the worker. Chaplin hurts people using the everyday artifacts that Scarry is everywhere cataloguing as the instruments of torture: her "model objects"[86] are also his objects of reinvention. The space in which torture takes place (as often as not a workplace, a small room, or a sweatshop) is confined and confining: the site of Chaplin's static camera, which does not tend to open onto wide vistas. As in the situation of the torturer, artifacts for Chaplin change the body of the worker as much as the other way around. For Scarry as for Chaplin, the body of the worker is absorbed into the machine. For both, the problem with the machine is that it reproduces itself rather than the desire of its maker, finally trying to replace the body of the worker itself.

Of course one may claim two or three problems with the analogies between Scarry and Chaplin, and between the worker and the immigrant: first, that the worker is not really tortured by the workplace and second, that the worker is not necessarily an immigrant. (Finally, one may further claim that merely living in America is not itself tantamount to torture for the immigrant.) While all these claims are arguable only in a critical universe unaccustomed to acknowledging the value of ethnicity, let us suppose for a moment a lesser case: rather than assuming the body in physical pain, let us assume instead that the rigors of the body are merely those recorded by Foucault in *Discipline and Punish* as a part of modern (post-Enlightenment) society, which is based on the penal-system dynamics of surveillance, conformity, and stillness. The body of the Western individual is in this case still submitted to the pain of conformity and stillness. Panopticon society makes the individual his own surveillance camera so that the society does not have to expend energy on actually surveying and punishing all its citizens at all times. Foucault's assertion is not that panopticon society is a possible dystopia—as in *1984*—but that the institutions of Western culture already operate according to the rules of the panopticon: certain discourses are disallowed, certain behaviors are characterized as perversions, and so on. For our purposes this means that the immigrant's body and mind are colonized and that the discourses they represent are repressed and replaced with self-surveillance or silence.

Tramp comedy—the comedy of transformation—is both analogous to and opposed to the alliance between the quotidian and torture. Chaplin's celebrated stare into the camera, for example, acknowledges not only a friendly companion—the audience—but also a means of surveillance whereby he is being watched and judged by an invisible entity that will determine his worth. Sometimes characterized as an act of rebellion (as I shall similarly characterize Groucho's stare in chapter 3), it is also character- ized as the reverse: submission to the dictates of the audience. But his response to being the center of surveillance is not to internalize guilt or maintain a self-surveillance but rather to stare back at the audience and refuse to recognize that audience as invisible and omnipotent. When we say that the tramp's wink at the audience is conspiratorial, we imagine that we are incorrectly assuming his behavior is harmlessly playful. Quite the contrary:

the wink is genuinely conspiratorial, an invitation to blow up Parliament. The entirety of *Modern Times,* like the bulk of Chaplin's films, is about surveillance in the story lines as well as in the imagery: the idle corporate president monitors the tramp's movements—via ubiquitous video monitors and screens at the center of the industrial panopticon—into the bathroom and sees a delinquent tramp smoking a cigarette. The institutions of incarceration and surveillance that proliferate throughout the film (juvenile authorities, mental institutions, prisons) are all subjects of Foucault's attention at one time or another. *Modern Times* can thus be characterized as a film about a person who does not realize he lives in the panopticon, even though all of his social contacts attempt to coerce him into panopticon behavior. In short, even as we reduce our definition of the comic's place in the machine from victim of torture to object of surveillance, we are still left with a comic mode investigating the unjust rigors of the workplace.

In some respects, Scarry and Chaplin are ambiguously opposed in their treatment of the body. The only real difference between the representations of slapstick and of torture is the failure of slapstick to register pain in any prolonged manner. Again, it is as if slapstick is an unacknowledged reenactment of the unconfessed tortures and rigors of the body. As torture transforms the everyday, so slapstick transforms both the everyday and torture. As torture objectifies the tortured object, so slapstick objectifies torture for a dispossessed group that must daily undergo its rigors in the forms of a more or less open industrial oppression and a more or less secretive political repression. Scarry's torturer imagines the world as an instrument of torture, while the tramp imagines all instruments of torture as devices for self-expression. While, for Scarry, torturing and creating are opposing activities, they are one and the same for Chaplin. Chaplin—and the slapstick mode more generally—creates through torture and through the exigencies of the body. The moment of creation as Scarry defines it is a dance of the creator in relation to the thing created: "Thus in work, a perception is danced; in the chair, a danced-perception is sculpted."[87] Remembering that one significant adjective applied to Chaplin is "balletic," we understand that the tramp's dance destroys things. If, for Scarry, capitalism increasingly denies the connection between artifacts and the human, Chaplin is able to re-envision artifacts through the very dynamic—torture—that serves as the model for denying life. Where objects are nearly sentient only in the imagination, the tramp is imaginative and the world sentient whether he is being cruel or sentimental. Even the elements of an oppositional duality connected by Scarry in the term "work" are linked in *Modern Times.* Scarry points out that the term is used "at once as a near synonym for pain,[88] and as a near synonym for created object."[89] Through the Chaplin oeuvre, Chaplin's aesthetic creations happen within the workplace: first, onscreen, in the guise of various familiar work sites, and second, behind the camera, in an aesthetic environment—the film studio—that is both workplace and artist's atelier.

In short, as body discourse illuminates slapstick humor, so slapstick comedy has something to add to the discourse of the body: the slapstick discourse is a fantasy of life without the torture of the machine, an optical illusion of dissociation that supports Scarry's assertions about the body trapped but does not allow the blithe separation of imagination and torture that informs Scarry's universe. Rather, Chaplin's trompe l'oeil is a trick that allows us to imagine freedom only through a satirical acknowledgment of the machine as torture device.

Finally, Scarry's model has implications for a wider arena in film than a single genre. If slapstick comedy offers an ideal aesthetic for immigrant self-projection, silent film offers an ideal medium. Though really a neo-Marxist critique meant to be universally applicable to all oppressed groups within the industrial machine, Scarry's model contains an excurse on silence and language that really begs to be read as a critique of the colonialization as well as of the colonization of pain. First, she offers an account of pain and voice that unintentionally offers some insight into the silence of silent slapstick: "The failure to express pain . . . will always work to allow its appropriation and conflation with debased forms of power; conversely, the successful expression of pain will always work to expose and make impossible that appropriation and conflation."[90] Further, "Physical pain is not only itself resistant to language but also actively destroys language."[91] In other words, Scarry associates pain with the absence of voice, suggesting that the physical absence of expression leads to the appropriation of the suffering person. Her model suggests the correctness of silent film as an immigrant medium because it is a perfect medium for expressing the desire of the silenced and the silencing of desire; it circumvents the need for language more than do other media of expression. Silent screen as silent scream. (Of course intertitles, and the apperceptive requirements of narrative, necessitate that the audience be in some sense "in language.") The absence of voice in the silent cinema means that, despite the intertitles and pit orchestra, the characters become artifacts very like the inanimate ones with which they interact, for an audience that perfectly understands what it means to be object-ified. (Slapstick in this sense merely dramatizes this silent film dynamic.) Without fear of committing too great an outrage, one might say that the Hollywood silent conventions—valorization of fewer and fewer intertitles, increasing reliance of character over plot in "quality" films, and a reduction of the Lasky–Famous Players–style reliance on great literature—was a response to the audience most attuned to silence, perhaps because their understanding of English was not very good (though remember that this audience would necessarily be bilingual when most nativists were not), but certainly because of the attempts politically and culturally to silence the immigrant and ethnic. What they saw on the screen was a valorization of the silence enforced on them by the American nativists, genteel reformers, and even the corrupt or repressive immigrants in the community who had obtained some power. To generalize further, it makes perfect sense that silent film narrative developed in Western industrialized countries, not so much because of industrialization per se—that would account only for the invention of the technology—but because these countries were also colonial powers, both externally and internally. Silent film would be attractively ambiguous: the cultural hegemony would see a medium for teaching immigrants how to behave, while immigrants would see a deep-structure enactment of their own silencing on the screen. The dependence of silent film on this contingency would, of course, not be recorded in the history books, not just because the stories were not overtly immigrant and ethnic (in fact many were) but because silencing itself would be silenced through such an act. The conversion to sound happened in the United States not merely because the technology was perfected. The technology was perfected when the depiction of immigrant repression gave way to ethnic repression after the closing of the "flood gates."

MODERN TIMES AND TRANSFORMATION

This chapter closes with a reading of Modern Times because, after having discussed the "lives" of Chaplin and the tramp, it seems appropriate to look closely at how the various themes and techniques we have hitherto referred to work within a single text. A reading of Modern Times reveals Chaplin films as structurally implicated in the theme of transformation. Chaplin films tend to be all of a piece in reproducing at several levels the same mechanism for an ultimately similar purpose: the fantasy unity of irreconcilable societal impulses. As a looser, feature-length production, Modern Times is a more challenging film to read; the shorts are uni-situational and so too patently susceptible to assertions about unity of theme, structure, and mode. The accusation leveled at Modern Times by contemporary critics, that the film is merely a compendium of situations, techniques, and gags from previous films (especially shorts), works to the obvious advantage of the Chaplin critic who wishes to claim a reading of one film as universally applicable.[92] One may thus relate through a reading of *Modern Times* a body of previous Chaplin films in ways that would be more tedious to discover and prove by reading all these films simultaneously.

The dominant theme of *Modern Times*—the oppression of the individual by the political-industrial complex—can be less mechanistically restated as the use of someone for something other than his intended use. The tramp works at several jobs in the course of the film, none of which suits him temperamentally, all of which he performs admirably but for a mistake or accident of some kind that serves as a parapraxis revealing his discontent. This reuse of the person by the state resembles the tramp's reuse of objects for purposes other than those for which they were intended. The tramp conceives of his body as a lamp or a projectile; the state more generally conceives of the tramp as part of a larger machine.. The difference lies in the ephemerality of the tramp's usages. While the state's use of the person is ineluctably and eternally repetitious, the tramp's transformations, because temporary, are eternally variable: the monkey wrenches can be Pan ears only momentarily. But the Pan ears are preceded and followed by other ironically insightful uses for factory equipment.

There exist two perspectives to any filmic joke situation: its existence as a joke independent of anything other than its immediate desire to make us laugh, and its relation to the significant theme(s) of the film. The joke is in part defined by the theme to which it relates. But the theme, because it is a part of a successful comic film, is in part structured by the structure of the joke. The structure of the central joke of the Chaplin oeuvre determines especially the theme of his most central and carefully planned works. This theme is not precisely about the transformation of one thing to another, because transformation in Western culture is conceived as magical and comic. Rather, *Modern Times* is about noncomic transformation—the inversion of things to a status other than their intended use.

Comedy of social inversion is rather standard fare; it is the norm from the social inversions of Aristophanes (as in the powerful women of *Lysistrata*) to the medieval plays and pageants about which Bakhtin speaks,[93] to Shakespearean elevations of low to high, masculine to feminine, slave to lord. The initial description of *The Taming of the Shrew*'s Christopher Sly could fairly sum up the assumptions underlying most comic social inversion:

> O monstrous beast, how like a swine he lies!
> Grim death, how foul and loathsome is thine image!
> Sirs, I will practice on this drunken man.

What think you, if he were convey'd to bed,
Wrapp'd in sweet clothes, rings put upon his fingers,
A most delicious banquet by his bed,
And brave attendants near him when he wakes,
Would not the beggar then forget himself?[94]

But these inversions tend to be temporary. The chorus of women are reconciled to the men at the end of *Lysistrata,* the feast of fools comes to an end and, presumably, Christopher Sly is returned to the sty the Lord assumes is his rightful resting place.

The cosmic inversions of the tramp's world, however, are portrayed in more durable pigments. The tramp lives in a world in which ethical as well as physical laws are *forever* transgressed and transgressable, not most by the tramp, but by the central representatives and authorities of his world: the cop, the factory owner, the shop manager, and so on. It is not a world in which the economically and culturally dispossessed usurp authority for a day in order that the inappropriateness of such rule might be made evident, but one in which the ethically low have permanently usurped authority, have *created* the idea of authority, usurping power and in so doing putting the lie to the very ethical strictures they pretend to represent. The world of the tramp is Manichean (and incidentally counter to the Hayes production code): unethical behavior (including the tramp's) is routinely rewarded, while ethical behavior, except at a very personal level, goes either unrewarded or punished.

For example, *Modern Times,* like most Chaplin films, is about the unrequited need for food and shelter. As Mast observes,[95] the film contains several scenes of people either eating or trying to cadge meals, often unsuccessfully: the tramp spilling the worker's soup, the tramp trying to eat with the aid of the eating machine, the Gamin trying to steal a loaf of bread, the tramp trying to get thrown back in jail (though he almost succeeds at this, and he tries to get in through the *illegal* device of eating), the tramp as waiter trying to serve a diner (who never receives his meal), the tramp trying to feed the master mechanic through an oil funnel, then through a chicken, always unsuccessfully. Even during the mock idyll in the shack by the sea, the tramp is not allowed to finish breakfast before he must leave for work. Other images of food frustration abound: the tramp is forced to become intoxicated by the burglars in the department store liquor department, a scene in which an excess of goods is quite as bad as a deficiency because this prank ends with his being fired. The Gamin even has her finger in her mouth in the photograph the juvenile authorities carry, making her appear more childish than her persona otherwise suggests, a bit like a starving waif. We even hear the frustrated carnal desire of an old roué in the nonsense song the tramp sings at the end of the film. (The Gamin is the final comestible for the state, the tramp, and, in the person of Paulette Godard, for Chaplin.)

But scenes of frustration alternate with instances of successful foraging and provisioning. The peculiarity of these successes is that they are almost always illicit. These scenes begin not with the tramp but with the Gamin, whom we first see stealing bananas from a boat. This sequence is followed by the tramp's aggressive acquisition of bread from a cellmate while high on cocaine, which he has mistaken for salt. The tramp also steals meals for the Gamin at the department store, selects a meal at a cafeteria in order to get arrested, and, for the same purpose, claims to have stolen bread that the Gamin has actually stolen. Finally, the tramp seems well fed only in jail (albeit after he has foiled an attempted escape; but even then he is high on cocaine). Almost every successful acquisition of food is in some manner illegal. Hunger thus becomes associated with all standardized, workaday livelihoods, while satiation is associated with criminality. The tramp's comedy of hunger becomes located in the criminal, a world in which virtue is *exactly* its own reward. In the tramp's *polis,* honesty is punished (in trying to return a red flag to its owner, the tramp is arrested as a communist agitator), and dishonesty rewarded.

The film's inversion and transformation of the workplace are more important than its handling of food, however, because they implicate the structure of the film: the order of the sequences, the contrast between certain shots. The structure of Modern Times is governed by the institutions in which the tramp finds himself and that he finds himself subverting again and again. The opposition between frustrated and satisfied desires is echoed in the contrapuntal relationship between institutions of work and detention: the tramp moves cyclically between remuneration and incarceration. Most frustrated desires are frustrated in institutional settings designed to create the conditions for instinctual satisfaction. Work is supposed to provide at least a competence for the worker: home, food, the ability to reproduce, and, perhaps, some cultural stimulation (or anaesthetization). But, though the tramp's intentions are good, he cannot hold a job for more than a day, and generally less than that. His job as assistant to the master mechanic lasts precisely half a day when the strike begins. His job as a dock worker lasts about five minutes. And each job ends in incarceration.

The factory at the beginning of the film is an environment in which all significant action is uniform movement. One does not choose how to move while working; one can choose only whether to work with the machine or in opposition to it. Eccentricity is defined as any human movement not serving the machine. When the tramp attempts to sneak a cigarette in the bathroom (the acres of porcelain reflecting a culture bent, among other things, on standardization in every bodily function), he is immediately caught by the televised president of the corporation, whose only official function is ordering the workers to increase their rate of production. Uniform motion becomes inscribed on the body of the worker in a manner that is locally destructive and ineffaceable. The tramp, unable to discontinue the motions of bolt-tightening, twitches during his break as if still tightening bolts, spilling a bowl of soup belonging to a co-worker in the process. The factory workers are lined up in rows; they repeat identical motions over and over to background music that emphasizes the repetitive quality of the work. The only change is the rate of production which, along with the parallel music, only crescendos. In keeping with the 1930s image of WPA and TVA projects, the size of the factory devices is enormous: the dynamos tower above the workers, the factory is itself palatial. The only small objects in it are the people and the artifacts (purpose unknown) they produce. Irony exists in the fact that while the scale of the factory is immense, the object of individual attention is so small as to seem the object of obsession. The real product is the panopticon sensibility that keeps the workers on the line and the audience in their chairs.

The institutions seem to become more humane in appearance as the film progresses: the tramp's gradual and utterly accidental upward mobility brings increased physical mobility. He moves from his soulless job in the factory to an outdoor job at the docks, to the rather more interesting job as mechanic's helper, to waiter, to singer. He even accustoms himself to prison so efficiently that he does not want to leave when pardoned. The opening factory sequences and the restaurant scenes that close the film compose a striking visual and aural contrast. Beginning as an assembly-line worker, repeating one motion over and over, the tramp ends his last venture in a restaurant/café as a singing waiter, the sound of applause still ringing in his ears. Unlike the movements of the assembly line workers, the motions of the restaurant inhabitants constitute the haphazard, purposeful, and confused din of people eating, dancing, and otherwise amusing themselves. These seem more the motions of life than the measured movements of the machine. The spaciousness of the factory is opposed to the compactness of the restaurant, with its low ceiling, cramped kitchen, and impossibly crowded dining area. The sequence further emphasizes the physical closeness of the clientele, crowding them together on the dance floor, so that the tramp cannot deliver a duck to an irate customer. In opposition to the panopticon quality of the factory video monitor, which observes all traces of disloyalty and eccentricity, the relationship between the tramp and the café audience is one of desired difference. For the tramp it is the difference between being either the object of surveillance or the object of spectatorship, between being accused of eccentricity and being encouraged in it. The café audience desires that he will be sufficiently eccentric to be entertaining, their applause validating his difference. That applause, and the tramp's song, mark the first time in his oeuvre, and the only time in this film (excepting the score), that Chaplin uses sound to portray a positive quality on the part of culture, standing in strong contrast to all his other uses of sound as insidiously human.

This visual difference between the two settings hints at other, less tangible differences. The president of the factory is perfectly dressed, dapper, and cold, while the café proprietor is fat, a bit sloppy though well-dressed, not rich though comfortably bourgeois, and obviously kind. (The proprietor is played by Henry Bergman, a long-time Chaplin repertory player who was extremely close to Chaplin.) Becoming a sort of fairy godfather, he gives the Gamin her first break as a dancer. At the factory, the tramp is obviously a loner, at odds with all parties, if not actually engaged in open hostilities. By the time he arrives at the restaurant he has acquired a friend in the Gamin, someone of supposedly similar sensibility: another loner, another eccentric, another character whose sense of personal freedom is impossibly ascendant over her need for security. Chaplin portrays the café as the scene in which human sympathy is finally possible for the tramp: food and entertainment provide a climate of gregariousness that fosters the possibility of warmth and intimacy.

But even the most benevolent institution, the café, cannot provide a permanently comfortable working environment for the tramp. He is still (if less) at odds with his fellow employees because of his inattention to the structural rules without which no institution can operate. The tramp enters through exit doors, knocking over waiter and tray. The café's encouragement of the tramp's eccentricity finally underlines the limits of cultural flexibility because, even in the best of circumstances, external societal forces (here in the form of delinquency officers) invariably push the tramp away from social comforts and back on the road. Although the jobs become more humane as the film progresses, each job loss is punctuated by actual or threatened incarceration:

factory	$\longrightarrow$	hospital
unemployment	$\longrightarrow$	prison
shipyard	$\longrightarrow$	arrest
department store	$\longrightarrow$	prison
factory (strike, unemployment)	$\longrightarrow$	prison
restaurant	$\longrightarrow$	arrest of Gamin

The conditions under which arrest occurs in each sequence vary: sometimes the tramp is seeking arrest, sometimes it is thrust upon him. His first confinement finds him not in jail, but in another equally futile institution: the psychiatric hospital. The last incarceration is only a threat of the orphan asylum. But the pattern is nevertheless striking. The repetition of this motif may or may not be intended as comic (though his longest stay in prison is so intended) as it is meant to be in films made after the Depression (*Take the Money and Run* [1969], *The Great Escape* [1963]). But more clearly evident at the ending of each job is the futility of attempting to acquire permanence, security, and sanity in the marketplace. Though the jobs themselves become better, the sense of the fatuity of work remains present. Work becomes—*causes*—its own obverse and complement: incarceration. It inverts itself, causing an instability it was created to forestall and prevent. When the tramp is not employed he goes to jail, almost as if prison is the home to which he returns after a hard day's work. It is as if to say that work and incarceration are associated as necessary alternatives—idleness is the only state not allowed in society. Or perhaps it would be better to say that even idleness must be physically surrounded by, and lent the legitimacy of, an institutional setting (remember the tramp's cell after he has thwarted the escape attempt—the cigars, the magazines, the meals in bed). And ironically, though institutions seem created in order to enforce nonidleness, or work, they really encourage idleness. The tramp is fired from all of this jobs—generally as a prelude to being arrested— for circumstances that are almost never his fault (though his sinking of a liner in a shipyard is perhaps arguably his responsibility).

The tramp is never jailed for a significant length of time. In *Modern Times* he seems to be incarcerated two or three times in as many days. He manages to make his first incarceration comfortable. But the same circumstance that renders comfort possible—his status as hero—is ultimately responsible for his release from jail; he is pardoned for a crime he did not really commit because of an act of heroism committed while drugged. The tramp even has trouble getting arrested and reincarcerated when he finds life outside the prison tougher than life inside; he has to try twice. And when he is finally arrested, a "lucky" accident ejects and frees him from the paddy wagon. Paradoxically prison, the lowest possible institution to which the citizen can appeal for safety and security—the minimal conditions of home—is not really accessible to its most desperate pursuers; it is as inaccessible as work.

The tramp, eager to comply with the social dictate that one must engage in enforced, institutionalized movement or idleness, is chronically and ironically thrust into extralegal circumstances that have none of the advantages of either work or prison, a liminal world not even supposed to exist. This extra-institutional idleness is movement between both institutions enforced by both the marketplace and the legal system. We are accustomed to the image of the tramp as a lonely figure moving of his own volition down rural, dusky California roads, even after it has been pointed out to us that, often as not, the tramp ends up in happier circumstances. We like to think of the tramp as reconciled to his lonesome fate because we do not like to consider that the reality of such a life is rather different, not quite so volitional. But even the tramp is forced down that road by a society that will not allow him to maintain the freedom of this unaffiliation with anything except the road. Forced freedom is extremely ambiguous at best.

As slapstick tends to be about individual physical movement, and Chaplinesque comedy tends to be about individual psychological movement conceived as the transformation of artifacts (including the self), so *Modern Times* is about the individual's social and spatial movement between institutions. This movement is thematized; it gets worked out by the plot in such a way that shiftlessness—an inherently valueless way of living—is transformed by the tramp into an intimately valuable ethos. Machines work because they move, and cause other things to move, at regular intervals. Similarly, the alternation between work and prison is a series of orders to move from one hot seat to the next. Movement denies time for reflection and fantasy. The capitalist tells the cigarette-holding tramp to stop malingering, and the policeman tells the tramp to stop fantasizing about a home in which one could remain benignly motionless.

The Chaplin moving picture thus becomes a film about two kinds of motion: socially determined and self-reflective. The tramp masters the second kind of movement, making shiftlessness homelike. Home, which does not really exist in the film except ironically, is replaced by movement, because home necessitates a kind of physical, moral, and intellectual stasis. But part of the comedy/fantasy of the tramp is his recreation of movement as homelike. Movement becomes both a reassertion of humanity and a re-connoting and reconnoitering of the kind of motion forced on him by the machine. For Chaplin, comedy analyzes the largest influences of mundane and unexamined life in such a way that their life-denying qualities are metamorphosed as life-affirming.

In other words, the largest transformation in *Modern Times* that reproduces the structure of the Chaplin joke is the tramp's comic inversion of consensually agreed-upon values. Chaplin comedy originates in the remaking of an accidentally malevolent world into an intentionally benevolent world (intended by the self). The act of perception by which this happens

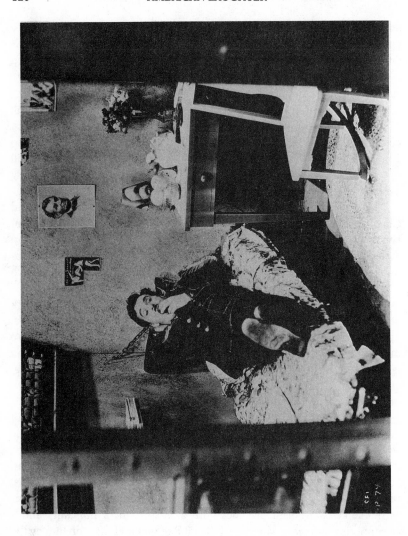

Figure 2.7 *Modern Times.*
© Roy Export Company
Establishment. Courtesy
of the Academy of Motion
Picture Arts and Sciences.

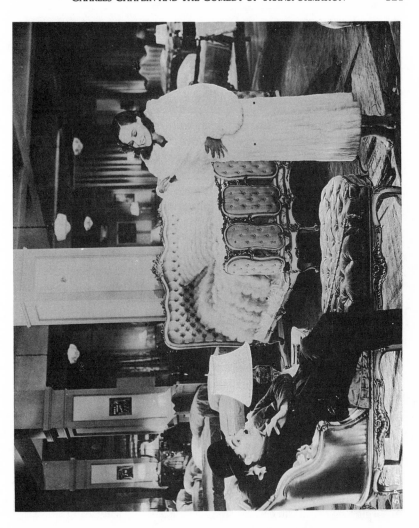

Figure 2.8 In *Modern Times* the institution—prison and department store—are reconfigured as home. © Roy Export Company Establishment. Courtesy of the Academy of Motion Picture Arts and Sciences.

is preternatural, if the actual act in which it results is not. Originally conceived as oppressive to the individual, the world is thus reconceived as an entity that utilizes its own oppressiveness as the very buffer protecting the individual from itself, turning the environment into the subject of comedy by protecting the self with what threatens the self. This makes a negative definition of the self positive, thus rendering difference attractive.

Of course, the tramp is turning a negative injunction to remove himself into a positive action. This is why the end of the film, and the end of so many Chaplin films, feels upbeat even though it is circumstantially pathos-laden: the tramp is forced on the road again, but it is a forcing to which he consents, which he makes his own, and which he himself has necessitated by following the Gamin. This is not subversive in a local way—the tramp merely follows orders dictated by the prevailing social codes. But in the sense that he refuses to understand by these codes that he is being punished he is approaching the subversive, not because he advocates the overthrow of those codes, but because he reinterprets them according to a radically individual light.

The easiest illustration of this transformation of values is located in the tramp's stylized treatment of institutions. We have spoken only of the ways in which these institutions manipulate the tramp. But the tramp manipulates the institution in return. His dependence on these institutions makes them subject to the same transformative faculty that works on bodies and inanimate objects. As a lampshade becomes a disguise and a boot becomes food, so the institution is made over as something unimaginably supportive. The factory becomes a nursery for a man with a nervous breakdown, and prison becomes a home for the tramp, as does the department store.

The institution's utility has in each case a very special quality: it suggests that the institution has been changed in a way that makes it more nurturing, more like the parental home than an indifferent purgatory. In constituting humane institutions as possible only through fantasy, the comedy recognizes that humanity is actually absent from plant, shop, and prison. The factory at the beginning of the film becomes for the lunatic tramp a fantasy of a nursery, with infant's toys and nurturing women equipped with breasts on which to fixate. The background music in this sequence emphasizes the childlike, regressed quality of the tramp at this point: it is the saccharine music signaling the presence of the nursery or the asylum. Later, jail becomes a place that feeds and shelters him from the world in comfort. The department store fills the same needs in a bourgeois dream of absolute luxury. The tramp's insanity transforms dystopia into utopia, searing deserts into oases of consumables.

Some of the comedy in this transformation of the workplace is located in the tension between the implied fantasy of the home and the graphically portrayed reality of the dehumanizing factory. Chaplin has been criticized for making the sets too large and streamlined, too old-fashioned an idea of the future for the tramp: the "little fellow" seems too anachronistic in the immensity and antique modernity of the settings.[96] But their enormity emphasizes the sense that any quality of the human brought to these settings is brought by the tramp and denied by the settings themselves.[97] A tension thus exists between the tramp's diminutive size and dainty motions and the cavernousness and precise movement of the institutions.

There is a further irony of identification at work between the character of the tramp and the factory settings. Our sympathies and sense of the reality of human feeling are with the tramp—he captures our sense of emotional reality. The factory, on the other hand, is more aligned with some version of industrial, objective, photographic truth. We do not know which reality to take as real: the personalized truth of the tramp, or the photographic, objective truth of the factories. They each lend an air of incredibility to the other.

The satire of the happy bourgeois couple—the smiling husband on his way to work, the wife happily skipping back into the house—further undercuts the possibility of middle-class domestic bliss by conceiving it as fantastic. The satirized component is not the happiness so much as what it ignores: two hungry victims of the Depression on the front steps. The couple's bliss is completely dependent on not acknowledging the starving couple in the same frame with them, almost underfoot. The tramp parodies the couple's bliss, imitating the saccharine, conventional motions of self-satisfaction. He desires a stable home but not at the expense of adopting a self-enforced ignorance of suffering. He knows ineluctably what the bourgeois couple can never afford to know about pain, hunger, and suffering: that they exist. Like the legal and marketplace institutions that promise what they deny, his vision of the world urges the tramp both to want a home for himself and the Gamin and to realize that the achievement of this goal is impossible.

Finally, Chaplin's use of sound elaborates the theme of ethical and economic transformation as a commentary about the film medium itself, as well as about industry. Sound in this film satirizes industry; sound is speech or noise that represents either social or industrial oppression of the individual: the phonograph that advertises the disastrous eating machine into which the tramp is forced, the television over which comes only orders to speed up the factory output, the radio that advertises gas pills at socially inappropriate moments. (The tramp's comic song is perhaps the sole exception.) But sound is also about the inappropriate use of film for some other use, or medium. All the examples of sound in this film are rationalized as being part of another medium: radio, television, phonograph. By using sound in a medium that

Figure 2.9 Ferdinand Leger's Cubist Charlie Chaplin. © 1996 Artists Rights Society (ARS), New York / SPADEM / ADAGP, Paris.

had depended for its aesthetic effects on silence, Chaplin is asserting that sound can successfully convey information only about tyranny or oppression. (Of the four sound films in which Chaplin subsequently starred, one was about fascism, and two others were about the disintegration and death of characters in revolt against an increasingly callous society.)

As *Modern Times* is about the oppression of the individual by industry and society, and about the strategies of re-perception through which the individual counters that oppression, so the jokes are not only the central devices of that strategy, but are also themselves about the arbitrary oppression of one object by another and the re-perception of that object by a creative sensibility that redefines and so momentarily liberates it. Chaplin's filmic world is one in which finally the whole range of artifacts—perhaps anything visible—ultimately requires a transformative liberation from at least the tyranny of our perception of them. This attempt at the iconic by a filmmaker often referred to as Victorian reflects, of course, a modernist sensibility.

3

— ◆ —

THE MARX BROTHERS AND THE
SEARCH FOR THE LANDSMAN

INTRODUCTION

Duck Soup (1933), so the critical narrative asserts, is the last in a series of Marx Brothers films made at Paramount Studios in which the protagonists' actions grow increasingly outrageous and antisocial. Afterward, under the tutelage of Irving Thalberg at MGM, the Brothers become more gentrified, or are at least placed in a more empathetic position in relation to the already genteel heroes and heroines of their films. While the Paramount films offered no characters with whom one would want to identify one's passional life, the later films find the Brothers less inclined to satirize the romantic leads. In the post-Paramount films the Brothers are eccentric characters given top billing as the feature attractions of the films, while in fact they move further and further from center stage until, by Copacabana (1947), and Love Happy (1950) they are mere sideshows meant to elicit more nostalgia than astonishment. In short, they are no longer the subjects of their own histories. Like the ethnic and immigrant, they are paid homage and then excluded from their own films.

Critics tend to perceive this movement as a degeneration in ethnic presence. Marx Brothers comedy, like the tramp's, gradually becomes more genteel, a move critics perceive as a falling away from their more characteristically detached and antisympathetic lampoons of all value. This critical sensibility, however, is itself both anarchic and reactionary: it enjoys the Brothers' destruction of society, but it desires only safely infinite repetitions of that destruction in a sort of nostalgia for nihilism. Joe Adamson gives a classic, even generous, assessment: "*A Night at the Opera* is the Marx Brothers decked out in refinery like a Christmas shopping window, going through some very funny motions against a stops-out backdrop of posh set design, realistically reacting extras. . . . This keeps them from being the figures of fantasy that Mankiewicz allowed them to be: Harpo can never step outside the bounds of reality any more."[1] Henry Jenkins especially, in a chapter on Eddie Cantor, argues that Hollywood comedy becomes "desemitized" in the early 1930s, becoming more Anglo-Saxon for a greater reception in the hinterlands.[2] But Adams's and Jenkins's assessment describes only one half of a dialectical process in which overt ethnicity disappears at the expense of critiques of and changes in the host culture. In the process Hollywood culture, and mainstream culture, internalize certain ethnic dynamics as well. For example, while the principal sign of the Marx Brothers MGM gentility in the 1930s is a kind of deference to the romantic couple, that romantic couple is, in another genre, destabilized through a kind of humor more characteristic of the Marx Brothers and other ethnic comics: screwball comedy. Because the newer gentility of the MGM Brothers includes taking the romantic couple seriously in a way they had not before, they may be seen as one of the last instances of pure new-immigrant ethnic comedy and one of the first attempts in the 1930s to evolve from team comedy into a comedy more congenial to a middle-class and intellectual audience. They attempt, in other words, to evolve a middle-class romantic comedy of assimilation. But because theirs is a comedy of social dissolution, a synthesis is difficult to achieve, which is why critics complain about the MGM films.[3] Though harbingers of screwball comedy, the Marx Brothers cannot become screwball comedians themselves.

By the time of the MGM films, the Great Depression, and the activation of the production code and other attempts at social control, ethnic codes dominated the Hollywood sound film even if ethnic images did not. Assimilation, accommodation, and acculturation became obsessive topics in American film for the next sixty years, from *A Star is Born* (1937) to *The Addams Family* (1991), and not just for a moment in the early 1930s, as Henry Jenkins implies. What critics call "desemitization" is in fact a representation—across a number of personae, films, genres, and decades—of various strategies of incorporation and resistance. Critics who notice one ethnic dynamic within a particular set of films then assume that any opposing dynamic across a number of films must as a consequence not be ethnic. This critical judgment, for example, fails to perceive that assimilation is itself an immigrant phenomenon that recurs in several careers before and after World War II. Chaplin moves from the savagery of *The Pawnshop* (1916) to the sentimentality of *City Lights* (1931). Jerry Lewis moves from the idiot-savant adolescent of his early career to the more thoughtfully urbane, if still inept, representative of the middle class. (The transition films for him are *The Nutty Professor* [1963], in which he plays both parts, and *The Family Jewels* [1965], in which he plays *all* parts.) Even the perennially disgruntled W. C. Fields makes motions towards respectability: *Never Give a Sucker an Even Break* (1941) begins with Fields playing a successful Hollywood star. Contemporary comics retain one voice for their nightclub show, and a more sanitized version for their films. It is as if comic ontogeny recapitulates comedic phylogeny; each artist, no matter his aesthetic ethos, begins as cultural critique and ends as an object of nostalgia for the critiqued culture.

This chapter will consider some dynamics that Henry Jenkins and other critics omit: the Marxian critiques that make "accommodation" and "resistance" simultaneous phenomena; the redefinitions of the American landscape as exotic; the "psychoanalyzing" of the comic moment. Through the Jewish institution of the *landsmannschaft,* the chapter will examine the Marx Brothers' attempt to build a community based on one of the few roads to authenticity: hostility. After the first section, which outlines the theme of the landsman in the films, the second section will contain a discussion of the attempt to find a landsman in the audience. The third section provides a psycho-analysis of ethnic separatism, and, finally, the last section discusses the reactionary quality of the landsman through an examination of gender.

THE LANDSMAN AND THE CRYPTO-ETHNIC

Every Marx Brothers film contains a doppelgänger of Groucho, someone Groucho might be were his gestures toward upward mobility in earnest. In *Duck Soup* Ambassador Trentino, though no arriviste, is the foreigner—the Sylvanian—in the Freedonian court. Like Rufus T. Firefly (Groucho), he wants control of Freedonia; like Firefly, he pursues Mrs. Teasdale as a stratagem based in realpolitik. In *The Cocoanuts* (1929) Groucho is just as invested in real estate fraud as the ostensible villain, Harvey Yates, is invested in jewel theft. This dynamic gets carried over to the MGM films, with Sig Rumann vying as Mrs. Teasdale's lover and the lead tenor's manager in *A Night at the Opera* (1935) and as the alter-ego hotel manager in *A Night in Casablanca* (1946). In *Animal Crackers* (1930) that character is Roscoe Chandler, a financier and patron of the arts: "I am just a lover of art, that is all. What people have given to me, I give back to them, in the form of beautiful things."[4] But Chandler is really Abie Kabibble, an arriviste with an assumed voice, a wealthy art patron eager to hide his origins, a fish peddler in the old neighborhood. Like Groucho, Abie is crashing a party to which he does not belong. Like Groucho, he convinces the guests that he is who he represents himself as being. Ravelli and the Professor (Chico and Harpo) question the authenticity of the art authenticator, revealing his real identity as the arriviste Abie the fish man, a fellow ex-denizen of the old neighborhood, by finding his birthmark. They blackmail him; then, after having stolen Abie's tie, 500 dollars, his garters (and, in the stage version, his teeth), the Professor steals the birthmark. Playing the traditional double's role of scapegoat, the ritual humiliation of this doppelgänger is explained as a deflation of social pretension.

The Marx Brothers' satire of the wealthy is always a satire of the pretensions of upward mobility and a denial of the existence of authentic gentility. Culture is always only veneer, the attempt to escape the consequences of a self that is neither genteel nor refined. The treatment of the arriviste cannot be easily dismissed as merely a xenophobic treatment of upwardly mobile ethnics because it appears in a film in which *everyone* becomes the object of similar criticism. Even the romance of the romantic leads is undercut in the dialogue and music. In the stage version of *Animal Crackers* (1928), the romantic couple's duet begins:

> All the boys I've known used to say
> I was made of stone.
> I would always leave them alone in despair
> I was on the pan
> I've been called an electric fan,
> Told I'm even colder than Frigidaire.[5]

Even romantic songs begin in the unsentimental language of the quotidian. In the Brothers' Paramount films the truest subversion lies in the fact that *all* the roles are satirized, not just those of the ethnics. More important, almost all the people in the films are depicted as arrivistes, in the sense that they all have something in their identities they wish to hide, something that does not harmonize with the conventional decor. In *Animal Crackers* the unveiling of a painting is spoiled because of its theft by different, respectable attendees of the party: once by the representatives of old money (they believe even Mrs. Rittenhouse [Margaret Dumont] is a social climber), once through the offices of the butler, and once by the romantic couple. Rittenhouse's genteel weekend party is overpopulated by amateur thieves with hidden agendas. The romantic lead wants to sell his paintings. Rittenhouse's daughter, Mary, wants to marry a penniless male artist. Even Mrs. Rittenhouse, like Abie, wants to enhance her prestige by featuring social lions and works of art. The only characters who seem to have no "hidden agendas" are the Brothers. (Hence, they have less desire to stay: "Hello, I must be going.") Their manifest agenda, though, involves an "outing" of guests like Abie through ritual torture and humiliation. And, as with Abie, they always hope to find a common origin, or way of being, in the other whom they torture.

It is as if the Brothers are attempting to found a *landsmannschaft,* an organization consisting of "individuals from the same village (*shtetl*) or region in the Pale."[6] The *landsmannschaft* was an attempt to maintain a recognizable bond apart from sanctioned identities; as an attempt to help the immigrant fit in, it emphasized a memory and history separate from American memory and history.[7] *Landsmannschaft* were forums for conducting business with people—landsmen—one might not otherwise meet, with an air of familiarity one might not otherwise assume. They allowed, for however brief a time, the fiction that identity was familial, independent of one's present economic and class definitions. In a world of tight collars and constricting belts, it was an ephemeral return to the more comfortable, if rougher, robes and tunics of the shtetl.

This *landsmannschaft* is, of course, not merely a Jewish phenomenon, but rather characterizes virtually every ethnic and immigrant group that comes to America. The Irish establish the Fenian Brotherhood, political clubs, and volunteer fire departments.[8] Italians maintain a close connection to *paisani,* folk from the same region as well as the same country.[9] Japanese Americans first established Gospel Societies,[10] then, at the turn of the century, workers' organizations such as the *Nihonjin Kutsuko Domekai,*[11] and, finally, Japanese Associations.[12] Polish Americans, among others, had their mutual aid societies.[13] Even those ethnic populations that considered themselves temporary "sojourners" in America formed close associations: the Chinese-American *huigans,* the largest of which became the Six Companies.[14] This is not to mention the various urban villages, with their coffinships, mutual benefit associations, politicas, and so on. These organizations were founded for various purposes—from establishing business and political connections to self-consciously attempting to retain some vestige of the *aud sod* in the new—and with various ideas about how one determined a countryman. Their common effect, however, was to establish neighborhoods in which ethnicity was preserved, so that the very urban landscape that was supposedly best suited to erasing ethnicity was in fact changed by it—the new-immigrant presence in New York, Boston, and Chicago being perhaps the best examples, but the African-American presence in those cities and in Memphis, New Orleans, and St. Louis, and the Asian presence in San Francisco being equally appropriate examples. Beyond all self-mythologizing claims of being frontier towns, or cities on the hill, the most significant difference between major American cities and many of their European counterparts was the former's degree of ethnic heterogeneity and the attempt by their various groups to retain some identity. The *landsmannschaft* sensibility of American film comedy was accessible to all these groups, even more because some of its specific ethnicity had disappeared, giving the dynamic a universal appeal.

Performances in the ethnic theater, which provided "a focus for social life" for the various social groups,[15] were sponsored by the various mutual benefit societies, social clubs, and ethnic organizations: the Magyar Egylet for Hungarian Americans,[16] the church and the coffee house for Italian Americans,[17] the temperance societies and the Finnish Socialist Federation for Finnish Americans,[18] and so on. Similarly, the Jewish *landsmanshaft* promoted itself on the stage.[19] Because this theater will be treated in the next section, it is only necessary here to assert that ethnicity, community, spectacle, and performance were conflated early on for a newly arrived immigrant audience. Though Jewish-American culture was as stratified as any, the fiction of community created on stage provided an escape through ethnicity from New-World social designations with which the audience did not feel comfortable.

The Marx Brothers play on this discomfort. Though they are German and French Jewish rather than Russian Jewish, the Brothers attempt to find an unofficial *landsmannschaft* with their audience, outside the political parties and outside the class, labor, and social divisions that militate against the integrity of the original ethnic group. Since the Brothers are second generation and can no longer depend on their ethnic identity as a center of value, and since there is no other sacrosanct dimension to replace religion or ethnicity, they define this *landsmannschaft* negatively: anyone unencumbered by mainstream social definitions may join. Of course, this stipulation only defines the Marx Brothers themselves, as they are the only ones with no social agenda in which they genuinely believe.

The Brothers respond to the alazon's official, public self by always assuming the existence of a more genuine other under the disguise of the dowager, gangster, or art connoisseur, Abie beneath the Roscoe. They attempt to locate that other person by creating a scenario in which an official response becomes impossible, replaced by the inappropriate response to an inappropriate provocation. The object of an insult, in acknowledging the slight, reveals an understanding of a world (often sexual) outside the sphere of the officially sanctioned and overtly inhabited. The landsman is glimpsed either when the official other capitulates by behaving anarchically or when his refusal becomes the occasion for anarchic retaliation. The Brothers' treatment of Abie and other authorities contains two related dynamics: the displaced desire to find someone who is more like oneself, a landsman, and a merciless satirizing of the other as social other. This satire is an infantile sadism that has at its root a desire to punish its object for not avowing identity with oneself as well as a desire to correct a condescending social ease by recreating it as dis-ease. When Sig Rumann and Louis Calhern maintain a traditionally condescending stance toward the Brothers, they play the perfect alazons to the Brothers' eirons. The Brothers cut off their coattails and lit cigars; they slap them (not once or twice, but three times) in a continued insult to the body. They paste their pants bottoms to newspapers. They chase their secretaries and, like Harpo with Lassparri, or Harpo and Chico with Trentino, desert to the opposition even while working for them. The Brothers invite the beleaguered party in authority to be either angry in his or her own world or anarchic in theirs—in other words, to be landsmen. The continued oppression of the villains is contingent on their inability or refusal to recognize that they are being oppressed, on their insistence that they inhabit a predictable world, a conventional film *sans* Marx Brothers. As long as they remain conscious of their status as ambassadors, impresarios, gangsters, or gamblers, however, they are abused in a way that constantly invites them to unburden themselves of social designations. In contrast to Abie Kabibble, for example, Louis Calhern's Trentino in *Duck Soup* is suave and debonair to the last degree. But, like Abie, and despite his urbanity, he is something of a failure, a schlimazel. He has failed to start a revolution in Freedonia, and failed to woo Mrs. Teasdale from Firefly. He has even failed to get any scandalously damaging information about Firefly (who is openly corrupt, repressive, and lecherous). Trentino and his various avatars are figures of pity rather than fear because, unlike Coyote or Iago, they are incompetent villains. The one momentary triumph against the Brothers in *Duck Soup* occurs when Edgar Kennedy laughs with Harpo and against himself, thus disarming Harpo for the moment it takes to pour water down Harpo's trousers. Kennedy is capable of momentarily simulating the self-irony necessary to enter the world of the Brothers, possibly because he was himself a Keystone Kop. The search for the self in the other—whether that other is an authority or the landscape—on which so much of comedy is predicated, is in Marx Brothers films motivated by and may be characterized as an immigrant point of faith: that even in an alien environment people and artifacts, despite their exotic facades, will be at bottom comfortably familiar. Marx Brothers comedy is based on a *potential* community of audience, object, and speaker. The attempt to find the self in the social other is like the traditional attempt to fit oneself into the New-World landscape: both are part of the same impulse to identify the ego with all that is not ego, with all that is overtly threatening in its strangeness to the ego.

The search for the landsman in the landscape certainly forces the Marx Brothers films to relocate ethnic Mott Street on the Upper West Side. But while critics routinely remark that the milieux the lower-class Brothers inhabit are most often the haunts of the wealthy, they do not at the same time notice that these milieux are always representations of center and margin, and always represent the Brothers as immigrants. In *Monkey Business* (1931) the Brothers are stowaways in the hold of a luxury liner bound from Europe to the United States; five years later Harpo and Chico are still shipboard stowaways—this time among operatic Italians—in *A Night at the Opera*. In both films, the Brothers become fugitives as a result of their illegal immigrant status; they are policed around the ship's deck in one film and a hotel room and opera house in the other. Two of their films find the Brothers in exotic locales particularly unsuited to nice boys from the Lower East Side: the Old West (*Go West* [1940]) and Casablanca (*A Night in Casablanca*). A sort of double jeopardy is at work here, in which the immigrants are Americans in a new environment either not at all American or super-American, either European or Western. In the first scenario, the journey to Europe is a *nostos* of the comic immigrant to the land of his origin (at least to the land of Chico's origin for *A Night at the Opera,* a fantasy Italy for a fantasy Italian). In the second scenario, the comic immigrant must journey in a direction that became a national imperative of the nineteenth century. Others of their films find the Brothers in intellectual and cultural milieux also (presumed) unsuited to their personae: the worlds of the opera (*A Night at the Opera*), the university (*Horse Feathers* [1932]), and high society (*Animal Crackers* [1930]). These films metaphorize the immigrant experience as a sense of placelessness. They are exposure nightmares; they recreate the experience of being physically, socially, and intellectually vulnerable to hostile environments that reveal the disjunction between one's inadequate personal resources, and the visible, yet inaccessible, abundance of goods.

Whatever the reason, several of the film's verbal and visual jokes refer to Groucho's fragmentation and loss of self; many jokes and gags are discussions of Groucho's absence. In the search for a disgruntled alter self (or "alte cocker"), one's *own* self—especially Groucho's self—may disappear entirely.

Duck Soup seems in some ways the Marx Brothers film most concerned both with the discovery of the self in others, and with the loss of the self to the world. In the first of his scenes, Groucho is waiting for himself in the production number staged to prepare for his entry. In another scene, each time Chico answers Groucho's phone, he insists that Groucho is not at home, until Groucho queries: "I wonder whatever became of me?" Almost immediately after, he slaps Zeppo's face for telling him a dirty joke that *he* had originally told Zeppo, saying "I should have slapped Mrs. Teasdale's face when she told it to me"—still another occasion on which he has forgotten himself.

"I wonder whatever became of me?" thus represents an admission of a divided self, half of which has unaccountably disappeared. This rather sophisticated admission of self-fragmentation might be a derivatively modernist representation of the world as fragmented. But the tone in which Groucho delivers the line has none of the angst we have come to associate with such modernism. The tone is insouciant, unconcerned, merely curious. The absent Groucho is the official Groucho: President Firefly, the official whose presence is constantly demanded on the phone, at state functions and inaugural balls, the Firefly who has not received an invitation to Mrs. Teasdale's reception. His verbally abusive self—the landsman—is present, but not his socialized self, which has been effaced.

Where is this Firefly to whom various persons, including Groucho, make application? He is located in part, as we have seen, as an alter ego in Trentino, who though only an ambassador, seems to have full presidential power in Sylvania. He is visually and aurally as ideal as Groucho is abrasive: he is well-groomed, traditionally handsome, tall, and possessed of a cultivated accent. He *appears* to be the perfect diplomat, in opposition to Groucho, who, as always, wears his seedy tails and carries "twofer" cigars. On the other hand, Trentino is dishonest, an adventurer who has tried to foment revolution in Freedonia and who attempts to gain the affections of Mrs. Teasdale for the political power she wields. Groucho succeeds at everything Trentino attempts, thus establishing kinship between Trentino's intentions and his own results. Groucho does in fact begin war and revolution in Freedonia, with his initial song and the declaration of war with Sylvania, and, of course, he wins the hand of Mrs. Teasdale. Both leaders use the two other brothers in civil service posts (spies and minister of defense) and both use the brothers as soldiers in a war that Groucho "wins." That Trentino should be represented as Groucho's dapper doppelgänger is an ethnic inversion of the normative representation of the Jew as insidious shadow.

Ultimately, however, Groucho is inscribed on the whole world of the film in and through the other members of the *landsmanshaft*: his brothers.

At Chicolini's trial, Groucho plays judge, prosecutor, and defense lawyer. He even refers at one point to Chicolini's brothers, who are waiting "for him with open arms in the penitentiary," so that he creates an image of himself as defendant and convict as well. At one point during the film, Harpo and Chico are dressed as Groucho in order to hoodwink Mrs. Teasdale into giving them the combination of the safe that contains the Freedonian war plans. The Brothers are not outfitted as traditional Grouchos: only the glasses, moustache, and cigar remain; the usual Groucho costume of tie, tails, and untidy white shirt is absent. The clothes are replaced by a neutral white nightshirt with nightcap that hides the hair, so that even Harpo with his blonde curls can convincingly pass as Groucho. This plot complication provides a rationale for the identical dress that initiates the famous mirror sequence following this scene. The masquerade reveals the Brothers as interested in defining identity as congruence or alienation through the other at several levels. At a primary level, Harpo and Chico assume versions of Groucho's persona in order to undermine that persona. Groucho asks Chico a riddle: "Now what is it that has four pairs of pants, lives in Philadelphia, and it never rains but it pours?" Chico responds: "'At'sa good one. I give you three guesses." Groucho then tries to guess the answer. (There is of course no answer.) Chico thus turns the riddle Groucho asks him into a riddle he is asking Groucho. Then he asks another, overtly insulting riddle. ("What is it got a big black moustache, smokes a big black cigar and is a big pain in the neck?") Insults are supposed to be Groucho's especial ken. This reversal happens because Groucho has momentarily reverted to his socially defined role as president of a country. Chico not only assumes Groucho's role as teller of riddles and dispenser of insults, but makes Groucho accept the role of receiver of a version of himself. Groucho is not only audience and straight man for Chico, he is also the punchline.

As a part of the assault on respectability, this masquerade is another search for kindred sensibilities. Comic deflation works through the comic's caricature of authority, caricature that reveals both the comic's (benevolent) likeness to, and the (insidious) artificiality of, that authority. But while authentic authority does not usually acknowledge the deflation, Groucho does. When Chico or Harpo turns the tables on Groucho's game, Groucho not only does not mind, but he plays along, allowing himself to be victimized in the way he is accustomed to victimizing others:

> *Firefly*: Just for that you don't get the job I was going to give you.
> *Chicolini*: What job?
> *Firefly*: Secretary of War.

Chicolini: All right, I take it.
Firefly: Sold![20]

Self-humiliation is the only possible response to an other whose most useful tool in his search for a kindred other is sadism. The fantasy is that, in an authoritarian world, the only way to be certain of an unmediated dialogue— unfettered by power relations—with the other is to accede to all demands, relinquishing all power.

The *attempt* to discover this self in an other is comic. (The discovery of its presence is epic, of its absence, tragic.) The Marx Brothers' attempt, however, involves insult and hurt, as if to avenge the senseless pain that history tends to disavow.

THE FICTION OF AUDIENCE

In George S. Kaufman's never-performed one-act play "Meet the Audience," a proposal of marriage by Mr. Winterbottom to Mrs. Teitelbaum is inter- rupted by "a hearty cough from the audience," then "[a] still bigger cough," "[a] hell of a cough," and so on, until in the end, with all the actors also coughing, three soldiers "level their guns at the audience, and fire."[21]

This antagonism between audience and performer is a dramatized version of a central part of the Marx Brothers dynamic. As their relation to authority within the films is antagonistically fictional, and their relation to their parents is (as every good post-Lacanian structuralist will observe) fictionally antagonistic, so their relation to their audience also depends on a fantasy hostility. Like the Margaret Dumont persona, the audience exercises an economic and hegemonic control over the Brothers. (Whom the fans would destroy they first ignore.) So, as with Dumont, the Brothers must antagonize the audience in order to keep its attention. Like the film dignitaries, the audience is an active foe in a passive stance. With the audience as with the villains, the Brothers are searching for empathetic landsmen in antagonists whose hostility is founded exactly on their desire *not* to be discovered as kindred. Thus, as with the authority figures in their films, the Brothers are attempting to establish a *landsmannschaft* with their audience, a society of hometown Jews with shared sensibilities.

The search for an audience landsman takes place in six ways: voice, puns and digressions, ad lib, breaking the theatrical fourth wall imagined as ghetto wall, doubling, and alien photography and visual anachronism. Because most of these methods have an explicitly sociolinguistic dimension, it is worth making one general observation before proceeding. The notion that, because immigrants and ethnics learn to speak in the dominant language, they are as a result completely appropriated is of course a simplistic elevation of the importance of *langue* (the language system) at the expense of *parole* (the particular use of language), in order either to justify the cultural hegemony of a language by its inevitability or to decry (more or less helplessly) the victimization of the subordinated ethnic group. My assumptions about language will be those of a certain line of contemporary socio- or ethnolinguistics that assumes that the analysis of the endurance of language systems is precisely half of the whole enterprise that includes the study—and valorization—of "variations of usage in differing circumstances, the changing meanings of words over time, the specialist practices adopted by specific social groups," and so on.[22]

Voice

In *Modern Times,* as we have seen, American film comedy conceives of the comic proletarian as essentially picaresque: a wanderer, a fugitive, immigrating within his own country, constantly and unsuccessfully locating his home in situations necessarily impermanent (a rotting house built over a river, the home furnishings section of a department store, jail). The thematic alliance of the dispossessed with the nomadic wards of Hermes is continued in Hollywood comedy sound films. The most notable comic teams travel: Laurel and Hardy (especially in *Sons of the Desert* [1934], *The Flying Deuces* [1939], and *Utopia* [1951]—this last the French cineastes' sense of the place this wandering should and does end); Abbott and Costello (*Abbott and Costello go to Mars* [1953], *Abbot and Costello in* (pick one) *Hollywood* [1945], *the Foreign Legion* [1950], *Alaska* [1952]); their co-equals Bob Hope and Bing Crosby (the *Road* pictures, the very titles of which reveal a kind of lebensraum); and their inheritors Dean Martin and Jerry Lewis (*Pardners* [1956], and the remake of *Nothing Sacred* [1937]: *Living It Up* [1954]).

But while the silent comedian tended to face that alien environment alone, or was at least billed alone (in practice Chaplin used villains like Mack Swain over and over again in what amounted to a repertory cast), the sound comedian tended to work with others as landsmen. This was true not only of the screwball romantic couple but also of the same-sex partner or sibling. By the early 1930s, Laurel and Hardy were no longer sui generis; there were Marx Brothers, Ritz Brothers, Olsens and Johnsons, and so on. Even Buster Keaton tried to pair up with a comic Italian, Jimmy Durante.[23] Sound comics tended to pair up or form teams, in part so that the plots of these sometimes plotless pieces would include some rationale for dialogue but more so because the infinitely ethnic resources of the vaudeville and Broadway stage could then be utilized for film.

Sound enabled the landsman's searches and subversions, enabled a Bakhtinian dialogism in which a multiplicity of voices compete for attention and primacy. One does not have to imagine a completely ethnic Hollywood waiting for a voice to allow it to speak; it had already spoken eloquently in images. But the parallel between the emergent technology and the newly arrived social unit became ever more visible. The positions of film and new-immigrant ethnicity at the end of the 1920s were roughly congruent. The children of new immigrants, now growing up, more often than not spoke only English at about the same time that sound precluded the possibility of American film "speaking" in any other language, as it had in the silent era. A large percentage of these children, unlike many of their parents, lost all contact with their home culture at about the same time as American film had to struggle to keep its international markets.

Despite the corporate urgency to make the early sound film conform to the standards of realism already established by the silent film, a sense of the arbitrariness of the language, of the changeability of the *parole,* was omnipresent in Hollywood: in the apparent carelessness, for example, of the Fleischer Studio dubbing, in which, not only do the animated lips not synchronize well with the voices, but the sound effects are incommensurate to the image. Large parties contain only five or six voices on the soundtrack; building crashes are dubbed with tympani, and so on. Moreover, there came to be a great variety of accents on screen, palpably different from the "legit" and Shakespearean stages. Even though a variety of parent tongues were becoming inaudible in the new, reverse Babel of U.S.A. culture, the country's single, hegemonic language changed, not in the direction of appropriation but in the direction of eccentricity and difference. Except in bastions of hegemony—the law courts, the university—eighteenth-century British English was only an echo, to be replaced by a language more tortured and tortuous. It was not merely the inclusion of words like "kosher," and not even the changes in grammar between the eighteenth and twentieth centuries that more and more distinguished American from British English in a manner that continued to elicit a now-familiar satire from the English. Rather, accents—the method as well as the matter of our articulations—changed.

The assertion that the Brothers' voices are "non-U" (non-upper-class) would be understatement; the Brothers' urban, Jewish, lower-class voices (or in Harpo's case, non-voice) insist on the presence of ethnicity as linguistic intervention. As in most dialect comedy, voice renders the Brothers'

landsmannschaft as a particular "speech community."[24] Like the most significant American comic heroes—from Sam Slick to Sut Lovingood to Woody
Allen to Garrison Keillor—the Marx Brothers' accents define them regionally
and economically: they are ethnic and poor, no matter their fictional position
within the story. Even the timbre of their voices demands attention. The
Brothers are thus set off from the wealthy societies they inhabit by their
accents.

Because of extrinsic social pressure to portray ethnics more benignly,
and because of increasingly intrinsic Hollywood codes of identification, the
film audience tended more to become a part of the new comic speech
community. The sound film not only enabled a new ethnic presence in film,
but also ensured that that presence could work dialectically against more
culturally normative voices. The tendency toward submerging the contemporary urban ethnic in various nineteenth-century fantasies of the orient (the
"sheik," the "vamp," the aristocrat) was itself submerged by the audience
expectation of hearing itself on screen. Conspicuous among the acceptable
regional accents was the ethnic accent, which promoted the urban ethnic in
a manner it could not in the 1910s, and would not in the 1920s. Although
mid-Atlantic accents among men were fashionable in the early 1930s, with
one or two exceptions they tended not to be as popular as regional accents
of various kinds. Warren Williams never attained the popularity of Gary
Cooper, Clark Gable, and others who incorporated the new urbanity. And,
of course, Cary Grant's accent was not traditionally American until Hollywood made it so. (As objects that, rather like cultural acceptance itself, had
to be attained, the leading actresses—Norma Shearer, Myrna Loy, Katharine
Hepburn, and so on—were more likely to speak in refined, "U" tones.) So,
though the early sound film conspicuously featured blackface comedians,
one may say that sound was in part responsible for the demise of minstrelsy,
as voice continued working against traditional types by creating new identifications that its audiences deemed more authentic. On the other hand, any
discomfort with the Marx Brothers and related comic types was also a
xenophobic response to difference. That such xenophobia existed was
evident in the fact that the Marx Brothers tended to play better in urban
centers than in small towns (as does Woody Allen today).

The Brothers impersonate two, perhaps three different ethnic accents,
a study probably equaled in humorous American literature only by the
similar exercise of *Huckleberry Finn*. Chico's accent is not Italian but pseudo-
Italian. Chico stands always in an ironized relation to his own character, as
if to say that an ethnic posture is always merely a posture. (In *Animal Crackers*
one character asks: "How did you get to be an Italian?") Groucho's wisecrack-

ing voice, on the other hand, being the accent of lower-class New York, is a genuine inflection, the impossible sound of the Lower East Side in a starring role. This ethnic inflection suggests membership in a speech community familiar with cynicism, hardship, and poverty. The irony and disaffection in Groucho's voice, so comic to audiences, is aggressive and hostile. This quality—present to some degree in Chico's voice as well—characterizes Groucho as a vaudeville comic accustomed to audience hostility. He delivers his one-liners in an offhand manner, as if careless whether his audience laughs or not. He is indifferent, even hostile, to the opinions of his audience, within the narrative as well as without:

> *Chandler*: Captain Spaulding, I think that [yours] is a wonderful idea.
> *Spaulding*: You do, eh?
> *Chandler*: Yes.
> *Spaulding*: Well, then there can't be too much to it. Forget about it.[25]

This vocal indifference is experienced by audiences as comic in part because it is threatening, a shared hostility.

The voice Groucho uses to disempower others reflects the same speech community that, in gangster films, seeks empowerment in that world through more violent means. The voice that for Groucho is deadpan is for the gangster dead serious. This is the wise-guy, fast-talking accent of Tony Camonte (*Scarface* [1932]), Rico (*Little Caesar* [1930]), and Tommy Powers (*Public Enemy* [1931])—two Italians and an Irishman. The foreign accent, or the American accent informed by immigrant parentage, becomes in the criminal a sign of resentful powerlessness. Though invested with the provisional, circumstantial authority of the jester or the criminal these characters cannot speak, except parodically, in the voice of the more truly empowered middle or upper classes. The gangster is always only a parodic version of upward mobility, from the original *Scarface* (1931) to Brian de Palma's remake (1983). The gangsters' "wisecracks" are the same one-liners produced by the new sound comedians, delivered with a defensiveness that reveals an unarticulated insecurity in both performers. Gangsters are also referred to as wiseguys: the one-liner substitutes for educated discourse, for refined speech, for reason. It is threatening, delivered with a staccato speed suggesting the sound of "tommy guns"—another noise so evocative of the early sound-film era.

In Marx Brothers comedy transgression against language, not against specific legal codes, is the most visibly resentful action allowed the anti-heroes (including Harpo, for whom *not* speaking becomes an aggressive act).

However, ethnic talk is potentially more subversive than ethnic violence because one cannot assume, as with merely violent action, that the speaker acknowledges the values against which his speech is directed. The Marx Brothers—like several early sound comics—do not try, as Camonte, Little Caesar, and Powers try, to gain entry into the cultural mainstream. For both the gangster and the comic, for example, clothes are problematic. But the gangster will not admit to a discomfort in donning the newer and fancier dress he has bought the right to wear. In a consciousness of their clothing that Groucho refuses, gangsters "shoot their cuffs" and wear loud colors, making their clothes icons of the absurd rather than absurdly iconic.[26] While the gangster films are thus comparatively conservative, reinforcing the sense that the conventional world for which the gangsters reach is valuable in proportion to the desperation, violence, and extremity of their attempts to reach it, the early comedy of the Marx Brothers is inherently radical in the sense that they do not act as if they wish to be included in that world at all. Their inertia is thus a form of radical action, as if they affirm a belief that any genuinely motivated action is motivated in the direction of conservatism and hierarchy. Comic speech is *contained* anarchy, more effective than the gangster's because motivated by the desire to replace power structures not with other structures but with critiques of power. Speech is a substitute for action; it is what one does instead of act. When the possibility of action is effaced by another mode, the desire for action's intended effect disappears as well, and an aesthetic gratification, an enjoyment of speech as speech or play, substitutes for it instead. Because its original ulterior motive has been effaced, this now disinterested play is capable of a kind of subversion inaccessible to mere violence. One cannot talk about the Brothers as spirits of anarchy, as incarnations of the surreal, without realizing that this anarchy and surrealism, as more or less explicit critiques of culture, could have occurred only in the voice of someone outside the high-culture discourse being critiqued, an ethnic voice.

Puns and Digressions

In his book *On Puns,* Jonathan Culler asserts, "Puns present the disquieting spectacle of a functioning of language where boundaries . . . count for less than one might imagine and where supposedly discrete meanings threaten to sink into fluid subterranean signifieds."[27] The pun thus works to erode traditional meaning, allowing the imposition of meanings outside accepted etymologies. Of course, since conventional etymologies will ultimately find the derivation of modern English in Old English, French, German, and other

Western European roots, puns become a vehicle for the conveyance not merely of some words into English but of a reordering of language.

Though puns and wordplay can be elitist,[28] this reordering of language often works in the service of class and ethnic interests, forcing its audience to re-envision the world through ethnic alienation. The "little man" phenomenon in American modernism, generally associated with such neo-genteel writers as Clarence Day and James Thurber, is most syntactically innovative in the writings of Dorothy Parker, S. J. Perelman, Moss Hart, George S. Kaufman, and other ethnic descendants—some of the most important writers for the Broadway stage, American film, and American magazines. The syntax of these writers most often works in the direction of a Hazlittian contrast of cultures. To take the simplest example, the title of a Perelman collection: *Dawn Ginsbergh's Revenge*.[29] Decades before Woody Allen, Perelman places a Jew in the semantic position of a "goy," satirizing both the upwardly mobile person, and the culture into which she is moving. The title is borrowed from the "bodice-buster," but the presence of "Ginsbergh" undercuts the already debased romance suggested. Ethnic deflation is present in the syntax of individual sentences like this one in "Puppets of Passion": "Such was Dawn of the flame-taunted hair and scarlet lips bee-stung like violet pools and so on at ten cents a word for a page and a half."[30] The first half of the sentence is the purple prose of the traditional romance while the second half undercuts the first by referring to the economy within which writing takes place. The ethnicity of this ironizing sensibility is more overt in sentences whose second halves contain Eastern European constructions: "Dawn always called her mother Uncle Nate—ask me why."[31]

Of course several of these writers—conspicuously Kaufman, Hart, and Morrie Ryskind—wrote for the Marx Brothers, often thematizing ethnicity and immigration in the Brothers' punning. This dynamic moves one further away from the plot with each ethnically motivated pun. From the stage version of *The Cocoanuts*:

> *Groucho*: We're going to have an auction.
> *Chico*: I came over here on the Atlantic auction.
> *Groucho*: We have a quota. Do you know what a quota is?
> *Chico*: Sure, I got a quota. (He takes the coin out of his pocket.)[32]

It is as if the further one moves from conventional language and plot, the closer the audience is moved toward the ethnic. The further removed from chronological narration, the more apparent is the history narration represses.

In *Monkey Business,* Chico and Groucho digress from their roles as stowaways pursued by the ship's captain, in order to participate in a history lesson:

> *Groucho*: Now, one night Columbus' sailors started a mutiny . . .
> *Chico*: Naw, no mutinies at night. They're in the afternoon. You know, mutinies Wednesdays and Saturdays.
> *Groucho, throwing down his cap*: There's my argument. Restrict immigration.

The comic bit thus digresses at least two removes from the plot: from a shipboard chase scene to a geography lesson to commentary on international relations. Several stories about immigration and movement are told at the expense of the gangster plot.

This digression from the plot is another antagonistic thrust at the audience meant to recreate it as countersocial. The Brothers, in the kind of move that critics of the canon traditionally abhor even in their own darlings, deviate from the plot of a film through the device of a pun for the sake of a joke or a comic skit. More generally, textual criticism, which has long turned away from plot and story in order better to exploit less visible narrative techniques, is guilty of an odd imaginative failure in objecting to the flimsiness of Marx Brothers plots, which are so constructed in order not to interfere with the elaboration of theme through comic technique. Digression is in fact thematically significant. One is *supposed* to be more or less contemptuous of the plots; audiences are expected to follow the divergence at the expense of the pleasures ordinarily provided by plot and character evolution.

This divergence reflects a Bakhtinian sense of the carnivalesque, an undercutting of the narratives that structure and define identity.[33] At the beginning of a comic sketch the Brothers seem to be aware of the conventions within which they should act, and to subscribe to them just enough to operate within the causal and motivational structure demanded by adherence to conventions. But all seem to forget the conventions and motivations in the elaboration of the sketch, opting instead for a series of nearly motiveless digressions. Chico is on trial for his life, and in an inexplicably short time he is taking bets on whether he will be found guilty. Harpo begins selling peanuts in a sketch that ends with the destruction of the peanut stand by a lemonade vendor. Groucho makes Herculean efforts to get to his inauguration on time, only to begin his term by asking Mrs. Teasdale to pick a card. This absentmindedness does not indicate any lack of intelligence or initiative. On the contrary, the Brothers are impossibly more aggressive and energetic than the characters they antagonize; they are too smart for the social situations they find themselves repeatedly transcending. They become diverted from original goals and social identities through excess rather than lack of consciousness.

Finally, this diversion derives from an irrationality in all "civilized" discourse that insists on one normative code of behavior, habit of thinking, or history, one "master code." To escape the plot of a film about presidents, countries, diplomacy, and war (or about universities, high society, high finance, etcetera) is to escape the narrative of history, or, perhaps more properly, to escape from the nightmare of history.

Ad Lib

Ad libbing onstage and in film is a special case of digression that throws into greater relief the performer's desire to find a community with an audience. The myth of the origin of the ad lib in the Marx Brothers' act defines the discovery of technique as a way to recoup an antagonistic audience, in this case an assembly of Texans that has deserted the Brothers to watch a runaway mule. When the audience returns, Groucho insults their town:

> "Nacogdoches
> Is full of roaches."
> It wasn't much as satire, but it relieved the boys so greatly that they proceeded to horse up the sentimental number until it became a shambles. Harpo was running up and down in front of the audience wiggling his fingers at his nose. . . . Groucho was singing mechanically and racking his brain for more insults. At the next break in the number he came forth with,
> "The Jackass / is the finest / flower / of Texass."[34]

The assumption that the audience is hostile was a fair defense against much of small-time vaudeville and small-town America. The Marx Brothers shamelessly exploited the potentiality of the direct address as a way of circumventing conventional modes of audience relation to the drama. After the Nacogdoches incident they continued to tailor their shows to include references to the locality in which they performed. But the Brothers also directed the action of their shows directly at a particular audience, at particular members of the audience: Harpo, for example, would climb a stage curtain in order to flirt with the women sitting in balcony seats. References were sometimes less topical but uncannily preconscious. One evening, in a complete non sequitur, "Groucho, out of the darkness, said in a bored way:

'I wonder what ever happened to Rhinelander?'" in reference to a racially motivated divorce case that had occurred four years before.[35] The audience signified its recognition of the name by responding with the biggest laugh of the evening.

Direct address is almost lost to cinema (except in such exceptional ways as the tramp's ambiguous glances at the camera). But even on film Groucho ignores filmic convention at moments, deviating from the plot in order to speak directly to his audience. In so doing, Groucho insults Chico several times to the audience: "There's my argument: restrict immigration"; "I have to be here but you can go out for popcorn till this thing blows over." At the end of *Monkey Business* Groucho becomes a radio announcer, giving us a blow-by-blow description of an otherwise pedestrian fight between Zeppo and Alky Brigs, filled with the kinds of quotidian references that would be familiar to a middle- or lower-middle-class audience. Groucho creates a momentary community with the audience by scapegoating someone in the film.

Appreciation for the Brothers' ad libbing derived from, if not the ethnic theater per se, then the kind of audience that had also attended ethnic theater, or whose parents had. As stage performers, the Marx Brothers were most successful in New York, the urban center with the most significant ethnic and immigrant population. Besides providing actors, the ethnic theaters provided several models for mainstream stage dynamics. Though more didactic there, the ad lib was more a part of Yiddish theater than of the genteel stage: "It was not unusual at this time for Yiddish actors to address the audience during some break in the performance—or sometimes, for that matter, in the middle of a scene. The relationship between actor and audience had some of the air of browbeating intimacy that frequently characterized the relationship between rabbi and congregation in a *shtetl* synagogue. Authoritative thundering from a stage, as from a pulpit, often had a dramatic effect upon one's listeners."[36] The liberty to change a part could in fact be seen as fundamentally ethnic, as a way of differentiating the Yiddish theater from other modes of presentation: "Then one day, during a rehearsal, Mogulesco [an actor] suddenly broke into a song and dance that he had inserted into the middle of a scene without Gordin [the writer's] prior knowledge. Gordin, who was not familiar with the ad-libbing propensities of Yiddish actors, interrupted him, and a quarrel broke out. 'Anti-Semite!' Mogulesco shouted at the playwright, and stormed off the stage."[37]

The stage performances of vaudeville comedy missed by literary America are a perfect trope for the ethnic life that remains untranslatable and unrecordable. These performances are difficult to discuss—they were by their nature ephemeral; references and asides disappeared as soon as they were spoken. They were not immortalized in folio because, though some acts would not vary at all for twenty years, a Marx Brothers performance would change a bit every evening. When, like *Animal Crackers* or *The Cocoanuts,* the stage plays were filmed, only traces of the original performance remained. The original dynamic relationship to the audience was almost completely lost. What in the theater could have been a more authentic contact must in film be a parody of authenticity. Eye contact between actor and camera, or between audience and screen, replaces eye contact between humans. Still, the effect is startling, as if it were an address to an authentic audience, as if we were real. The wider gap—the increased technological barrier—over which the performer has to cross makes the failure to cross it more prominent, as if what was always the point—the attempt rather than its failure or success—highlights more starkly the need and possibility for such a bridging. The enterprise is successful insofar as our attention is called to, and our laughter results from, the attempt.

Other comics break the sanctity of the proscenium arch in the same cautious way: Olsen and Johnson perpetrate all manner of outrage on the stage and film audiences of *Hellzapoppin* (1942); Hope and Crosby speak to the audience only to assure them that their studio is paternalistically presiding over the outcome of the film. As Paramount contract players, when they survey a distant peak, they remark to the camera, "It may be a mountain to you but it's bread and butter to me." The comic ending in precapitalist and capitalist culture must be also a happy ending, to atone for the stylistic chances that comedy takes. The ephemeral ad lib thus becomes the way the industry assures the audience that both they and the filmmaking audience will continue after the film has ended.

Theatrical Fourth Wall/Ghetto Wall

Ad libbing is already a denial of the existence of a proscenium arch, the tool of an urban culture accustomed to crowded urban spaces in which the privacy assumed by the walls of the Edwardian middle class is simultaneously desired and ridiculed. The Brothers further denied that arch on stage by directly addressing the audience in a manner that assumed an equal response from the audience itself. Not surprisingly, the Brothers' vaudeville and Broadway performances were even less controlled than their films. The Brothers diverged not only from the plots but also from the scripts whenever

they had the desire, in a *meshuggah,* parapractic performance of the unconscious. In a frenzy of Artaudian surrealism, they tore clothes off women,
insulted people in the audience, and misbehaved in a fashion that at the same
time conjured up and denied the presence of an audience in a denial of the
invisible partition between audience and actor. The Brothers' wildness
presented an image of the ethnic as bad Jew refusing silence and valorizing
loudness and impolite, *hamishe* behavior as ways of overcoming arbitrary
social distinctions. *The fourth wall was thematized as ghetto wall.*

Like the ad lib, this closer, more assaultive relationship with the
audience had been present in Yiddish theater from its inception in the
United States. Yiddish audiences were boisterous, conflating the action on
stage with the actors themselves: "[W]hen Jacob P. Adler was playing in *The
Yiddish King Lear* and his daughter begrudged him a bowl of soup, a
spectator couldn't bear the old man's sufferings. . . . [asserting] 'Leave those
rotten children of yours and come home with me. My wife is a good cook;
she'll fix you up.'"[38]

Despite the assertions of critics like Richard Dyer, who finds the origin
of the star system in a moment of Anglo theater at which actors become more
important than their roles,[39] the real desire to conflate the world on stage
and the world offstage was a phenomenon of the urban ethnic theater. One
can see this ethnically sanctioned conflation of audience and actor in, for
example, the Friar's Club, a *landsmannschaft* of show-business people that
has, since its founding in 1904, taken on a particularly ethnic cast.[40] The
Friar's "roast," the series of insulting speeches that commemorates the
friendship of the object and the speakers,[41] taking place on a dais in front of
other show-business "personalities" who compose the audience, places the
private lives of the objects of insult on display, conflating in several ways
stage and auditorium.

The denial of social/aesthetic divisions between actor and actor, and
actor and audience, led to mistreating actors on stage or to inviting nonactors
to participate in the improvisation. In a Kaufman play, *Stage Door* (1937),
one of the hard-boiled actresses tells an untalented, unemployed thespian,
"Cheer up, Mary Lou. Someday the people on the stage will sit and watch
the audience and you'll be a sensation." The Brothers treated the cast offstage
as if they were on, and onstage as if they were off, conflating the real and the
stage/film world in the treatment of actors. The Brothers mistreated nonactors in the same way, stripping a visiting British show-business agent in
their rooms, or directly insulting the audience, including it in the stage
proceedings. The Brothers even disrupted other acts, as when Harpo, unusually drunk, wandered on stage during a love duet and, while the male

Figure 3.1 *Duck Soup* © by Universal City Studios, Inc. Courtesy of MCA Publishing Rights, a Division of MCA, Inc. Courtesy of the Academy of Motion Picture Arts and Sciences.

Figure 3.2 *Duck Soup* © by Universal City Studios, Inc. Courtesy of MCA Publishing Rights, a Division of MCA, Inc. Courtesy of the Academy of Motion Picture Arts and Sciences.

Figure 3.3 *Duck Soup* © by Universal City Studios, Inc. Courtesy of MCA Publishing Rights, a Division of MCA, Inc. Courtesy of the Academy of Motion Picture Arts and Sciences.

Figures 3.1-3.3 The first illustration is a shot from *Duck Soup*. The last two are photographed during breaks between shooting. In a modernist denial of the theatrical fourth wall, the simulacrum of aggression onstage spills offstage.

lead was singing, bellowed, "You can't insult that girl!"[42] As they became upwardly mobile, moving from vaudeville to Broadway, the stage-play became even wilder and more assaultive.

The favorable audience response to Marx Brothers chaos depended on the belief that these people were who they represented themselves as being, that they were not acting but being. Their offstage behavior (or the stories spread about their behavior) reinforced this conviction, which would occasionally elicit a landsman's impulse in the audience to cross the ghetto/fourth wall. Composer Harry Ruby, after waiting in vain for a promised birthday present, walked on stage during a performance:

> The first scene in *Animal Crackers* reveals Captain Spaulding being feted by the natives. They sing the famous song, "Hooray for Captain Spaulding. . . ," and a group approaches to present him with a treasure chest. On the night after Ruby's forlorn birthday Groucho opened the chest and Ruby stepped out.
>
> "Where's the bathrobe?" demanded Ruby, and stood his ground belligerently.[43]

The gesture confirms a sense that at least part of the pleasure in watching the Marx Brothers is a narcissistic fantasy of conflating the public and the private—on stage as well as off.

Doubling

As Ruby desired to imitate the staged outrageousness of the Brothers, so the audience desired to see the Marx Brothers double for each other and, finally, to double for the Brothers in a kind of self-abasement that is also an emotional release. Doubling has been a standard comic device at least since *The Odyssey*. But the wrinkle in the Marx Brothers' oeuvre is that, as Hollywood is in fact composed of landsmen, the Brothers are also brothers offstage. They use their physical resemblance to each other (obscured by the costumes they wear) to complicate the skits: all four (badly) imitate Maurice Chevalier; Groucho and Chico rip up their tenor's contract in unison; the three Brothers dress as bedridden Grouchos in *Duck Soup* (and Groucho and Harpo imitate each other in the mirror scene in the same film); all four escape from a ship in identical Russian aviator uniforms; three Brothers dress identically as doctors, all of whom are named Steinberg (the model skeleton is also so named); each Brother performs a version of "I Love You" at different moments in *Horsefeathers*.[44]

The sibling similarity is stressed in the mythology of the Brothers' stage career. When Groucho was ill, Zeppo acted Groucho's part; the audience could not tell the difference. In one stage gag Harpo pulled a rope across the stage during a love duet:

> His face was serious, the veins stood out on his forehead from the weight of the task, and his progress was laborious.
>
> The gag was timed so perfectly that the last note of the song coincided with Harpo's disappearance into the wings. At the exact moment when he departed at the right, he appeared again at the left, fighting as hard to resist the pressure as he had previously done in exerting it.[45]

Harpo also disguised Walter Winchell as Harpo in order to get the journalist, against Shubert's orders, into a Shubert theater where they were performing. In another show, "Margaret Dumont was supposed to open a big chest the explorer, played by Groucho, had brought back from Africa. Then she would tell of the ivory and precious stones inside. When she opened the chest, a parade of Grouchos walked out of it. All the musicians and stage hands, unbeknownst to her, had been made up as Groucho."[46] Groucho's insistence on likeness as a narrative strategy is a part of his famous letter to Warner Brothers when they tried to sue for exclusive rights to *Casablanca*:

> You claim you own Casablanca and that no one else can use that name without your permission. What about "Warner Brothers"? Do you own that, too? You probably have the right to use the name Warner, but what about Brothers? Professionally, we were brothers long before you were. We were touring the sticks as The Marx Brothers when Vitaphone was still a gleam in the inventor's eye, and even before us there had been other brothers—the Smith Brothers; the Brothers Karamazov; Dan Brothers, an outfielder with Detroit; and "Brother, Can You Spare a Dime?"[47]

This insistence on *landsmannschaft* has greater cultural reverbera-tions; in much popular culture one may see the effect of the Brothers' self-multiplication, of their attempt to find versions of themselves in an otherwise remote world. The world responds by looking like Groucho; he stops having to recreate the world in his image because the world learns to recreate itself in his. The duck on *You Bet Your Life* is only the most obvious of examples.

Examine the photograph in figure 3.4. A Hollywood costume party featured in *Life Magazine* is the occasion for the appearance of the world as

Figure 3.4 Reproduced by permission of *Life Magazine*. © Bert Granet.

Groucho. The birth of Groucho is celebrated by a fiction that the world ultimately *becomes* Groucho (an assertion characteristically denied only by Groucho, who attended this party dressed as Harpo).

The more ideal cinema icons are not nearly as imitated as the Marx Brothers. Cary Grant and Jimmy Stewart, though somewhat imitated, were not adopted by popular culture in the way especially Groucho and Harpo were. The plastic glasses, eyebrows, and nose that may or may not have been modeled on Groucho's inevitably suggest him now. Chaplin is imitated in the same way but, like most popular icons, in the singular, not in the plural.

The representations of Groucho are as often as not representations of plurality as if, finally, he represents the entire community of landsmen for which he had always searched.

But that community is never nostalgically hospitable. In opposition to portrayals of other comics, representations of Groucho routinely emphasize the neutrality of his features and the impassivity of the face, despite the outrageousness of his antics or appearance. Groucho does not call attention to the fact that he is joking, in the hysterical manner of comics from vaudevillians through Jerry Lewis. (This is one reason the jokes come too quickly to catch them all in the early films. He does not wait for the significant pause during which the audience is more or less coerced into laughing.) The mask Groucho wears is modernist: emotionally neutral, alienated from its own body and the opinion of the world, like the Magritte paintings in which a number of identical subjects inhabiting a single canvas, uniformly dressed, uniformly gaze in different directions but not at each other.

Alien Photography and Visual Anachronism

Among the Indians, or, The Country Peddler, a Yiddish-language skit about two Jewish peddlers "making good" in Indian territory, was performed in 1895 at the Windsor Theatre in New York. The comedy derived from opposing dynamics, the first of which we have already treated: the discovery by the audience that the Indians were in fact implicitly Jewish landsmen (or at least spoke in "broken utterances . . . based on Yiddish").[48] The second dynamic— the incongruity between the person and the setting, the Jew "among the Indians"—is worth examining further because it allows the defining of a broadly-used mise-en-scène as ethnic.

Eddie Cantor plays a version of this visually displaced Jew in most of his films. Like *Among the Indians, Whoopee* (1930), his most famous film and stage success, takes place in an extremely postmodern West. The surreal quality of the landscape is made even greater both by the presence of the small, popeyed, adenoidal, hypochondriacal Jewish actor, and by the two-strip technicolor process, reminding one more of *Three Amigos* (1986) than of William S. Hart. (Gregg Toland is co-credited for the photography in this and other early Cantor films.) The fact of his being dressed in this film as a woman, an African American, and a Native American only reemphasizes his Jewishness. Other of Cantor's films find his diffident second-generation Jew in Spain (*The Kid from Spain* [1932]), ancient Rome (*Roman Scandals* [1933]), Alexandria (*Kid Millions* [1934]), and Baghdad (*Ali Baba Goes to Town* [1937]). Despite the fact that he is a solo act, Cantor's films tend to call

attention to Cantor's ethnicity and, more interestingly, to conflate the ethnic
with the national identity: Cantor is very obviously an American Jew on
foreign soil. As a consequence, the mise-en-scène and character behave as
two levels of discourse about American ethnicity. While the mise-en-scène
tends to orientalize (sometimes, as in *Whoopee,* in an explicitly racist manner), the ethnic character Cantor plays tends to affirm not just the possibility
of ethnic durability, but the defining of the American as ethnic. These films
retrospectively explain the eccentricity of any "stranger in a strange land"—
from Odysseus to Aeneas to Gulliver to Jack Crabbe—as the result of
diaspora.[49]

The studio system's tendency to control the mise-en-scène by shooting
on sound stages, generally attributed either to technological limitations or to
a desire to enforce ever greater visual control over the already very formulaic
genre system, can be also thought of as a desire to stylize a world not in which
ethnics and immigrants may feel comfortable but in which their concerns
are in some way being "played out." The tendency of 1930s comedy to
represent a stylized version of an orientalized non-U.S.A. culture is almost
obsessively reproduced by other comics and other films of the era: *The
Diplomaniacs* (1933) begins in a barber shop set on an Indian reservation,
and even normative romances, such as *One Night of Love* (1934), starring
Grace Moore, contains a *Duck Soup*-like fantasy version of Milan. *Ambassador
Bill* (1931) sets part Native-American Will Rogers down in Freedonia's
nearest neighbor, Sylvania. The most famous feature films of Laurel and
Hardy, comic stars more generally associated with more realistic milieux, are
often set in fantasy scapes: *Swiss Miss* (1938), *Babes in Toyland* (1938), and
especially *The Bohemian Girl* (1936).

The Bohemian Girl is typically concerned with ethnic differentiation
and nostalgia. Beloved in nineteenth-century America, the original operetta
is about a white princess kidnapped by gypsies who finds herself unaccountably dreaming of "marble halls." Too easily dismissed as a fantasy of youth
and adolescence, it also displays an ethnic ambivalence and nostalgia that
makes its way into the national film culture at some point through the odd
amalgamation of the real and fantastic that is the aesthetic of Disney and
science fiction, moving into the culture at large.

This tendency to represent ethnicity within an exotic and eccentric
world is even more a part of the American animation aesthetic. The Fleischer
and Warner Brothers companies especially tended to represent overt ethnicity in such films as *Romantic Melodies* (1932), in which you can see Hebrew
letters on the ambulance picking up a vagrant German brass band. Fleischer
(who made films for the same studio—Paramount—for which the Marx

Figure 3.5 *Ambassador Bill* © 1931 Twentieth Century Fox Film Corporation. All rights reserved. Courtesy of the Academy of Motion Picture Arts and Sciences.

Figure 3.6 Even those comic figures who, like Will Rogers and Laurel and Hardy, we do not associate with exotic milieux, are often placed in fantasy landscapes. *The Bohemian Girl* © LAUREL AND HARDY CHARACTERS licensed by Larry Harmon Pictures Corporation, Hollywood, California 90028 USA. Courtesy of the Academy of Motion Picture Arts and Sciences.

Brothers worked), Warner Brothers (whose gangsters and golddiggers conduct their own discourse about ethnicity), and even Disney (despite his anti-Semitism) all represent the world as an impossible marriage between animals of different species, between animals and humans, and between live action and animation. That this mixture refers to ethnic and racial miscegenation is being made overt even decades later, in *Who Framed Roger Rabbit?* (1988).[50] The humans are present in an animated world that means an orientalized version of the ethnic, but, in Fleischer, the humans are often ethnic or play ethnics as well: Ethel Merman as herself (*You Try Somebody Else* [n.d.]), or Arthur Tracy in Italian street singer drag, singing "Santa Lucia" (*Romantic Melodies* [1932]).

Live-action comedies reproduce a popular-culture version of a fantasy landscape that conflates United States culture and a host of other cultures. 1930s comedies set in fantasy lands are always satires both of American administrations (whether Hoover or Roosevelt) and of foreign governments, both conceived as merely archaic (*Duck Soup, Never Give a Sucker an Even Break*), or as some version of fascist (*Ambassador Bill*). *Duck Soup's* Balkan Sylvania further and explicitly signifies an American corporation. This conflation of countries only makes cultural sense as an ethnic attempt at accommodating the old nation and the new.

Finally, of course, by the 1930s this eccentric mise-en-scène is so ingrained as to allow its redefinition as a place to which "real" Americans go in order to resolve some personal conflict: Shirley Temple in *The Blue Bird* (1940), Judy Garland in *The Wizard of Oz* (1939), Will Rogers in *Ambassador Bill* and *A Connecticut Yankee*. By the 1950s, this fantastic mise-en-scène, when not part of an overtly satirical piece, becomes the visual field of both the musical and the fantasy/science fiction genres—the creation of visual worlds in which the rules of representation can be invented by the filmmakers.

The mise-en-scènes of several Marx Brothers films are fantasies unconcerned with "faithfully" reproducing the periods in which they are set. In *Horse Feathers* the classroom contains a poster of a pin-up girl rather than an anatomical outline. In *Animal Crackers* Groucho, the African explorer, enters Mrs. Rittenhouse's Long Island estate "carried in a sedan chair by four Nubians."[51]

Set in a simulacrum of Europe, *Duck Soup* contains some of the most significant anachronisms in the Brothers' oeuvre. Freedonia is a small, independent European duchy: the flag is heraldic rather than abstract, the setting Balkan, the official titles British, the cutaway coats Edwardian, and the architecture (done in expansively imaginative glass shots) medieval.

Several centuries of European political protocol are disjunctively and mal-adroitly suggested. The anachronisms are purposely egregious, even by Hollywood, *Day of the Locust* standards. (The apotheosis of this egregiousness is the plethora of uniforms Groucho wears in the final battle.) This freakish representation of political officialdom forces a juxtaposition of European and American history and politics. We see a European mise-en-scène, but hear American accents, ideals, and buzzwords in an economic matriarchy fi-nanced by an American millionairess, Vera Teasdale (Margaret Dumont). The film thus becomes simultaneously a burlesque of Balkan politics and Amer-ican pretensions to European high culture. Of course, Hollywood costume dramas are also being satirized—the sloppiness and inattention to detail that result in such Ruritanian incongruities as peasants in Tyrolean costume buying peanuts and lemonade from a turn-of-the-century American vendor whose stand is located beneath the (Tudor) window belonging to the president of a Balkan kingdom, who is himself dressed in old-fashioned tails.

The previous generation of new-immigrant theatergoers, especially the Jewish segment, would have seen plays that the cultural hegemony would define as unintentionally kitschy in some of the same ways that *Duck Soup* intends: Jacob Gordin's *Der Yiddisher Kenig Lear,*[52] or his *God, Man and Devil,* "a retelling of the Faust story."[53] In these great illustrated classics, Western canonical stories are imposed upon ethnic characters. In Marx Brothers works, the ethnic (or merely marginal) characters impose themselves on a canonical universe. Groucho is a Yiddisher explorer ("did someone call me schnorrer?"), as well as a hotel owner, university president, and ruler. But his refusal to be constrained by the stories imposed on him becomes the meta-plot of the films. In refusing to take the plots of the films seriously, the Brothers are also refusing to subscribe to criteria by which such plots are judged.

More generally, the Brothers satirize upward mobility out of the ethnic enclave as well as the object of that move: gentility. They isolate one of the pretensions of upward mobility and carry it to the furthest extreme of its appearance, without granting any of the presumed legitimacy of the preten-sion. The satire is the fantasy of a dispossessed ethnic who, though he cannot imagine himself as a ruler, also cannot imagine that the world could be run any way but badly by anyone concerned about the appearance of gentility. The unrealized alternative is a world without rulers, only brothers or landsmen. The degree to which the fantasy is staged as absurd is the degree to which it is acknowledged as impossible. The Marx Brothers are a fantasy of not feeling shame at the gaps in one's education in the hegemony, of instead turning the tables and assigning shame to the cultural hegemony that imposes shame on the suppressed minority.

THE SEARCH FOR THE OTHER THROUGH THE LOOKING GLASS

We have shown that the ethnic voice disrupts authority, but we have not shown why. Having established the *landsmannschaft* as an important socio-logical phenomenon, we may discuss it as a psychoanalytic dynamic. Our starting point is provided by the mainstream culture itself, which has in all eras clinically defined ethnicity as a pathology, from the German accusation of a Jewish thinking, to the American castration of African Americans, and more generally to the American eugenics movement.[54] In the present section, the attempt to wrench the psychoanalytics of ethnicity away from the domain of the pathological will necessitate a conversation that, while occasionally appearing to have left ethnicity behind altogether, de-objectifies ethnicity, allowing it to read psychoanalysis itself.

Social uniformity is an important concern of 1930s world cinema in various ways—from the enforced movement of Eisenstein away from formal-ism, to American and Soviet social realism, to Jean Renoir's absorption with the disappearance of the *elan* of class distinction. It is an implicit concern in the one new major genre to emerge with the coming of sound in America: the musical, with its goose-stepping chorus girls and its reductions of complex psychologies to still another set of Hollywood formulae.

The mirror scene in *Duck Soup* is a countermoment in this filmic tendency to valorize uniformity in physical motion. It opposes Leni Riefenstahl's and Busby Berkeley's use of uniformity in film in the 1930s, which emphasized the way in which large groups should work together—like clockwork, like machines—for the greater good. The dance sequences in a Berkeley film are almost always conventional spectacles surfeiting their narratives; the mob movements in Riefenstahl propaganda films are almost always spectacular conventions surfeiting history. The mirror scene's unifor-mity is a *divergence* from the plot of the kind we have discussed in earlier chapters and an evasion of the strictures of history. In contradistinction to the musical and the crowd, the mirror scene allegorizes uniformity as an escape from historical necessity into the fairyland of aesthetics and play. It metaphysicalizes the search for the landsman, becoming a fiction of redemp-tion through self-multiplication and fragmentation. Deity, not the devil, is legion.

Groucho looks for someone in the mirror who is like Groucho; he finds the landsman for whom he searches in the rest of his films. This search for a landsman is reinterpreted here as a quest for someone who can reproduce, even if only in fictions and dreams, the motions of one's own life. The comedy of four ethnic Jewish men is an attempt to discover, through fraud, deceit, and the infliction of pain, more than simply an empathetic other in the official other, rather one's whole identity in the other. Though the great official fear of romantic Anglo-Saxon life (documented, for instance, in "The Student of Prague" (1913) or Poe's comic-macabre story "William Wilson") is the discovery that someone else is just like you, the more palpable fear of a heterogeneous but repressive society in which difference is the ground for exclusion is that no one else is like you, that those with whom you have identified yourself have changed in their upward mobility.

Along with the Marx Brothers, and a little after Bakhtin,[55] Jacques Lacan is another 1930s intellectual interested in the totalitarian development of social uniformity. ("Le stade du miroir" was published just a few short years before the establishment of Vichy France, and not long before de Man was publishing anti-Semitic articles in fascist journals.[56]) Writing safely at the heart of a number of mainstream cultures he, like the Brothers, is intrigued by identity formation. Lacan discusses the developmental stage at which self-identity becomes integrated: the moment of the development of the ego, the moment in childhood during which we become aware of a self. He calls this moment the mirror stage, because it is in the mirror image of ourselves that we receive the first clue about who we are. This idea of the self has several properties that break down into three developmental stages: (1) it postulates a split self, because our picture of ourself—mirror-derived—comes from outside; (2) because it is an image, it is a false idea of self; it is not actually us; and (3) this image implies a loss, because with it comes the realization that we are not the world. The mirror stage is about the way in which identity is predicated on a fiction: identity derives from a perceived image of ourselves, from our simultaneous ability and inability to differentiate ourselves from that image and so from the world.

Duck Soup's mirror scene is a fantasy reversal, a neutralization, of Lacan's mirror stage. The scene denies our difference from the world, asserting instead that the world *is* like us in some essential way. The mirror is not false; its image is not glass but flesh and blood, interested in being who we believe it to be: ourselves. In the mirror scene, comedy reconstitutes the unity of our identity with the world. Identity is not dependent on a false image—it is not a mirror, it is Harpo acting the part of a mirror. It is not a false, externalized sense of self, because this *imago* is authentically giving—or trying to give—back one's own identity to oneself. Finally, self-identity is not a split with the world because in recognizing Harpo as attempting to be himself in play, Groucho is able to rejoin the world—he is able to join in the perpetuation of the illusion.

The Marx Brothers thus offer a model for reading psychoanalysis—Freudian or Lacanian—backward, as a fantasy of escape from the dialectic it erects. While not exactly transforming fiction into fact, the mirror scene legitimizes a fiction that the world non-psychotically reflects and fulfills one's own desire. Of course this is a fantasy of escape. Being an alien in a culture with inadequate coping mechanisms of its own provokes the fantasy creation of an escape hatch from the oppressive culture.

The briefest complete description of the mirror scene would sound something like this: Harpo/Pinky, a spy, in trying to evade Groucho/Firefly, the president, smashes into a full-length mirror. While trying to leave he is interrupted by Groucho. Standing opposite each other, identically dressed as somnambulist Grouchos, the two stare at each other for a moment. Then, to evade capture, Harpo tries to fool Groucho by imitating the latter's movements. He is a mirror. Each imitation is more and more expert, more and more occult, so that Groucho cannot catch him out. Finally, Groucho walks through the "mirror," trying to trick Harpo into confessing himself not a mirror. But when Harpo begins to make errors in reflection, Groucho helps him out. The scene ends when Chico, also dressed like Groucho, strolls into the scene.

In a shot-by-shot description, of the sequence one may trace a dialectical change, mediated by the mirror, in the relation between Groucho and Harpo. (See endnotes for a shot-by-shot description.[57]) This dialectic initiates a descent, by perfectly traceable stages, into the metaphysical.

In this analysis I will discuss the four comprehensive categories that refer to the fantasy recouping of the identity traits lost in the mirror stage: split self, false self, lost world, and exposure (of the fantasy as fantasy, of film as film).

The World Regained

The mirror sequence, like most of the Marx Brothers skits and many of the tonier vaudeville acts, and unlike most of today's standup comedy, is a traditionally motivated activity. As a spy, Harpo must steal the war plans; as president, Groucho must stop him. Groucho must fool Harpo into exposing himself as Harpo, while Harpo must resist discovery. This first section of the sequence reveals the camera as diegetic fact in the creation of a mirror of the mind. The camera work reinforces the sense of traditional reality. From the beginning of the sequence the camera is very particular about recording circumstantial reality. We see Harpo break the mirror, Groucho come down the stairs, and Harpo hide past the mirror frame and

Figure 3.7

Figure 3.8

Figure 3.9

Figures 3.7-3.9 The anti-dialectic of the mirror. The sequence moves backward through a regaining of the world, a protecting and healing of the self, and exposure. *Duck Soup* © by Universal City Studios, Inc. Courtesy of MCA Publishing Rights, a Division of MCA, Inc.

doorjamb. In opposition to other moments in the film, like the musical numbers, the camera is static, reminding one of Rollie Totheroh's camera. Once the scene begins, the mise-en-scène does not change at all until the end. Nothing distracts us from the action; what we see is really happening.

But this represented reality evinces some odd qualities. There are some elisions in editing: we do not see how the shards of broken glass are removed. They disappear without filmic comment. And, making us question this "narrative space," a "real" mirror room waits behind the reflection of the room in which the camera sits. Even when absent, the mirror still reflects a chair, a desk, and other items of furniture. Some of the reflected objects are curiously self-referential: a mirror wall-sculpture and a curtain that hides either a window or perhaps another mirror or painting that, as in *The Lady from Shanghai* (1948), would create an infinite series of digressions on the theme of reflection. A little out of the reach of the "mirror," in the camera-side room, a small wall mirror is just out of reach of the mise-en-scène. These objects all appear in their appropriate places in the new mirror room. This uncanny resemblance of things behind the portal to things in front of it is of course parallelled by the more active reflectivity of Harpo. Harpo's imitation of Groucho is not dependent solely on his momentary resemblance to him. Its success is provided for in another way: Harpo shares with mirrors the quality of silence.

Because language is so important to a Marx Brothers film—even its lack in Harpo signifies much—the mirror scene seems an odd reversion back to the silent era: an investment of value in the play of silence. (One suspects that any sound actually made in this scene has been removed from the soundtrack, so that we are actually left with a silent one-reeler.) Irony exists in the fact that the only person in the film who cannot talk makes the most noise. Just before the mirror scene Harpo does battle with a radio that will not stop broadcasting, having mistaken it for the safe containing the war plans. Similarly, a piano, harp, music box, and grandfather-clock music reveal his presence in Mrs. Teasdale's house. Unless it is the priapic honk or the heavenly harp, sound victimizes Harpo.

The breaking of the mirror is the nadir of Harpo's journey through Freedonia. The good fortune of which the broken mirror is a harbinger resides in the new dynamic produced by his imminent contact with another human being whom he can victimize with the vulnerable affection that hides a child's potential malevolence. For the most part, Harpo must utilize objects as instruments of aggression in order for them to work for rather than against him. Harpo can become a medium for a hostile universe, which expresses itself against others through him. It is as if, by virtue of his own sympathetic malevolence, Harpo is the conductor of an aggressive malevolence latent in the inanimate universe. This sympathy is not quite a humanizing of objects and artifacts, as in so many silent films. He desentimentalizes Chaplin's ability to transform the purpose of things. But he at least raises them from their status as merely and conventionally useful for what they are.

As conduit for an active world, Harpo recoups the world for us. When one is antagonistic to Harpo, or even when one ignores him, he becomes a conduit for a universal malevolence. But this "channelling" of the inanimate universe, though usually malevolent, is a precondition for the ability to mirror back desire that will be evidenced in the mirror scene. It creates in the audience a disposition toward recognizing the universe as animist. Harpo's cruelty and casual assaultiveness are the measure of our alienation from the phenomenal world. The latent malevolence in the world is a magic that represents a desire for revenge. The loss of speech enables this magical hostility, as if giving up the realm of the symbolic allows access to the everyday artifacts produced by the unempowered as tools for revenge. Silence, usually the sign of cultural disempowerment (ethnics do not speak until they speak English), is reimagined in Harpo as the sign of potency beyond the symbolically phallic. Silence, the language of insufficiency, is reimagined in his character as the medium of revenge. The question of the mirror scene is whether, once having established oneself as powerful, one can use "silence, exile, and cunning" for a cooperation that is not also appropriation.

Protected Real Self

The segment of the mirror scene that extends from the beginning of the mirroring effect to Groucho's walk through the mirror begins as a straightforward ratiocinative relationship between them: Groucho is trying to discern whether Harpo is in fact a mirror. The skit is characterized almost throughout by so superlative a mirroring effect by Harpo that, as the sequence progresses (it is long, taking about two minutes), our questions about how the trick works begin to pull us away from the plot. The ambiguity of the two Brothers' activity is reflected in audience curiosity and detachment.

The scene is hence a meditation on reflection. "Reflection" as an intellectual process pretends to hold an object in psychological suspension, without deciding to decide about its meaning along any possible axis of judgment, in essence, suspending belief. In this scene, the object of reflection is oneself, and not only oneself, but a self that is at the same time reflecting on the self reflecting on the self. (Remember, in this split second, Harpo has to decide to take advantage of Groucho's doubt, which is a reflection on Groucho's reflection of him.) Because the mirror is a nonverbal game of infinite removes, the scene offers itself as self-consciously dialectical and ratiocinative. The moment seems intellectualized for us because Groucho is testing Harpo, forcing him into error, forcing him to show himself as human, as not-mirror. This activity is still somewhat plot-oriented, still a marginally rational thing to do. In opposition to the child who wishes to prove that the *imago* is a fragmented part of himself, subject to the laws of the subject's ego, Groucho tries to prove that his *imago* is *not*. Of course, in this reverse model he fails—the *imago* at this point of the scene mirrors him, as far as he can see, perfectly.

The conscious reflection of the audience begins as meditation on a number of ambiguities, almost too numerous to mention, that arise in confronting an improbable premise. How much does Groucho know about Harpo? About the mirror? How much does Harpo know about Groucho? How can Harpo "read" Groucho so well, so instantaneously? How can the rooms be so identical? The greatest ambiguity is in the nature of the space between Groucho and Harpo; we cannot tell whether, during Harpo's aping of Groucho, we and they are observing a mirror or a portal. We cannot determine whether we are seeing simultaneity or its simulacrum, a causal chain in which Harpo is following Groucho's movements an imperceptible moment after Groucho makes them. Are we supposed to be seeing Harpo's prescience at work? If we were to verbalize the overt plot line, it might sound rather as if Harpo were magically reproducing Groucho's motions. Or we may be watching a series of conventions carried out quite independent of each other: two people performing identically choreographed movements, two members of a chorus line facing each other.

Harpo's representation of reality—his imitation of Groucho—quickly crescendos. It becomes more ingenious: the tempo increases, the imitation is more precise. (Every comic equation, from the eiron/alazon relationship to the "principle of three" to Bergson's metaphysics, is an attempt to account for this crescendo.) A dialectic is at work in this skit in which Harpo not only meets each new, more difficult, qualitatively different challenge with a never varying degree of finesse, he also makes the trick by which he succeeds appear more metaphysical each time. Harpo's increasingly fine imitation produces a more perfect mirror. Groucho speeds up his movements, inventing a choreography of the increasingly unexpected. But Harpo's mimicry suggests that however inventive and accelerative his brother is, Harpo would remain infinitely capable of sustaining his half of the charade.

As a perfect mirror, Harpo reflects not only appearance but also disappearance and reappearance. Groucho, not immediately realizing this, walks away from the mirror (off camera) in order to fool Harpo/mirror by reappearing suddenly and unexpectedly within the mirror frame. Groucho then peers out slowly past the edge of the frame again with his spectacles awkwardly perched on his nose, not expecting to find Harpo and not expecting to find *his* spectacles similarly placed. Of course they are, making Harpo's motions seem, again, more magical than deft. The emotion of the scene derives from the representation of mechanization as magic. As the artifact to be repetitively reproduced, Groucho is the speeding up of the assembly line; he is the cynical assumption that the worker will not run away and save himself from mass production.

Harpo's show is a parody of this desire to approach Andre Bazin's limit of total cinema.[58] Like Groucho's, our initial suspension of disbelief—that Harpo could successfully imitate Groucho—is the first in a series of increasingly difficult situations that must elicit a degree of belief if we are to derive amusement from the scene. But we willingly accede to this suspension for our yield of pleasure. We are gulled, our gullibility is revealed to us, and this self-exposure is sufficiently pleasurable that we desire gulling over again. This pleasurable mystification of identifications is abetted by the camera, which seems to encourage our identification with Groucho. It records Groucho thoughtfully planning each (increasingly clever) step of his strategy. The camera remains more or less stationary just over Groucho's shoulder, staying with Groucho when Harpo disappears behind the wall. Some of the trick editing—the speeding of motion in the scene, designed to make Groucho appear even faster than he is—seems similarly sympathetic to Groucho. The camera physically and figuratively places us at Groucho's point of view. We initially want Groucho to win the contest.

But, though the camera is on Groucho's side, it faces Harpo. The superlativeness of Harpo's performance enforces our identification with him. The physical identicalness of the Brothers makes it harder for us to decide whom we wish to win the contest, so that the antagonism that we are supposed to feel against one side or the other begins to disappear in ourselves as audience as well as in the characters. As the brothers then abandon their mutually antagonistic roles, *we* are tricked by the illusion of simultaneity into abandoning our sense of the traditional relationship between the good guy and the bad. We are left with either an ambivalent sense of ego-identification or its complete erasure. Our ambivalence about the film's motives for keeping up the charade means that we are split between believing the plot and believing in the attractive relationship. We are faced with an allegory about competing fictions: between an un-comic common sense and a fantasy we can't believe in for too long; between the dictates of the historical record and the immanent off-the-record. It is as if we begin to realize that the point of doing history is no longer truth but pleasure, as if pleasure has become an ethical imperative.

Healing the Split Self

Up until the point at which Groucho steps through the mirror, the rule— unrealized until transgressed—has been that the Brothers cannot touch each other. Neither has been able to step over the threshold into the other's world, the easiest test of the mirror that Groucho could make. At this point the rules change. If the first stage was about mirror as camera, and the second stage about portal as mirror, the third stage is about the camera as portal. From being impressed by Harpo's imitation, Groucho advances to abetting that imitation actively, enhancing the charade through his own desire to identify himself as the world. He becomes the ideal film audience, himself patching any cracks in Harpo's narrative of himself.

Stepping through the mirror fulfills the great post-Freudian wish to reverse consciously the process by which the unconscious is formulated, like other moments in film that suggest the desire to reverse maturation: the home-movie sequences in *Rebecca* (1940) and *Adam's Rib* (1949), in which the married couples, in formal attire, watch earlier, pastoral versions of themselves. It is like other moments that suggest the eruption of the feared and desired fantasy versions of the self: the dream sequences in *Spellbound* (1945), for example. Of course those moments are fraught with a sense of the uncanny at confronting a version of the self over which one has no control, that is absent from the mirror scene: the meetings of the king and Rassendyll in *The Prisoner of Zenda* (1937) and of the student and his double in *The Student of Prague*. But these moments generally show up the limitation of this special effect: one film character cannot really enter the world of the other, at least until Groucho steps through Harpo's mirror.

When Groucho puts foot across that threshold to circle Harpo, the sequence transcends classical, Bergsonian, and Freudian explications of the comic, as well as cinematic norms. Until that point, it is possible to argue that the skit is accessible to interpretation by three theories. First, the two actors seem in the beginning to compose the classical eiron/alazon configuration: Harpo punctures the futile, hubris-ridden intelligence of Groucho, and Groucho's contemptuous nod as he walks past the frame the first time implies an egotistic sensibility begging for deflation. Second, Groucho is the man with a fixation: to reveal Harpo as not a mirror without actually touching Harpo to discover the truth. He represents Bergson's human as machine, repeating in futile fashion the same motions long after they have been proved anachronistic. Finally, the desire to prove Harpo a fake is (very loosely) allied with Freud's use of comedy as a way of revealing competition while neutralizing both audience and object. It is a way of ridiculing the object and castrating the audience, which sides with you against the object of desire.

But Groucho and Harpo outgrow the eiron/alazon relationship as the skit progresses because they both cease taking their parts seriously, especially Groucho who, in an increasingly aggressive way, helps Harpo to fool himself. When he walks through the mirror and then helps Harpo pick up his hat, he becomes, if anything, more the eiron in showing up Harpo's masquerade as artifice. But in reality he is no more eiron at this point than is Harpo, because neither of them is at all invested in the antagonistic personae that initially defined their relationship. They have achieved a state of play in which Groucho wants Harpo to succeed as much as Harpo does. Remember that both actors work with equal care to keep up the charade. Groucho must know the routine as well as Harpo in order to achieve their degree of precision.

The fantasy is similarly revealed as anti-Lacanian, as if, like Alice, one could go back into the mirror and pluck out a more benevolent identity, even erase identity altogether. At some point Groucho stops trying to prove that Harpo is Harpo, and instead tries to maintain the fiction—with only ostensible irony—that Harpo is Groucho. He begins to trust that Harpo will not reveal the world as other than Groucho. In a state of play, what in Shakespearean romantic comedy would be called the green world, the ambition and drive that characterize the real world become lost. Instead, the world is aestheticized, rendering one identityless, or identified with the universe: Marx Generica. The moment Groucho helps Harpo pick up the hat, subject and object cease to exist as we understand them. There is no distinct actor or acted upon, only the fulfillment of the desire for a something beyond identity. The discovery of the other as self is the discovery that the world is to be identified with the ego, which becomes both self and world. The need for mediation breaks down when the other is identified—correctly—as oneself.

Groucho's handing the hat to Harpo indicates that the roles are reversed: it is now the former who wants to escape detection. In other words, Harpo is trying as hard as Groucho to discover whether the person before him is a fake Groucho, an impostor. The mirror is more real than the thing it ostensibly reflects. Harpo, who is at least a reflection, seems more substantial, more real, than Groucho. Groucho's need for sustaining the illusion that he exists is evident in his refusal to recognize Harpo's errors in reflection, which come with greater frequency toward the end of the scene. Harpo can now taunt Groucho with errors that show the illusion as illusion.

Finally, this moment represents an audience desire for a permeable medium. It is a desire about "breaking through" that becomes a motif, a string of notable filmic moments—from *Sherlock, Junior* (1924), in which the audience enters the film, to *Rear Window* (1954), in which the real world has become a metaphor for the film world so that the interpenetration of both worlds may be consummated. Jimmy Stewart physically enters the world behind the window and nearly dies; the murderer enters Stewart's space and nearly kills him. This interpenetration is most dangerous in films that are more standard or made by more orthodox sensibilities. In a Marx Brothers film, however, it is harmless, a sort of game without any real consequences. In the Hitchcock film, a potentially harmless situation—a man looking out his own window—is imbued with a danger it would not otherwise have. Marx Brothers comedy exists in a state of potential danger—Harpo being caught as a spy stealing war plans, for example—that it is constantly defusing.

The movement through the mirror is metaphor: it fictionally acknowledges moments historically unrecognized, openings we know are there but cannot speak to publicly, but whose existence informs all behavior. The opening of the portal constitutes the relaxation of several sphincters whose existence has been obscured. The moment is an allegory of Platonic learning: Groucho enters the portal as light enters the eye, whose sphincter must enlarge to allow the entrance of more light where there is darkness. It is an allegory of photography and film, the opening of the aperture to let in light. It is the wished-for moment when the projector lens will widen so that the image will cover not just one wall (*Persona* [1966]) but four (*Sherlock, Junior*). The projector's world is our world; it yields us the fantasy that collision with a concrete object affords not pain and death but the entrance to another world. The existence of a subject and a technology are precisely those things that the classical Hollywood cinema teaches its devotees to forget.

Exposure

Even when he walks through the mirror, Groucho cannot touch Harpo. You cannot touch an illusion, just as you cannot touch the figures on the screen. Touching means it is not cinema anymore. When Groucho grabs Chico at the end of the sequence, the illusion of simultaneity vanishes, the allegory of cinema ends. The dream-landsman is thus undercut in the end by the unacceptable inclusion of a *second* version of Groucho in Chico. (The assertion that Chico's Groucho makeup makes him another mirror forgets that two mirrors facing each other should be able to produce the illusion of infinite Grouchos. This the two subordinate brothers cannot do.) The fantasy of unified identity ends with an intrusion of plot that reveals identity to be what we had known and repressed: division.

Chico's intrusion in the sequence as a third Groucho reestablishes the primacy of cause and effect. Chico's capture dissolves to a shot of his face in a newspaper headline—"Chicolini under arrest: Faces court-martial for treason"—as if, rather than the attempted stealing of the plans, the treason had been the return to the plot, the upsetting of the scene. (One notices for instance that it is not Harpo who is on trial.) The courtroom trial is open to the public; in contrast to the intense privacy of the mirror scene, the courtroom drama is a very social affair. In a reversal—or even collapse—of Hegel's and (Karl) Marx's categories, the mirror scene reduplicates identity first as farce, then as tragedy. When Groucho grabs at Chico the scene represents the way in which comedy limits itself, the way in which a true dialectic of fantasy ends. Two Grouchos are comedy, three a return to narrative.

Why *must* the scene end? We must refer back to the fact that we are a part of the Brothers' dialectic: we come to expect the least expected behavior from them, so that *we* are disappointed when we do not receive the dramatic stimuli we have come to expect. The point at which the dialectical process of the comedy has been successful—the point at which we as audience have come to expect the opposite of our expectations—is the moment of synthesis between expectation and desire, resulting in an expectation and a wish for each moment to be more amusingly surprising than the last. This is the moment at which we begin to become disappointed with any part of the film that does not provide us with that immediate gratification, any part of the film that does not include the Marx Brothers. We become surprised at their absence rather than at their presence. We become disappointed at the intrusion of the serious and conventional at those moments we expect the comically surprising.

But though we all want the skit to go on ad infinitum, as Groucho and Harpo do, we are securely insecure in the knowledge that the continuation of the scene would be a repeated gratification that would inevitably kill desire. At the moment the dialectic produces a successful synthesis—laughter—we are left in danger of finding the Marx Brothers themselves less humorous. It is not possible self-consciously to expect their jokes and still find them amusing. The mirror scene could not plausibly be spun out for eighty minutes (or a lifetime) because the delight of having replaced certainty with controlled anxiety would be replaced by the inability to bear for too long the repetition that in our culture is defined as neurosis. Only children and neurotics repeat a word over and over until it loses its meaning.

The psychoanalytic fantasy of discovering a landsman becomes politically volatile if one considers that the lesson of American culture is that nationally ascribed identity is exactly as arbitrary as the names assigned to the immigrants at Castle and Ellis Islands. Conceived as a strategy of libido containment (as Freud conceived it), humor is harmless, even conservative. Conceived as a fantasy of escaping containment it is much more: a model and a spur for, if not immediate action, then a kind of anarchic sensibility that might precede action. As a fantasy of pre-mirror stage, pre-oedipal identity—of a reconstituted identity—the landsman is a way of exploring alternatives to traditional power structures. A moment's satiation in front of a mirror explicates, justifies, and prepares for a life of antagonisms in front of the camera.

TERMAGENT IMMIGRANT *IMAGOS*: REPRESSING THE FEMININE ETHNIC

The search for a landsman is an explicitly masculine endeavor, an attempt at self-creation without the feminine, a male parthenogenesis. Women were, of course, not allowed membership in most *landsmannschaft*.[59] Though the *landsmannschaft* attempts to maintain itself as a third term, apart from leftist and nationalist agendas, this sexism is a kind of bridge to the New World, precipitating the revelation that subversion is always complicit in creating the structure it seeks to topple.

The reactionary face of the *landsmannschaft* can be seen in Hollywood in several ways: in the conservative politics of the heads of most of the studios (including the attempt to assert that the structure of family should substitute for more empowering structures, like unions[60]—a strategy particularly hard on working women[61]); in the sexism of such organizations as the Friar's Club (despite its own avowals to the contrary); and so on. To say that the Marx Brothers are sexist is not precisely to say that they fit themselves into Anglo-American sexism, but rather that Anglo-American culture, like Italian-American, African-American, Jewish-American, and others, has a stake in the repression of the feminine. In fact, hyphenated American cultures emphasize a repressive dynamic—the culture of shame—that is only a small footnote in the official Victorian handbook. Richard Sennett, in elaborating the problematics of ethnic assimilation, asserts that "Dependency, which is at the very heart of the extended family, appears as perhaps the ultimate weakness in American terms."[62] For Groucho (and S. J. Perelman and George S. Kaufman), the fantasy of the *landsmanshaft* is an instantaneous victory through revolution and parricide over the ethnic shame John Murray Cuddihy describes.[63]

Historians contradict each other in describing immigrant feminine accommodation and assimilation. Some perceive the ethnic woman as a well-kept secret, secreted in a sort of ghetto seraglio, subjected (or subjecting herself) to the whims of an atavistic, old-country patriarchy and less able as a result to climb out of the patriarchal cave.[64] Others, from Herbert Gans and Maxine Schwartz Seller to more recent feminist historians, conceive an ethnic woman who in many ways much more easily adapts to the New World, embarrassing the newly arrived male immigrant, whose working wife is at odds with the Old-World vision of the sole breadwinner.[65] (This despite the fact that, of course, women worked extremely hard under Old-World patriarchy.) On the one hand, immigrant women worked as wage earners almost as much as men (in marked contrast to genteel, middle-class women[66]), and immigrant men, like the host culture, were often embarrassed by this fact.[67] Further, the only work available to a statistically overwhelming number of immigrant women of several ethnic designations was prostitution, creating further cause for shame in the ethnic community.[68] (The press, of course, sensationalized the issue even more.[69]) On the other hand, ethnic mothers were perceived as embarrassingly atavistic in their behavior, feeding their children according to Old-World customs,[70] overprotecting their children,[71] unwilling or unable to learn English language or customs; in the end they are perceived as aggressive and unfeminine. The constant in both equations is the shame caused the ethnic man by either the working wife or the atavistic mother consequent on ideas and styles of negotiating the New World. The man is either ashamed his wife or mother is unassimilated or ashamed that she is more assimilated than he is.

The Marx Brothers and American comedy are central supports in the bridge between Old- and New-World patriarchies because they connect this immigrant shame to other issues: second-generation shame of the immigrant parents and unease at mainstream feminine representations. To assert that the Marx Brothers are sexist is to miss the extremity of their attack on the feminine: the excess of sadism, humiliation, and physical and verbal abuse of every kind. It is to miss the fact that their sadism has as its object precisely those women—Margaret Dumont and Thelma Todd—who in other antifeminist (film) texts would be rewarded for one or another kind of conventional femininity, either maternal or sexual. It is to miss the Brothers' resemblance to burlesque comics commenting on the ingenues and soubrettes, insulting the inaccessible.[72] It is, in other words, to miss the fact that misogyny in the Marx Brothers is so energetic as to be overdetermined, derived from a desire to acknowledge and erase the ethnic mother/wife and the genteel culture simultaneously, to identify the feminine as a different, if still patriarchal, conflation of maternal and sexual from other mainstream American representations, to conflate the ethnic with the mainstream feminine, the lover with the mother.

For the Marx Brothers, as for much of ethnic America by the 1930s, shame defines the relationship to both parents. The traditional representation of the father, Frenchy, is a too perfectly straightforward Freudian scenario of the sons' scapegoating and exaggerated contempt for the father. In this tableau Frenchy Marx is the eternal pantaloon eternally cuckolded by the sons, who have banded together for this purpose. The story of the Brothers and Frenchy is thus the Freudian myth of the brothers who kill the father, sharing the mother between them.[73] (Like Frenchy, the villains in the Marx Brothers' films are almost always the losing rivals for the hand of Margaret Dumont, always unctuous authority figures intent on upsetting the benign matriarchy created by Dumont's wealth and plenitude.) In Kyle Crichton's biography of the Brothers, Frenchy's Alsatian accent is comic-German, like Sig Rumann's or the Captain's in *The Katzenjammer Kids*: "'Py golly!' Papa would explode disgustedly, getting back to the boardinghouse after an unsuccessful day. 'Dot Shoolius.'"[74] The Brothers' biographies recreate the father as a parody of his parodies. In the films the face changes but the paternal phallus lingers on.

The mythology of the Marx Brothers' mother, Minnie Palmer, contains (as mythologies often do) both versions of shame at the feminine; she is drawn as an embarrassingly *hamishe* woman invested in her son's success in a New-World enterprise. She invents the idea of the Marx Brothers and then attempts to include herself in that success in an unassimilated fashion. The ambivalence of the Brothers is visible in the comedy with which they surround first her, then her screen substitute, Margaret Dumont. (The vision of the Marx Brothers posed in an ironically adoring tableau around Minnie resembles Groucho's stance as a mangy lover toward Dumont's screen persona.) Their relation to her is simultaneously adoring and satirical. Minnie is created, first by the Brothers and then by a credulous public, as a backstage mother. She is agent, critic, oracle, and, almost incidentally, mother. She directs the first part of their career with an iron fist in an iron glove. During their vaudeville career, Minnie sometimes sang in the Brothers' act. But while

Figure 3.10 Marx Family. Reproduced by permission of Culver Pictures.

the Brothers are allowed comic ad libs and on-stage disasters, Minnie is not. Middle-aged, perceived as untalented, and unconscious of that perception, she played a slapstick version of Margaret Dumont in family stories:

> The boys had lost their battle to relegate Mama to the ensemble, and she and Hannah were listed for a duet. . . . [T]hey rustled daintily forth from the wings to find that a stagehand had blundered. Two chairs were called for and only one was there. The ladies became panicky and lost their heads. Instead of standing for the number, they sat down gingerly on the lone chair. As the years passed Minnie had grown stouter; Hannah was always a doughty package. They tinkled their guitars, opened their mouths to sing, and—*crash!* The chair gave way and they descended.[75]

On stage Minnie is not a landsman but a greenhorn, oblivious of the codes (and chairs) she is breaking.

Margaret Dumont is treated on screen like a benighted Minnie whom the Brothers could savage to their heart's content. The fact that she is the physical and cultural opposite of the small, gregarious, card-playing, guttural, *hamishe* Minnie should be no real objection to such an argument: the Brothers would have to be attacking a physically disguised version of their mother in a cultural displacement upward. A certain logic adheres to the attacks on the genteel dowager Minnie might have enjoyed becoming.

Figure 3.11 From Minnie Marx to Margaret Dumont: the fantasy continuation of maternal plenitude as stage prop. *Duck Soup* © by Universal City Studios, Inc. Courtesy of MCA Publishing Rights, a Division of MCA, Inc. Courtesy of the Academy of Motion Picture Arts and Sciences.

Despite this displacement, the Brothers tended to describe Minnie as having the very qualities for which Dumont is satirized. Like Mrs. Claypool in *A Night at the Opera,* or Mrs. Rittenhouse in *Animal Crackers,* Minnie was pretentious and upwardly mobile. Like Mrs. Rittenhouse, she kept a large house open to guests of all stamps. Like the Dumont persona and, apparently, like Dumont herself, she often did not understand the Brothers' humor, even on occasion berating them from the audience for diverging from their script. Dumont towers over the Brothers while Minnie was diminutive. But all mothers once seemed ample and expansive.

Unless Dumont is some version of a mother whom the Brothers approach with ambivalence, it seems all the more odd that the Dumont persona should be so important an object of ridicule in a film ethos populated by more traditionally beautiful, scheming "golddiggers." She does not seem sexual in the customary Hollywood fashion; large and stately, she is satirized for a lack or overabundance of conventionally attractive secondary sexual characteristics (*Groucho*: "I can see you bending over a hot stove. Unfortunately, I can't see the stove" [*Duck Soup*].) While other women in Marx Brothers films are teased for being golddiggers, Dumont, like the screwball heiresses of the 1930s, is criticized for having *too much* money, for relying on her fortune for her status, her attractiveness, her "splendid insularity." (*Groucho*: "Listen Giuli—making love to Mrs. Claypool is my racket; all you're after is two hundred thousand dollars" [*A Night At the Opera*]). Too much money, too much bulk, too much dignity, too much authority: the incongruities in Groucho's relation to Dumont are more understandable if we think of the relationship as a satire of that psychoanalytic sacred cow— maternal plenitude. We more easily understand Dumont's accommodation and forgiveness, her blindness to her own interest despite the fact that Groucho is so obviously after her money and her self-respect. Her nonobservance, her refusal to participate in the Brothers' jokes, her refusal to acknowledge that they are occurring, makes her splendidly ambiguous. Dumont is a male fantasy of a mother whose rules hide an indifferently maternal breast that punishes, accepts, and forgives all at once. She is the fantasy of a parental despot all of whose rules are suspended for oneself. She secretly enjoys the obscenity that she forbids everyone else, including the arch-rivals: brothers and father. (Of course, this desire for a wealthy, sexualized mother also reflects its opposite: an anxiety in the immigrant community that successful women are prostitutes.)

Further confusing life, text, and performance, Dumont was a proper, if humorless, Lady Bracknell offstage as well as on. As a result, the sons' ambivalent response to matriarchy, offstage, becomes a lower-class response to upper-class chauvinism. Dumont was reputed by the Brothers never to have known why their humor was comic; she often had to ask Groucho to explain the lines to her. Further, the Brothers boasted about having played innumerable cruel, sexually humiliating tricks on her on and off the set:

> Her first piece of armor was a whalebone body corset. . . . To this structure she added dresses with loose sleeves after Harpo stuck his foot up her arm. Long trains were discarded because Groucho had a habit of following her off the stage, leaping from one side of the train to the other. One night, he leaped on the train itself and Miss Dumont found herself on the stage in her whalebone corset.[76]

Offstage, the Brothers continued the torment. They posed as johns in her hotel room in order to convince the house detective that she was a prostitute.[77] Another actress, no longer disturbed by them, advised Dumont, "Don't resent it. Tell them to do it some more and that you love it."[78] The rape analogy is self-evident. Aggressively physical, the attacks are sexually motivated. Calling them sexist would be a gross understatement. Like the coercions in *The Taming of the Shrew,* the attacks resembled brainwashing— an attempt to engender complacency and compliance in the subject.[79]

And though the feminine romantic leads in the Marx Brothers films are generally insulated from such assaults, other women are not: Raquel Torres in *Duck Soup,* Thelma Todd in *Monkey Business* and *Horse Feathers,* and even Lois Collier in MGM's *A Night in Casablanca.* These women, however, make more sense as objects of attack in a patriarchy that enforces the suppression of feminine sexuality, since they are presenting themselves as having desire. This treatment of Dumont and the golddiggers is of course the most sexist view of women imaginable: it implies an inability to perceive women as separate from men and an inability to see that relation as anything other than mercantile, a view we see as "ethnic."

The limit of Marx Brothers satire, then, reveals the way in which the sexism of one culture is analogous to the sexism of another: the comedy of the Brothers is based on a series of embarrassments caused by the feminine. Minnie's stature as founder and first agent of the Brothers is impossible for both the older, traditional culture, and for the new, genteel culture to assimilate. The satire of the ethnic feminine is accompanied by a similar satire of the culturally central feminine. At a certain point in her career, Minnie Marx changed her name to Minnie Palmer. Among the stories told about this change—that the new name sounded more genteel, that it derived from her affection for the Palmer House in Chicago—is the myth that she in fact named herself after a British singer she liked. Whether the story is true, it suggests a link with European women performers of an earlier moment—about 1905 to 1920—a wave of aging actresses and demimondaines attempting to capitalize on their nationality and their fame in American vaudeville: Lillie Langtry, Mrs. Patrick Campbell, Jessie Millward, Olga Nethersole, and so on.[80]

The tableau of Groucho and Margaret Dumont as lovers is a satire of this British invasion of the previous generation. Though Groucho was not so much younger than Margaret Dumont, the moments at which the former woos the latter are reminiscent of a thirty-year-old Lionel Atwill playing opposite a Langtry in her sixties.[81] Minnie Marx is satirized insofar as her pretensions toward upward mobility are coincident with the downward mobility of these English actresses. Ironically, Margaret Dumont as satire of both kinds of mobility makes Minnie the co-equal of Langtry and Campbell, making of Langtry, Dumont, and Minnie Marx a sort of "ladies' auxiliary" to the Brothers' landsmannschaft. The satire is thus in part absorbed in revealing the hamishe Minnie beneath the aristocratic Margaret.[82]

However, this landsmannschaft repression of the feminine is in the end an erasure of the ethnic feminine; there is not enough control by women in the narrative to suggest even the desire to become a third or fourth cultural term. Chapter 4 will explicate how, in screwball comedy, the ethnic feminine resurfaces in an explicitly orientalized fashion as a kind of sanctioned revenge on the repressing cultures.

4

— ◆ —

Unlikely Ethnic Heroes: William Powell, Myrna Loy, and the Fantasy of Assimilation

INTRODUCTION: HISTORY AS GHETTO

It was written by a Latin
A gondolier who sat in
His home out in Brooklyn
And gazed at the stars.
— Irving Berlin, "The Piccolino," 1935

In the last chapter, we saw that the Marx Brothers' strategy of bringing along their audience on their self-imposed exile from consensual reality, though a structuring fantasy, was in thematic opposition to melting-pot ideology. Though this fantasy reflected to some degree the idea of Hollywood as "an empire of their own," it could not, as a segregationist gambit, address the problems of assimilation. A different genre, one that could discuss inclusion and assimilation as viable strategies, would be required. In fact, several genres in the classical cinema—the western, the science-fiction film—allegorically and literally confront "aliens." My topic in this chapter is the genre most often discussed as being able to incorporate differences and negate oppositions: the screwball comedy, a kind of green world that enables a fulfillment of melting-pot ideology through a fantasy interrogation of it called "passing."

In the classical era of Hollywood, assimilative tendencies and failures were both glaring in public life and better hidden in the movies. For the film moguls, for instance, success meant a leap into the public eye in a way that made them seem ridiculous or menacing. Louis B. Mayer and others are remembered for tyrannizing their studios and subordinating art to the dollar. Samuel Goldwyn is memorialized for his uninformed oxymorons, the most famous of which, "include me out," might summarize the immigrant paradox. Conversely, Irving Thalberg is often criticized in retrospect for his attempts to inject a rather pathetic and overblown sense of "culture" into films (for example, his decisions to make Norma Shearer a star, inject romantic plots into Marx Brothers films, or remove Erich Von Stroheim from the production of *Greed*). Harry Cohn is best remembered for his obscenities and for an egotism and anti-intellectualism that made Louis B. Mayer "look like a dreamer."[1] These studio "bosses" and the rest of ethnic Hollywood produced films in their own images, films containing a barely suppressed concern about inclusion into what the ethnic or immigrant perceived to be the cultural mainstream. The films portray in disguised manner the tensions implicit in becoming Americanized: the choices one must make between the older culture and the new and between viewing oneself as either American or ethnic; the choices, based on the tension between shared sensibilities and disparate backgrounds, that the ethnic must favor in pursuing his object of desire, or even in favor of desire. In other words, the partial exclusion of the ethnic in film reveals an absorption with the subject by the ethnics who are making those films. The disproportionately ethnic Hollywood requires a disguised version of the problems of ethnicity because the standard solution to becoming American is to leave the older ethnic identity at Ellis Island. Ethnic filmmakers, or any filmmakers concerned with nonparticipation in the perceived cultural mainstream, often choose leading actors and actresses who earlier played roles as villains, ethnics, or eccentric character actors. Further, and paradoxically, these filmmakers portray America in screwball comedies as a cultural Middletown that while providing ethnic strategies for assimilation, provides no ethnics. The protagonists, because they are beautifully and ideally regular in appearance, suggest a world void of ethnicity except in anti-heroes, gangsters, and subordinate, character actors. While they recreate more viable versions of the problem of assimilation, immigrant and ethnic filmmakers also recreate the world from which they are excluded.

I will discuss William Powell and Myrna Loy as paradigmatic masculine and feminine versions of the disguised ethnic for these reasons: (1) their careers begin, like those of Chaplin and the Marx Brothers, before sound and the 1930s, so that one can chart the change in new-immigrant representation through their changing personae; (2) their careers begin slightly earlier than those of the actors and actresses we best remember from the 1930s, so that they may be taken as paradigmatic for those other stars; and

(3) their pairing in the Thin Man films, though perfectly typical of the genre, is, given their previous personae, a distinctly surreal representation of the desire to conform.

UNLIKELY ETHNIC HERO: WILLIAM POWELL IN LATIN DRAG

One of the superlative recent methods for demonstrating the culturally constitutive effect of a "disguised" ethnicity has been that of Werner Sollors, who, while using primary literary texts to explicate ethnicity, avoids ghetto-izing it.[2] This chapter will embark on an analogous program, which is to examine the development of two actors' film identities over time to see how their change, their use by the film community, is a negative, mirror, or fantasy image of the kinds of changes elicited from the ethnic and immigrant by the perceived necessity for a social homogeneity.

William Powell is my first subject of choice because he would seem to be the worst possible candidate for the examination of an ethnic underside in American film. He is too paradigmatic, too idealized, too perfectly and seamlessly the romantic lead. In conversation, colleagues have correctly pointed out that, if anything, Powell and the screwball comedy seem to reflect the latent Anglophilia of Hollywood and of American culture. But, though Anglophilia exists in American film, it is derivative—being Anglophilic is not the same as being Anglo.[3] Anglophilia transforms its subject for its own purpose. (Who would argue that even the admiring representations of British culture in, say, *The Scarlet Pimpernel* [1934] or *The Dawn Patrol* [1938] are not ridiculously exaggerated?) In a paradigmatic fashion that will be emu-lated in some or all respects by Clark Gable, Cary Grant, James Cagney, and Humphrey Bogart, the Powell persona arrives at its status as romantic lead from a foreign shore, a tainted member of the "criminal" class that is composed largely of character actors. Within a few years, however, Powell will work his way out of the character-actor class, becoming the lead player in his filmic universe.

Lifting the Stain

In the 1936 feature film *My Man Godfrey* William Powell plays Godfrey Smith, a butler for the dissolute Bullock household. He is discovered by one of the Bullock daughters, Irene, who takes him away from the city dump where he and the poverty-stricken forgotten men of the mid-1930s Depres-sion make their home. Irene is in search of a forgotten man, whom she needs in order to win a scavenger hunt, which she tactlessly describes to Powell as something like a treasure hunt except that "you try to find something that nobody wants." She gives him a job as a manservant and immediately falls in love with him, though it seems more like puppy love than any identifiably adult emotion. But Godfrey adamantly refuses to begin an affair with a daughter of the house, not even giving in to Irene's avowal that hers is a mentor's interest.

Of course Godfrey Smith is really Godfrey Parke, of the Boston Parkes. His true identity is revealed during the course of the film, and he and Irene marry and live happily ever after. This is a frog-prince tale in which the proletarian is discovered to be an aristocrat in disguise who can choose to resume his real person at any time (the only codicil being that he do it by virtue of money he has earned himself rather than with the parental fortune). The frog was never really a frog, and Godfrey Parke was never really a poor man. Because of Powell's characteristic self-possession, it is even difficult to believe in the desperation that would have allowed him first nearly to take his own life and second to eke out an existence on his city dump. The mise-en-scène supports the contention that Godfrey Smith was never really a believable derelict. We learn about his patrician origins only about halfway through the film, but after the first scenes we see Powell in his customary habitat. He inhabits the haunts of the wealthy, even if he does so as a butler. He is desirable to women, even if only as a protégé and potential gigolo. His clothes include waistcoat, tails, and white tie, even if they are only livery. Godfrey's diction never includes slang or street argot. His accent is mid-Atlantic, which is to say one of a very few identifiably cultivated American accents. And of course the history of the William Powell character in other sound films convinces us that in fact this man must be a gentleman in some way the film's introduction conceals from us. Audiences are too much influenced by such films as *Manhattan Melodrama* (1934), *The Thin Man* (1934), and *Libeled Lady* (1936) not to be startled at the beginning of *My Man Godfrey* when Powell appears unshaven, unkempt, and badly dressed; he seems more like his previous celluloid avatars when he is dressed as a butler. Our sense of the gentlemanliness of Powell's previous roles, as much as his comportment in this, enforces a sense that Godfrey Smith was never meant for the city dump but for the haunts of the wealthy, for "dash and cash, not trash."

The decision to make Powell a romantic leading man was consciously taken, insofar as that was possible, by Paramount, which was founded and run in large part by Jesse L. Lasky and his son. Beginning in business with Samuel Goldfish (Goldwyn), Lasky ultimately committed himself to a partnership with Adolph Zukor to form Paramount–Famous Players–Lasky. Lasky, who originally started in vaudeville as an impresario, had to sell out of Paramount in the early 1930s because of the Depression, subsequently going to work for Warner, Fox, and RKO. He was, therefore, a prime example of the problematically self-made ethnic. The studio that actually made *My Man Godfrey*—Universal—was formed by Carl Laemmle, a German immigrant who began his business career in film by investing in the nickelodeon boom. He sold his interest in Universal in 1935 for five million dollars when the Depression nearly bankrupted him. The director of *My Man Godfrey,* Gregory La Cava, was of Italian origin, the son of Pascal Nicholas and Eva Wolz La Cava. His father, a "musician and linguist, was the only Italian in [an] Irish town."[4] Powell stated about the degree of La Cava's involvement in the film: "Probably, no one ever lived who was like Godfrey. But La Cava, the director, made the man seem quite plausible. Actually, that was La Cava's picture. Every morning he'd give us some dialogue that he'd written during the night, and it was good dialogue."[5] Myron and David O. Selznick, agent and producer, respectively, for some of Powell's transition films, were the sons of Lewis J. Selznick (née Zeleznick), a Russian-Jewish immigrant who moved from the jewelry business to the film business. They were in part responsible for the conscious decision to change Powell's image. David collaborated on the script for the single film he believed would do this: *Street of Chance* (1930).

Sound films like *My Man Godfrey,* in which we see a gentlemanly William Powell, are the end result of a rather surprising ontogeny. In fact, Powell's whole early career was spent playing foreign villains, revolutionaries, and gangsters. In Powell's first film role he played one of Professor Moriarty's henchmen in the John Barrymore silent version of *Sherlock Holmes* (1922). He continued in a series of interesting and villainous "foreign" roles: Francis I, enemy of Mary Tudor in *When Knighthood Was in Flower* (1922); "the treacherous Duke of Orleans" in *Under the Red Robe* (1923); the Spanish Captain Gaspar deVoca in *The Bright Shawl* (1923); "the evil Tito" on location in Italy for *Romola* (1924).[6] He moved gradually out of period pieces to play more modern villains: a fortune hunter in *Dangerous Money* (1925), the "lead heavy" in *Too Many Kisses* (1925), and even Nick Di Silva, an American gangster, in *The Beautiful City* (1925). After a few sympathetic roles, he returned as Boldini, another ethnic villain, in the 1926 *Beau Geste,* and as another poor American—George Wilson, Jay Gatsby's murderer—in *The Great Gatsby* (1926). Also in 1926, Powell played Trent Regan in a film called *New York,* a role his biographer Charles Francisco describes as "a neighborhood boy who grew up to be a gun-toting gangster. He would get fourth billing, behind Ricardo Cortez, but Powell would win the girl both men loved—only to shoot her to death in a jealous rage before the picture's final frame."[7] As the title suggests, *New York* is rather oddly like a film Powell would make some eight years later, *Manhattan Melodrama*—except that in the latter film Powell would play the role of the good neighborhood boy who grows up to be the district attorney. Over the course of the film, he would be responsible for incarcerating and executing his closest friend, who may be precisely described as "a neighborhood boy who grew up to be a gun-toting gangster." In the later film, Powell would thus have the opportunity of symbolically dissociating himself from the villainy of the ethnic roles.

The transition to sound at first increased the ambiguity of the Powell persona. In his first sound film Powell was cast in an ambiguous role: "Before the final frame he would commit an unforgivable act. But his unselfish reason for doing it would gain him the sympathy of the audience."[8] Francisco finds that Powell's transition into sound film, when "movie fans . . . were surprised to find that he didn't sound the way he looked," provided the occasion for his transformation into a sympathetic persona. But, as we have been implying, that sympathetic persona had become increasingly evident in his silent films: "that trim mustache, which had made him look so excitingly wicked, now seemed downright classy in combination with that deep voice."[9] After 1930 Powell, then, is almost permanently the suave leading man we recognize in the Thin Man films and *My Man Godfrey*. In actuality, though, the self-conscious attempt to remake Powell as a screen hero—"to present him in an excellent film in which his character undergoes the same moral and ethical regeneration"—in *Street of Chance* occurred after the fact.[10]

So it is only after a film metamorphosis engineered in part by Paramount–Famous Players–Lasky, in part by audiences—a metamorphosis sustained at MGM—that Powell appeared both suave and sympathetic to film audiences. Before that he has a history of playing foreign subversives and villains, American gangsters and fortune hunters, and the occasional cowboy villain. This sea change might be dismissed as a product of the new sound technology, which allows the gentility of that mid-Atlantic accent to appear. But subsequent films, such as *My Man Godfrey,* continue to feature as subject this metamorphosis from rich to poor, grasping to comfortable, ethnic to nonethnic. Powell's character plays out in each film the fantasy of a one hundred-minute transformation into the ideal American, just as the film director he plays in *The Last Command* (1927) is determined to play over again in America the Russian revolution, himself now generalling the generals.

The Powell persona was ultimately adopted in the early 1930s by MGM, a studio originally owned by two Jewish businessmen, Samuel

Goldwyn and Louis B. Mayer. The transformation of the Powell persona merely refracts the unconsciously engineered transformation of ethnic to nonethnic through the consciously contrived transformation of character actor status to star and leading man. This political unconscious is the local version of a fantasy life in which film moguls at Paramount and MGM participated at wider levels when they created out of the Southern California farms and wilderness a city that they controlled and in which they could then feel at home as founding fathers and natives. They created from the material of the villain, the ethnic, and the revolutionary a romantic protagonist. Powell is just one example of a general trend in the 1930s toward this valorization of the urban, ethnic anti-hero. As Charles Francisco says about Powell's role in *Street of Chance*, "It was the type of role that most of Hollywood's bad men—Clark Gable, James Cagney, Humphrey Bogart, and others—would later use to begin the transition from villain to hero."[11]

Well after his initiation into sound films in ambiguous roles, Powell starred with Clark Gable and Myrna Loy in *Manhattan Melodrama*. It is an important film because it was popular, had pretenses to social relevance, and brought together for the first time William Powell, MGM, director William S. Van Dyke, and Myrna Loy. (Even Nat Pendleton, a minor crook in this film, would later figure as Guild, the simple, vaguely Irish detective in the Thin Man series.) It was produced by David O. Selznick, who, as we have shown, had been partially responsible for the conscious Hollywood decision to convert Powell from villain to romantic lead. *Manhattan Melodrama* marks one endpoint in Powell's transition from urban, ethnic villain to protagonist, a "dead end" in the imagination of American filmmakers who attempted to live out in their characters a fantasy of belonging to a society they have created but from which they have excluded themselves. The fantasy fails, or becomes a fantasy of failure, in this film because of a traditional and very overt pairing of ethnicity with a sympathetic but fatal taint of moral ambiguity. This pairing derives from a sense that the American requirements of social and economic upward mobility can be fulfilled only through either denying one's origins or denying social and ethical strictures. Ethnic characters ultimately betray either their friends or society.

Manhattan Melodrama is about two boys, friends and orphans, one Irish Catholic and the other Protestant, who are born and raised on Manhattan's Lower East Side. One grows up to be the governor who sends his friend, a gambler and a murderer, to the electric chair. William Powell is Jim Wade, the upright friend, Clark Gable is "Blackie" Gallagher. As governor, Wade is torn by contradictory ethical claims. While he does not want to be responsible for the death of his friend, whom he saved in childhood from drowning, he must mete out justice both as the district attorney who prosecuted Blackie Gallagher and as the governor who refuses to commute the death sentence. The ethical demands are further confused here since Blackie is being tried for murdering the man who is trying to blackmail Wade. Wade does not know that Blackie murdered the blackmailer to protect his friend until Wade has already won a guilty verdict and is elected governor on the success of this case. When he makes this discovery, he is even more confirmed in his belief that Blackie should die, because a motive has been established that renders the latter's guilt unequivocal. The issue is complicated still further by the fact that the blackmail material the murdered man used involves the district attorney's friendship with Blackie and Wade's possible suppression of material about still another murder Blackie has committed.

In the film only Protestants are reflective, so only Protestants leave the ghetto. As a child in the initial melting-pot scenes, Wade is the only Protestant in a group that includes Irish, Italian, and Jewish children. In this, as in most Hollywood films, the Protestant is an ethnic type only when viewed as one of several possible types and especially when he is a poverty-ridden or lower-middle-class ethnic. But as a member of the new "chosen people" (in the best Puritan tradition), he has a unique destiny. Of all the types, he is the only one who escapes the Lower East Side. Blackie becomes wealthy, but it is a precarious wealth: he never quits gambling, he murders to retain his status, and, of course, he dies in the electric chair. Only Wade successfully manages to escape his earlier environment. He does so spectacularly, too, becoming first assistant district attorney, then district attorney, then governor. It is as if the film concludes that the only good ethnic representative is one from the mainstream: an Anglo.

One of the issues of the film, then, is assimilation, defined here as the exchange of such human values as personal loyalty to friends and origins for social and ethical values that identify oneself with the society of one's choice. Successful assimilation in this film means a real, if unacknowledged, rejection and repudiation of the family and friends with whom one grew up. For Wade, this is only made easier by the fact that his parents die early in the film. Blackie seems to feel the death of his foster father, an immigrant, more than Wade.

Wade and Blackie are constructed as opposing fields in the same ethnic tension. On one end is Wade, who desires to join the mainstream political elite on their own terms; he must believe in those terms and his power to uphold them. On the other end is Blackie, who does not really want to assimilate; rather, he gains intraethnic success, continuing his identification, now seen as criminal, with the original ethnic groups.[12] Blackie retains the friends of former days; Wade does not. This split has the effect of identifying criminality with ethnicity, as Wade is honest while Blackie is not. But, of course, Blackie is the more sexually charismatic of the two characters. He is attractive to Eleanor (Myrna Loy) because he is exciting, while Powell is attractive, to a lesser degree, because he is stable. Loy and Gable are allowed the prolonged screen kisses that Loy and Powell are not. It is as if the charismatic criminality seen in other gangster films of the early 1930s (and later) is explicated here: retention of one's original ethnic status is identified with individuality, sexual aggression, and lawlessness. Delinquence precedes tumescence. As in other gangster films, Blackie's individualism is attractive. It is ethically antisocial, but it also seems grounded in a way Wade's sanctimoniousness is not. One is encouraged to feel that because Blackie knows and participates in life's underside, he recognizes how Wade's sense of civic duty is ultimately unrewarding to the ethnic group, and so meaning-less. Blackie indicates his sense of the grotesqueness of equating his anti-assimilation with marriage and social responsibility when Eleanor asks him to marry her. He asks her, "Say, what're you trying to do, make an honest man outta me?" The phrase, traditionally used about women marrying, has a further relevance when applied to a male criminal; it indicates how equally incongruous to Blackie are the pictures of him either legally married or legitimately employed and how intimately these two societal functions are bound.

Other Powell films address various dichotomies associated with ethnicity. Of the more prominent films, *Mr. Peabody and the Mermaid* (MGM, 1947), as its title suggests, is about the encounter of the exaggerated exotic with the exaggerated mundane. *I Love You Again* (MGM, 1940) features a Powell with a split personality: he plays a confidence man who wakes up after several years of amnesia to discover that he has been living as a respectable, small-town businessman. Others of Powell's films suggest class, legal, or ethnic dichotomies in their titles: *The Hoodlum Saint* (1946), *The Baroness and the Butler* (1937), *Double Wedding* (1937), and even *The Great Ziegfeld* (1936).

In light of Powell's film career, then, one must revise one's sense of the meaning of the transformation of Godfrey Smith to Godfrey Parke. It is true that Smith has always been Parke, but it is also true that this duality is a fantasy wish by the makers of *My Man Godfrey* to have always been Parke rather than Smith. It reflects a fantasy about recreating not only one's persona but one's very origins. But the fantasy reveals an anxiety about a potential truth: that one was Godfrey Smith all the time—the "newly revealed" identity is in fact the *real* sham. When the makers of *My Man Godfrey* become a part of the film's context, the film seems concerned more with the insecurity that one's true origins will be revealed as base than with a hope that those origins are in fact aristocratic, or at least "native."

We know in more textual ways as well that the film is the reverse of what it seems, that the story about weaning oneself away from old family money and values conceals a story about acquiring wealth and status. For instance, Godfrey's economic success depends on an ambiguous plot detail. Irene's sister Cornelia (Gail Patrick), who dislikes Godfrey, plants her pearl necklace in his room (under his bed) and summons the police to find the thief. Godfrey, however, having discovered the necklace and anticipating such a move on Cornelia's part, has hidden it elsewhere. Wisely investing the money he raises with the necklace as pledge, he becomes a successfully independent businessman, apparently over the course of a summer. He is never depicted as a thief, and he ultimately returns the necklace. Whatever moral ambiguity might attach to the act of keeping the pearls is more than compensated for when he helps Mr. Bullock out of his own financial difficulties. The attempt is to allow Godfrey to be completely and morally self-made. Further, Godfrey does not have to rely on his family, Irene, Cornelia, or a bank for money, having come by it, if under peculiar circumstances, on his own. In other words Godfrey Parke, however much a part of the personality of the character, is not allowed to intrude in any way on the capitalist nativity of Godfrey Smith. Godfrey, at the film's end, even opts to keep his new name and remain in Manhattan as the owner of a nightclub rather than return to Boston and the Parkes' more substantial interests. The plot twist concerning the necklace, otherwise so ridiculous, makes sense only as an attempt to allow Godfrey Smith an economic self-creation.

In short, Godfrey is the best of both possible worlds: derived from a family who has been here probably longer than the Bullocks (who came here, as Mrs. Bullock says, not on the Mayflower, but on the one after that, evoking the origins of a group in an immigration that did not result in immigrants), he is nevertheless economically an immigrant, or immigrantlike: a new man with a new name and a new economic identity. (Tommy Gray, a friend of Godfrey Parke, explains their acquaintance away by inventing a family for Godfrey Smith that includes an Indian wife and five children, again inventing an origin outside the perceived cultural mainstream. Hearing this story, Mrs. Bullock remarks that Godfrey *does* have rather high cheekbones.) By 1936 the Powell persona has completely and unproblematically erased the stain of ethnicity, while allowing its trace to remain a subject of discourse in his films.

I would like to recall "the mystery of milady's necklace" to mind for a moment because it provides a connection between class division and criminality in such a way that the apparently guilty party—the butler—is innocent, while the wealthy and spoiled patrician is guilty of robbing herself. This patrician guilt brings us to the Thin Man films.

Visiting the Old Neighborhood

The strategy of the Thin Man films, which is to reduce the difference between the ethnic hero and the perceived cultural mainstream, works in a threefold manner: the films depict a cultural mainstream that is actually criminal while allowing the ethnic world merely to appear criminal; the Nick Charles persona itself bridges the gap between mainstream and ethnic worlds; and, most significantly, the hero foists his latent ethnicity onto the character actors. Nick Charles, the detective hero, derives from the ethnic working class and he marries into money. Further, because the Thin Man films crosspollinate the detective story and the romantic comedy, murder and marriage, they allow the creators of Powell's persona to correct the errors committed by the villains and fortunehunters of his silent film career and resolve the assimilation dilemmas of such ambiguous roles as the attractively villainous Tito and the moral but trite Jim Wade.

Nick Charles looks like a gentleman, or better, a dandy, always perfectly and expensively dressed. (Powell's previous detective avatar, Philo Vance, carried a cane.) Nick's trousers are invariably and perfectly creased, his moustache perfectly straight, narrow, and even, resembling the pencil that might have drawn it. Like a long string of Hollywood heroes (Melvyn Douglas, Warren William), he is even attractively heavy and solid. But though his hat brim snaps crisply, the hat itself is often white, in opposition to the respectable grey and black fedoras of most male denizens of 1930s, 1940s, and 1950s films. (The other justly famous, flamboyantly white fedora belongs to Joseph Cotton, who plays the Merry Widow strangler in Hitchcock's *Shadow of a Doubt* [1943].) Nick's drinking leaves him a little physically off balance. He walks and moves with the awkward grace of a clown on a tightrope. These one or two peculiarities in appearance alert us to the fact that Nick's *almost* conventional gentlemanly appearance is superficial.

Nick lives in a fictive world in which class conventions are breaking down, in part through his agency, and are being replaced by an immanent criminality. The detective's cynicism, though constituting a fixed social hierarchy whose criterion is the law, recognizes not a fixed society, but rather individuals who are constantly crossing insecurely from one side of the law to the other. Confirmed and suspicious criminals are almost never guilty (at least of murder) in the Thin Man films: wealth and status, on the other hand, almost invariably guarantee guilt. In *The Thin Man* the guilty party is a prominent lawyer, Herbert Macaulay. In other films he or she is the heiress to a fortune, the socialite boyfriend of the accused woman, a doctor, a wealthy patron of the arts, and even a district attorney.[13] This plot element inverts a social assumption and a film convention equating crime with the lower, ethnic classes: the association between lower-class origins and crime found in *Manhattan Melodrama* is broken in such a way that a new convention is erected in which only the wealthy are guilty.[14]

To complicate matters further, the law is not the most important filmic evaluative dimension. In its editing, *The Thin Man* tries to maintain a physical distinction between the wealthy and the poor, criminal, or ethnic, separating them in different sequences, different spaces. At a party thrown by the Charleses, Nick is at pains to sequester his "tonier" guests in private rooms. But even this segregationist impulse is contradicted by the tendency, when wealthy and poor must inhabit the same frame, to crowd them together for the sake of humor. And in contrast to the attempt to hierarchicalize the classes, other values are obfuscated in such a way that several positive values accrue to the criminal. Criminals and cops, for example, tend to be more trustworthy than the wealthy, to know more, and to be less narcissistic. More important, they are comically eccentric. Lieutenant Guild is a second-generation Irish cop, without the accent but with more than a little obtuseness and self-aggrandizement. The Charleses throw a Christmas party for Nick's old friends, all obviously denizens of a Runyonesque, extralegal world, with names already behind quotational bars: "Studsy" Burke, "Shep" Morrelli, "Rainbow" Benny, and "Face" Peppler. (Other suspiciously foreign names are Nunnheim, Jorgenson, and Wolf.) Physically, the actors are no match for the lead players. They tend to extremes, being gaunt or fat, tall or short, bald and loud. Several have comic ethnic accents.

So that he might appear ideal, or at least so that his eccentricity might seem ordinary in a world populated by more extreme eccentrics, the protagonist's eccentricity is projected onto the characters who constitute his world. Character actors act quirkily so that protagonists do not have to do so. That the character actors are projected distortions exorcised from the protagonists can be inferred from their affinities to the protagonists. Sometimes the character actor is the almost allegorical voice of conscience that speaks for the hero when the hero is completely ambivalent (Walter Brennan towards Gary Cooper in *Meet John Doe* [1941], for example). Sometimes he or she parallels the absurd situation of the protagonist in an even more absurd fashion that removes the onus and embarrassment from the protagonist. (Edward Everett Horton's pursuit by Ginger Rogers's formidable friend Alice Brady saves Fred Astaire's face to some degree in *The Gay Divorcee* [1934].) Sometimes the character actors are even more exaggerated versions of whatever identifies the protagonist with a certain class or subculture (the seven professors of *Ball of Fire* [1942], who, as Sugarpuss O'Shea [Barbara Stanwyck] observes, are more like the seven dwarves). Sometimes the character actors create an ethos in which the protagonist can act in an absurdly liberated manner of which he would otherwise be incapable (Cary Grant's aunts and brother in *Arsenic and Old Lace* [1944]; Cary Grant's teenage nemesis, Shirley Temple, in *The Bachelor and the Bobby Soxer* [1947]).

Eccentricity makes any identification with these denizens of a filmic demimonde impossible. As embodiments of eccentricities that the protagonists (and, by extension, the characters) are not allowed to possess themselves (poverty, criminality, foreignness), the character actors are exaggerations, or minimalizations of the desirable real. Most of the audience repudiates any conscious identification with the character actors, however much we may like and be amused by them. We like the bumbling of Edward Everett Horton, though we may think he is pompous, and the appealing acerbity of Eric Blore. As a consequence, the audience learns to identify not only with the protagonists but *against* these eccentric filmic groups.[15] They are, in Dickensian fashion, physically exaggerated extroversions of recognizable psychologies. Cesar Romero's Jorgenson in *The Thin Man,* for instance, is visually slick, fine-featured, and "foreign" in the fortune-hunting way Powell's persona once was. The trace of Powell's celluloid origins thus remains in his films even though it has been erased in his characters.

Dashiell Hammett's novel *The Thin Man* contains some direction for the tension in the series between revealing and effacing origins. In both the novel and the films, Nick tends to obfuscate when confronted with questions about himself, denying his origins while raising them as an issue. His jokes raise a subject and then negate the possibility of discovering any important truth connected to that subject. When, early in Hammett's novel, Nick claims immigrant Greek parentage, and further claims that his patronymic was changed to Charles from Charalambides by the immigration authority who was unable to pronounce the Greek name, his deadpan manner prevents any determination of this assertions's truth value. As Dorothy Wynant correctly points out: "I never know when you're lying."[16] In both the film and the novel, Dorothy asks Nick whether the tales he told her when she was a child about his detective adventures were true or not. He answers in both versions that they were *probably* not. And there is some discrepancy about the kind of time Nick spent with Mimi Jorgenson when he was working on a case for her then-husband, Clyde Wynant. When she asks him in the present whether he likes her and he answers no, she accuses him of joking with her. He "neither confirms nor denies" the accusation. We do not know his genuine origins or the nature of his original liaison with Mimi. Stories about the past, or about origins, are neither confirmed nor denied, so that one does not have to define oneself finally as a part of or apart from the perceived cultural mainstream.

In other ways the changes in Nick's character throughout the film series are calculated to efface the memory of any eccentricity in the original persona, as if the Powell persona's original transition from villain to hero is replayed within the history of the Charles role, so that Nick becomes decreasingly eccentric. As a premise of the first film, Nick has gone from professional sleuth to professional husband, allowing the emphasis, in genteel fashion, to shift from the public economic person to the private sentimental self. As an ongoing tendency of the films, he is forced to drink less and to become ever more of a parent and spouse figure, in stronger and stronger contrast to his professional stance. The laissez-faire relationship that exists between his marriage and his work at the beginning of the series is with each entry ever more jeopardized. And, as familial responsibilities increase, Nora becomes increasingly protective of Nick and their child. When Nora carries a babe in arms she loses her status as companion in arms. Even Nick's jokes about his access to her wealth disappear, as if their off-color quality is no longer appropriate in their new, more traditional domestic menage.

Of paramount importance is Nick's ability, in a world that is split between native and stranger, cop and robber, ethnic and nonethnic, to be a part of both worlds, to maintain the ambiguous relation to society and the ironic relation to himself necessary to retain a nearly objective view of all levels of society. It is as if Blackie and Jim Wade have formed an uneasy alliance in one persona. Several Powell films are predicated on his ability to maintain, or try to maintain, divided loyalties: from the detective films, in which he is called upon to be knowledgeable of the world of crime while living in the world of fashion, to *Manhattan Melodrama,* where the split takes the form of divided loyalties, one to society, one to his friend. One of the more interesting and overt divisions occurs in *I Love You Again,* in which he plays both a gangster and a pillar of society. The most interesting plot complication in this film is that the crook is the more sympathetic version of himself. The crook, who resurfaces after years of an amnesia in which he believes himself to be a stuffy businessman, must, in order to obtain his wife, divert himself from his original intention of stealing his own money and instead save himself from himself and his gang, whom he has rounded up for the purpose of bilking himself. The split almost always refers to a class difference that implies a sexual and ethnic difference as well. (Even in *Manhattan Melodrama* Powell will finally gain or lose Myrna Loy according to which loyalty—friend or state—he valorizes.)

Though Nick, as a detective, is on the opposite side of the law from the villains and gangsters of his earlier film life, he seems to be great friends with the criminals he has put away, refusing to repudiate the connections he made early in life. In each Thin Man film this acquaintance becomes the occasion for high comedy in two ways: first because the characters are eccentric in and of themselves, and second because they are often allowed to interact with the tonier family and friends of Nora, or with Nora herself. In film after film, she refers to her impressions of his acquaintances as a valid tie to him. During the Christmas party peopled with Nick's criminal, cop, and reporter friends, most of whom are in eccentrically advanced stages of inebriation, Nora remarks, "Oh Nicky, I love you, because you know such lovely people." The remark is only partly ironic; the meeting between cultures that had been at one time cause for anxiety has been transformed into an occasion for celebration.

Still, Nick's criminal friends are paradoxically a part of the background Nick must overcome: he must want more to associate with them than to use them professionally. Nick has no use for the criminals he has put behind bars, but they still attend parties he throws for them, or he attends their parties (which seem for the most part to be thrown in his home anyway). They have become for him both aestheticized and personalized, both further from him and closer to him than when he was a detective. In *Libeled Lady,* Powell is a "libel man" who cultivates women professionally. But it is on one of his jobs that he becomes romantically involved. Powell, and other characters in other screwball comedies, learn, or have thrust upon them, the ability to turn their vocations into avocations, into occupations with a private value quite different from the commercial value that underlies their initial connection to their jobs. The hero undergoes a rite of passage into the middle or upper classes by virtue of the fact that he conflates the economic and intrinsic values of people.

Nick's relation to the wealthy characters is also complex and might best be exemplified by his relation to the murderer, who is always patrician and who is always Nick's mirror image. Like Nick, the murderer is intimate with, and so reduces the difference between, two carefully delineated worlds.

The murderer is familiar with the psychologies of patrician and criminal and with how the behavior of the patrician class is criminally hypocritical (even as he or she partakes in that hypocrisy). Like Nick, the murderer is also aware of how the law works and of how to work on both sides of the law. Many times the murderer has a sexual interest in the other side of the law—a woman for whom he has murdered, a woman he has murdered, a gangster boyfriend for whom she has murdered. The gangsters and fast women are in Nick's past while they are in the murderer's present, but both Nick and the murderer have a stake in both legal and nonlegitimized sexuality. And yet each case further enhances the reputation of the detective while utterly destroying the reputation of the murderer—Nick is upwardly mobile while the killer is downwardly mobile.

Of course, the similarities between Nick and his criminals are reinforced by the conventional bonds between murderer and detective: the detective is the murderer in retrospect; he must think as the murderer would think, must reproduce the crime in his imagination the way the murderer must have produced it before the murder. The murderer and the detective both act in a world in which appearances are necessarily false—the murderer assuming an air of innocence that rightfully belongs to all characters but him/herself, the detective assuming that all characters are potentially guilty, that all protestations of innocence are suspect. Like all film doppelgängers at least since *The Student of Prague* (1913), the murderer and the detective know each other but cannot coexist, and their meeting is necessarily a catastrophe for at least one of them. (Holmes and Moriarty going over the falls.) Also, though both the murderer and the detective work in the world of illusion, the detective operates to destroy an illusory world while the murderer is the creator of an illusion.

In contrast to the patrician murderer, ethnic and lower-class characters are perfect suspects because they are already guilty, at least of poverty and its attendant extralegal behaviors. One of the most important components of a crime—motive—is always present for them in a way it is not for the wealthy; it is built into the fabric of their economic being.[17] By definition more likely suspects than the wealthy, the poor ethnics in the Thin Man films act guilty even when they are innocent. They are often killed because they are knowledgeable about the film's murders (as in *The Thin Man,* in which two people, a gold-digging secretary and a stool pigeon, are killed, the first because she knows who killed Wynant, the second because he knows who killed her). They are knowledgeable both about a kind of world that the patricians are not supposed to know and about the ways that patrician world is in any case invested in the lumpenproletariat criminal world. It is an odd kind of awareness of the other—the knowledge that one is perceived as part of a slum that is attractive exactly because of its seediness. Again, to be aware that this is how one is perceived is to be aware of one's own guilt at belonging to the wrong class. This perception cannot but be mixed with a certain perverse pleasure, because this lower-class sensibility is of course a part of the attraction for the patrician. A moment in *Gold Diggers of 1933* perfectly sums up the reality and perversity of this pleasure. Joan Blondell, accused of mercenariness by the stodgy banker she loves, confesses herself not good enough for him when he professes his love for her. When she calls herself "cheap and vulgar," he protests that every time she says that he will kiss her on the mouth to make her stop. She repeats the self-accusation several times, to the osculatory pleasure of both parties. "Slumming" expresses perfectly the tendency for the bourgeoisie to see the lower class as an object of tourism. ("Puttin' on the Ritz" is the theme song for such a sensibility, with its attendant sense of Harlem Blacks as spectacle.) This plethora of potential culprits is an attempt first to erect class distinctions and then to confuse them even further; the wealthy are as guilty, if not more guilty, than the poor. Where the poor aspire economically upward, the rich aspire emotionally downward—an interesting dichotomy in which an emotional life is one of the advantages of poverty. The rich cannot afford to be anything but conventionally happy with conventional toys.

The William Powell persona and *The Thin Man* are representative of the kinds of solutions to the dilemma of ethnic and immigrant acceptance that more generally characterize the American screwball genre. They attempt to represent tensions between acquiring money and acquiring culture, between the persistence of origins and the insistence of the present, between assimilation and acculturation, and between opposing cultural milieux and classes. Like other American film genres, screwball comedies suppress overt representation of ethnic and immigrant issues, but they are in part strategies for overcoming problems of assimilation in the face of a culture that only partially and minimally acknowledges the ethnic's presence as part of the perceived cultural mainstream.

MYRNA LOY AND THE ART DECO EXOTIC WOMAN

Figure 4.1 depicts Nora Charles, wealthy, poised, and relaxed, in the bar scene that introduces her to us in *The Thin Man*. But Nora does not wear that dress in the bar scene. Nor does she ever stand at the bar. And Asta is not engaged to another dog until the *next* film. Actually, this is Louis

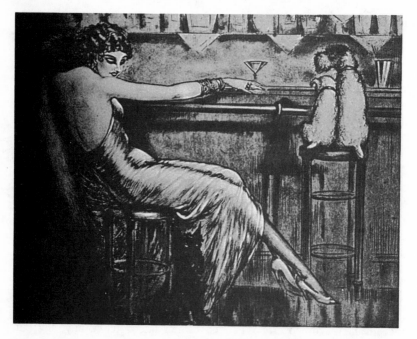

Figure 4.1 "Le Cocktail," by Louis Icart. © 1996 Artists Rights Society (ARS), New York / ADAGP, Paris.

Icart's "Le Cocktail." Produced one year before the publication of Dashiell Hammett's novel and two years before the release of the film, it has no causal connection to *The Thin Man* at all.

Still, the resemblance to Myrna Loy's opening sequence is astonishing. It results from the use of Art Deco in Hollywood to perform a number of industrial and psychic tasks best suited to this aesthetic and from Loy's conformity to a number of Art Deco ideals. Essentially, Loy is a reflection of Hollywood's use of Art Deco to propagate a certain vision of women as apparently free but literally hobbled to prevent any menace, a vision of ethnics as apparently represented but recoded in a way that neutralizes them as well, and a vision of the ethnic woman as a menace in need of suppression. As one might infer, the point of pursuing a "reading" of Loy is to demonstrate a methodology for connecting ethnic with gender concerns. One great advantage of the Hollywood Deco style is that it allowed a conflation of otherwise aesthetically incompatible foreign elements and motifs in the body of the Art Deco woman. As suggested in chapter 3, Hollywood sometimes cultivated anachronism for the sake of comedy.[18] But even unintended anachronisms are part of a style, the purpose of which is the conflation of all foreign cultures. This conflation, in its benevolent aspect, had the effect of reproducing the ideology of the melting pot in miniature. However, this also meant that nothing was distinctly Western or American. As a consequence, Deco allowed for the representation of the tension between assimilative and segregative tendencies in a feminine body that reveals a complex psycho-analytic.

Art Deco and the Feminine

The distinctive image of Myrna Loy is possible only through the prior existence of orientalism, Art Deco, the various symbolisms, cinema villains and vamps, haute couture, and certain lines of decadent and neoclassical movements (Ingres to Klimt to Beardsley to Icart). An exhaustive list of influences is the work of semiotics, but I will briefly trace one cluster of correspondences that seems to me most significant for the purpose of connecting feminine with ethnic representation: fin de siècle haute couture to Art Deco to orientalism to Myrna Loy.

To understand feminine ethnic representation in Hollywood one would then begin not in America, but in France, with Denise Boulet, who in 1905 wed Paul Poiret, an early French couturier who designed women's bodies. In an era when women still wore corsets emphasizing larger busts and buttocks, Poiret's wife was petite. At about the same time Hollywood was being founded, Poiret redesigned the corset, converting it from the S-shaping vehicle it had been to one that flattened the hips and buttocks, liberating the waist. Then he redesigned dresses in empire style, further constraining women within a tubular construction.[19] This construction of the feminine along constrainingly slim lines not only, as one critic asserts, "paralleled the evolution of the major arts"[20] but was a predetermining factor in the Art Deco movement, a movement thus inseparable from the feminine, as the Italian Renaissance is inseparable from the masculine form.

In 1910 Poiret took *le vague,* this new classicizing line with its new slimness, to an extreme. By further narrowing the lines of the dresses he created the aptly nicknamed hobble skirt, "a garment so narrow that walking was almost impossible."[21] The effect was, of course, further to deemphasize maternal lines, lending a sense of woman as androgynous adolescent not only in appearance but in movement as well. The hobble skirt was an instant sensation and a controversial success.

This Deco shape—a compression and elongation of the Victorian woman's body—would remain a representational norm for at least the

Figure 4.2 The Art Nouveau construction of the feminine along confiningly slim lines. Paul Poiret's "hobble skirt." Reproduced by permission of Fashion Research Centre and Museum of Costume, Bath.

next three decades. Sheared away from previously accreted meanings—mother, womanhood, domestic angel, and so on—this new body fit a new aesthetic of the first third of the century whose strength was the economic manipulation of visual symbols. Whatever its relation to the Vienna Secession, the various Weimar movements, or Bauhaus, nonarchitectural Deco as revealed in America in the first third of the twentieth century was an art movement that was actually a poster aesthetic that was really an advertising strategy of the 1920s and 1930s. Art Deco romanticized and then sold soap, tires, and train tickets. It succeeded the various symbolisms as a compromise between representation and abstraction, and succeeded Art Nouveau as a marketing rhetoric. It was a distinctly modern development of nineteenth-century "symbolism"—especially in such artists as Sir Edward Burne-Jones and Gustave Moreau—which featured beautiful human bodies subordinate in interest to some legendary or mythological figure or symbol.

The point of much symbolism was to render legend contemporary. The point of Art Deco was to render contemporary artifacts legendary. It is no accident that Deco evolved with modern advertising and about the same time as the first great advertising houses and first great film stars (like

Chaplin). Art Deco (depending on whether you were listening at one end to the pre-Raphaelite version or at the other to Beardsley-like decadents) rendered legend marketable and merchandise legendary. Substitute a show poster of Josephine Baker for, and as a mirror image of, Franz von Stück's "Salome." Substitute product for myth (an "exotic" dancer for an exotic dancer), or "logo" for emblem, and you have advertising (figures 4.3a-b).[22]

The general argument, now traditional among film theorists, is really that of Roland Barthes, who asserts that capitalist societies create their own mythologies in order to erase both the past and a truer sense of relations between people.[23] Art Deco artifacts thus became floating signifiers without clear referents or with unstable referents. Deco was an inside-out shadow of Symbolism, of the impulse to valorize a contemporary aesthetic vision by representing the past. Instead of selling aestheticism itself, Deco sold things by connecting them to the graphics of the avant-garde and the "great Western tradition."[24]

Especially in America, Art Deco painting was in style foreign and avant-garde but unthreatening: French in derivation, influenced by the Ballets Russes, influencing Eastern European art, and connected to both Italian Futurism and Nazi social realism in its tendency to idealize and reinterpret its own culture's myths and legends in a simplified neoclassical style, Deco was accessible as an avant-garde in a way the various other modernisms were not. In fact, the value of Art Deco for its consumers resided in its ability to be avant-garde while circumventing completely the difficult-to-watch wrenchings of reality that were intrinsic to expressionism, surrealism, or cubism.[25]

Hence, the Poiret-inspired woman's body was compressed—"streamlined"—in order to sell things, reduced to zero in order to allow it to mean only what it sold. Breasts, for example, were reined in so that the feminine would not also mean the maternal. Streamlining the body, reducing its complexity, the absolute number of planes it contains, provided an analogy to the things sold: cars, trains, planes, etcetera. But such streamlining had opposing meanings for artifact and consumer. For the product—the car, the plane, the train—the greater the compression, the more power the engine, and so the greater mobility. But if Art Deco meant greater freedom of movement for its artifacts, it did not for the women it portrayed. The putative freedom of the Deco body (whose owner was to be identified with, for example, her newly won suffrage) was bound by its marketability. The woman's body, emptied of its traditional significance, was refilled with marketplace significance. No longer maternal, it represented only desire: the desire to possess. The ultimate refinement of modern advertising would of course be to associate the woman's body directly with the product, so that *everything* that can be bought is by definition feminine.

Figure 4.3a Franz von Stück,
"Salome." © Städtische
Galerie im Lenbachhaus,
München.

Figure 4.3b Substitute a cabaret
poster of Josephine Baker for
Franz von Stück's "Salome," or
a product for a myth, or a logo
for an emblem, and the result is
a more referential and authoritative advertising. Paul Colin,
"Josephine Baker." © 1996 Artists Rights Society (ARS), New
York/ADAGP, Paris.

Art Deco and Ethnicity

After 1909, when the Ballets Russes came to Paris, Poiret, who had made women mince as if they had bound feet, reintroduced oriental costuming, *chinoiseries*: "bejewelled turbans and bead-trimmed tunics worn with slave bangles and harem slippers."[26] The European fascination with the colonial East, represented for at least two centuries on stage and in print, made its way into the clothing salons of the wealthy bourgeoisie.[27] Natacha Rambova, "Mrs. Rudolph Valentino," was one of Poiret's customers. For Rambova, née Winnifred Shaughnessy, escape into the exotic was a way out of a stifling middle-class atmosphere. The adopted daughter of a rich American perfume manufacturer, Rambova ran away from her English school, becoming a *danseuse* under the direction of Theodor Kosloff for an imperial Russian ballet troupe. Returning to America, she found work as a set and costume designer, especially for the actress Alla Nazimova and then for her husband, Valentino. Her most famous film work was for Nazimova's *Salome* (1923), which she designed after the Beardsley drawings for Wilde's play. For the film, Nazimova, the epitome of the exotic for American audiences, gathered a lesbian, exotic, orientalized, decadent coterie that meant for Rambova ART. (The conflation of ethnic, "oriental," and exotic in this text was extreme: a Russian expatriate in America playing a Jewish maiden in Roman Palestine in a play by an Irish expatriate in England designed [after an English artist's drawings] by an Irish-American ex-expatriate to Russia.) Rambova gave Myrna Loy her first screen test, for a Valentino film, *The Cobra* (1925). (She finally decided not to use the younger actress, though she gave her a walk-on part in a later film.)[28]

The attempt by these two women to take Art Deco at its word as a liberating aesthetic was unsuccessful in Hollywood. *Salome* bankrupted Nazimova, while Rambova ultimately left Hollywood to become a fashion designer, opening her own dress shop at 6 East Fifty-Second Street.[29] Using Art Deco to empower women economically by allowing them a wider range of self-representations on the screen could not work in a patriarchy as circumscribed as Hollywood. Loy, for her part, would come to represent a different use of the aesthetic: more ambiguous, more about commerce, less about liberation.

The use of ethnic motifs intertwined with, and parallelled, the use of women: transmuted into the exotic, ethnicity, now signifying the things it sold, belonged to the artist and the audience, not to the ethnic. The exotic included the internal colonial as well as the colonial; Edward Lucie-Smith refers to "the cult of the negro which swept the world of high fashion during the 1920s and 1930s."[30] As one can tell from Figure 4.3b, Josephine Baker is a prominent motif in Deco art. (Like other American modernists, Baker and jazz had to go abroad in order to become acceptable in the United States as "art." Figures like Baker represented a link between the orientalizing of Black culture and the decadence of exotic women.) While Art Deco had in common with Symbolism an almost complete disregard for socially responsible representation of ethnicity (or, most of the time, of anything else), its use of ethnic influences was pandemic: "examination of the style's standard repertoire of motifs . . . reveals influences from the world of high fashion, from Egyptology, the Orient, African tribalism and Diaghilev's Ballets Russes."[31] In fact, by stylizing the accoutrements of ethnicity, Deco allowed its audience to maintain a safe distance from it. While using the patina of exoticism to sell everything, Deco aestheticized colonialism. Like the woman's body, ethnic motifs themselves became floating signifiers because they were streamlined in such a way that their original frames of reference disappeared. In America, as a mass-merchandizing strategy, they became an extraordinarily efficacious way to bring a tourist's view of the world back to this country. The Deco version of oriental motifs shows no hint, for example, of discomfort with—or awareness of—Japanese empire-building in the 1920s and 1930s, or the struggle between warlords and communists in China, or the effects of various immigration exclusion and disenfranchisement laws practiced specifically against Chinese Americans and other Asian communities well into this century. Instead, stylization replaced the social realities of the present with the past.

Representation of "Third-World" culture, or any lower-class exotica, was of purely aesthetic concern. One of the most delightfully artless accounts of this delectation of the exotic lower classes by the Western upper classes, though about European rather than African workers, is contained in this description of couturière Elsa Schiaparelli: "She brought a sense of fun to fashion, and travelled far and wide in search of ideas for clothes. . . . After seeing old women in the Copenhagen fish market wearing newspaper hats, she had a fabric made with a newspaper print which she used for scarves, blouses and hats."[32] It made sense that Art Deco, the style of the wealthy or at least of twentieth-century upward mobility, retained in mass merchandizing the wealthy person's point of view, one inclined to see the Third World in an exploitatively decorative manner. Art Deco used the Third World to sell its products, but, more importantly, it purveyed a special, reified vision of the world as merely consumable.[33]

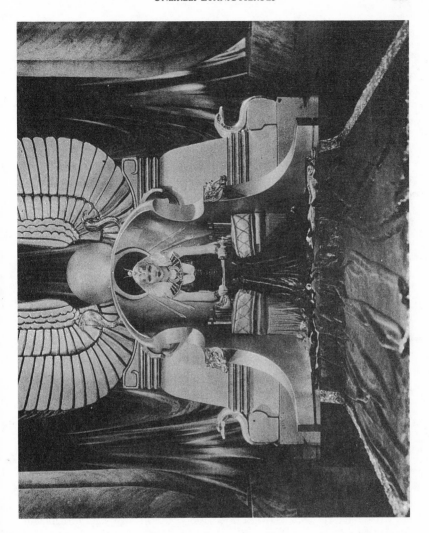

Figure 4.4 As spectacle, the filmic East is an orient devoid of political uncertainty. Whatever anxiety the narrative may contain, the story of Cleopatra is absolutely self-assured as visual presentation. *Cleopatra* (1934) © by Universal City Studios, Inc. Courtesy of MCA Publishing Rights, a Division of MCA, Inc.

Hollywood and Art Deco

Every observation Edward Lucie-Smith makes about the appropriative tendency of Art Deco is also true, film critics have noted, about Hollywood. Most film critics have noticed that the "classical Hollywood style" is a style of appropriation disguised as an art of decoration, an "apolitical" art with a decidedly conservative bent in its neoclassicism. Hollywood, especially the more upscale studios, tended to portray a classist vision of society. With some notable exceptions—film noir, for example—Hollywood tended to portray wealth and upward mobility rather than the plight of the working classes. More simply, Hollywood used the Art Deco trappings of wealth to sell Hollywood and Hollywood's vision of the world. Glossy Art Deco graphics became especially and appropriately associated, on the one hand, with the prestige studio—MGM—and on the other hand with the most traditionally "corporate" of the studios, RKO. And stars as well as sets were Deco-influenced, as if the studios picked stars who conformed to Deco style, or created them using Max Factor's Deco palette, which contained not only color but better-defined, harder, and more "streamlined" contours. Stars become generic Deco works, sculpturesque pieces, often self-created, as in the case of Joan Crawford.

Deco conservatism in representing the individual dovetailed nicely with Hollywood's need through the 1920s to remain noncontroversial. As a vehicle for reification, Art Deco, by importing films like L'Inhumaine (1923), was a perfect style for Hollywood, and indeed the influences were reciprocal: "Rather than attempting to impress the spectator with the status of the sitters, [Deco] portraits now concentrated on the idea that the image was the reflection of a superior personality, and showed a being from another world who had, just for a moment, condescended to make an appearance in this one. Glamour was the stock-in-trade of the Hollywood stills photographer, but also of the Art Deco portraitist."[34]

Deco Exotic, with its overtones of innocuous libertinism, tourism, and avant-gardism, so suited Hollywood that the industry continued to be dominated by it even after it had begun to wane as a fashion. By the time Loy arrived in the late 1920s Deco chinoiserie had become a cliché: it symbolized the way in which women were conspicuous consumers, willing to spend (men's) money on haute couture. As the 1920s rolled into the 1930s, Hollywood continued to portray Deco Asians in beautiful films such as Shanghai Express (1932), while women in the audiences were removing oriental baubles for more austere decoration. In the years of The Bitter Tea of General Yen (1933) and The General Died at Dawn (1936), the ornamental

Figure 4.5 Joan Crawford. Reproduced by permission of Culver Pictures.

quality of Poiret gave way to the "common sense" styles of Coco Chanel.[35] In film, therefore, it became easier to depict the orientalized woman as a villainess because anyone dressing that way was first passé and second an economic drain.[36]

The Hollywood Oriental Femme Fatale

What had Natacha Rambova seen in the nineteen-year-old Loy? While it must have been obvious that this woman was from Montana, Loy had been introduced to Rambova as an exotic performing in the *Thief of Baghdad* prologue (1924).[37] Loy was the perfect Deco subject: a white woman able to pretend to the role of oriental. Deco style seems to imitate Loy because Loy is a Deco mold, a Deco figurine in lines and poses.

Though not tall, the body is slim, alternately giving the appearance—in a sort of fort/da game—of both an anemic athleticism and a manipulative vulnerability so important to the 1920s woman. A Deco flapper: liberated in theory but constrained by binding brassieres that flatten breasts in a boyish, androgynous fashion. (The binding itself seems a vague displacement upward of the "oriental" binding of the feet.) In the 1930s, women who could afford plastic surgery bought the Myrna Loy nose because it was small. The physical operation had to be one of removing, of shearing away and diminishing.[38] (Ultimately, the Deco body sold itself into disappearance.) Loy is small, so she can be built on: clothes can drape over her, jewelry made to drip or drop off her. A young dancer in the days of Diaghilev, appearing in Poiret-inspired film prologues, scouted by Natacha Rambova, Myrna Loy is an Art Deco bibelot whose career originated as much in the Ballets Russes and the 1925 Paris International Exhibition of Decorative and Industrial Arts as in any real acting ability.[39]

In these "prologues," Loy had already begun living the crossover career Rambova had wanted. Loy became more successful in the later 1920s and 1930s, as Rambova's film career was on the wane. As a wealthier version of the same dynamic, Rambova must have seen Loy as a middle-class analogy to herself. In fact, Loy would make a success of the orientalized Deco persona because she would not be as threatening. The number of seminal silent and early sound films in which she appears, even with second or third billing, is astonishing: *Ben Hur* (1925), *Don Juan* (1926), *The Jazz Singer* (1927), *Noah's Ark* (1928), *The Desert Song* (1929), *A Connecticut Yankee* (1931), *Love Me Tonight* (1932). And in most of those films (the notable exceptions are *Love Me Tonight* and *The Jazz Singer*), Loy portrays a Deco exotic, from a black French waitress in *Ham and Eggs at the Front* (figure 4.7) to Morgan le Fay in *A Connecticut Yankee* (figure 4.10).

Figure 4.6 Myrna Loy is an Art Deco figure. Reproduced by permission of Culver Pictures.

208 AMERICAN LAUGHTER

Figure 4.7 The Deco exotic in blackface. *Ham and Eggs at the Front,* © 1927 Turner Entertainment Co., All rights reserved. Courtesy of the Academy of Motion Picture Arts and Sciences.

Of course Loy had been an exotic before her film career, a "chorus"·girl dancing in the live programs at Graumann's Egyptian: "I started at the Egyptian in the prologue for De Mille's first *Ten Commandments*. . . . The dance was supposed to be Egyptian to complement the picture's Biblical sequences, so we rehearsed all those square movements associated with ancient Egypt. We wore little pants and sort of Egyptian halters and headdresses."[40] Obviously Poiret-inspired, this "prologue" was like others in which Loy appeared; for *The Thief of Baghdad* Loy danced "barefoot, with skirts that whirled around and bells on [her] ankles"; still later she was a bacchante.[41] Even as a sixteen-year-old Loy had a Deco sensibility, creating her own costumes for local theatrical productions, mixing and matching motifs: the neoclassical (or Native American) headband, the slave bangles, the toe shoes, the conflation of all ethnicities into one. Loy played several variations on the flapper in her films, and several films feature her as a demimondaine, or in a specifically (and naughtily) Parisian setting (*So This is Paris* [1926], *New Morals for Old* [1932], *Topaze* [1933], *Love Me Tonight*). But it is as a Deco exotic that she is most often used in the early part of her career.

For 1920s and 1930s actresses Deco Exotic, an extremity of style—turbans, large costume jewelry, harem pants, and so on—became associated with comic types, prostitutes, and femme fatales, wasters of men's money and substance; loud dress was mercenary, narcissistic, or both. And Hollywood was particularly interested in the use of white women as exotics.[42] Hollywood's use of Loy is typical, if exemplary. It is possible to trace several strains of this exotic woman through the history of American genre films, from filmed melodrama to postmodern dark comedy; from Theda Bara in *A Fool There Was* (1915), to Marlene Dietrich in *Shanghai Express* (1932), to Shirley Maclaine in *My Geisha* (1962) to Phoebe Cates in *Princess Caraboo* (1994). Their particular ethnic designation is almost irrelevant in their films, or at least very subordinate to the quality of "exotica." One runs across some significantly bizarre entries: Ruby Keeler as "Shanghai Lil," for example, bewitching sailor James Cagney in a foreign port in *Footlight Parade* (1933). It is impossible to convey a sense of the complex bizarreness of that song, of Keeler's flat, nasal voice attempting an oriental accent through the patina of "cultivated" mid-Atlantic American, but by way of a New York Yiddish accent and syntax at moments when she pronounces such syntactic and dipthongal delights as "I miss you velly much a *long* time." The pleasure goes far beyond a connoisseur's delight in kitsch. This camp reverberates. Marlene Dietrich in *Kismet* (1955) and *Touch of Evil* (1958) does, respectively, neutralized Asian and Latina versions of her blue angel. In fact, the list of white women who play fantasy exotics as well as ethnic women who play alternative ethnicities is virtually endless. Mariann Oshana's *Women of Color: A Filmography of Minority and Third World Women,* an annotated bibliography of over 300 pages recounting minority characterizations in American film, contains a wealth of examples.[43] Her list includes a significant percentage of occidentals in exotic roles, including not only Rita Cansino (Hayworth) and Dorothy Kaumeyer (Lamour), but Gene Tierney, Katharine Hepburn, Loretta Young, Barbara Stanwyck, Yvonne De Carlo, Rhonda Fleming, Debra Paget, Maureen O'Hara, Suzanne Pleshette, Sylvia Sidney, Gale Sondergaard, and Judith Anderson.

Though the history of visual arts in the West is filled with examples of occidentals in exotic regalia (from English eighteenth- and nineteenth-century portraiture to *Lawrence of Arabia* [1962]), Deco is *specifically* designed to encourage the kind of slippage in signification that allows for the transformation of occidental into oriental. Where the model of a portrait plays at being oriental for a moment, the actor or actress *is* that oriental. Its floating signification allowed Deco orientalism to become a sign of the white woman as an exotic. Film stories almost never present a homogeneous Latino/a, Asian, or African culture but rather show the interplay between the white and the exotic, the attempt at assimilation of one or the other. Plots in films as different as *Bird of Paradise* (1932) and *Flying Down to Rio* (1933) both hinge on the desire to pair Dolores Del Rio with an Anglo-occidental. In *The Black Watch* (1929), miscegenation is sidestepped by asserting that Myrna Loy's Yasmini is really part white, being descended from Alexander the Great (a gambit used again in *The Man Who Would Be King* [1975]). Deco re-presents the low immigrant as high art. Where Powell is a fantasy about being white, Loy is a fantasy of punishment for not being white.

Without yet discussing the reason for the vision of all these occidentals in oriental garb, we might first give as one more proof of the significance of the phenomenon the fact that ethnic women, as a tendency, do not last as long as occidentals in top-billed positions. The list of women who remain for a moment in star positions, only to fade to black, or to parts for blacks, is several times larger than the list of top-billed white women.[44] To take one of the more dramatic examples: Anna Mae Wong had a rather long career (from 1920 to 1961). But though she was one of the most long-lived ethnic stars, her career as a major name stretched only from the late 1920s to the early 1930s, after which she played character roles, making only three films and some television appearances from 1942 to 1961. During the height of her popularity she played roles complementary or even subordinate to both Loy and Marlene Dietrich, who both went on to play exotic roles when Wong's career waned.

Figure 4.8 While both Myrna Loy and Anna Mae Wong begin as exotics, Wong's career wanes as Loy's waxes. *The Crimson City* © 1928 Turner Entertainment Co. All Rights Reserved. Courtesy of the Academy of Motion Picture Arts and Sciences.

Anna Mae Wong's version of Art Deco does not work because she is authentically Asian; history begins to creep back into her character with an unacceptable realism, a history that would, by the 1920s, include the Chinese Immigration Exclusion Act, the ill treatment of Chinese in the United States, the special exclusion of Chinese women, and the subsequent picture bride and prostitute phenomena. Like Rambova's, Wong's career must fade in a climate in which Loy's can flourish.

MYRNA LOY, MASOCHISM, AND THE EXOTIC WOMAN

Deco provides a vehicle within which whites can play out a fantasy of otherness, historically irrelevant to the authentic experience of ethnic alienation, under the rubric of "exotica." Filmmakers use the floating signification that exotic Deco affords its constituent elements in order to create safely fantastic versions of exotic terrains, a consensual fantasy for ethnics and nonethnics alike. But these worlds are displaced versions of more authentic ethnicities—the old country for the first generation, the old neighborhood for the second. The external reason for this displacement has to do with the ideology of the melting pot, or of that masterfully disguised version of segregation, the triple melting pot, both of which require the repudiation of earlier identities. The psychological (and hence, more subtly ideological) compensation for this political need to relinquish the neighborhood is a fantasy of a punishing white/exotic woman. If the Marx Brothers are a fantasy of pleasurable liberation from identity and guilt, then Myrna Loy and other actresses are the agents of a pleasurable expiation, a pleasurable suffering; in short, a masochistic pleasure. At this point, my argument will move to a schematic theorization of the role of the exotic in masochism, in order to justify the generalizing of a psychological process into a sociological one, carefully distinguishing between different psychological accounts (for example, Freud, who locates essential identification between the masochist and the father; and Gilles Deleuze, who finds the strongest identification between the masochist and the mother), choosing between them or offering an alternative, and, finally, carefully explicating the relationship between masochism and the filmgoing experience.[45]

First, let us add to the various etiologies and creation myths about filmgoing—Jean-Louis Baudry's connection of the filmic experience to Plato's allegory of the cave and Freud's dream screen, Bazin's myth of total cinema, and so on—the masochism of filmgoing.[46] Think of the filmgoer, bound and shackled to the seat of his[47] own volition as Baudry asserts, helpless in a mechanical process that proceeds mechanically with or without his assent. This filmgoer watches only what is on the screen, as the denizen of Plato's cave and the masochist watches what will happen to him,[48] and believes himself to be enjoying the experience.

To take the most straightforward description of masochism for a moment: Theodor Reik, deriving his operational paradigm from Freudian psychoanalysis (principally from "A Child Is Being Beaten") describes "the passive nature, the feeling of impotence, and the submission to another person, the cruel, humiliating, and shameful treatment by this person, and consequent sexual excitement."[49] Some of this description seems an intuitively correct account of the filmgoing situation, at least of the classical Hollywood variety: the passivity, the submission, and the sexual excitement. But the rest—the humiliation and shameful treatment—seems inimical to traditional descriptions of the filmgoing experience, most of which dwell on the feeling of power given the filmgoer, as if the camera were simply a prosthesis or weapon. At least this seems inimical until one remembers the originary milieu of early filmgoers: the nickelodeons and their disreputable aura and lumpenproletariat atmosphere. And even now filmgoing—especially Hollywood filmgoing—seems in some way shameful.

Reik refers to three distinct "characteristics" of masochism: fantasy, suspense, and demonstration. Of the three, demonstration is extremely tertiary, overlooked, as he admits, by most writers on the subject. Because it has to do with a kind of exhibition by the masochist, it does not really fit with any notion of audience, though it certainly would apply to the makers of film, whose lives are represented filmically and extrafilmically. But the other two characteristics are patently filmic: fantasy and suspense are themselves film genres. Add to this Baudry's sense of the filmgoer chained to his seat like the denizens of Plato's cave, and his general sense of the discomforts of the filmgoer, and one begins to perceive a certain plausibility in an otherwise unlikely argument. Even more important, if one contrasts to his sense of helplessness the masochist's ability to initiate the masochistic situation, remarked by all commentators, then the masochistic ambivalence in relation to power is even more pertinent to the situation of the filmgoer, whose power, as one of initiation, prosthesis, and mental focus, is similarly ambiguous.

Having for a moment cultivated the outrageous, I would like more modestly to maintain this line of inquiry as background to a specific argument. New-immigrant Hollywood ethnics create an anachronistic screen version of ethnicity in genre films about exotic lands and/or characters—one conspicuous feature of which is the punishing exotic woman—in order to enact a ritual of pleasurable self-punishment to which a large new-immigrant ethnic audience can respond. This genre I will call "exotic masochism."

To return to Reik for a moment as a way of charting the etiology of this response: of the two remaining characteristics of masochism, fantasy and suspense, the former is the most pertinent for my purposes, as well as the most important to Reik.[50] Of the three representative instances of masochism Reik recounts, two are overtly exotic (the last is about a visit to a butcher shop): one is about being sacrificed to "an ancient barbaric idol, somewhat like the Phoenician Moloch,"[51] and the other is introduced by a male client's asking a prostitute for "Russian Lessons."[52] (This last exotic reference, in one sense perfunctory, is curiously revealing as well. Reik asserts that "Russian Lessons" is a code: "The phrase is used in certain newspapers of [one patient's] country to advertise masochistic practices. In the patient's imagination the term connotes the terrors of pogroms and scenes in Russian prisons which he has read about."[53] In other words, marketplace masochism is envisioned as the anti-Semitic persecution that sent the families of the film moguls to America.) Putting aside for a moment the crucial questions of gender that are the focus of all psychoanalytic inquiry on the topic (for example, Can women be masochists?), one important quality of the masochistic scenario is thus its air of the exotic. That this is not merely a secondary quality is attested to by the fact of its pervasiveness in the literature, from Gaylyn Studlar's recent book on Marlene Dietrich, back to Reik, who continually if unconsciously returns to it when he refers to such phenomena as the "Aztec," "Marsyas," and "Laocoon" "cycles" of fantasy scenarios.[54] The first cycle begins: "An English officer has been captured by an ancient tribe of Aztecs," sounding precisely like the conceit of heroic imperialist genre films such as *Gunga Din* (1939), *She* (1935, 1965), and, most specifically, *King of the Khyber Rifles* (1954) or its 1929 avatar, *The Black Watch,* a Myrna Loy vehicle.

In the literature of masochism, the element of foreignness derives from anywhere; the writings of the eponymously seminal Leopold von Sacher-Masoch are perhaps the most fecund in this respect, exploiting Greek and Roman mythology and history, biblical stories, ethnic folklores of various kinds from Slavic to Jewish, and class differences.[55] Like practitioners of Art Deco, Sacher-Masoch eclectically uses motifs "from Egyptology, the Orient, [and] African tribalism."[56] His *Venus in Furs,* the prototypical text of masochism, compares its heroine to Salome, Judith, Delilah, Venus, Catherine the Great, the Amazons, Circe, and Lola Montez, all of whom would in one way or another be exotic to a Galician scholar. (Not to reiterate other excellent descriptions of the story of *Venus in Furs,* I will merely summarize it as the story of Severin, a man who seeks punishment at the hands of a woman,

Wanda, whom he tries to construct as exotically cruel. She adopts that exotic pose so well that, by the end of the novel, she utterly rejects her creator, converting him into an abuser of women.[57])

For reasons I will try to explain shortly, Hollywood presents a version of the dominatrix that resembles in several respects Sacher-Masoch's classic version, Wanda von Dunajew. As with Powell, I will take Loy as representative of a whole class of actors to whom I have referred or will refer in passing: designed and designing women constructed between the wars, from the 1910s and 1920s vamp (who, like Wanda, is ersatz exotic—Theda Bara, famously anagrammatized as "Arab Death"—and, who like Sacher-Masoch, is imported originally from the Carpathians: the vampire), to the interwar Anna Mae Wong persona. Loy plays the classic dominatrix in an era that desires her. Though she is not its star, one of her first films, alliteratively echoing Sacher-Masoch's famous novel, is called *Satan in Sables* (1925). Loy's exotics are even more the women of the Sacher-Masoch school than the Dietrich that Studlar brilliantly describes.[58] Like Severin's Wanda, Loy is redheaded, and her exotics wear furs. Among her more revealing roles is one she did not get: she was almost cast "as the ruthless trapeze star" in *Freaks* (1932), a role finally assigned to the Russian Olga Baclanova.[59] Loy did play orientals and other "exotics" in a significant percentage of her films.[60] These women are cruel and cold (to use Deleuze's words) in their "oriental" splendor.

Loy's dominatrices' power is frequently absolute. She is not a passive odalisque, even less a succubus; in her propensity for "coldly" manipulating men she often resembles the similarly capricious Empress Catherine of Sacher-Masoch's *Venus and Adonis*. Like Catherine she is sometimes (as in *Mask of Fu Man Chu* [1932] or *The Black Watch*) an oriental princess with a satrap's right and ability to sexually abuse her serfs and slaves.[61] These princesses carry whips or have the whipping done for them (*Mask of Fu Manchu, A Connecticut Yankee, The Black Watch*). Their power over the men who come to them seems either merely sexual (*The Squall* [1929]), or sexual and hierarchical (*The Black Watch, A Connecticut Yankee, Mask of Fu Manchu*). In those films in which she dresses or is made up exotically Loy acts with overt cruelty, as in *Thirteen Women* (1932), *The Black Watch, A Connecticut Yankee,* and *Mask of Fu Man Chu.*

Yet like Wanda, who vacillates back and forth between cruelty and kindness, Loy's cruelty is ambiguous: it may or may not hide an attraction for the victimized male, who is, like Severin to Wanda, ambivalently attracted to her. This ambivalence defines Loy as dominatrix rather than, strictly speaking, sadist (as Studlar and Deleuze assert about other women). In *The*

Figure 4.9 Myrna Loy in *Mask of Fu Manchu* © 1932 Turner Entertainment Co. All Rights Reserved. Courtesy of the Academy of Motion Picture Arts and Sciences.

Figure 4.10 Loy as the exotic dominatrix of Sacher-Masoch's fantasy seducing Will Rogers. *A Connecticut Yankee* © 1931 Twentieth Century Fox Film Corporation. All rights reserved. Courtesy of the Academy of Motion Picture Arts and Sciences.

Black Watch, for example, Loy/Yasmini temporizes with the life of Victor McLaglen/King long enough to get herself killed in the final reel. In these films Loy tends to be an object of simultaneous fear and fascination, a thing to be embraced warily, as in *The Black Watch* or *The Squall.* More often than not, she is destroyed by the man over whom she wishes to exert power.[62]

Who Creates Loy?

That Hollywood exotic Deco should be an imaginative version of various mother countries is surprising only because it erupts in popular culture. We find the same imaginative perversions less surprising when produced by high-culture expatriates: Nabokov's Nova Zembla, Joyce's Dublin, and Stein's America are all *nostoi* to land masses mapped more in the unconscious than on any firmer ground. In short, we should be surprised only at our own surprise that Sacher-Masoch's desire as a member of a cultural elite to represent ethnicity, and Hollywood's desire to repress the same, meet at some point in similar interests and technique.

Our surprise should abate even more in counting the connections between the sociology of the Hollywood moguls and that of Sacher-Masoch. In common with most Jewish immigrants, most of the moguls were from (or their parents were from) Eastern Europe, in or near Galicia. While Sacher-Masoch was not himself an immigrant, he was a citizen of Galicia, a region in which ethnicity was, if anything, more vexed than in America. Competing with ethnic strife were national considerations; Galician land was contested and/or appropriated by nearly every country surrounding it: Austria, Hungary, Poland, Russia, and Germany. Galicia had a ubiquitous Jewish population, and, though his portrayal of them in his most famous text is rather clichéd, Sacher-Masoch was evidently sympathetic to the plight of Galician Jews and had written, among his collections of folk stories, one called *Jewish Tales* that, according to Wanda von Sacher-Masoch, was favorably received.[63] Rightly or wrongly, Reik refers to Jewish masochism and Jewish self-hatred in his *Masochism and Man.*[64] According to Deleuze, Sacher-Masoch was involved in the Pan-Slavic movement, an attempt to allow Slavs of the various countries, pales, empires, and palatinates that made up the surreal chessboard of Carpathian geopolitics to maintain an autonomous national identity, or at least to identify with Russia as the hegemonic Slavic country.[65] Further, travel to foreign countries is, as one might expect, a dominant motif intimately connected to masochistic scenarios in both *Venus in Furs* and *Venus and Adonis.* As Wanda's cruelty and detachment increase, she and Severin (though unlike new immigrants because not economically motivated) become peripatetic, emigrating from Russia to Italy, with plans to settle in Turkey or somewhere further east. The reasoning is quite specific:

> "A golden dream . . . will never come true."
> "And why should it not be feasible?" I began.
> "Because slavery does not exist any longer."
> "Then let us go to a country where it does, to the Orient or Turkey,"
> I said eagerly. . . . "I want your power over me to become law."[66]

More specifically, at least two of the early film moguls—Adolph Zukor and Marcus Loew—were not merely, like many immigrants, clothiers, but furriers, spending some portion of their lives with Sacher-Masoch's primary fetish.[67] One can attach a psychic or economic significance to the adoption of this Old-World symbol of wealth and decadence. Finally, Reik discusses anachronism in the masochistic fantasy, a technique we have reviewed in relation to Chaplin and the Marx Brothers, but which is also present in the depiction of ethnicity in the Hollywood film more generally.

Though the film audience is construed as ethnic male in need of assimilation, its identification is with the maternal, not the paternal (as Deleuze, Studlar, and Silverman assert, against Freud and Reik). One may therefore valorize the observation that several (perhaps most) of the film moguls and much of the rest of Hollywood had, like the Marx Brothers, *luftmenshn* (airheads) for fathers and strong authority figures for mothers. One might further generalize that, unlike the traditional Anglo household in which the mother was hemmed in by the "cult of pure womanhood," several ethnic families—including Jewish, Italian, and African-American —asserted a primacy of place of the mother that was not a part of the Anglo ideology. Studlar's argument about the cross-dresser might then equally apply to the ethnic: "Like the wish and counter wish for fusion with and separation from the mother, the wish to become the opposite sex is an ambivalent one. The desire to cross the anatomical boundaries of gender identity may be interpreted as a primitive, literal representation of the wish to subvert the polarized gender-role stereotypes fostered by a patriarchal society."[68] The ethnic is also torn between two untenably polarized identities that, like the two genders, can be represented as primary social constructs.

As Deleuze's masochist attempts to escape patriarchy, so Hollywood and its audience submit to the exotic feminine as an ethnic escape from patriarchy. Because the exotic is represented as feminine, Loy's sexual loyalty is exogamous: the potential mate, as a white man, represents the betrayal of the feminine ethnic family to patriarchy. When Loy plays a half-caste, she represents miscegenation between white man and native woman, the only kind whose representation would be acceptable. Some of these films include *Cameo Kirby* (1930), *The Woman in Room 13* (1932), *The Black Watch,* and *The Barbarian* (1933). In the last she stresses the Egyptian birth of her mother; in *The Black Watch* she stresses her white heritage through Alexander the Great. It is as if Loy is a concave mirror, the upside-down reflection of an authentic history in which personal loyalty is to the ethnic family, while national interests oppose ethnic interests. That inverted image reflects a fantasy of evading the inevitable dichotomy between nation and ethnic home. Exotic Loy's ethnic family often *is* her nation—in *The Black Watch, Mask of Fu Man Chu, The Desert Song* (1929), and *Isle of Escape* (1930)— though this fantasy unity is ambivalently represented as villainous plots to conquer the world.

One may speculatively assert that the invention of an exotic dominatrix works as an economical conflation of politics and psychology: it represents the desire for the mother as the desire for assimilation. To be an immigrant or second-generation ethnic is to be outside both the realm and the parental realm. To be an immigrant is surely to be grabbed from the motherland and transported to the strange land in which one becomes an adult away from the parent. To be the child of immigrants is to be always confronting the notion of rejection by either the family or society.

But the axis of decadent exoticism and femininity is ambiguous: it both critiques and supports patriarchal and cultural hegemony. The obverse of the fantasy escape from Anglo and patriarchal hegemony is a kind of orientalism that reinscribes patriarchal structures. Linking ethnicity and femininity enables an aesthetic/psychic economy: the artist creates two targets of repudiation in one person. The historical justification for this economy is one early-twentieth-century intellectual tendency to link ethnicity and femininity as decadent influences. Bram Dijkstra, in discussing early-twentieth-century race ideology, asserts that

> The characteristic link between women and the "degenerate races," so apparent to Carl Vogt, also caught Weininger's attention. He insisted that Jews, blacks, and orientals had, through inbreeding or the inability to respond to evolutionary impulses, become effeminate and had consequently degenerated. Judaism, especially . . . "is saturated with femininity." Like women, Jews were unable to recognize the link between individual evolution and property, for, said Weininger, "property is indissolubly connected with the self, with individuality."[69]

Loy's *A Connecticut Yankee* illustrates this conjunction between Jew and woman. Loy, as the unmanning Morgan le Fay, dressed in a fantastic medieval lady's costume, "cold" manner, and cruel command, is again a Severin fantasy. In this film le Fay is allied to Merlin. But this Merlin looks and acts like a stage Jew, right down to some alchemical contraption on his forehead that resembles *tefillin*.

Of course their collusion is connected to the overthrow of the rightful, Anglo-American axis constituted by King Arthur and Boss Hank (Will Rogers, as archetypally American as one might fear). One will be coerced, the other seduced. Hank is in fact effeminized by Morgan's ambiguously real affection for him:

> *Morgan/Loy*: Bedeck him in fine raiments, in silk and velvet, and return him to me.
> *Hank/Rogers*: I like to do my own bedecking.

Hank is then obscured from the camera by a number of ladies-in-waiting, who proceed to "bedeck" him. For Edward Said, the desire to see the exotic is the desire to repudiate any extreme impulses in one's own person or culture.[70] This repudiation occurs for the new immigrants, who, in (at best) ambivalently embracing the ideology of assimilation, are further constrained to repudiate any of the habits with which earlier residents of America already identify them, in part by finding these film exotics exaggeratedly comic.

Of course it makes sense that the cruelest Loy characters are oriental in the strictest racial sense; Asians, furthest away geographically from America, and, for the most part, with the least geopolitical influence in the West, are the easiest targets. Further, Loy's most villainous Asian role—Fah Lo See (in *Mask of Fu Manchu*)—is specifically Chinese, arguably the most vulnerable of the new immigrants, with a history of racial oppression in this country in some ways worse even than the treatment of African Americans. Chinese women were an even smaller minority, because they were not allowed in any great number into the country.[71]

We Are All Second Generation

In summarizing Loy's very overdetermined meanings as a white woman playing exotics, one may ultimately assert that the structures of the ethnic dilemma imposed on ethnic filmmakers and audiences are refracted onto the audience at large, back into the culture. This refraction occurs in three ways.

First, as ethnic woman, Loy represents the revenge of the culture still and always left behind, revenge over the too-successful *appearance* of assimilation. In *The Squall,* gypsy Loy/Azuri ruins the lives of the landowners by seducing them away from their modern-dress wives and lovers, away from their poses as reasonable modern husbands. For the entire male audience— ethnic and Anglo-identified—she is the woman with whom one may transgress. But Loy also represents the punishment for that transgression.[72] In other words, the Loy exotic forces the larger audience to internalize as an orientalized sexual ambivalence the same structures of ambivalence and punishment the immigrant must feel.[73]

Second, as Anglo woman playing ethnic, Loy is a dominatrix punishing the desire to be Anglo, to be equal. Further, the fact of a white woman playing exotic indicates that the exotic woman represents not only the old but the new country. Though she is a version of the old country re-imagined by the implicated ethnic groups, her very exoticism also accurately represents the structures of exclusion and alienation to which ethnic groups are submitted in this culture. (Were all groups acceptable, all groups would be understood, and none would be exotic, which is to say, imagined.)

Though one might point to occasional filmic examples of Loy's exotics and demimondaines being accepted by other characters as "one of us" (for example, *Topaze*), it is her audience that understands best the white woman under the mask. Characters in the films do not generally know Loy's character is white, but filmmakers do, and so—because of fan magazines, publicity stills, and the like—do audiences. (Again, the critics' negative reviews of Loy playing native can adequately stand for all extra-filmic information. She is transparently playing a role.) The entire audience (or that portion that reads fan magazines), both minority and white, maintain a simultaneous focus on Loy as both white and not white and find that ambiguity desirable.

Third, as half-caste, Loy represents the obsessive—and finally apocalyptic—attempt and failure to be Anglo: the failure to assimilate, including the danger of miscegenation. The desire to unite "East" and "West," "white" and "dusky," and the thwarting of this desire, are the subjects of several Loy films. In *The Desert Song* her birth as a half-caste is Loy's/Azuri's defining feature; she is introduced in an intertitle by that characteristic. Again, she is in her own person the product of the attempt to amalgamate races. But again, in film after film (*The Desert Song, The Barbarian, The Black Watch, Thirteen Women*) she is the ocular proof that such attempts are generally doomed to failure—the mixing of the races breeds the femme fatale who can only visit destruction on the white woman who supplants her and/or on the white father who sired her. Playing the Javanese Ursula in *Thirteen Women,* Loy tries to kill all her racist sorority sisters. In *The Desert Song,* she tries to have her lover killed.

The plots of several of her films are, therefore, directly or indirectly, about Loy's attempt to find a way to fit into a hegemonic culture that rejects her; they are about her stance between two cultures for which (like Powell) she has divided loyalties. *The Black Watch,* for example, is the story of a woman who can embrace her English lover only at the expense of destroying the nearly emergent Indian nation she represents and leads. Of course, as in most of her films, Loy/Yasmini is also destroyed in the last reel. As a woman and ethnic in a patriarchal hegemony, she must be contained, but not before she has represented the two opposing cultures as equivalent and embattled forces. Films such as *The Black Watch,* derived from stories about European imperialism (*King of the Khyber Rifles*), become in America near-allegories illustrating the contradictions of melting-pot ideology. Loy/Yasmini, as Indian descendant of Alexander the Great, explains her near-hieratic interest in British officer King:

> *Yasmini:* There is a prophecy that when one of Alexander's line shall find a mate or deign to rule these tribesmen, that conquest will be fulfilled.
> *McLaglen/King:* So that is the reason these hillmen acclaim you as their goddess.
> *Yasmini:* I have looked long for that mate who would fulfill that prophecy. A leader, strong, brave, white.

Played out obsessively in several Loy films, this desire to fulfill the dictates of the melting pot—to have it both ways—would in the Loy persona have to await one more change, in which, transformed back into the white woman, she would be able finally to find "a leader, strong, brave, and white." This leader would be Nick Charles.

From Hammer to Anvil

The Loy we want to remember is not the dominatrix of the silent and early sound films, but the Nora Charles we construct retrospectively: genteel, soft-spoken, supportive, sympathetic, funny. Erasing the temptress, we remember only the wife and mother. Critics invariably discuss the limitations of Loy's earlier career—the succession of oriental vamp films—while, in fact, the earlier films contain a greater variety of roles than her films from *The Thin Man* on. (Loy played in nearly twice as many films—eighty—before

Figure 4.11 Myrna Loy as wife: genteel, sympathetic, supportive, white. *The Thin Man* © 1934 Turner Entertainment Co. All Rights Reserved.

The Thin Man as after—forty-three.) The very vehemence and universality of
the assertion that the later roles are broader suggests a broad critical repression. (Other industrial repressions are more subtle. Garbo cannot become a
mother figure, so she must quit films altogether. We take her reclusiveness
as the confirmation that her version of Deco will be erased.) At some point
the fantasy of the exotic dominatrix becomes unsatisfactory because (as Reik
asserts) a sense of reality creeps into the film or persona, so the fantasy
changes. But Loy will keep vestiges of her persona because of the coincidence
of the desire of both capitalism and ethnics within capitalism to retain,
transform, and suppress their respective histories. Humor, as discussed
earlier, is a tool for this appropriation, holding in tension the opposing
desires to remember and repress, here submerging, but not obliterating, the
masochistic scenario. The comedies foreground the humor of the masochistic scenario, while submerging its less assimilable aspects. As a result, Loy
comedies of the 1930s often lampoon their predecessors: *Topaze* and *Love
Me Tonight* satirize the melodramatic love triangle, while *The Barbarian*
satirizes orientalism.[74] A comparison of two films released the same year
(1932) reveals the way the transition works. Loy played both Valentine in
Love Me Tonight and Fah Lo See in *Mask of Fu Manchu* for MGM. She objected
to Fah Lo See as a sadistic and sexually voracious woman. But as Valentine,
a role she describes as a breakthrough,[75] she establishes her comic persona
by responding to a breathless request for medical help—"Valentine, Valentine, could you go for a doctor?"—with: "Yes, bring him in." For Valentine,
men are consumable, even comestible. In *Love Me Tonight* she is still the
"nymphomaniac" she does not want to play in Fah Lo See, but it is a comic
version. This fragment of Valentine's dialogue reveals the overtly aggressive
sexuality of Fah Lo See, but the controlling, voracious mulatto has not been
erased, but repressed. She remains a threat, however subliminal.

   Loy's new persona is a fantasy comprehending and appropriating its
previous self.[76] After her oriental sirens, the Loy persona becomes who Loy
always was—an Anglo—who now resonates an exotic note that has stopped
(ap)pealing. Her screen marriage to William Powell works like this: a white
woman who played oriental sirens becomes white again, marrying a Northern European-derived American who played Italian villains but who now
plays an urban white man of uncertain parentage. In the process two things
happen: the fantasy of perfect assimilation is, as with Powell, accomplished
again—the marriage of two ex-ethnics. And, as with Powell, the stain of
ethnicity now adheres to the character actors. This fantasy assimilation is
complete and satisfactory until after World War II, through six Thin Man
films and eight other films in which they appear together. In the process, the

meaning of the ideal romantic relationship and marriage is converted, for two generations of Americans at least, in the screwball genre.

As with the Powell persona, Loy's new persona is a control of the orientalized ethnic, but now with a gender spin. Gayatri Chakravorty Spivak asks, can the subaltern speak?[77] For Loy (and Garbo, Stanwyck, Davis, etcetera) the answer is that, when spoken even by ethnic men (perhaps especially then), the subaltern ethnic ultimately resolves into an Anglo-American because, as conceived by the male speaker, that is who she always was.

As with Loy's change from Anglo to exotic, Deco is the vehicle for this retrotransfiguration. Long after her sea change into the perfect wife, and well into the 1930s, Loy remains a Deco figurine. But, as with the last change, the Deco clothes and body allow a certain ambiguity in the meaning of the change so that, though Loy moves from "hammer" to "anvil," Deco is obfuscatory enough that the anvil retains some of the quality of the hammer. The ideal dominatrix becomes the ideal wife, while one wonders how much of the dominatrix is still implicit in this vision of wife.

The metamorphosis of Loy's persona does not require a great deal of elaboration because it follows rather closely the metamorphosis of the Powell persona. Though Loy plays a number of serious dramatic parts, the metamorphoses of her persona are, like Powell's, most often identified under the aegis of comedy, as a way further to displace the threat she embodies after the pleasure has disappeared.

As if to reveal her roots in Symbolism and Deco, Loy's transition films often make her French, even Parisian.[78] The ambiguity always implicit in the masochistic relationships intensifies at this time. Three films especially of her transitional period, *Topaze, Love Me Tonight,* and *New Morals for Old,* share the tactic of first opening with Loy in an ambiguous and incorrect light, though they do this in opposite ways. In the first Loy sequence of *Love Me Tonight* we take Loy to be a golddigger; she is really rich and merely asking for her own money. In the opening sequence of *Topaze* we take her to be the wife of Baron de Latour-Latour, when a casual remark informs us that she is his mistress. In *New Morals for Old,* Robert Young mistakes "Myra" for a French demimondaine when they meet. Because she has not yet spoken during his attempts to speak broken French to her when he (and we) first see her, we also do not know whether she is French. Loy's persona is gradually changing; the placement of Loy at the beginning of these films is meant to bank on the audience's presuppositions about her persona. Audiences should be surprised before the revelation of her character in *Topaze* and after in *Love Me Tonight.*

Sports **BOSTON AMERICAN** Comics

13 WEDNESDAY, JUNE 24, 1936

ANN MARSTERS IN HOLLYWOOD

Myrna Loy Off Screen Not at All Oriental, Just Nice

The Boston Evening American presents herewith the 18th story in a series of intimate glimpses into the life of filmland's capital—"ANN MARSTERS IN HOLLYWOOD." Miss Marsters is being given entree to all of the studios, and is writing her stories from behind the scenes in the land of make-believe. These stories will appear daily.

By ANN MARSTERS

Hollywood, Cal., June 24—In this land of glamorous girls and romantic young men, I have discovered again and again that the clear and simple fact is, "they aren't at all like that."

I mean—should you ask me if a certain star is REALLY as mysterious, as regal, as aloof as she appears on the screen, the answer would have to be—a thousand times "No."

At the moment I'm thinking, in particular, of Myrna Loy.

That name itself has a mysterious sound that goes very well with her slightly drooping eyelids and her slow, baffling smile. When she is alone, you might imagine her in a languid pose with a faint smile about her lips as she meditates on her own unguessable thoughts.

But what do you suppose she was doing when I first saw her? She was curled up on a sofa in her dressing room at Twentieth Century Fox studio, with her auburn head bent over a small loom.

She was weaving bright-colored yarn in and out, in and out. She was so intent upon her work that her lips were pressed together like a little girl's who is struggling over her arithmetic.

Freckled Face, Friendly Smile

I said hello, and she looked up and smiled—a wide, friendly smile. I saw a face that was vivacious and vivid—and there was not a trace of the "exotic" in her blue-gray eyes. There was a myriad of freckles beneath her camera makeup, and they were dotted generously over her arms and hands.

And she was dressed in the most unalluring way you can imagine—in a house dress and an apron.

I'm really not trying to destroy your illusions about one of Hollywood's foremost Glamour Girls. Myrna Loy is so much nicer and sweeter and more real than what your preconceived idea of her may be.

You would like her as a person—not as a mysterious being who has stepped from the land behind the moon.

Myrna herself laughs at the word "glamour."

"I don't believe there is any such thing," she said. "At least it has no substance, it's not a part of any woman's real personality. I know that that word has been woven around many actresses—but it's very easily brushed away when you get close enough to them, when you get to know them as they really are.

"Perhaps some women pose in their own lives—but I'm sure I couldn't, and I don't think it would be any fun at all."

Weaves and Weaves, Something Comes Out

Myrna laid aside her loom and put her yarn back in her work basket, where already there were several 4 by 4 squares of completed weaves.

"I haven't any idea what I'm making," she laughed. "But I like to do this to pass away the time between scenes. Perhaps when I get enough squares finished, I'll sew them all together and see what happens."

It was now "between scenes" of "To Mary—With Love," in which Myrna Loy will appear with Warner Baxter. It's the story of a married couple's troubles and how they are solved over a period of years.

"Warner Baxter and I go to the Dempsey-Tunney fight in the picture," said Myrna. "And it's not a fake—we see the actual fight."

It doesn't sound quite possible—somehow—but it is. Anything can happen in Hollywood, you know. At least, almost anything—and I learned that by a bit of movie magic, it is possible to reproduce any important event of the past 15 years and play modern actors and actresses against them.

Doesn't Like to Talk Just About Herself

But that's getting away from the subject of Myrna Loy. She doesn't, as a matter of fact, like to talk about herself. Not because she wants to appear mysterious, but because she is naturally a little shy.

You may have a delightful conversation with her—if you are prepared to do most of the talking. Myrna will keep on listening and smiling at you—and when says it slowly, in a soft, sweet voice.

She is more loquacious about her work than about anything else.

"I've been working steadily for weeks and weeks," she said, "and I love the type of roles I've been doing.

"For a while, you know, I was definitely 'typed' as a slant-eyed Oriental, and I think it would have killed my career before very long if I hadn't got away from it.

"I've been Chinese, Hindu, Javanese, Malayan, and heaven knows what. I used to think such roles were fun—and I even studied Oriental philosophy.

Continued on Page 24, Column 2

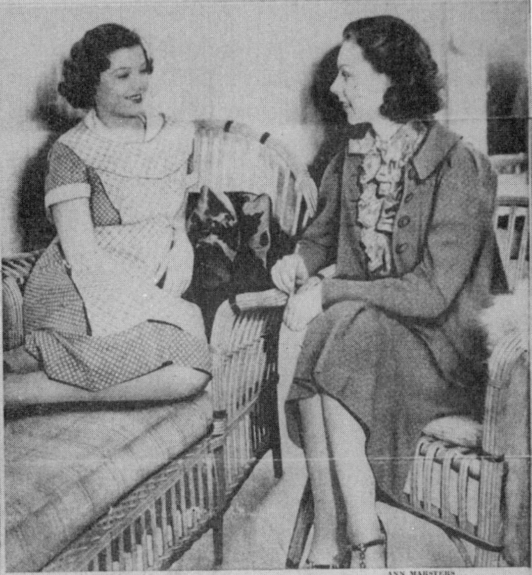

MYRNA LOY — ANN MARSTERS

Although she doesn't like to talk about herself, Myrna Loy does have an occasional word for her art, and Ann Marsters, Boston Evening American feature writer, enjoys her confidence in the star's dressing room at Hollywood. Work, then more work, is Myrna's keynote, but she didn't become sensationally popular until she essayed dramatic roles. Then her stock with film fandom went skyrocketing, Ann is told. Between scenes she weaves with a loom—what, she doesn't know—but it usually turns out to be something.

Lawmakers Ready To Quit Tonight

Lawmakers are picking up their desks in the State House today in anticipation of final adjournment tonight.

Principal piece of legislation awaiting their approval is Governor Curley's supplementary budget of $1,092,687.

Several amendments were proposed during Senate debate yesterday, but most of them were voted down.

The debate was marked by a sharp clash between Senator William A. Davenport of Greenfield and Senator Joseph C. White of Jamaica Plain over White's motion

Twin Daughters Put in Incubator

New Bedford, June 24—Weighing one pound and six ounces and one pound and two ounces, the twin daughters of Mr. and Mrs. Eli Margolis are in a special incubator in St. Luke's Hospital.

Born Saturday, the twins weighed a total of three pounds and two ounces, so now physicians and nurses are watching them carefully to help them win back their birth weight.

Their father owns a restaurant.

Cone Leads in Florida

Tallahassee, Fla., June 24 (INS)—Fred P. Cone, Lake City banker, was leading Judge W. Raleigh Petteway, of Tampa, by 39,841 votes early today in the run-off

Figure 4.12 As with Powell's, the transformation of Loy's persona is an acknowledgment that ethnicity is undesirable. Reprinted with the permission of the *Boston Herald*, June 24, 1936.

Like Powell, Loy contends with doppelgängers. Loy the oriental dominatrix is always contrasted to a sympathetic double—Irene Dunne, Ann Harding, Louise Fazenda, among others. Like Powell, Loy exorcises this persona by appearing as a contrast to other ethnics at various points in her career, becoming the Anglo doppelgänger who earlier haunted her. Loy's *Desert Song* is to *The Barbarian* and *Arrowsmith* (1931) as Powell's *Street of Chance* is to *Manhattan Melodrama*. While Powell is making *Street of Chance* Loy is making *The Barbarian,* in which she is a gentlewoman carried off by Arab Ramon Novarro, and *Arrowsmith,* in which she is featured as a rich New York widow stranded in the West Indies during a plague. Further, after Loy's metamorphosis, her doppelgängers echo her original roles. The Thin Man films almost always contain a woman who is either ethnic or who is hiding a background at odds with her present position. Though the parts tend to be small, the actresses are notably talented. In *Shadow of the Thin Man* (1941), Claire Porter (Stella Adler), a woman of refinement caught among gangsters, is revealed by Nick to be a swindler. As their conversation proceeds, her accent degenerates from cultivated mid-Atlantic to something derived from a rawer clime, perhaps the Lower East Side. As he leaves her apartment, Nick comments, "Don't look now but your accent is showing." In *After the Thin Man* (1936) the demimondaine chanteuse is "Asian" (Penny Singleton, about to suffer *her* sea change). *Another Thin Man* (1939) contains another such woman, Dorothy Walters (Ruth Hussey), as well as an odd, revealing twist in which, after the genteel daughter of C. Aubrey Smith is unmasked as her father's murderer, *her* accent slips into that of a gangster's moll. Even when the upbringing is good, the accent reveals the true origin of the killer.

The year before *The Thin Man,* Loy's demimondaines are more sympathetic—in *Penthouse* (1933) and *The Prizefighter and the Lady* (1933)—while in 1934 she begins to play a string of unassailably good women: in *Night Flight* and *Men in White,* for example. In several of these and similar films Loy, like Powell, becomes comedic. But the comedy is more equivocal: Loy relinquishes power in relinquishing her ethnicity, but only with a struggle.

As the comedic Loy of the early 1930s resolves into the atavistic spouse of William Powell, her purpose becomes clearer: to reclaim the history of the ethnic woman while making accessible the white woman, both of whom must be overcome in some fashion by her somewhat less than reputable husband/lover. She is, in other words, a controlled version of the ruling mistress disguised as its opposite—the caring wife. Every emotion that seems true in Fah Lo See is feigned in Nora. Her indifference to Nick's fate ("I wouldn't be a widow long") and her coldness (again, Deleuze's word) hide an intense affection. Her desire to control is really a desire to compete at his level. Her attractiveness to men is merely a sign of both Nick's power and her fidelity to him. Her jokes at his expense are signs of love.

Nick's and Nora's too-slight disparity in social standing in the Thin Man films obscures the need to make the inaccessible white woman accessible. Because class disparity is more greatly emphasized in Powell's and Loy's non-Thin Man films, the motif of the accessible/inaccessible woman is more readily apparent. In *I Love You Again,* an ex-con man re-wins the heart of a dissatisfied small-town wife; in *Double Wedding,* a bohemian wins the heart of the businesswoman; in *Love Crazy* (1941), a husband suspected of philandering wins back his wife. Even Loy's films with other leading men— *Wife vs. Secretary, Test Pilot* (1936, 1938, both with Clark Gable), and *Lucky Night* (1939, with Robert Taylor)—all have her reenacting the thaw of the dominatrix.

In Loy's ethnic films, the hero becomes double, descends in his affection for her, risking miscegenation and ethnicity while ultimately reaffirming his whiteness by repudiating her in the last reel. In the Powell-Loy films Loy remains the unified object that tests the duality of the Powell persona. Only this time the man ascends to meet her, sloughing off his ethnicity, again reaffirming his cultural centrality. She still serves to reaffirm the cultural centrality of the white man, not this time through being repudiated, but by accepting him. Though she seems to have more power in the later films, this is a sentimentalization: she has the power only to accept or to repudiate Powell. And, given the limits of the screwball comedy, even this is not a choice.

Still, the diegetic control of the woman is ambiguous in the screwball comedy because it contains trace elements of the masochistic relationship, remarked by all scholars, in which the man must ritually humiliate himself, so that Powell spends a significant amount of time wooing his wife while in drag in *Love Crazy.* Nora/Loy remains vestigially a dominatrix, spending much of *The Thin Man* testing her husband for a sublimated, cultural potency. The sadistic sensibility remains vestigially as a sense of humor that is often about her husband's death:

> "How did you like Grant's Tomb?"
> "I loved it. I'm having one built just for you."

But the comedy changes the polarity of Loy's domination. It allows the substitution of a neo-construct for a construct, the perfect wife for the femme fatale, the ambiguous sadistic masochist for the ambivalently masochistic sadist, the anvil for the hammer. Nora's neutralization as the Thin

Man series progresses is the continuation of a dynamic that has been occurring in her transition from vamp to wife. From the mid-1930s on, she is no longer the mover of events but rather the ironic commentator on those events, the wooed rather than the wooer. As the comedy of the West rises when the West passes, so Loy becomes more comic as her roles become more harmless. It is perhaps noteworthy that the bulk of her ethnic roles are played out at Warner Brothers, the more hardboiled of the studios, while the perfect wife years occur at MGM, the more soft-focus studio. She dissolves from goddess of a dangerous exoticism into the hearth-goddess of a neutralized domesticity until, by *The Best Years of Our Lives* (1946), she presides over an empire of impotence.

CONCLUSION: TOKEN MISCEGENATION

The much-remarked resolution between disparate classes in the comedy of remarriage seems far less remarkable when, in remembering the Hollywood tabloids that contextualize the films and actors, one realizes that audiences understand lead actors and actresses always belong to the same world of glamour. Leading man and lady are united in spite of class differences because they really belong to the same representational world. As Stanley Cavell asserts (if in a slightly different context), these people have known each other before. This hermetic unity of the leads has as its obverse the character actors, whose meaning is limited to the meaning they carry for the leads. The differences in representation (not to mention pay scale and other indices of power in the industry) between character actor and romantic lead are structured by an immigrant industry as a reinforcement of and gloss on the way our culture historically represents immigrant and ethnics. Just as Powell, in *Manhattan Melodrama,* is supposed to represent the kind of persona that can escape the ghetto of representation, so the marriage between Powell and Loy represents the margin of tokenism within which assimilation is permitted. In short, the relationship between lead and character actor reproduces the politics of tokenism.

To use the Charles marriage as paradigmatic of the relationship between lead and character actors: for Nick and Nora Charles, Cavell's sense of characterological foreknowledge has specifically ethnic implications. As already observed, the Charleses' is a mixed marriage, miscegenation between an oriental vamp, an Italian-American gangster, a half-Egyptian American tourist, a Russian Bolshevik Hollywood director, an African-American *jeune fille,* a George Eliot Italian stage villain, a South Seas siren, an Anglo from

Montana, and so on—a sort of two-person League of Nations. As such they are an ideal of successful assimilation: even more than Hollywood itself, they are not merely constituent elements of a larger society; they *are* that larger society, complete with an independent economy (they are wealthy during the Depression), diplomatic relations with other classes and nations (from the extremely wealthy to the lumpenproletariat), and—since the conceit of the films is that Nick is a detective—the means for internal policing. Most important, however, they have a shared language, understood only by themselves, consisting of insults and hidden codes.

However, the insistent repetition of jokes about fidelity and money reveals these subjects to be sources of anxiety. There is always some comic ambiguity about Nick's current faithfulness to Nora. In *Another Thin Man*, when Nick jokes that a phone call means a tryst with a mysterious woman, Nora remarks that she does not know why she always assumes he is joking. Friends and acquaintances who do not know Nora assume that she is a mistress and not his wife; they promise to keep Nick's philandering with her a secret. The marital tension engendered by Nick's premarital sexuality also remains a part of that running joke. Acquaintances drop hints to Nora about Nick's previous life, making her extremely curious.

A similar dynamic holds true of Nick's relation to his wife's wealth. He jokes about his reasons for marrying her, always maintaining that he married for her money:

> *Nora*: You know, that sounds like an interesting case. Why don't you take it?
> *Nick*: I haven't time; I'm much too busy seeing that you don't lose any of the money I married you for.

(The parody of the Thin Man characters in *Murder by Death* [1976] has the Nick Charles character run completely through his wife's fortune.) Nick's jokes about Nora's wealth are, like jokes about Nick's origins and his sexuality, simultaneously obscurantist and revelatory. The source of the wealth is a source of mild discomfort that is assuaged by comedy.

The attempt to erase anxiety about money and fidelity through linguistic irony is only partially successful because, like all such evasions, the strategy always recalls what it attempts to erase. Another, more visual attempt at such erasure is a characteristic cultural response to ethnicity. The world of the character actors provides the climate within which the relationship is worked out, and made a metaphor for assimilation in corporate America. The Charleses inhabit identically glamorous worlds only because the character actors constitute a background for that glamour, shouldering the burdens of eccentricity repudiated by the lead characters.

These burdens, shared by wealthy and poor figures alike, suggest that there is not nearly as much difference between the groups as critics traditionally suggest. We know that the two screwball protagonists, most often derived from two different worlds, are represented by the two distinct groups—poor and rich, stuffy and free, powerful and powerless. But often, there exists a compulsion visually to force those two groups together, as in the Christmas party the Charleses throw, in which the Wynants and Nora Charles are thrown together with the fight promoters and small-time hoods that Nick invites. (Of course one group is going to be feminine and one masculine, because the groups are always identified with their respective protagonists, but the values associated with femininity and masculinity change from film to film.)

The identification of the protagonist with his or her respective group almost always illuminates and intensifies, for a while, his or her difference from his or her romantic counterpart. The group serves as an alternate avenue from the love affair. It often, for example, includes the buddy, or, for the female lead, the other, older woman, so that homoerotic undertones conflict with the heterosexual romance. But the dichotomy is often, perhaps usually, illusional—the important members of the group are sympathetic to the opposing protagonist, as in It Happened One Night (1934), Ball of Fire (1942), Woman of the Year (1942). Thus, because screwball comedies attempt different strategies to force disparate classes and societies into each others' company, they tend to be thematically about a heterogeneous culture trying to become homogeneous but physically and visually about a homogeneous culture trying to appear heterogeneous.

However, if the differences between the two protagonists and between their groups prove largely illusional, there is another difference that is extremely important. The two subordinate groups of character actors have more in common than not and are to be differentiated from the group composed of the leading protagonists. The differences in class between the two groups are counteracted by our sense that they both belong to the same underclass of character actors, a class with physiognomic and behavioral features that, as I have already suggested, sets them apart from the protagonist class. The members of the groups are as a tendency not as photogenic as the leading protagonists. Physically, the protagonists are almost always specimens of perfect health and beauty: the broad chest and black hair of Clark Gable, the litheness of Carole Lombard, the facial beauty and physical trimness of Katharine Hepburn, the robustness of Cary Grant. In other words, the same externalized kinds of characteristics—the same cartooning and caricaturing—meant to distinguish the physical and intellectual inferiority of the ethnic (say Thomas Nast representing the popish menace) from the intelligent progressive American are used to distinguish the character actor from the leading characters.

We can consciously identify more closely with the protagonists not only because they are more attractive but because they seem more whole, less like exaggerated eccentrics than the character actors. Attractiveness and wholeness characterize the superiority of the protagonists over the character actors. Not that the protagonists are without their own eccentricities, but this behavior is safely contained in generally attractive persons or personalities. This manic behavior, because it appears in Cary Grant or Carole Lombard, is something that the audience would like to emulate because it seems clever rather than ridiculous. It is ridiculous behavior undercutting an ideal exterior, the sum total of which presents us with the illusion of a psychologically complex person. The eccentric behavior of the character actors, on the other hand, merely repeats the eccentricity of their physical appearance. These character actors develop in as exaggerated a manner as they do because of the fear that their exaggerated qualities still exist in latent form in both the protagonists and the American audience.

The "realistic" stage or cinema comedies of other countries do not axiomatically include characters as exaggerated as American character actors. In British "little comedies," for example, eccentric characters are given their own genres; so too in puppet theater, *folies*, harlequinade, commedia dell'arte, French bedroom farce. But American comedy tends to place its exaggerated versions of life in the same films as its idealized versions as if, on the one hand, it fears to allow the idiosyncrasies fully to exist in the ideal characters, and on the other, as if it is afraid to sever completely those idiosyncrasies from the world in which the main characters exist because such a truncation would entail too great a falsification of that world. (The early Thin Man films contain a scene in a cabaret or club or dive that has some ethnic "flavor." In the first film it is Studsy Burke's Irish dive, in the second it is a Chinese night club, and so on.) So the screwball world is split into idealized character and ridiculous character as much as it is into rich and poor, good and bad (and these latter designations more often than not coincide with that of idealized/ridiculous). A split identification occurs in which unconsciously we are forced to credit the possibility of ourselves as eccentric as much as we consciously would like to credit ourselves as ideal. This split is much like that which the immigrant and the children of immigrants must face in this country: a choice between the laughably old and the ideal new, the well-dressed American and the comically accoutered and accented foreigner. Of course the choice in the films is not really a choice. We must identify consciously with the protagonists. They have all the money, power, and fun. But the two groups still represent alternatives that are parallel to the immigrant choices because the immigrant also really has no alternative. In a culture that defines social acceptance as rejecting part of one's identity—the ethnic part—then the alternative is really not between retaining ethnic identity or Americanizing oneself, but between successfully or unsuccessfully assimilating. In other words, the choice between two modes of adjusting to mainstream culture is set up in such a way that the audience's choice has been predetermined. There really is no contest between Barry Fitzgerald and Cary Grant, or between Marjorie Main and Irene Dunne. The character actors are not merely adjuncts to the plot, then, but tools for assuring that the audience will, no matter what the peculiarities of the lead characters, make the right identification.

The opposition group/romantic couple is a fantasy of an easy choice because the films see even this choice as spurious, since the romantic other and the group are placed in an apparent opposition that is belied by more fundamental ideological similarities: shared nostalgia for childhood (the two opposing fathers in You Can't Take It With You [1938]), shared assumptions about the benevolence of a paternalistic society (Peter Warne and Mr. Andrews in It Happened One Night). In other words, assimilation of one group into another is not really necessary because all groups are, in all important ways, already alike.

Finally, the separation into two groups—leading and character—one of which, fictionally, has derived from the other, lends a sense that assimilation is inevitable, if limited in scope. After all, the significant time we spend with the charismatic leads assures less time spent with the character actors. This is an elitist vision of success, in which only two persons can succeed, while others (like Carlo in My Man Godfrey) fail conspicuously. In a very direct way, this vision of assimilation into American culture is historically real. The number of ethnics in our culture who succeed is also tokenist, probably in an even greater ratio than portrayed in film. But, more important even than the fact that the films reflect in a distorting lens the historically real, is the fact that temporal representation of characters in a film genre is, from the beginning, structured by an ethnic sensibility. The length of the celluloid strip devoted to a particular character is in direct proportion to that character's ability to assimilate.

— ◆ —

CONCLUSION

If, as Judith Mayne articulates on behalf of most film scholars, it is true that cinema is "an extension of the nineteenth-century realist novel into the realm of the image and sound,"[1] the Hollywood version of *Oliver Twist* was read by Minnie Marx, produced by Lewis Selznick, written by Leopold Sacher-Masoch for the screen, and acted in by Gallagher, Shean, and Paul Robeson. All the parts are cast to the "wrong" actors: Fagin is played by William Powell, Oliver by Chico Marx, Bill Sykes by Charlie Chaplin, and Nancy by the daughter of Fu Manchu.

And if Félix Guattari and Gilles Deleuze are correct in asserting that minority literatures are characterized by deterritorialization, politicization, and collectivization, then Hollywood film comedy has about it the aura of a minority literature.[2] Further, the aura of the minority overarches all aspects of the industry: the classical Hollywood style, the studio system, even the dialectic created between the studio system and the independent filmmaker, conceived as outsider against insider. (That this dialectic remains after the studios themselves have all but disappeared is proof enough that the structure and the intention outweigh their concrete embodiments.)

Evidence of the absorption with ethnicity is everywhere in Hollywood three quarters of a century after the end of new immigration. The classical Hollywood style continues to mix its ethnic metaphors in now traditional ways: containing African-American actors (Eddie Murphy, Richard Pryor) in genre films and roles created for white actors;[3] creating fantasy landscapes that work either as overt allegories of race (*Alien Nation* [1988], *Blade Runner* [1982]), or as displacements of ethnicity (*The Neverending Story* [1984], or any fantasy in which a contemporary sensibility intrudes on an archaic society). We now call this pastiche of elements postmodernism, itself a style characterized by a leveling of all constituent styles. But this leveling was the thrust of the immigrant and ethnic filmmakers' version of culture; for these filmmakers, all cultures were to be valued equally, both because the codes, only newly known, were only partially understood, and because of their desire to dehierarchicalize for the sake of self-promotion. Postmodernism at national and international levels finds its origin in the immigrant and ethnic desire to diminish the value of social hierarchy.

It is not just a matter of an Italian- or Japanese-American inhabiting the place an Anglo used to occupy. Rather, the interesting question is how ethnicity continues to redefine the culture with every succeeding wave of immigrants, every new valuation of ethnicity. The Hollywood version of American ethnicity—that black men can inhabit contemporary white genre roles, or that ethnic Americans were always interested in becoming some normative version of Americans (*The Godfather* [1972], *Mobsters* [1991], *Ragtime* [1981]),[4] should be examined equally with the more independent, confrontational cinema of Spike Lee and Julie Dash, which claims a separate film aesthetic for a separate culture.

Ethnicity as a structuring device can be seen everywhere still in standard Hollywood film genres, and not only because most of those genres came into existence at the formative moment during which urban immigrants and ethnics still comprised the largest audiences of film. Ethnicity informs the logic of horror films, from the unconsciously racist allegory of King Kong as African American to the very self-conscious allegories of *Alien Nation* or *Enemy Mine* (1985). The most significant commentators on the Hollywood musical discuss how that genre is almost always a false avenue for establishing community, cynically playing on the audience's desire to belong to the community of the film, always discussing the repression or appropriation of differences.[5] The gangster film is already being examined elsewhere as a ground for displaying ethnic difference,[6] though this is a late move, considering that since at least *The Godfather* gangster films have been foregrounding not only ethnicity but also how ethnicity structures the genre, for example in referring to previous texts in which ethnicity played an important role. (John Singleton's African-American *New Jack City* [1991] refers to Brian De Palma's Cuban-American *Scarface* [1983], which in turn refers to Howard Hawks's Italian-American *Scarface* [1932].)[7] In their reliance on a breathtaking number of Italian, Italian-American, and foreign-film cultural codes (Machiavelli, subtitling, classical Roman history, Mafia semiotics) Francis Ford Coppola's first two Godfather films can only be understood as attempts to recreate their audiences as Italian-American. One might even account for the western genre's tendency to view the world as split between insiders and outsiders less as derived from Natty Bumppo's antisocial tendencies and more as a strategy of sublimated expression for audiences and filmmakers for whom social acceptance is a foregrounded anxiety. The recent rediscovery of the independent African-American cinema of the 1910s through the 1940s, and its concomitant alterity to the classical Hollywood codes, will inevitably lead to theorizing about the constructional quality of the African-American film presence.

The assertions made in this book about one medium are equally true of other media. In *Crashing the Gates,* Robert C. Christopher ties together some of these media: politics, industry, entertainment.[8] His work is a good beginning because it acknowledges an ethnic presence in American self-representation. But the effects of that presence are still to be weighed. American popular culture must continue attempting to absorb ethnic variety, from overt political repression to representation in the fashion industry ("[Christy] Turlington is not blond, blue-eyed or all-American-looking. Photographer Arthur Elgort calls her combination of blue-green eyes, dark hair, olive skin and remarkable cheekbones 'unspecified ethnic,' which gives her a broader appeal").[9]

In the end, no account of the structure of any medium of expression in America, perhaps especially the Hollywood film, will be able to leave out the originative importance of the ethnic and the immigrant. The most significant theorist for the reading of the ethnic and immigrant voices in culture will probably be Mikhail Bakhtin, whose notions of heteroglossia and dialogism—notions about the multiplicity of voices at various levels of signification—lend themselves well to the authentic "Hollywood babel." Though like most formalist film theories, however, it is not particularly interested in ethnicity, Robert Stam's very complete account of Bakhtin and film is tailor-made for interpreting ethnicity: "Bakhtin foregrounds the human capacity to mutually 'author' one another, the ability to dialogically intersect on the frontiers between selves."[10] A moment later, Stam describes a Bakhtin who sounds as if he is himself describing the Marx Brothers' *landsmannschaft*: "One becomes 'oneself' not by shedding others to disinter an originary essence, but rather by revealing oneself to another, through another, with another's help." Stam's filmic Bakhtin is interested in "layering of meaning upon meaning, voice upon voice."[11] But except for some very few pages on Brazilian cinema and individual films like *Sweet Sweetback's Baadasssss Song* (1971), Stam is not really interested in ethnic voice per se, except as a class phenomenon.[12] As yet an enormous amount of work remains to be done in theorizing the interrelation between filmic representation and the various ethnic groups that constitute the different voices and positions in and out of the classical Hollywood style.

Perhaps the most important work will have to do with "reappropriation" by implicated ethnic groups. As with the Egyptian takeover of dynastic cultures, the Greek erasure of Minoan culture, the Roman revision of Greek gods, and the medieval appropriation of Roman and Byzantine rites, the contemporary industrial West has not been influenced, nor even metamorphosed by the cultures it has appropriated, but invented by them, created by cultures whose prior existence has been the precondition for its own heterogeneous avatars. However, the modern folk whose cultures have been appropriated may—unlike, say, first-century Greeks— reappropriate their culture because of folk and popular culture's persistence in a media culture not so easily destroyed by fire and salt. The interesting questions will have to do with whether or not cultural artifacts warped out of all visible recognition as ethnic can be reabsorbed, and whether such reabsorption is worthwhile.

NOTES

INTRODUCTION

1. Foster Rhea Dulles, *America Learns to Play: A History of Popular Recreation, 1607-1940* (New York: D. Appleton-Century, 1940).
2. "[T]he character of [America's] amusements, in so far as the urban population was concerned, could not but cause serious misgivings" (Dulles, 229).
3. "Recreation became a primary concern of the twentieth-century social movement to reform the evils of urban life" (Dulles, 227).
4. Jill Norgren and Serena Nanda argue convincingly that even the genteel ideal of equality in American law militates against diversity: "The spread of the norm of equality has made egregious forms of subordination illegitimate" (*American Cultural Pluralism and Law* [New York: Praeger, 1988], 8).
5. In the second chapter of *The Decline and Fall of the Roman Empire,* Edward Gibbon refers to the extension of Roman hegemony across Europe and Asia: "It was by such institutions that the nations of the empire insensibly melted away into the Roman name and people" (Edward Gibbon, *The Decline and Fall of the Roman Empire* [New York: The Modern Library, 1932], 25-26). Elsewhere, Anthony H. Birch, in *Nationalism and National Integration* (London: Unwin Hyman, 1989), refers to the nineteenth-century version of hegemonic extension. He quotes John Stuart Mill on representative government: "Nobody can suppose that it is not more beneficial to a Breton . . . to be a member of the French nationality . . . than to sulk on his own rocks, the half-savage relic of past times"(39).
6. Marxist and neo-Marxist accounts tend to place ethnic and nationalist revivals in the hands of an educated intelligentsia. See, for example, Miroslav Hroch, *Social Preconditions of National Revival in Europe: A Comparative Analysis of the Social Composition of Patriotic Groups among the Smaller European Nations,* trans. Ben Fowkes (Cambridge: Cambridge University Press, 1985), whose analyses of nationalist "patriots" tend to favor the notion, for example, that

activist students came from "families of artisans and merchants. Less than a fifth of them came from peasant families" (53).

7. Richard Butsch's work, though in many ways useful, still offers a fairly classic account of the critique of hegemony in entertainment studies:

> Hegemony varies in strength; it is never total, secure, complete but is susceptible to attack, degeneration, undermining, displacement. . . . A group of children playing a street game without standardized equipment, grounds, or rules have greater power over their leisure practice (which is thus less hegemonic) than do children playing in a Little League game, whose equipment, organization, and rules are specified by centralized and commercial authorities.

("Introduction," in Richard Butsch, ed., *For Fun and Profit:The Transformation of Leisure into Consumption* [Philadelphia: Temple University Press, 1990], 8). Players can be greater or lesser victims of hegemony, but not its controllers. And though Butsch mentions some "resistance" by women, he is virtually uninterested in ethnic resistance, mentioning the Yiddish theater only in passing.

8. Wayne Franklin, *Discoverers, Explorers, Settlers: The Diligent Writers of Early America* (Chicago: University of Chicago Press, 1979), 179. The critics with whom he finds fault are themselves almost canonical: Sacvan Bercovitch (*The Puritan Origins of the American Self* [New Haven, CT: Yale University Press, 1975]), David L. Minter (*The Interpreted Design as a Structural Principle in American Prose* [New Haven, CT: Yale University Press, 1969]), and Richard Slotkin (*Regeneration Through Violence: The Mythology of the American Frontier, 1600-1860* [Middletown, CT: Wesleyan University Press, 1973]).

9. See, for example, Benjamin B. Ringer and Elinor R. Lawless, "The 'We-They' Character of Race and Ethnicity," in *Race-Ethnicity and Society,* ed. Benjamin B. Ringer and Elinor R. Lawless (New York: Routledge, 1989), 141-44.

10. Barbara Christian, "The Race for Theory," in *The Nature and Context of Minority Discourse,* ed. Abdul R. JanMohamed and David Lloyd (New York: Oxford University Press, 1990), 40.

11. Althusser asserts:

> And just as any "history" which does not work out the concept of its object, but claims to "read" it immediately in what is visible in the "field" of historical phenomena, is still willy-nilly tainted with empiricism whether intentionally or no, any "political economy" which goes to the "things themselves," i.e., to the "concrete," the "given," without constructing the concept of its object, is still willy-nilly caught in the toils of an empiricist

ideology and constantly threatened by the re-emergence of its true "objects," i.e., its objectives (whether these are the ideals of classical liberalism or those of a "humanism" of labour, even a socialist one).

(Louis Althusser and Etienne Balabar, *Reading Capital,* trans. Ben Brewster [London: NLB, 1970], 183).

12. Fredric Jameson, *The Political Unconscious: Narrative as a Socially Symbolic Act* (Ithaca, NY: Cornell University Press, 1981), 20. Without meaning to, Jameson almost incidentally formulates the problem of ethnic representation with some elegance: "Pluralism means one thing when it stands for the coexistence of methods and interpretations in the intellectual and academic marketplace, but quite another when it is taken as a proposition about the infinity of possible meanings and methods and their ultimate equivalence with and substitutability for one another"(31).

13. Terry Eagleton, *Criticism and Ideology: A Study in Marxist Literary Theory* (London: NLB, 1976), 43.

14. Lary May, *Screening Out the Past: The Birth of Mass Culture and the Motion Picture Industry* (New York: Oxford University Press, 1980); and Orlando Patterson, *Slavery and Social Death: A Comparative Study* (Cambridge, MA: Harvard University Press, 1982).

15. Michel Foucault, *The History of Sexuality,* vol. 1: *An Introduction,* trans. Robert Hurley (New York: Pantheon Books, 1978).

16. John Murray Cuddihy, *The Ordeal of Civility: Freud, Marx, Levi-Strauss, and the Jewish Struggle with Modernity* (New York: Basic Books, 1974).

17. It is perhaps important to distinguish from the outset between new immigrants and new ethnics. The subject of this book, new immigrants, were largely Asians and Southern and Eastern Europeans who arrived in the United States between 1880 and 1920. New ethnics, which include Latin Americans and the newer Asian communities, are a post–World War II phenomenon.

18. Jameson, 56.

19. Jameson writes: "What Althusser's own insistence on history as an absent cause makes clear . . . is that he does not at all draw the fashionable conclusion that because history is a text, the 'referent' does not exist. We would therefore propose the following revised formulation: that history is not a text, not a narrative, master or otherwise, but that, as an absent cause, it is inaccessible to us except in textual form" (Jameson, 35).

20. Neal Gabler, *An Empire of Their Own: How the Jews Invented Hollywood* (New York: Crown, 1988); Lee Lourdeaux, *Italian and Irish Filmmakers in America: Ford, Capra, Coppola, and Scorcese* (Philadelphia, PA: Temple University Press,

1990); John Russell Taylor, *Strangers in Paradise: The Hollywood Emigres, 1933-1950* (New York: Holt, Rinehart, Winston, 1983).

21. Wayne Franklin notes a similar impulse to erase the uncomfortable reminders of failure in the earliest colonial North American settlements. He is worth quoting at length because his language is suggestive:

> In a very real sense, the most fully extreme records either were not composed at all, or were lost along with their authors—for in this much, at least, Poe's "MS. Found in a Bottle" . . . is a good guide to the probable and the possible. The large textual gap thus created surrounds whatever records we do have with a significant silence that is the purest expression of the settlement account as a form. Against the projected plot of an explorer, or even the contingent tale of a settler like Columbus, the untold and hence plotless fate of a lost traveler suggests a range of experience, and of potential art, far more devastatingly historical. The ruins of a scheme are reflected in this ruinous state of speech, this failure of narrative to embrace a failure in life. . . . If the fate of unfortunate travelers is known, the simple pattern of their experience may be so subversive of a survivor's ideal action . . . that it can enter the latter's text only in a modified form. Likewise, those whose fate is *not* known weaken a narrative structure which well may be designed, given a writer's purpose, to support an undertaking sorely taxed with acknowledged disasters. (Franklin, 143-44)

One notices that Franklin is in some way pointing to the unspoken and unspeakable history to which Jameson alludes. The language is strikingly similar, too. Rather than rifts and discontinuities in narrative we get "textual gaps" and a "ruinous state of speech." Finally, Franklin asserts that it is important to include *some* account of that history which is less fortunate in outcome.

22. Abdul JanMohamed and David Lloyd, "Introduction," in JanMohamed and Lloyd, eds., 4.

23. Nancy Hartsock, "Rethinking Modernism: Minority vs. Majority Theories," in JanMohamed and Lloyd, eds., 34.

24. Ethnicity as mediating between the individual and the nation is, roughly, the assumption of social historians such as John A. Armstrong, *Nations Before Nationalism* (Chapel Hill: University of North Carolina Press, 1982), and Anthony D. Smith, *The Ethnic Origins of Nations* (New York: Basil Blackwell, 1986).

Of course, in talking about the group as an organic psychological whole, I will inevitably be accused of a falsifying anthropomorphization of the group. There is no way of answering such an objection except by asserting that in bourgeois societies represented as democracies or republics, the practice of referring to the *body* politic already commits a similarly indispensable rhetorical error.

25. Oscar Handlin, *The Uprooted: The Epic Story of the Great Migrations that Made the American People* (2nd ed. Boston: Little, Brown, 1973).

26. "[T]hose who, despite their marginalization, in fact constitute the majority should be able collectively to examine the nature and content of their common marginalization and to develop strategies for their reempowerment" (JanMohamed and Lloyd, eds., 2).

27. See, for example, Lourdeaux's *Italian and Irish Filmmakers in America* for an example of film and ethnology, and several feminist texts on immigration for this same generalizing tendency: Elizabeth Ewen, *Immigrant Women in the Land of Dollars* (New York: Monthly Review Press, 1985); and Doris Weatherford, *Foreign and Female: Immigrant Women in America, 1840-1930* (New York: Schocken Books, 1986).

28. Robert C. Christopher, *Crashing the Gates* (New York: Simon and Schuster, 1989).

29. Thomas Cripps, *Making Movies Black: The Hollywood Message Movie from World War II to the Civil Rights Era* (New York: Oxford University Press, 1993), viii.

30. I shall explore the notion of dialogism more in chapter 3.

31. This argument is in opposition to a certain strain of ethnology that believes "ethnic identity and modern nationalism arise out of specific types of interactions between the leaderships of centralizing states and elites from non-dominant ethnic groups, especially but not exclusively on the peripheries of those states" (Paul R. Brass, *Ethnicity and Nationalism: Theory and Comparison* [New Delhi: Sage Publications, 1991], 8).

32. Anthropologists at least acknowledge that ethnic influence is bi-directional. Michael Banton, for example, briefly discusses "the failure to acknowledge that the receiving group undergoes change in absorbing the other" ("The Direction and Speed of Ethnic Change," in *Ethnic Change*, ed. Charles F. Keyes [Seattle: University of Washington Press, 1981], 33).

33. Roland Barthes, "Myth Today," in *Mythologies*, trans. Annette Lavers (1957; New York: Hill and Wang, 1972), 109-59.

34. Ernest Gellner, *Nations and Nationalism* (Ithaca, NY: Cornell University Press, 1983), especially 92-93. Gellner views the role of ethnicity in the state with contempt: "[Late industrial society] . . . will have to respect cultural differences where they survive, provided that they are superficial and do not engender genuine barriers between people" (121).

35. Alan Trachtenberg, *The Incorporation of America: Culture and Society in the Gilded Age* (New York: Hill and Wang, 1982), 143-44, my emphasis.

36. Gellner, 56.

37. Smith argues for the "durability of ethnic forms and contents, in the heart of the modern era" (16).

38. As, regrettably, in a certain obvious kind of Marxist critique, which conflates the forest and the trees by subsuming ethnicity and immigration under the class struggle: "Clearly, the act of leaving one country and settling in another is a case of uprootedness in the most literal sense. Yet, such a condition is virtually endemic to all modern societies where, in the process of modernization, traditional forms of social organization have been torn asunder, leaving individuals with a diminished sense of identity and belonging" (Stephen Steinberg, *The Ethnic Myth: Race, Ethnicity, and Class in America* [Boston: Beacon Press, 1989], 56). In correcting the "romantic" ethnic criticism of the 1960s and 1970s, Steinberg is willing to ignore the way in which immigration and ethnicity are the models and emblems of existential angst, the founding rather than peripheral phenomena of modernism.

39. Werner Sollors's *Beyond Ethnicity: Consent and Descent in American Culture* (New York: Oxford University Press, 1986) is a conspicuous exception. But this excellent book is about the only recent text on ethnicity that makes use of anthropological speculations going on since about 1980. Some of the more pertinent observations are being made by Michael Banton, who asserts, for instance, that "The implication of a uniform process of change is misleading, *as the failure to acknowledge that the receiving group undergoes change in absorbing the other*" (Banton, 33, my emphasis). Or, from George De Vos: "Today's ethnic minorities are not content to remain mute: they too seek to be heard. The defeated and the oppressed are themselves contributing to the writing of history, adding their own interpretations, and, where facts fail, creating or deepening their own sustaining mythologies" ("Ethnic Pluralism: Conflict and Accommodation," in *Ethnic Identity: Cultural Continuities and Change,* ed. George De Vos and Lola Romanucci-Ross [1975; rpt. Chicago: University of Chicago Press, 1982], 7).

Finally, in a different move, Charles Keyes describes how newly dominant cultures invent a mythology that gives them primary claim to recently acquired territory: "Tausug [the recent emigrant] myths now stress that they are of local origin and link themselves to Islamic origin themes. Samal, who were probably the aboriginal inhabitants of the region, are characterized in Tausug mythology as poor Muslims who are therefore morally inferior to the Tausug" ("The Dialectics of Ethnic Change," in *Ethnic Change,* ed. Charles F. Keyes [Seattle: University of Washington Press, 1981], 20). This mythmaking occurs in the relationship between Puritan and Native American cultures.

The problems of these excellent studies for my purposes are, first, that they represent an anthropological line of inquiry that tends not to be thoroughly explored (the sources are all article length), and, second, that they are again more interested in ethnic boundaries than in the dissolution of boundaries.

40. Stanley Cavell, *Pursuits of Happiness: The Hollywood Comedy of Remarriage* (Cambridge, MA: Harvard University Press, 1981).

41. Scholars are still asserting that "[t]he immigrants who were now settling fast around the county [sic] were very fond of these short films because they would not only introduce them to scenes of American life, but their simple subtitles would help them learn to read English" (Grayce Susan Burian, "Stanley and Aileen: Children in Vaudeville," *Journal of American Culture* 7, nos. 1-2 [Spring/Summer 1984]: 10).

42. For example, Daniel J. Leab, *From Sambo to Superspade: The Black Experience in Motion Pictures* (Boston: Houghton Mifflin, 1975), and especially Thomas Cripps, *Slow Fade to Black: The Negro in American Film, 1900-1942* (New York: Oxford University Press, 1977) and *Making Movies Black*.

43. See Lester D. Friedman's excellent *Hollywood's Image of the Jew* (New York: Frederick Ungar, 1982) and Patricia Erens's thorough *The Jew in American Cinema* (Bloomington: Indiana University Press, 1984). Of course, historians of ethnicity are not alone in defining film through ghettoizing: witness Vito Russo's *The Celluloid Closet: Homosexuality in the Movies* (New York: Harper & Row, 1981).

44. Randall M. Miller, "Introduction," in *The Kaleidoscopic Lens: How Hollywood Views Ethnic Groups*, ed. Randall M. Miller (Englewood, NJ: Jerome S. Ozer, 1980), 5.

45. John Izod, *Hollywood and the Box Office, 1895-1986* (New York: Columbia University Press, 1988), 11.

46. Take for example Patricia Erens's assertion: "Despite their small numbers in the United States, Jews have enjoyed an advantage unequalled by any other ethnic group in America—a virtual control over their own self-image on the screen" ("Between Two Worlds: Jewish Images in American Film," in Miller, ed., 114).

47. African-American film aesthetics is one significant exception to this assertion, an addition to the growing body of work on the image of the African-American in film. See, for example, Gladstone L. Yearwood, *Black Cinema Aesthetics: Issues in Independent Black Filmmaking* (Athens: Ohio University Press, 1982); Thomas Cripps, *Black Film as Genre* (Bloomington: Indiana University Press, 1978); and the generation of writing that has emerged since Melvin Van Peebles's *Sweet Sweetback's Baadasssss Song*. The other significant exception is the collection edited by Lester Friedman, *Unspeakable Images: Ethnicity and the American Cinema* (Urbana: University of Illinois Press, 1991).

48. Izod, *Hollywood and the Box Office: 1895-1986*; Leo Handel, *Hollywood Looks at Its Audience: A Report of Film Audience Research* (Urbana: University of Illinois Press, 1950); Michael Wood, *America in the Movies: Or, "Santa Maria, It Had Slipped My Mind"* (New York: Columbia University Press, 1975); Brian Neve, *Film and Politics in America: A Social Tradition* (New York: Routledge, 1992); Gorham Kindem, ed., *The American Movie Industry: The Business of Motion Pictures* (Carbondale: Southern Illinois University Press, 1982).

49. Even a history of film and sociology would find a wealth of interest in ethnicity in the plethora of studies done over the last sixty years on the "effect" of film on audiences. To take one example at random: Ruth C. Peterson and L. L. Thurstone, *Motion Pictures and the Social Attitudes of Children* (New York: Macmillan, 1933) contains such chapters as "Attitude toward Germans," "Attitude toward Chinese," "Attitude toward the Negro," and "*The Birth of a Nation* and the Negro."

50. Garth Jowett, *Film: The Democratic Art* (Boston: Little, Brown, 1976); Friedman, *Hollywood's Image of the Jew.*

51. Robert C. Allen, "Motion Picture Exhibition in Manhattan, 1906-1912," in Kindem, ed., 12-24.

52. Thomas Elsaesser and Adam Barker, ed., *Early Cinema: Space, Frame, Narrative* (London: BFI, 1990).

53. Charles Musser, *Before the Nickelodeon: Edwin S. Porter and the Edison Manufacturing Company* (Berkeley: University of California Press, 1991); Charles Musser and Carol Nelson, *High-Class Moving Pictures: Lyman H. Howe and the Forgotten Era of Traveling Exhibition, 1880-1920* (Princeton, NJ: Princeton University Press, 1991).

54. Charles Musser, "Ethnicity, Role-Playing, and American Film Comedy: From *Chinese Laundry* to *Whoopee* (1894-1930)," in Friedman, ed., *Unspeakable Images*, 50.

55. Musser, *High-Class Moving Pictures*, 21.

56. Ibid., 171. Musser elsewhere states about one genteel exhibitor exhibiting to the middle class, non-ethnic audience, that "Howe's miniature, less ambiguous in its educational aspirations, catered to people with a more fastidious temperament" (21).

57. Again, this tendency is in marked contrast to contemporary historical practice: "Today, however, historians portray unprivileged people as creative, autonomous agents rather than victims of circumstances beyond their control" (Pauline Maier, "A Marketplace of Human Souls" [review of Peter Kolchin, *American Slavery, 1619-1877*], *New York Times Book Review*, September 5, 1993, 9).

58. JanMohamed and Lloyd, eds., 6.

59. Ted Sennett, *Lunatics and Lovers: A Tribute to the Giddy and Glittering Era of the Screen's "Screwball" and Romantic Comedies* (New Rochelle, NY: Arlington House, 1973); Penelope Gilliatt, *Unholy Fools: Wits, Comics, Disturbers of the Peace: Film and Theater* (New York: Viking Press, 1973), who divides comics into physicists, cogitators, farce-makers, scamps, and disrupters; Steve Seidman, *Comedian Comedy: A Tradition in Hollywood Film* (Ann Arbor, MI: UMI Research Press, 1981); Raymond Durgnat, *The Crazy Mirror: Hollywood Comedy and the American Image* (London: Faber and Faber, 1969); Gerald Mast, *The Comic Mind: Comedy and the Movies* (Indianapolis, IN: Bobbs-Merrill, 1973); and Gerald Weales, *Canned Goods as Caviar: American Film Comedy of the 1930's* (Chicago: University of Chicago Press, 1985).

60. Most extremely, Henri Bergson states that "a cut-and-dried agreement among the persons will not satisfy [society], it insists on a constant striving after reciprocal adaptation. Society will therefore be suspicious of all inelasticity of character, of mind and even of body, because it is the possible sign of a slumbering activity as well as of an activity with separatist tendencies, that inclines to swerve from the common centre round which society gravitates" ("Laughter," in *Comedy,* ed. Wylie Sypher [New York: Doubleday, 1956], 73).

61. Thomas Schatz, *The Genius of the System: Hollywood Filmmaking in the Studio Era* (London: Simon and Schuster, 1989); Charles Higham, *The Art of the American Film* (Garden City, NY: Anchor Press, 1974); Cavell, *Pursuits of Happiness;* and Seidman, *Comedian Comedy.*

62. Seidman, 64-71.

63. See especially David Bordwell, Janet Staiger, and Kristin Thompson, *The Classical Hollywood Cinema: Film Style and Mode of Production to 1960* (New York: Columbia University Press, 1985).

64. Henry Jenkins, *What Made Pistachio Nuts? Early Sound Comedy and the Vaudeville Aesthetic* (New York: Columbia University Press, 1992), 172-84.

65. Ibid., 283. Jenkins's very language suggests an ethnic agenda that he himself does not pursue. One of his operative metaphors for comedy is itself drawn from the language of immigration. In speaking of an early-twentieth-century critic, for example, he asserts that "Gags . . . often failed to provoke strong emotional responses if they are not fully *integrated* into the narrative" (52); "Mass market magazines provided an *alternative voice*" (38); "The shift between the loosely structured slapstick shorts of Chaplin and Keaton and their 'mature' feature films . . . reflected these performers' *assimilation into the mainstream* of the classical Hollywood cinema" (97; my emphases); and, in articulating his thesis, "My central claim will be that anarchistic comedy

emerged from the classical Hollywood cinema's attempt to *assimilate* the vaudeville aesthetic" (24). But the hidden metaphor is rarely actualized.

66. David Marc, *Comic Visions: Television Comedy and American Culture* (Boston: Unwin Hyman, 1989); Stephen Neale and Frank Krutnick, *Popular Film and Television Comedy* (New York: Routledge, 1990); and Andrew S. Horton, ed., *Comedy/Cinema/Theory* (Berkeley: University of California Press, 1991). Horton's anthology contains one rather predictable essay on Jewish humor: Ruth Perlmutter's "Woody Allen's Zelig: An American Jewish Parody" (206-21).

67. In *Subversive Pleasures: Bakhtin, Cultural Criticism, and Film* (Baltimore: Johns Hopkins University Press, 1989), Robert Stam points out that "bakhtinian formulations have the advantage of not restricting liberatory struggle to purely economic or political battles; instead, they extend it to the common patrimony of the utterance" (8).

68. Jenkins, 282. Like Musser and others, Jenkins posits the formative moment of cinema at a moment of his choosing.

69. Robert C. Allen, *A Horrible Prettiness: Burlesque and American Culture* (Chapel Hill: University of North Carolina Press, 1991).

70. For example, Allen's treatment of Ada Menken (99).

71. Musser, "Ethnicity, Role-Playing, and American Film Comedy," in Friedman, *Unspeakable Images*, 48-49. This is essentially the thesis of older texts such as Albert McLean's *Vaudeville as Ritual* (Lexington: University of Kentucky Press, 1965), but with an ethnic flavor. In his more recent discussion of ethnicity in silent film Kevin Brownlow also sees ethnic representation as victimization (*Behind the Mask of Innocence* [New York: Knopf, 1990]). This tendency probably derives in large part from Richard Dyer's theoretical work, *Stars,* as well as Dyer's practical work in reading the ethnic imagery of Marilyn Monroe and Paul Robeson. (Richard Dyer, *Stars* [London: BFI, 1979].) His work on Monroe and Robeson can be found in Dyer, *Heavenly Bodies: Film Stars and Society* (New York: St. Martin's Press, 1986), chaps. 1-2, respectively.

72. Renato Rosaldo, "Politics, Patriarchs, and Laughter," in JanMohamed and Lloyd, eds., 144.

73. Robert Stam, *Reflexivity in Film and Literature: From Don Quixote to Jean-Luc Godard* (Ann Arbor, MI: UMI Research Press, 1985).

74. A predecessor text that examines the history of ethnic comedy is Maureen Waters's *The Comic Irishman* (Albany: State University of New York (SUNY) Press, 1984).

75. Though I hasten to add that some of these revisions—particularly those of Charles Musser and Henry Jenkins—are in part influenced by my own earlier

work, particularly that on the Marx Brothers and on screwball comedy. See Mark Winokur, "Unlikely Hero," *Cinema Journal* 27, no. 1 (Fall 1987): 5-22; and "Smile Stranger: Aspects of Immigrant Humor in the Marx Brothers' Comedy," *Literature/Film Quarterly* 13 (1985): 161-71.

76. Cavell, *Pursuits of Happiness.*

77. Another advantage to the generic division of comedy is a certain synthesizing faculty: an ability to include various partial explanations under one aegis. In some ways, the observations about comedy presented here are extremely traditional and unoriginal. The immigrant comics are little more than expert eirons (the deflators); the secondary, authoritarian members of the screwball world are more often than not alazons (the deflated). My explanation of immigrant comedy shares a great deal with the Platonic theory of comedy as the laughable ugly, the comic unacceptable. Middle-class, or screwball, humor is a category of social corrective Meredith and Bergson would appreciate. The idea of a trinity of characters—included, semi-excluded, and excluded (immigrant, bourgeois, intellectual)—would roughly correspond to a similar trinity in Freud—object of desire (woman), desirer (wooer), and audience (rival)—but without the obligatory sexual differentiation.

78. Dyer, *Heavenly Bodies,* 3.

79. Ibid., 9.

80. Ibid., 102.

81. The immediate theoretical precursor is the work of Richard Dyer. The real influence is Roland Barthes's work, especially the semiotics of *S/Z* or "The Face of Garbo." Roland Barthes, *Mythologies,* 56-57; *S/Z,* trans. Richard Miller (New York: Hill and Wang, 1974).

82. Such theorizing still needs to be done. The normative stance in relation to comic stereotyping can be briefly found in Musser, *Before the Nickelodeon,* 275, 303, 313, 344, 351, 365, and passim. Still, anyone who browses briefly through, say, the *Variety* film reviews can readily see that an enormous number of films made in the 1920s and 1930s investigate ethnicity and immigration.

83. For instance, Jenkins, *What Made Pistachio Nuts?*

84. André Bazin, "The Myth of Total Cinema," in *What is Cinema?,* trans. Hugh Gray, vol. 1 (1958-65; Berkeley: University of California Press, 1967), 17-22; Irwin Panofsky, "Style and Medium in the Motion Pictures," in *Film Theory and Criticism: Introductory Readings,* ed. Gerald Mast and Marshall Cohen (New York: Oxford University Press, 1985), 215-33; and Jean-Louis Baudry, "The Apparatus: Metapsychological Approaches to the Impression of Reality in Cinema," trans. Jean Andrews, *Camera Obscura* 1 (Fall 1976): 104-28.

CHAPTER 1

1. Jose Rabasa, *Inventing America: Spanish Historiography and the Formation of Eurocentrism* (Norman: University of Oklahoma Press, 1993); Clive Bush, *The Dream of Reason: American Consciousness and Cultural Achievement from Independence to the Civil War* (New York: St. Martin's Press, 1977); Frederick Jackson Turner, *The Significance of the Frontier in American History* (Madison, WI: Silver Buckle Press, 1984); Richard Slotkin, *Regeneration Through Violence: The Mythology of the American Frontier* (Middletown, CT: Wesleyan University Press, 1973); Leo Marx, *The Machine in the Garden: Technology and the Pastoral Ideal in America* (New York: Oxford University Press, 1964); and Benedict R. O'G. Anderson, *Imagined Communities: Reflections on the Origin and Spread of Nationalism* (1983; rpt. New York: Verso, 1991), 188.
2. Anderson, 187.
3. Rabasa, 16.
4. The metadiscourse of America should have seduced film theorists before now because its most significant tropes are visual: "landscape" and "space."
5. Fredric Jameson, *The Political Unconscious: Narrative as a Socially Symbolic Act* (Ithaca, NY: Cornell University Press, 1981), 25.
6. Note, for example, the tone and pronominal usage of critic-historian A. L. Rowse as he discusses the contest over America between Spain, France, and England: "[W]hat would have happened if we had not conducted the struggle unitedly, consistently, with Elizabeth's firm grasp of power, we may observe from the case of France" (*The Elizabethans and America* [London: Macmillan, 1959], 6). This is a delightfully overt piece of chauvinism. Even later, though, the same assumptions about where the culture derives are being made: "During the nineteenth century, the Americans, exploring their own continent as their Elizabethan ancestors had explored the Atlantic and the Eastern Seaboard of America, recapitulated both the psychological and physical nature of the Renaissance discovery experience" (Bush, 9). Sherman Paul's *Repossessing and Renewing: Essays in the Green American Tradition* (Baton Rouge: Louisiana State University Press, 1976), an anthology of essays about the "organic tradition" in America, begins: "This collection is an informal account of the Emersonian tradition and of some of the critics who have fostered it" (xiii). David R. Williams's grandly titled *Wilderness Lost: The Religious Origins of the American Mind* (Selinsgrove, PA: Susquehanna University Press, 1987) fails to treat any other religion than American Protestantism very seriously; those religious origins culminate in final chapters on Hawthorne, Melville, and Oliver Wendell Holmes. Kenneth Lynn (*Mark

Twain and Southwestern Humor [Boston: Little, Brown, 1959]); Henry Nash Smith (Virgin Land: The American West as Symbol and Myth [New York: Vintage, 1950]); Howard Mumford Jones (The Frontier in American Fiction: Four Lectures on the Relation of Landscape to Literature [Jerusalem: Magness Press, 1956]); Roderick Nash (Wilderness and the American Mind [New Haven, CT: Yale University Press, 1967]) work the same neo-Puritan vein, although Jones, one of the earliest of the critics of the American landscape genre, does treat "distaff" influences in his discussion of the Mediterranean treatment of the New World. Finally, the attempt at an alternative history attempted here informs other such works as John Armstrong's Nations Before Nationalism (Chapel Hill: University of North Carolina Press, 1982), which contextualizes pre-Enlightenment Western Europe in Muslim and Slavic cultures.

7. Comparison of Puritan and dynastic rhetorical self-justification is more than preciously ironic. The Capetians justify their usurpation of the Carolingians through the same rhetoric appeal to the Old Testament that justifies the Puritans: "[L]ike the people of Israel . . . the kingdom of France [is] a peculiar people chosen by the Lord to carry out the orders of Heaven" (quoted in Anthony D. Smith, The Ethnic Origin of Nations [New York: Basil Blackwell, 1986], 59). A standard component of any ethnie is a sense of ordained uniqueness. The Puritans are merely the group whose demi-divinity has been recognized as such by the official culture.

8. In a conversation with noted anthropologist Alan Dundes I asked what texts existed documenting the influence of Native American myths on colonial oral tales. He stated categorically that no such influence existed; the influence was all in the other direction. I asked him how he knew this, and he replied that no research had been done because none need be done. A profound truth about history should be observed in this tautology, (self-)created by the fact that anthropologists did not begin to record Native American tales until the latter half of the nineteenth century. Any similarities between Native American and European tales could thus be attributed to the fact that Native American culture had become by this time "contaminated" by the west.

9. Elsewhere than in film and literary studies this methodology is standard practice: "The comparison of events along the historical vertical axis is one of the commonest procedures of historical research: we confront prior with subsequent occurrences and we establish the similarities and differences between them" (Miroslav Hroch, Social Preconditions of National Revival in Europe: A Comparative Analysis of the Social Composition of Patriotic Groups among the Smaller European Nations, trans. Ben Fowkes [Cambridge: Cambridge University Press, 1985], 20).

10. John Donne, from "Elegy 19: To His Mistress Going to Bed":

O my America! my new-found-land,
My kingdom, safeliest when with one man manned,
My mine of precious stones, my empery,
How blest am I in thus discovering thee!

(quoted in Walter Blair and Hamlin Hill, *America's Humor: From Poor Richard to Doonesbury* [New York: Oxford University Press, 1978], 3).

11. L. Sprague de Camp and Willy Ley, *Lands Beyond* (New York: Rinehart, 1952), 165.

12. While these four responses do not correspond precisely to Rabasa's four "moments" in the invention of America, there is some overlap in the sense that each response is a kind of projection, and I am arguing that my fourth response, like Rabasa's fourth moment, allows a space for ethnic difference (Rabasa, 16-17). The first three responses correspond roughly to Lawrence Fuchs's three models for assimilating immigrants: the Pennsylvania, Massachusetts, and Maryland "ideas," respectively (*The American Kaleidoscope: Race, Ethnicity, and the Civic Culture* [Middletown, CT: Wesleyan University Press, 1990], 8).

13. Richard Slotkin, *Regeneration through Violence*; Annette Kolodny, *The Lay of the Land: Metaphor as Experience and History in American Life and Letters* (Chapel Hill: University of North Carolina Press, 1975); Jenny Franchot, *Roads to Rome: The Antebellum Protestant Encounter with Catholicism* (Berkeley: University of California Press, 1994).

14. See especially Edward Dudley and Maximillian E. Novak, eds., *The Wild Man Within: An Image in Western Thought from the Renaissance to Romanticism* (Pittsburgh, PA: University of Pittsburgh Press, 1972).

15. The one story William Bradford tells "rather of mirth than of weight" is about the Puritan administration's repression of revelry during an attempt by one faction to celebrate the "day called Christmas Day" (*Of Plymouth Plantation* [New York: Random House, 1981], 107).

16. Marianna Torgovnick, *Gone Primitive: Savage Intellects, Modern Lives* (Chicago: University of Chicago Press, 1990). Torgovnick accounts for the Anglo-American tendency to orientalize across a number of disciplines and media, tracing the tendency throughout the twentieth century in forms as disparate as anthropology and the avant garde.

17. One might assign different groups different strategies for assimilation into the landscape of the New World: Spanish exploration as the discovery of utopia or the Puritan settlement as the creation of utopia. Such generalizations would be, like all such cultural generalizations, both true and false. One could justify them only as "tendencies" plagued by significant exceptions (Roger Williams

for the Puritans, the California missions for the Spanish). A scholarly agenda like this would in the end almost certainly reveal one underlying truth: all such tendencies to assimilate the landscape were present in all their manifestations, some of which were then either encouraged or suppressed, depending on the requirements of the particular group.

18. Thomas Morton, *New English Canaan* (1637; rpt. New York: Da Capo Press, 1969).

19. Wayne Franklin states that "the explorer's future always serves as the final scene of his play, the time of comic resolution." This is the future against which the comic sensibility struggles. He continues: "Having admitted time into America by making the prospect of delight a temporal concept, the explorer has allowed the later perversion of his plotted history" (*Discoverers, Explorers, Settlers: The Diligent Writers of Early America* [Chicago: University of Chicago Press], 81).

20. Morton is a minor footnote in the battle, partly waged by means of satire, between the Puritans and the Anglican Church, waged from about 1588. Charges levelled at the Puritans included those usually made against religious zealotry: extremism, hypocrisy, obsession with minutae (William P. Holden, *Anti-Puritan Satire: 1642-1772* [New Haven, CT: Yale University Press, 1954], 40-41, 44). By the seventeenth century, chapbooks were delineating Puritans in the same manner that the *fabliaux* of a previous century had painted church prelates. One poem, titled "The Puritan," contains this verse about the willing seduction by a dissenter of someone in the same congregation:

> He laid her on the ground,
> His Spirits fell a ferking,
> Her Zeal was in a sound,
> He edified her Merkin
> Upside Down.

(J. Woodfall Ebsworth, ed., *Choyce Drollery: Songs and Sonnets. Being A Collection of Divers Excellent Pieces of Poetry, of Several Eminent Authors. Now First Reprinted from the Edition of 1656. To Which are Added the Extra Songs of Merry Drollery, 1661* [Boston: Robert Roberts, 1876], 195-96).

21. Bishop Joseph Hall, *Mundus Alter et Idem* (Frankfurt, 1605).

22. Printed between 1684 and 1695 and reprinted in John Ashton, ed., *Humour, Wit, & Satire of the Seventeenth Century* (London: Chatto and Windus, 1883), 34-37. While it does not describe streets paved with gold, they are "pav'd with pudding-pies / nay powder'd beef and bacon" (35).

23. Ebenezer Cooke, *The Sotweed Factor: Or, a Voyage to Maryland* (London: B. Bragg, 1708). As a repudiation of the official story, it was (as Wayne Franklin

asserts) an antidote to the tendency toward a militant forgetfulness, a refusal to read in the national past the record of any terminal disorientation. The suffering of the "pioneers" became, by a kind of sacrificial arrogation, acts of "pious devotion to the brighter American future enjoyed by their memorialists (Franklin, 13). Franklin cites John Underhill's *Newes from America* (1638) as an example of the early whitewashing of history:

> Nowhere else can one find a better example of the discoverer's desire to stop American time, to retreat into a world of categorical design which is free from the narrative implications of his real career. In the midst of a war . . . Underhill finds in the snatch of a future horizon the necessary oblivion for a historical struggle which he would rather forget. The defense of genocide by an argument from cultural imperatives lies implicit in this uncanny, almost accidental, mix of modes. As Wood pushes to one side of "the pathe" any natural evil, and crowds the traveler's way with presumed delights, so Underhill and a hundred apologists after him insure the safe passage of European culture to America by defeating the natives in deed and word. No less than Wood, Underhill offers a prospect into (and of) America, a shortcut revealed by sharper weapons but a duller wit. His own "mount" (and that of the reader) is a bloody pile of corpses. (43)

24. For example, J. M. Powell, *Mirrors of the New World: Images and Image-Makers in the Settlement Process* (Folkestone, England: Dawson, 1977):

> [Samuel Waldo] suddenly appeared in Germany, proclaiming himself a "Royal British Captain [and] hereditary lord of Broad Bay, Massachusetts," and advertising splendid terms to all who would return with him to what were supposed to be his ancestral lands in Maine. His and Massachusetts's *Werber*, knowing a good thing when they saw it, then went seriously to work. They picked up every footloose vagabond they could find, bamboozled respectable families by fancy enticements, and packed off several hundred "freights," as they referred to fare-paying adult immigrants, to rallying points along the Rhine, whence they were relayed, under increasingly sordid conditions, to the Dutch shippers, who reduced even the more affluent of them to beggary before sending them on to New England. (50)

Another example among scores tells of a state's exploitation of foreign labor markets:

> Between 1680 and 1740 South Carolina was enthusiastically
> presented in several languages and by a wide range of private and
> officially-sponsored authors. Unlike the highly successful propa-
> ganda for Pennsylvania during this period which emphasized
> favourable economic prospects and religious attitudes, the litera-
> ture which marketed the idea of South Carolina portrayed its
> physical environment as a definite terrestrial paradise.

(Bernard Bailyn, *The Peopling of British North America: An Introduction* [New York: Alfred A. Knopf, 1986], 71).

25. Sarah Kemble Knight, *The Journal of Madam Knight* (Boston: D. R. Godine, 1972); *William Byrd's Histories of the Dividing Line Betwixt Virginia and North Carolina* (Raleigh: The North Carolina Historical Commission, 1929).

26. It is by no means the only repudiation of the landscape by early settlers and explorers. Franklin recounts the complaints of Thomas Harriot in *A Briefe and True Report* (1588):

> The bad reports [of the new world] . . . have resulted from bad
> men . . . or from the acute sensitivity of those English voyagers
> who have had "a nice bringing up, only in cities or townes,"
> and who (having not found in Virginia "any English cities, not
> such faire houses, nor at their own wish any of their old
> accustomed dainty food, nor any soft beds of downe or feath-
> ers") discovered that "the countrey was to them miserable, and
> their reports thereof according." (Franklin, 166-67)

The undercut pastoral ideal continued to be a subject of comedy, most famously in the beginning of Augustus Baldwin Longstreet's "Georgia Theatrics," where the narrator's pastoral idyll is suddenly interrupted by an interjection from an unknown and unseen speaker: "Boo-oo-oo! Oh, wake snakes, and walk your chalks!" (*Georgia Scenes* [1835; rpt. Savannah, GA: Beehive Press, 1975], 4).

27. Early critics such as Constance Rourke (*American Humor: A Study of the National Character* [1931; rpt. Garden City, NY: Doubleday, 1953]) fail to mention Cooke's poem. More recent writers, always in the hope of delimiting an unproblematically American canon, perpetuate this error. Neil Schmitz, in *Of Huck and Alice: Humorous Writing in American Literature* (Minneapolis: University of Minnesota Press, 1983), asserts, "The humorous tradition in American literature begins effectively in the Jacksonian period, with Davy Crockett" (25). Even writers whose whole point is that American humor is inclusive fail to include it, such as the otherwise intensely interesting Jesse Bier (*The Rise and Fall of American Humor* [New York: Holt, Rinehart and Winston, 1968]).

28. Edward Tyson, *Orang-Outang, sive, Homo Sylvestris: or, the Anatomy of a Pygmie* (1699; facs., London: Dawsons, 1966).

29. M. St. Clare Byrne, ed., *The Elizabethan Zoo* (London: Fredrick Etchells and Hugh Macdonald, 1926), 24.

30. Unlike the Puritans and most early settlers, for whom Native Americans were often at best subversive, at worst dangerous, the very earliest humorists—Morton and Cooke—tend to find in Native Americans a source of proto-Rousseauean value, either as occasions for contemplation or as playfully abandoned. The overabundance of wildlife is very like the superabundance portrayed in the anonymous "Wonderful Hunt" (1809) or the much more famous T. B. Thorpe story, "The Big Bear of Arkansas" (1841) which, like *Life on the Mississippi* some forty years later, even contains ubiquitously phallic mosquitoes, notable in Cooke for number and persistence, if not for size. Blair and Hill describe "The Wonderful Hunt," an 1809 story in which a hunter tries to shoot a buck (19); T. B. Thorpe, "The Big Bear of Arkansas," *Spirit of the Times* (New York), March 27, 1841.

31. Harry B. Weiss, *A Book about Chapbooks: The People's Literature of Bygone Times* (1942; rpt. Hatboro, PA: Folklore Associates, 1969), 124.

32. Or, as William E. Lenz says about how Brackenridge's *Modern Chivalry* quickly goes out of fashion: "The literary conventions of the Old World prove inadequate to the New" (*Fast Talk & Flush Times: The Confidence Man as a Literary Convention* [Columbia: University of Missouri Press, 1985], 360). It is more correct to say that such repudiation lessens in the American scene, although it remains in the travel narratives. But the difference between Mrs. Trollope and Cooke is the difference between the tourist and the prospective settler. Trollope is the greater aesthete; she is more adventurous and less ambivalent. Cooke has an economic stake; he is hopelessly ambivalent and quite timid.

33. Wayne Franklin charts this change from the imposed fabulous to the native realist in serious colonial writing as occurring even earlier. In comparing William Penn to the earlier Christopher Carleill, he asserts that "Penn's writings in support of the undertaking are less conceited in their idea of America: the fact of established colonies there has made almost unnecessary those acts of metaphoric settlement which characterize the earlier work. Magical transformation seems in Penn's case to be the result of a chronicling rather than a fabulating mind, an accurate reflection of achieved change" (103). Yet Franklin's argument continues by asserting of Penn's pragmatic writings that "one must note the ways in which this topos, when used in retrospective narrations, *exerts a subtly idealizing force on the matter to be recorded*" (103, my emphasis).

34. Blair and Hill, 9-10.
35. For example, Blair and Hill, 35-36. Diction remains important in establishing other colonial comic personae. Maureen Waters asserts that of primary importance in the establishment of the comic Irishman is the brogue (Maureen Waters, *The Comic Irishman* [Albany: State University of New York Press, 1984], 1).
36. "Davy Crockett as Demigod," *The Parade of Heroes: Legendary Heroes in American Lore*, ed. and sel. Tristram Potter Coffin and Hennig Cohen (Garden City, NY: Anchor Press, 1978), 32.
37. One manifestation of this impulse to contrast the two cultures appeared in a theatrical tradition in which European culture was implicitly opposed to native culture. This tradition flourished to approximately the middle of the nineteenth century, when it was more or less appropriated by the novel, first in Nathaniel Hawthorne's *The Marble Faun* and later by Henry James. Plays such as *The Politician Outwitted* (1789) featured an American bumpkin among a Europeanized population a year before the more highly touted— and more relevantly named—*The Contrast* (1790). But, partly because the contrast was implicit in the earlier plays, the superiority of the adoptive European values remained unquestioned. The relationships between the dandies of the main plots and the bumpkins of the subplots very rarely attained the kind of ironic commentaries of the lower on the higher classes of even such minor Renaissance comedies as Robert Greene's *Friar Bacon and Friar Bungay* (c. 1589-90).
38. In another history of ethnicity, someone will document the Jacksonian and antebellum eras as ethnically constitutive, a moment of significant ("old") immigration and cultural change. In *Yesterdays: Popular Song in America* (1979; rpt. New York: Norton, 1983) Charles Hamm asserts about popular music:

> As early as the first decades of the nineteenth century, it was becoming clear that Americans liked novelty—songs in musical styles drawing on the various schools of national song brought to America by new immigrants. . . . Americans . . . preferred the fresh and "wild" sounds of Irish and Scottish song, the cloying seductions of the new school of Italian opera, the exciting and amusing minstrel songs combining the neo-African sound of the banjo with Irish-Scottish melodies. (99)

One can document as an ethnic phenomenon traditionally high-culture opera production, which begins in America at the same time as old immigration. The first production of non-English opera in America outside of New Orleans occurs in 1825 with *The Barber of Seville*. The most enduring success is *The*

Bohemian Girl, an 1843 production about a child stolen away from the parental palace and made to live a false life in a different culture but who waxes nostalgic about the old home: "I Dreamt that I Dwelt in Marble Halls."

39. Though utterly uninterested in ethnic journalism, John Tebbel and Mary Ellen Zuckerman, in *The Magazine in America: 1714-1990* (New York: Oxford University Press, 1991), document the rise of a "Golden Age" for magazine publication in America as roughly contemporary with the era of "old" immigration: "To reach a new literate mass readership, an extraordinary explosion . . . of magazines occurred between 1825 and 1850. . . . Reliable statistics are difficult to come by . . . but roughly, the number of magazines rose from about 100 in 1825 to about 600 in 1850" (11). They are ludicrously unaware of possible connections between a new population and new interests in fiction and international politics (10-11).

40. Frank Barna, "The Frontiersman as Ethnic," in *Ethnic Groups in the City: Culture, Institutions, and Power,* ed. Otto Feinstein (Lexington, MA: Heath, 1971), 151-64. Barna further asserts, "It was this area which gave rise to men like Davy Crockett, Andrew Jackson, and Daniel Boone. In many respects they are typical of the southern Scotch-Irish" (160-61). Mark Derr avers that the Crockett family fled Scotland by way of Ireland (*The Frontiersman: The Real Life and Many Legends of Davy Crockett* [New York: William Morrow, 1993], 37). Later, in order further to distinguish the Scotch-Irish from the English, Barna states, "Perhaps their 'democratic fervor' spurred them to fight in the Revolutionary War, though it appears that their hatred of the English had more to do with their taking up of arms" (161). It is certainly true that, in seventeenth- and eighteenth-century English chapbooks, the most ridiculed groups are not inhabitants of the New World, but rather nearly everyone else, conspicuously the French, Scots, and Irish.

41. Thomas Chandler Haliburton, *The Clockmaker: Or, the Sayings and Doings of Samuel Slick, of Slickville* (Paris: Baudry's European Library, 1839), 194. Slick's inversion of the axes of cultural value is positively hermeneutic. Clive Bush argues that one representative of the American "dream of reason" is David Rittenhouse, the eighteenth-century creator of orreries that linked cosmic timeliness to social organization ("This cosmic sense turns naturally into social sense" [68]). The running joke (so to speak) of the Slick narratives is that his clocks break down, presumably like Enlightenment ideology.

42. Gardiner calls for us to "go back to the day when things were newer—but not so quiet as they are now" (review of *The Spy,* in *North American Review* 15 [1822], 254). Oh, for the sedateness of America in the 1820s.

43. Lenz, 44.

44. Blair and Hill, 158-59 (my emphasis). Another excellent chronicler of American humor, Jesse Bier, notices the jump that another American comic subgenre had over other another major American movement:

> [American humor] is not merely allied with the movement of Realism in American literature and culture, but is part and parcel of it. American humorists have consistently given their minority realist report on American life. It is no coincidence either that a great many of our comics have risen from the lower class, from frontier or immigrant quarters, conditioned to disabusement and resilient clarity. Furthermore, humorists, as in the Local Color movement, spearheaded Realism itself, and figures like Bret Harte and Mark Twain are pertinent in this connection. Moreover, in their advanced use of real speech and dialect (as in the early "southwest" humorists), in all their antirhetorical devices, and in their combativeness, they foreran the Realists by a full generation. (*The Rise and Fall of American Humor*, 8)

45. One of the more famous descriptions is of Sut Lovingood, "a queer-looking, long-legged, short-bodied, small-headed, white-haired, hog-eyed, funny sort of a genius, fresh from some bench-legged Jew's clothing store" (George W. Harris, "How Daddy Played Hoss," in *Oddities of Southern Life and Character*, ed. Henry Watterson [Boston: Houghton, Mifflin, 1883], 416).

46. Georges Louis Leclerc, Comte de Buffon, *National History, General and Particular*, trans. William Smellic (London, 1812), quoted in H. S. Commager and E. Giordanetti, *Was America a Mistake?: An Eighteenth-Century Controversy* (New York: Harper and Row, 1967), 64.

47. Alexander Saxton asserts, for example, that the Crockett autobiography and narratives were for the most part patently spurious, fabricated by ghostwriters (*The Rise and Fall of the White Republic: Class Politics and Mass Culture in Nineteenth-Century America* [London: Verso, 1990], 81).

48. J. Hector St. John de Crèvecoeur, *Letters From an American Farmer* (New York: Dutton, 1957), 21. Romanticism nourishes the satire that will kill it, although this *spirituelle* recurs even in the writing of Mark Twain who, though satirizing such romanticism in Cooper, draws on some of the latter's romantic values—for instance nostalgia—but within a realist aesthetic.

49. Thomas Jefferson, *Notes on the State of Virginia*, ed. William Peden (Chapel Hill: University of North Carolina Press, 1954), 164-65.

50. Blair and Hill, 128.

51. "Henry Clay and John Quincy Adams . . . were involved in a vicious assault on Andrew Jackson's character, proclaiming him a drunkard, a gambler, a cockfighter . . . and a wife-stealing adulterer. Not content with that array of

charges, they went on to spread rumors that his mother had been a prostitute and his father a mulatto who had sold his oldest son into slavery" (Derr, 140).

52. Martha Hodes, "Wartime Dialogues on Illicit Sex: White Women and Black Men," in *Divided Houses: Gender and the Civil War* (New York: Oxford University Press, 1992), 230.

53. Oddly, not only are the British not attuned to the nuances of the new ethnicity in New World representation, but their comic literature reflects some rather odd notions about ethnicity. Though the representation of America in eighteenth- and nineteenth-century British jest books is rather sparse, it is characterized largely by stories about Ben Franklin in Europe or by undifferentiated black stereotypes, as in "Life in Philadelphia," a British jest-book entry that sounds like a minstrel turn (*The New Comic Annual* [London: Hurst, Chance, and Co., 1831], 148-61).

54. Bush, 191.

55. Stephen Steinberg, *The Ethnic Myth: Race, Ethnicity, and Class in America* (1981; rpt. Boston: Beacon Press, 1989), 7. Steinberg is a presumably Marxist critic who can still oxymoronically assert that "[d]evoid of its invidious implications, the claim that the nation was founded by white Anglo-Saxon Protestants is reasonably accurate" (8), when such an assertion is by definition invidious.

56. Bush, 348.

57. Ibid.

58. Saxton, 173.

59. Chip Rhodes, "Education as Liberation: The Case of Anzia Yezierska's *Bread Givers*," *Science and Society* 57, no. 3 (Fall 1993): 303.

60. Elsewhere Rhodes asserts, "[T]he novel seems to suggest that Reb's thickheadedness, stupidity and selfishness have to do with his individuality, not his cultural determinates" (301).

61. Except in sociology, colonial multiethnicity has been largely unacknowledged; its extent has remained largely unknown. In a few pertinent passages of *The Peopling of British North America*, Bernard Bailyn opposes New England, which remained genuinely homogeneous in the eighteenth century, to New York, in "the settlements scattered from the Hudson River south to the Delaware," where one

> would have found ethnic diversity of the most extreme kind, and not a single expanding network of communities impelled outward by the dynamics of a distinctive demographic process, but half a dozen different demographic processes moving in different phases at different speeds.
>
> Small migrant flows over many years had produced New York's population of 1700. Originally people had come from

New England, from England, from France, from the German
principalities, from Brazil, indirectly from Africa, and from Virginia and Maryland. . . . In the Hudson Valley there were Dutch,
French, Walloons, Palatines, and English. Manhattan, with a
population of only five thousand, was dominated numerically by
the Dutch but politically, socially, and economically by the
English and French; it had a small community of Jews. (95)

Despite this, New England remains overwhelmingly the place we look for
patterns of American settlement and models of cultural progress.

62. John Higham, *Send These to Me: Jews and Other Immigrants in Urban America*
(New York: Atheneum, 1975), 15.

63. Steinberg, 33.

64. Leonard Dinnerstein and David M. Reimers, *Ethnic Americans: A History of
Immigration and Assimilation* (New York: Dodd, Mead, 1975), 37.

65. Glenn C. Altschuler, *Race, Ethnicity, and Class in American Social Thought,
1865-1919* (Arlington Heights, IL: Harlan Davidson, 1982), 43.

66. Quoted in Fuchs, 57.

67. Bailyn, 100-1.

68. Altschuler, 56.

69. As contemporary immigrants must choose between industrial and
postindustrial poverty.

70. Bailyn, 65-86.

71. Ibid., 73.

72. Higham asserts, "[A] dependence on unskilled immigrant labor encouraged
the introduction of automatic machines and processes" (23).

73. Irving Howe, *World of Our Fathers* (New York: Simon and Schuster, 1976),
35. The language used for immigration from Asia was just as hyperbolic:
"America is a veritable human paradise, the number one mine in the world.
Gold, silver, and gems are scattered on her streets. If you can figure out a way
of picking them up, you'll become rich instantly to the tune of ten million
and be able to enjoy ultimate human pleasures" (quoted in Yuji Ichioka, *The
Issei: The World of the First Generation Japanese Immigrants, 1885-1924* [New
York: The Free Press, 1988], 11).

74. As movie audiences learned to read film, they laughed at the earliest and
strictest representations of the myth of transformation created by, or under
the authority of, the beneficiaries of that myth—the small number of immigrants who *did* rise above a sea of anonymity, overwork, ill health, and
death, those for whom magical transformation worked. As present-day
audience members, we laugh at those "lacunae" in silent films and early sound
films in which time and effort collapse, where a man becomes a lawyer in a

four-week summer course in order to defend himself at his own trial. (Comic glosses on this phenomenon still surface on occasion, as in the 1978 film *Movie-Movie*.) But we laugh from the vantage point of a culture that still celebrates the individual entrepreneur as culture hero, whether he is selling nostalgia for an unproblematically successful corporate capitalism (Steve Wozniak, Lee Iacocca) or the ethic of violence that allows for this success (Bernard Goetz, Oliver North). We still conceive of the exception as the rule, or worse, as if it *should be* the rule, because we cannot admit that such exceptions work only because they are exceptional.

75. Terry Ramsaye, *A Million and One Nights: A History of the Motion Picture* (New York: Simon and Schuster, 1926); Lewis Jacobs, *The Rise of the American Film: A Critical History* (1939; rpt. New York: Teachers College Press, 1967), especially 74-75; Lary May, *Screening Out the Past: The Birth of Mass Culture and the Motion Picture Industry* (New York: Oxford University Press, 1980).

76. For these neoconservative revisionist film histories, see especially Charles Musser, *Before the Nickelodeon: Edwin S. Porter and the Edison Manufacturing Company* (Berkeley: University of California Press, 1991); and Musser and Carol Nelson, *High-Class Moving Pictures: Lyman H. Howe and the Forgotten Era of Traveling Exhibition, 1880-1920* (Princeton, NJ: Princeton University Press, 1991); for my analysis of these revisions, see the introduction.

77. May, 253-55. In a table on the "Birthplaces of Movie Personnel" (255), May finds that around the year 1920, 484, or about one-quarter, of the 1,914 movie personnel polled were foreign born. Further, May finds that 64 percent of the movie personnel were urban born, which suggests that a large number of those who were native born were the children of immigrants.

78. "Even as late as 1912 while some 5 percent of New York City audiences comprised the business class, and 25 percent were clerical workers, about 70 percent continued to be the oldest audience of the motion picture, the working class" (John Izod, *Hollywood and the Box Office: 1895-1986* [New York: Columbia University Press, 1988], 38).

79. The bickering between the Cohens and the Kellys, for example, can be, if not completely dismissed as an unrealistic version of the traditional animosity between the Irish- and the Jewish Americans, at least defined according to anthropologist Anya Peterson Royce's metonymic definition of the stereotype: "Stereotypes generally pick out some conspicuous attribute or attributes and let it or them stand for the whole" (*Ethnic Identity: Strategies of Diversity* [Bloomington: Indiana University Press, 1982], 147).

80. Neil Schmitz, in *Of Huck and Alice*, notices this homology, but attributes it to an unexplained "American" impulse: "There has always been, after all, a fascination in American art with the destruction of things. . . . We like to look

at the event of demolition, feel the release of all that power, see things fly. . . .
We are indeed a short technical distance in [Sut Lovingood's] "skeers" from the
kinetic bedlam of silent film comedy (55-56).

81. In contrast, say, to Georges Méliès, who played with size in *The Man with the Rubber Head, The Conquest of the Pole,* or *A Trip to the Moon,* and with fairy-tale transformation.

82. Izod, 10.

83. Daniel Boorstin, *The Americans: The Colonial Experience* (New York: Random House, 1958), 165.

84. Boorstin, 166.

85. Bela Balazs, *Theory of the Film: Character and Growth of a New Art,* trans. Edith Bone (1945; rpt. New York: Dover, 1970).

86. Justin Kaplan, quoted in "If You Wish You'd Said It, You Can," *The Memphis Commercial Appeal* (November 25, 1993), C15.

87. Anderson, 40.

88. Ibid., 39.

89. Félix Guattari and Gilles Deleuze, "What Is a Minor Literature?" *The Mississippi Review,* 11, no. 3 (Winter/Spring 1983): 13-33.

90. See, for example, Editors of Cahiers du Cinema, "Young Mr. Lincoln," in *Screen,* 13, no. 3 (1972): 13-35.

91. Werner Sollors, *Beyond Ethnicity: Consent and Descent in American Culture* (New York: Oxford University Press, 1986), 31.

92. [T]he less frequently reported fact was that the theater catered to him [the lower-class audience member] through necessity, not through choice. The blue-collar worker and his family may have supported the nickelodeon. The scandal was that no one connected with the movies much wanted his support—least of all the immigrant film exhibitors who were working their way out of the slums. The most frequent complaint against nickelodeon audiences—voiced with monotonous regularity in trade journals, personal correspondence, and in Congressional testimony—was that moviegoers as a group lacked "class."

(Russell Merritt, "Nickelodeon Theaters," *A.F.I. Report* [Washington, DC: American Film Institute, May, 1973], 5).

93. In a certain social-psychoanalytic manner it was perfectly sensible that the oedipal struggle for control would result in the moguls' attempt to take the place of the genteel ethnologists. Izod quotes one of Carl Laemmle's perorations against the Edison trust that sounds positively Miltonic in its phallic rebellion: "I wll rot in Hades before I will join the Trust. . . . How is *your* backbone?" (26; emphasis in original).

94. Samuel Goldwyn's *Behind the Screen* (New York: George H. Doran, 1923) is rather interesting as a study in tone. Still another rags-to-riches tale, it is told in the diction of a Dickens, a duke, or a Damon Runyon.

95. Richard Maltby, "The Political Economy of Hollywood: The Studio System," in *Cinema, Politics and Society in America*, ed. Philip Davies and Brian Neve (Manchester: Manchester University Press, 1981), 54.

96. Leonard Dinnerstein, Roger L. Nichols, and David M. Reimers, *Natives and Strangers: Ethnic Groups and the Building of America* (New York: Oxford University Press, 1979).

97. Stanley Cavell, *Pursuits of Happiness: The Hollywood Comedy of Remarriage* (Cambridge, MA: Harvard University Press, 1981). An extended explanation of this critique appears in chapter 4.

98. By the mid- and late 1920s native-born citizens increasingly represented the ethnic population. While the rate of immigration in the United States decreased from 10.4 per thousand in the decade 1901-1910 to 0.4 per thousand in 1931-1940 (with a huge decrease at the end of the 1920s), the rate of births to immigrants stayed relatively stable in the same period. While the number of immigrants admitted to the United States fell drastically, from nearly 9 million in the decade of 1901-1910 to under 1 million in the decade of the 1930s, the "native white population of foreign or mixed parentage" grew from 15,600,000 in 1900 to 23,100,000 in 1940 (U.S. Department of Commerce, Bureau of the Census, *Statistical History of the United States from Colonial Times to the Present* [Stamford, CT: Fairfield Publishers, 1965] and *Statistical Abstracts of the United States*, 84-85).

99. Richard Krickus, *Pursuing the American Dream: White Ethnics and the New Populism* (Bloomington: Indiana University Press, 1976).

100. Maxine Schwartz Seller, "Introduction," in *Ethnic Theatre in the United States*, ed. Maxine Schwartz Seller (Westport, CT: Greenwood Press, 1983), 8.

101. Richard Sennett and Jonathan Cobb, *The Hidden Injuries of Class* (1972; rpt. New York: Vintage Books, 1973), 27-28.

102. Everett Stonequist, *The Marginal Man: A Study in Personality and Culture Conflict* (New York: Scribner, 1937).

103. Barbara Miller Solomon, "The Intellectual Background of the Immigration Restriction Movement in New England," *New England Quarterly* 25 (1952): 47-59.

104. Without any awareness of so doing, one sociologist makes vaudeville *exactly* co-extensive with new immigration: "the 1880s to the 1920s" (Robert W. Snyder, "Big Time, Small Time, All Around the Town: New York Vaudeville in the Early Twentieth Century," in *For Fun and Profit: The Transformation of Leisure into Consumption*, ed. Richard Butsch [Philadelphia: Temple University Press, 1990], 119).

105. Eric Anderson presented a paper at the 1993 American Studies Association convention in Boston on the presence of a plains Indian aesthetic in Krazy Kat comics, entitled "Ectoplasms, or the Trickster Inside Krazy Kat." And even legitimate theater was occasionally recreated as a Bakhtinian polyphony. How else are we to read the successful run in America of the Italian Ernesto Rossi as the Danish prince in an English play? (See Marvin Carlson, *The Italian Shakespearians: Performances by Ristory, Salvini, and Rossi in England and America* [Washington, DC: Folger Books, 1985], 132.)

106. For example, Gracye Susan Burian, "Stanley and Aileen: Children in Vaudeville," *Journal of American Culture*, 7, nos. 1-2 (Spring/Summer 1984): 9-15; or Jill Dolan, who, in speaking of burlesque, asserts with evidently no sense of audience whatsoever, "If the humor was reassuring, the fears it assuaged were those of the dominant white male majority" ("'What, No Beans?' Images of Women and Sexuality in Burlesque Comedy," *Journal of Popular Culture*, 18, no. 3 [Winter 1984]: 37-38).

107. The analogy here is with Mikhail Bakhtin's assertion that Rabelais's prose reflected the change from a medieval belief system to a Renaissance "carnivalesque" skepticism (*Rabelais and His World*, trans. Helene Iswolsky [Bloomington: Indiana University Press, 1984]).

108. Theodor Reik notwithstanding. Theodor Reik, *Jewish Wit* (New York: Gamut Press, 1962).

109. Dinnerstein et al., in *Natives and Strangers*, provide a chart of the "[m]ain sources of European [i]mmigration to the United States," from which the following was excerpted (87):

	1841-1850	1851-1860
Denmark	5,074	4,738
Germany	434,626	951,667
Great Britain		
England	32,092	247,125
Scotland	3,712	38,331
Ireland	780,719	914,119
Netherlands	8,251	10,789

110. In "Vaudeville in Los Angeles, 1910-1926" (*Pacific Historical Review* 61, no. 1 [February 1992]: 103-13) Stan Singer even asserts that there were radical differences between Los Angeles and New York vaudeville. Another critic asserts that, in America, "[m]iddle-class Victorians found their culture of restraint and self-discipline challenged by brash comedians, singers, and dancers from the Lower East Side" (Robert Snyder, *The Voice of the City: Vaudeville and Popular Culture in New York* [New York: Oxford University

Press, 1989], 120). It is only fair to assert here that Snyder, like Henry Jenkins (*What Made Pistachio Nuts? Early Sound Comedy and the Vaudeville Aesthetic* [New York: Columbia University Press, 1992]), sees the intrusion of film as the chief cause of an absolute decline in ethnic representation.

111. Elaine Aston, "Male Impersonation in the Music Hall: The Case of Vesta Tilley," *New Theatre Quarterly* 4, no. 15 (August 1988): 247.

112. Laurence Senelick, "Wedekind at the Music Hall," *New Theatre Quarterly* 4, no. 15 (August 1988): 327.

113. Senelick, 327.

114. Michael Diamond, for example, discusses the presence in music hall "Jingos" of a "popularity aroused by the nationalist and anti-Russian elements to the Suez deal" ("Political Heroes of the Victorian Music Hall," *History Today* 40 [January 1990]: 34).

115. Senelick documents that Frank Wedekind wrote sketches in "the 'Anglo-American' style (for which read slapstick)" (326).

116. Say, for example, the "cabaret artistique" as described by John Houchin, "The Origins of the Cabaret Artistique," *The Drama Review* 28, no. 1 (Spring 1984): 5-14.

117. Dinnerstein et al., *Natives and Strangers,* 164. It is not too far-fetched to ask whether the thirteenth-century Chinese *tsa-chü* or *yüan-pen* forms of vaudeville, with their variety formats and mixes of song, narrative, and comedy, are not, in some circuitous fashion, influences on contemporary theater. Elsewhere Dinnerstein states that "in the early decades of the twentieth century [the Jews] made up half the actors, popular songwriters, and song publishers in New York City" (Dinnerstein and Reimers, *Ethnic Americans,* 44). More lyrically, Robert W. Snyder remarks that "vaudeville had to have as many voices as the city where it thrived. They swelled together in a chorus that was rarely in unison" (xiv).

118. Seller, 8.

119. Ibid., 3-17.

120. This is true even in the most recent texts by Henry Jenkins (*What Made Pistachio Nuts?*) and Robert C. Allen (*A Horrible Prettiness: Burlesque and American Culture* [Chapel Hill: University of North Carolina Press, 1991]).

121. Maxine Schwartz Seller asserts in her introduction that "observers who approached the ethnic theater free of negative stereotypes . . . often came away with admiration for the quality of the performances and increased understanding of the ethnic community" (10).

122. John Dimeglio, *Vaudeville U.S.A.* (Bowling Green, OH: Bowling Green University Popular Press, 1973); Douglas Gilbert, *American Vaudeville, Its Life and Times* (New York: McGraw-Hill, 1940); Albert McLean, *American Vaudeville as Ritual* (Lexington: University of Kentucky Press, 1965); and Shirley Staples,

Male-Female Comedy Teams in American Vaudeville, 1865-1932 (Ann Arbor, MI: UMI Research Press, 1984). Even Allen's otherwise marvelously researched *Horrible Prettiness*, which *does* interest itself in nineteenth-century popular stage representation, ignores ethnicity.

Gilbert provides one of the best summaries of the variety house, though it is fairly generic. At some point in the study of popular culture some enterprising historian or anthropologist will resuscitate the variety hall for scholarship as a respectable "art form" that precedes vaudeville as vaudeville precedes film, or as Southwestern regional humor precedes *Huckleberry Finn*. But for now, Gilbert still sums up one current attitude toward variety:

> That is what your grandpappies laughed at. The seventies were
> the cowbarn days of vaudeville. The audiences (all male) were
> none too bright, a mental condition hardly improved by alco-
> holic befuddlement. Jokes had to be sledge-hammered home.
> The days of personalities, subtlety, wit, expert dancing, and
> superb technique were to come. (26)

123. Robert C. Allen, *Vaudeville and Film 1895-1915: A Study in Media Interaction* (New York: Arno Press, 1980), 23-24.

124. "The curtain rose on a group of harvesters, boys and girls, busy about a haystack. Smirks and gestures of a purport easily grasped by those in the audience not too drunk to understand were a prelude to the exit of all but one couple. This couple repaired to the back of the haystack. Then the others returned, and the boys, one by one, with simpers, gigglings, and pointings and suggestive calls visited the girl behind the stack. As each returned to the stage his expression registered what had happened. The finale was the exit of one of the boys in disordered clothing" (Gilbert, 11).

125. This excess is a far cry from Roland Barthes's vision of a desexualized striptease, and Laura Mulvey's notion of filmic voyeurism. "Striptease," originally published 1954, reprinted in *TriQuarterly* 63 (Spring/Summer 1985): 31-33; Laura Mulvey, *Visual and Other Pleasures* (Bloomington: Indiana University Press, 1989).

126. Marybeth Hamilton, "Mae West Live: *SEX, The Drag*, and 1920s Broadway," *TDR* 36, no. 4 (Winter 1992): 98. Without really intending to, Hamilton also makes reference to an orientalized interest in sexuality on the legitimate stage. *SEX* takes place in part in Trinidad; the contemporaneous *Shanghai Gesture* in the "far east." *Lulu Belle* is "the tale of a mean, merciless, unrepentant mulatto hooker seducing black and white lovers from Harlem to Paris" (98).

127. This wealth of orientalizing is quite apart from the well-documented "coon songs" and black-face performers cited, for example, in James H. Dormon, "Shaping the Popular Image of Post-Reconstruction American Blacks: The

'Coon Song' Phenomenon of the Gilded Age," *American Quarterly* 40, no. 4 (December 1988): 450-71; and Janet Brown, "The 'Coon-Singer' and the 'Coon-Song': A Case Study of the Performer-Character Relationship," *Journal of American Culture* 7, no. 1 (Spring/Summer 1984): 1-9.

128. Gilbert, 249.

129. Channing Pollock, *The Green Book Album* (December 1911), 1209; rpt. in *Selected Vaudeville Criticism,* ed. Anthony Slide (Metuchen, NJ: The Scarecrow Press, 1988), 58.

130. Gilbert, 135-51.

131. Snyder, "Big Time, Small Time," 120.

132. Staples discusses the class consciousness of the vaudeville moguls:

> Keith's insistence on polite behavior and the earmarks of status betrays, perhaps, his own class-sensitivity. A former circus grifter, his personal fortune had risen with the variety business; he wanted vaudeville to be not only wholesome but also high-class, presumably because its status mirrored his own. Like Keith, most of the successful vaudeville producers had begun in the humblest capacities in the entertainment business, and they were anxious, self-conscious arbiters of the vaudeville audience's taste. (76-77)

133. Allen, *Vaudeville and Film,* 296.

134. Frederick Snyder, "American Vaudeville: Theater in a Package," Ph.D. diss. Yale University, 1970; quoted in Allen, *Vaudeville and Film,* 8-9.

135. Perhaps it is best to quote Robert Snyder to demonstrate the kind of criticism that sees ethnicity as unproblematically cohesive:

> Whatever their origins, one factor united the vaudevillians: one way or another, all of them were beyond the pale of native-born, middle-class society. In his book *Vaudeville U.S.A.,* historian John Dimeglio asserts that the majority of New Yorkers who entered vaudeville were from "underprivileged circumstances." Bill Smith, a writer who covered the vaudeville scene as a journalist, asserts that "most performers came from working-class families." Biographies, interviews, correspondence, and newspaper clippings confirm this point. Vaudevillians often seem to have been from an immigrant, ethnic, or working-class background. Blacks were also present, although the widespread practice of putting only one black act in a show limited the extent of their opportunities. (45)

136. Gilbert, 243.

137. Jenkins, 37, 41, 45, and passim.

138. McLean, 112-13.

139. Ibid., 3.

140. Robert C. Allen, "B. F. Keith and the Origins of American Vaudeville," *Theater Survey* 21, no. 2 (November 1980): 106.

141. Ibid., 106-08. For example, "P. T. Barnum was instrumental in the transformation of the American museum from temple of science to palace of freaks" (107).

142. Ibid., 112-13.

143. This upward mobility is not true of all the American arts at all times, but rather of local arts that aspire to a more universal appeal. The actors and producers of off-Broadway shows in the 1940s and 1950s, especially the subscribers to the Strasberg "method," became in fact less "intellectual" as the years went by while also attempting to create a greater mass appeal for the kind of theater they professed. Marlon Brando went from *A Streetcar Named Desire* (1951) to *Bedtime Story* (1964; with David Niven); in his last film—*Going in Style* (1979)—Lee Strasberg appropriately co-starred with George Burns, a perennial vaudevillian. (Of course, in a rather surprising moment, Clark Gable is virtually a method actor in *The Misfits* [1961].)

144. Gilbert, 322.

145. Saxton, especially chapter 7, "Blackface Minstrelsy" (165-82).

146. Gilbert, 62.

147. Staples, 31.

148. Joe Welch, in "Troubles," *American Popular Entertainments: Jokes, Monologues, Bits, and Sketches,* ed. Brooks McNamara (New York: Performing Arts Journal Publications, 1983), 40.

149. Staples, 47.

150. Ibid., 76-77.

151. This explanation of vaudeville and early cinema as palliative social measures to decrease the pain of social inequity, though probably acceptable, is still, however, too unexamined. To say that the customer enters the theater for a couple of hours in order to forget troubles that he or she must subsequently resume on leaving the premises is hardly more than descriptive. One wonders why such palliative measures work, what it is about them that is efficacious, and even whether they do work efficaciously.

CHAPTER 2

1. For example, virtually all the reviews in *Variety* of the early films center (often rather unfavorably) on the physicality of the films: "[*Work*] is the usual Chaplin work of late, mussy, messy and dirty" (*Variety,* June 25, 1915).

2. From James Agee's seminal "Comedy's Greatest Era" (*Agee on Film*, vol. I [1946], rpt. in *Film Theory and Criticism: Introductory Readings*, ed. Gerald Mast and Marshall Cohen [Oxford: Oxford University Press, 1974]): "Funny as his bout with the Murphy bed is, the glances of awe, expostulation and helpless, almost whimpering desire for vengeance which he darts at this infernal machine are even better" (446).

3. Gerald Mast, *The Comic Mind: Comedy and the Movies* (Chicago: University of Chicago Press, 1979), especially 61-104.

4. Charles J. Maland refers rather vaguely to Chaplin's "interaction with objects," in *Chaplin and American Culture: The Evolution of a Star Image* (Princeton, NJ: Princeton University Press, 1989), 30.

5. Albert McLean, *American Vaudeville as Ritual* (Louisville: University of Kentucky Press, 1965). For McLean, vaudeville is the ritual enactment of the American myth of success.

6.   Even as a Lancashire Lads beginner . . . as fate would have it, he planned to start a comedy team called the Millionaire Tramps. And though the team did not materialize, it nicely anticipated the irony of his later position—being a millionaire by way of his portrayal of a cinema tramp. (Paperback editions of his autobiography often carried the additional title: *Memoirs of a Millionaire Tramp*.)

    (Wes D. Gehring, *Charlie Chaplin: A Bio-Bibliography* [Westport, CT: Greenwood Press, 1983], 6).

7. Ibid., 9.

8. Carlos Drummond de Andrade, "Song for That Man of the People Charlie Chaplin," trans. Thomas Colchie, *Paris Review* 28 (Summer/Fall 1986): 152-59.

9. "Charlie is a little usurper. Having come at the beginning of the film industry, he monopolizes it. When in class someone asks, 'Tom, who invented the movies?' the answer is always, 'Charlie.'" *Le Disque Vert*, 3rd series, vol. 2, nos. 4-5 (Paris: Disque Vert, 1924), 23.

10. See especially Charles J. Maland, "The Immigration and Naturalization Service Interview with Charles Chaplin," *Cineaste*, 14, no. 4 (1986): 10-15.

11. From the autobiographical *My Wonderful Visit* (London: Hurst & Blackett, 1922), published in the United States as *My Trip Abroad* (New York: Harper & Brothers, 1922):

        "Oh, do you think Jewish people are clever?" she asks, eagerly.
        "Of course. All great geniuses had Jewish blood in them. No, I am not Jewish," as she is about to put that question, "but I am sure there must be some somewhere in me. I hope so." (209)

12. Reginald R. Chaplin, "Charlie Chaplin's Ancestors," *Historical Journal of Film, Radio and Television 5*, no. 2 (1985): 211. From the first issue of the *New Yorker*, which evidently did not know what to make of Chaplin: "A mad sensualist, emerged, sadistic, yet possessed of a cruel love of checking himself back into intelligence. At 3 A.M. he was a wistful, bewildered lad of the East End. If words of the kabala had come from his hard mouth, I should not have wondered. He seemed a Jew." Apart from other phrases connoting crypto-anti-Semitism like "mad sensualist," "sadistic," and "cruel love," the article is in part about Chaplin's ability to disguise himself, an archetypally Jewish ability ("Funny Legs," the *New Yorker* 1 [May 23, 1925], 10). Finally, by 1985, one critic unproblematically reads Chaplin as part of a history of Jewish humor: Morris Dickstein, "Urban Comedy and Modernity: From Chaplin to Woody Allen," *Partisan Review, 52*, no. 3 (1985): 271-81. Of course, reading Chaplin as simply Jewish is as problematic as eliminating Jewishness from his identity altogether.

13. Gehring describes Chaplin's Dickensian sense of his own childhood as described in *Charlie Chaplin's Own Story* (ed. Harry M. Geduld [1916; rpt. Bloomington: Indiana University Press, 1985]) this way: "Chaplin's story even has a nasty Fagin (Mr. Hawkins) who steals a child (young Chaplin) away to slave for him, as well as an Artful Dodger (Snooper) who, of course, steals purses" (123). At least two critic-biographers believe this version of Chaplin: "He and Dickens particularly are of the same stock, filled with the same humanism. . . . They share too the same ingenuous sentimentality, the gift of pathos exploited. . . . Jo the crossing sweeper, Oliver Twist and Smike are blood brothers of the Kid, indeed of Charlie himself" (Peter Cotes and Thelma Niklaus, *The Little Fellow: The Life and Work of Charles Spencer Chaplin* [London: Paul Elek, 1951], 9).

14. Charles Chaplin, *My Autobiography* (New York: Simon and Schuster, 1964), 122-31.

15. Cotes and Niklaus, 23.

16. "Chaplin, taking a serious view of his responsibility for his young half-cousin . . . continued to urge Betty to take American citizenship. When she countered that he had never done so, he would only reply that he was too old" (David Robinson, *Chaplin: His Life and Art* [New York: McGraw-Hill, 1985], 497).

17. Chaplin, *My Wonderful Visit*, 47.

18. Chaplin, *Charlie Chaplin's Own Story*, 159.

19. Abraham Cahan, *The Rise of David Levinsky* (New York: Harper, 1966); Anzia Yezierska, *Bread Givers* (Garden City, NY: Doubleday, Page, 1925).

20. Leonard Dinnerstein, Roger L. Nichols, and David M. Reimers, *Natives and Strangers: Ethnic Groups and the Building of America* (New York: Oxford University Press, 1979):

Unlike so many foreigners [British emigrants] spoke English as a native tongue and did not feel as strange in the United States as did members of other national minorities. Immigrants from the United Kingdom were often welcome in America because they had valuable skills. . . .Even in growing cities experienced English workers soon found themselves at the top of the working class. Thus their cultural similarity and relatively easier economic adjustment made their experiences considerably less harsh than those of the Irish or even of the Germans and the Scandinavians. (100-1)

21. In the popular press, his Englishness was not necessarily an asset. In a negative review of *A Woman* (1915), Englishness and transvestitism are equated: "Chaplin in a woman's dress, with his English ideas of comedy" (*Variety,* June 16, 1915).

22. Maland, 11. Maland goes on to quote one magazine review: "From a penniless immigrant . . . to the highest paid movie actor—is the story of Chaplin's rapid rise to success."

23. Maland quotes Chaplin as having asserted, apropos of some English criticism: "They say I have a duty to England. I wonder just what that duty is? No one wanted me or cared for me in England seventeen years ago. I had to go to America for my chance, and I got it there. Only then did England take the slightest interest in me" (128). Maland then goes on to assert that the American press loved this affirmation of the myth of American self-reliance and success. As if acknowledging this mythos, Chaplin seems to define the old country as tragic, the new country as comic. He sometimes goes so far as to minimize the origins of his art in England: "Everything I know and don't know . . . I learned [in the United States]. . . . Sir Herbert Tree has taught me many things, but not in England" (Konrad Bercovici, "Charlie Chaplin: An Authorized Interview," quoted in Gehring, 106).

24. Robinson, 51-52. Robinson also quotes a Miss Edith Scales, who describes a youthful Chaplin's behavior in the witness box: "Charlie first went into the witness box, but no one could understand his cockney accent. The sergeant kept touching him on the shoulder and saying, 'Will you speak a little more clearly please?'" (49-50).

25. Robinson, 602.

26. Dinnerstein et al., *Natives and Strangers,* 107.

27. J. P. Telotte, "Arbuckle Escapes," *Journal of Popular Film and Television* 15 (Winter 1988): 172-79, asserts that Arbuckle contains some Derridean tensions, both within his comedy, and between his screen persona and the press representation of his life. Certainly the pathos of his post-scandal life is founded in his screen persona.

28. To cite one example: in *Fatty's Plucky Pup* Arbuckle bathes his dog in a clothes washtub as if it were a shirt.

29. James R. Quirk, "Mabel Normand Says Goodbye," *Photoplay* (May 1930), 182.

30. It is probably important to assert here, however, that although Chaplin is the best example of the repression and displacement of immigrant tensions onto silent comedy, most other silent comedians participate in this dynamic, whether they are immigrants or not. Chaplin's informality in relation to the camera (raising the audience to the level of performer's intimate) transgresses the genteel proscenium arch in a way that most of the silent clowns duplicate at one time or another. As the tramp is often referred to as Charlie, so Fatty Arbuckle, Mabel Normand, and other comics are recognized by their "real" names (*Mabel's Busy Day* [1914], *Fatty's Plucky Pup* [1915], *Mabel, Fatty and the Law* [1915]), as if even the titles and intertitles are thematically tied to this confusion and conflation of representation and history. Chapter 3 will argue that the revelation of names has more to do with ethnic unveiling than with the endings of Victorian romances.

31. Critics are eternally arguing over the facts of Chaplin's early life, including whether he is Jewish, how deprived his childhood was, and even the existence of at least one of his marriages (to Paulette Godard). As Gehring romantically asserts, "Like Pan, the Greek god of fields and forests to whom Chaplin's comedy persona frequently is compared, mystery seems to have surrounded the creator of the tramp from the beginning" (3). Articles such as Harold Manning and Timothy J. Lyons, "Charlie Chaplin's Early Life: Fact and Fiction," *Historical Journal of Film, Radio, and Television*, 3, no. 1 (1983): 35-41, merely throw into relief the need for elaboration. This tendency toward biographical opacity can be seen in other comic American characters, from Krazy Kat, who has only an eternal present, to Dagwood, whose patrician roots were quickly obscured under a protracted suburban present, to film comedy teams of the 1930s through the 1950s.

32. It is rather interesting to contrast Chaplin's biographies with that of another emigré of the previous century. T. Edgar Pemberton's *John Hare: Comedian, 1865-1895* (London: George Routledge and Sons, 1895) begins: "Now that the inevitable has happened, and following the example of his famous brother and sister artists, Mr. John Hare has determined to cross the Atlantic and give American audiences a taste of his quality" (7). The biography, while alluding to the difficulties of life in the theater, takes great pains to deny the suffering of its subject. Poverty and change are not so clearly memorialized as they are in Chaplin's biographies.

Another, more comprehensive text, Montrose J. Moses's *Famous Actor-Families in America* (New York: Thomas Y. Crowell, 1906), includes the family trees of acting nobility, and contains the assertion, "The history of the drama in America is a part of the history of the English drama; our actors were mostly of English origin, our early theaters subjected to all the conventions that marked the London stage" (4). Such an assertion would within a decade be almost impossible to make.

33. Parker Tyler's reading of Chaplin's career begins with the conflation of child, private adult, and filmmaker: "Chaplin's epic of the child aristocrat, the great artist, and the frustrated lover, has taken place" (*Chaplin: Last of the Clowns* [New York: Vanguard, 1948], 19).

34. The Chaplin narrative, and early American film, re-invents self-reflexivity in such a way that, in the twentieth century, the American narrative will be identified closely with the experience of the writer at several levels of production: advertising, creation, performance. As an immigrant, Chaplin performs a fictionalized version of himself in the 1910s, re-enacting himself in a way acceptable to both immigrant and mainstream cultures. Except for Gertrude Stein, high-culture narrators like Fitzgerald, Hemingway, and Faulkner will re-enact themselves in prose fiction only from the 1920s. The impulse to identify the American narrative as a fictionalized elaboration of the writer's life begins, not with expatriates to Paris, but with the Hollywood immigrants a decade before.

35. Chaplin, *Charlie Chaplin's Own Story*, 42.

36. Ibid., 36.

37. Ibid., 25.

38. Ibid., 35.

39. Ibid., 91-92.

40. The public relations aspect of Chaplin's life and work are the entire focus of *Chaplin and American Culture*. More generally, critics often complain of the fictional quality of the celebrity's account of his own life. David Robinson gives quite compelling evidence that this autobiography is not really Chaplin's doing at all but the unauthorized work of Rose Wilder Lane, a "representative of the *San Francisco Bulletin*" (and daughter of children's-book author Laura Ingalls Wilder) (180); Maland follows Robinson on this point. Chaplin critics especially lament the lacunae in his memory. But it is part of the process of fame to be the subject of discussion. The criticism and the lamentations are part of the larger process of notoriety. They imply a desire to get at the truth of the life of the celebrity, which is itself only an acknowledgment that that life has become interesting and significant. The dispute over authorship only throws into relief the fact that, finally, only the story is interesting, not its status as fiction; it is, in fact, more interesting if fictional.

41. Lary May, *Screening Out the Past: The Birth of Mass Culture and the Motion Picture Industry* (New York: Oxford University Press, 1980): "So in the great campaign against the movies in 1908 [Charles Sprague] Smith spoke for regulation and gained support of the producers. . . . Adding legitimacy to the voluntary Board was the list of local notables on the executive committee. Nearly all of them were wealthy Protestants, with a few German Jews" (55).

42. Chaplin, *My Wonderful Visit,* 5.

43. Nathan Glazer and Daniel Patrick Moynihan, *Beyond the Melting Pot: The Negroes, Puerto Ricans, Jews, Italians, and Irish of New York City* (1963; rpt. Cambridge, MA: MIT Press, 1970), 16.

44. Lynn Hollen Lees, *Exiles of Erin: Irish Migrants in Victorian London* (Ithaca, NY: Cornell University Press, 1979), 88.

45. Maureen Waters, *The Comic Irishman* (Ithaca, NY: State University of New York Press, 1984), 10.

46. Ibid., 30.

47. Ibid., 42.

48. Ibid., 44. Interesting how this sounds precisely like American minstrelsy.

49. Even if that point of view is itself self-contradictory, like the Progressive politics with which Gehring identifies him in "Chaplin and the Progressive Era."

50. Thomas F. Pettigrew, "Ethnicity in American Life: A Social-Psychological Perspective," in *Ethnic Groups in the City: Culture, Institutions, and Power,* ed. Otto Feinstein (Lexington, MA: Heath, 1971), presents the most complete case that the major strategies for assimilation—the melting pot, the triple melting pot, and pluralism (all ethnic designations remain absolutely separate) are failed strategies (29-37).

51. Dinnerstein et al., *Natives and Strangers,* 111.

52. Ibid.

53. Of course, hegemonic restrictions could not immediately erase difference, even after the introduction of sound in film: "Just as Hollywood has become a veritable babel of the movie world with foreign talkies running riot in all the studios, so has New York suddenly become the show window of foreign movie product. There have been German (of course!), French, Italian, Spanish, Polish, Yiddish, Swedish and Hungarian talkies presented within the last few months" (Herman G. Weinberg, "Notes from America," *Close Up* 8, no. 3 [September 1931]: 191). The tendency to allow ethnicity even at home is now discouraged by a new generation of neoconservative thinkers such as Richard Rodriguez, who believes his own experience of being forced to speak English at home, though painful, was both salutary and inevitable (*Hunger of Memory: The Education of Richard Rodriguez* [Boston: D. R. Richard Godine, 1982]).

54. Charles F. Keyes, "The Dialectics of Ethnic Change," in *Ethnic Change,* ed. Charles F. Keyes (Seattle: University of Washington Press, 1981), 15.

55. These contested meanings are mainly immigrant, but also include gender conventions: the films are interested, for example, in definitions of homosexuality. Homosexuality is intermittently an issue across the Chaplin oeuvre and may, in some sense, be the most interesting transformation of all. Though William Paul cites only instances from *City Lights* (1931), and though Stanley Kauffmann "can't remember this element in another Chaplin picture," it is present at least as a conventional homophobia in intertitles—"Count Rendered: just a nice boy who rides horseback with both legs on one side" (*Caught in a Cabaret* [1914]); and "Next day a fairy floated into the studio" (*The Masquerader* [1914]). The latter film, and *A Woman* (1915), contain more interesting discurses on transvestitism. In both films, Chaplin is in drag, and, unlike Milton Berle, he is rather beautiful. (See William Paul, "Chaplin and the Annals of Anality," in *Comedy/Cinema/Theory,* ed. Andrew S. Horton [Berkeley: University of California Press, 1991], 109-30; and Stanley Kauffmann, "City Lights," *Film Comment* 8, no. 3 [Sept-Oct 1972]: 18.) Stephen Neale and Frank Krutnik, in *Popular Film and Television Comedy* (New York: Routledge, 1990) briefly allude to the transvestitism in *A Woman* (1915) (127). Henry Bergman appears in drag in *The Rink* (1916). There is even a recognition that transvestitism is a significant motif in the contemporary popular criticism; of "The Five Funniest Things in the World," the fifth is "for a man to assume women's clothes" (Homer Croy, *Photoplay,* September 1918).

56. As a child actor Chaplin is supposed to have ad libbed a scene in which he played an animal by lifting his leg and making a motion as if to urinate.

57. Gilberto Perez Guillermo, "Charlie Chaplin: Faces and Facets," *Film Comment* 8, no. 3 (Sept.-Oct. 1972): 11.

58. David Aberbach has written an excellent article on the tramp and criminality: "Charlie Chaplin: Of Crime and Genius," *Encounter,* 60, no. 5 (May 1983): 86-92.

59. Robert Sklar, *Movie-Made America: A Cultural History of American Movies* (New York: Random House, 1975): "When one understands that Chaplin's consciousness was English—and working-class English—before it was American, some essential elements of his comic repertoire begin to fall into place. No comedian before or after him has spent more energy depicting people in their working lives: his first motion picture was prophetically titled *Making a Living*" (110).

60. John Higham, *Strangers in the Land: Patterns of American Nativism, 1860-1925* (1963; rpt. New York: Atheneum, 1974): "By 1870 about one out of every three employees in manufacturing and mechanical industries was an immigrant—a proportion which remained constant until the 1920s" (16).

61. Fatty Arbuckle's failed career is perhaps an even better index of the relationship between pathos and employment. One *Photoplay* article (March 1931) is significantly titled: "Just Let Me Work."

62. Alan Trachtenberg, *The Incorporation of America: Culture and Society in the Gilded Age* (New York: Hill and Wang, 1982), 71.

63.   But reality quickly makes Charlie land on his feet. Then, because he has fought so many times, been defeated, given life to objects, verified the fourth dimension, animated lifeless matter, and spontaneously enlivened a broom, a policeman, flower, a bench, a brick, a Ford, a ladylove, and a telephone, he went to Jerusalem as a good Israeli! There he met a little German Jewish woman, and Mr. William Shakespeare. A Jew renders comic even the most tragic circumstances.
    (Florent Fels, "That Damn Old Silly Charly Chaplin—To Him," in *Charlot,* ed. Franz Hellens, *Le Disque Vert,* 3rd Series, vol. 2, nos. 4-5 [Paris: Disque Vert, 1924], 29-33).

64. Mast, *The Comic Mind,* 50.

65. After Mast, the most typical use of Bergson in relation to Chaplin is contained in Wes D. Gehring's *Charlie Chaplin: A Bio-Bibliography.* Gehring briefly discusses "mechanical inelasticity" (21-22). One should probably assert that these critics use Bergson without any sense of the discrepancy between his theory and Chaplin's praxis.

66. Henri Bergson, *Laughter* (1900; rpt. in *Comedy,* ed. Wylie Sypher [Baltimore: Johns Hopkins University Press, 1956]), 79.

67. Ibid., 64.

68. In fact, audiences know perfectly well that the pain is real, as we know from the absorption with the on- and off-screen tribulations of film personalities from Fatty Arbuckle to John Landis. We are fascinated with such anecdotes as that of how Keaton broke his neck on the set of one his films.

69. Mast, *The Comic Mind,* 57.

70. Most recently among serious commentators, Fredric Jameson finds Bergson conservative: "[T]hus for Bergson comedy has the function of preserving social norms by castigating deviancy with ridicule" (*The Political Unconscious: Narrative as a Socially Symbolic Act* [Ithaca, NY: Cornell University Press, 1981], 107).

71. This summary is only a bit reductive: Bergson's ideal behavior does not mean one behavior, but rather a flexible range that changes momentarily.

72. Or, at least, the most famous films are singled out by critics for this quality. Gilbert Seldes, for example, spends a great deal of time describing Chaplin's use of objects, especially the clock, in *The Pawnshop* (*The Seven Lively Arts*

[New York: Harper and Brothers, 1924], 361-64). Gehring offers a general discussion of Chaplin in relation to "incongruity theory" (14-15).

73. These categories are as follows:
     1. Use of objects to evade authority:
          a. Use of objects to disguise self (lampshade to become lamp);
          b. Use of objects to impede progress of others (chairs near the end of *Modern Times*);
          c. Use of objects to hurt pursuing others (gas lamp over head to anaesthetize);
          d. Use of objects to increase speed of evasion;
          e. Use of body (of pursuer) to evade pursuer (walking over person as gangplank in *A Day's Pleasure* [1919]).
     2. Use of objects for pleasure, or for survival of self or of other:
          a. Use of objects to appear wealthy or middle class (dress, dressing stick as cane-lighter in *Sunnyside*)—this is still disguise.
     3. Mistaking one object or person for another:
          a. Lunch bell for fire alarm: the not serious for the serious.
     4. *Our* mistaking one object for another:
          a. Fishing for seasickness in *The Immigrant*;
          b. Cocktail mixing for crying in *The Idle Class*.
     5. Transformation of the body of the tramp:
          a. Superstrong or efficient: "his ability to carry a limitless number of chairs in *Behind the Screen* (1916)" (Gehring, 155), or shuffling cards (*The Immigrant*) and money (*Monsieur Verdoux*) at an incredible speed; or the incredible speed with which he lays bricks;
          b. Super-flexible: any drunk scene, as *Tango Tangles* (1914);
          c. Super-lucky, -intuitive, or -natural: skating in *Modern Times*.

74. Sigmund Freud, in *Jokes and Their Relation to the Unconscious,* trans. James Strachey (New York: W.W. Norton, 1960), proposes the paradigmatically psychological origin for the social utility of humor: "When the [sexual aggressor] finds his libidinal impulse inhibited by the woman, he develops a hostile trend against that second person and calls on the originally interfering third person as his ally. Through the first person's smutty speech the woman is exposed before the third, who, as listener, has now been bribed by the effortless satisfaction of his own libido" (100).

75. Dinnerstein et al., *Natives and Strangers,* 108-9.

76. For example, Peter Brunette mentions Scarry in passing, though he is really much more interested in applying Bakhtin's notion of the carnivalesque to

the Three Stooges ("The Three Stooges and the (Anti-) Narrative of Violence," in *Comedy/Cinema/Theory*, ed. Andrew Horton [Berkeley: University of California Press, 1991], 182).

77. Michel Foucault, *Discipline and Punish: The Birth of the Prison*, trans. Alan Sheridan (1975; trans. New York: Vintage, 1979); *Madness and Civilization: A History of Insanity in the Age of Reason*, trans. Robert Howard (1965; trans. New York: Vintage, 1988); and *The History of Sexuality*, vol. 1, trans. Robert Hurley (1980; New York: Pantheon Books, 1986).

78. Hélène Cixous and Catherine Clément, *The Newly Born Woman*, trans. Betsy Wing (Minneapolis: University of Minnesota Press, 1986); Helen Wilcox, Keith McWatters, Ann Thompson, and Linda Williams, eds., *The Body and the Text: Hélène Cixous—Reading and Teaching* (New York: St. Martin's Press, 1990); and Eve Kosofsky Sedgwick, *Between Men: English Literature and Male Homosocial Desire* (New York: Columbia University Press, 1985).

79. Elaine Scarry, *The Body in Pain: The Making and Unmaking of the World* (New York: Oxford University Press, 1985).

80. "[T]hat a picture from a Sears Roebuck catalogue should appear on the wall of a hut in Nairobi, that Sony recorders are prized in Iran, are events sometimes greeted by Western populations with bewilderment" (Ibid., 243).

81. Ibid., 41.

82. Ibid., 41.

83. Agee, 442.

84. Scarry, 255.

85. To the objection that slapstick comedy existed before and after silent film one may respond that such an observation ignores the fact that slapstick is more popular at this moment in this medium than at other times and in other places. It may be objected that Scarry's notion that the body at work is in pain, correct or not, is not applicable specifically to the immigrant but to the whole of the working class. But—and again—the working class in America between 1880 and 1920 was largely ethnic and/or immigrant.

86. Scarry, 177, and passim.

87. Ibid., 290.

88. She further defines the pain of work as "controlled discomfort" (171).

89. Ibid., 169.

90. Ibid., 14.

91. Ibid., 172.

92. David Robinson, *Chaplin: The Mirror of Opinion* (London: Secker and Warburg, 1983), for instance, remarks that Meyer Levin "saw the film as a kind of anthology, a collected complete edition of Chaplin's earlier work" (106). Also according to Robinson, critic Otis Ferguson "pointed out that the film

really takes the form of several one- or two-reelers from which he proposes as suitable titles, *The Shop, The Jailbird, The Watchman, The Singing Waiter*" (106).

93. See especially Mikhail Bakhtin, *Rabelais and His World*, trans. Helene Iswolsky (Bloomington: Indiana University Press, 1984).

94. William Shakespeare, *The Taming of the Shrew*, in *The Riverside Shakespeare*, ed. G. Blakemore Evans (Boston: Houghton Mifflin, 1974), Induction i. 34-41.

95. Mast, *The Comic Mind*, 111.

96. Robinson, *Chaplin: The Mirror of Opinion*, cites Otis Ferguson: "*Modern Times*, he quipped, was the last thing they should have called it: its times were modern many years before, when the movies were young. The antiquity of the sets, the characters, the handling of performers and groups irked him" (106).

97. An analogous enormity dwarfs the women in the factory setting of Eddie Cantor's *Palmy Days* [1931]; by extension, so does the Broadway "follies" stage.

CHAPTER 3

1. Joe Adamson, *Groucho, Harpo, Chico, and Sometimes Zeppo: A History of the Marx Brothers and a Satire on the Rest of the World* (New York: Simon and Schuster, 1973), 283.

2. Henry Jenkins, *What Made Pistachio Nuts? Early Sound Comedy and the Vaudeville Aesthetic* (New York: Columbia University Press, 1992), 172-84. See this volume's introduction for a more detailed account of Jenkins's argument.

3. The most notable of such critics is Gerald Mast, *The Comic Mind: Comedy and the Movies* (Chicago: University of Chicago Press, 1979), 285-88.

4. George S. Kaufman and Morrie Ryskind, *Animal Crackers* (1929; rpt. London: Samuel French, 1984), 14. This is the script of the stage play.

5. Ibid., 41.

6. Michael R. Weisser, *A Brotherhood of Memory: Jewish Landsmannschaft in the New World* (Ithaca, NY: Cornell University Press, 1989), 4.

7. Weisser finds the *landsmannschaft* even more separatist: "[P]eople who joined a *landsmannschaft* and kept it at the psychic core of their existence were at the same time rejecting the larger society and resisting its opportunities for assimilation" (5).

8. Lawrence Fuchs, *The American Kaleidoscope: Race, Ethnicity, and the Civic Culture* (London: Wesleyan University Press, 1990), 44, 49.

9. Ibid., 5.

10. Yuji Ichioka, *The Issei: The World of the First Generation Japanese Immigrants, 1885-1924* (New York: Free Press, 1988), 23.

11. Ibid., 94.

12. Ibid., 156-57.

13. William I. Thomas and Florian Znaniecki, in *The Polish Peasant in Europe and America*, ed. and abr. Eli Zaretsky (Urbana: University of Illinois Press, 1984), talk specifically about the function of the Mutual Aid Society to preserve Polishness (253-55).

14. Shih-shan Henry Tsai, *The Chinese Experience in America* (Bloomington: Indiana University Press, 1986), 46-47.

15. Maxine Schwartz Seller, "Introduction," in *Ethnic Theatre in the United States*, ed. Maxine Schwartz Seller (Westport, CT: Greenwood Press, 1983), 9.

16. Ibid., 193.

17. Ibid., 240.

18. Ibid., 122-23.

19. "In order to fund themselves, they often gave benefits, and by the early years of this century, the majority of weeknights in Yiddish theater were sponsored in this fashion" (Nahma Sandrow, *Vagabond Stars: A World History of Yiddish Theater* [New York: Harper & Row, 1977], 82).

20. Kaufman and Ryskind, 130.

21. George S. Kaufman, "Meet the Audience," in *By George: A Kaufman Collection*, ed. Donald Oliver (New York: St. Martin's Press, 1979), 21-25.

22. Penelope J. Corfield, "Introduction: Historians and Language," in *Language, History and Class*, ed. Penelope J. Corfield (Cambridge, MA: Basil Blackwell, 1991), 13. The last ten years have brought the study of various national and international "Englishes," from African-American English to Irish English to pidgin English to various colonial Englishes. See especially John Platt, Heidi Weber, and Ho Mian Lian, *The New Englishes* (London: Routledge, 1984); and Manfred Görlach, *Englishes: Studies in Varieties of English, 1984-1988* (Amsterdam, John Benjamin's, 1991). In *Toward a Social History of American English* (Berlin: Mouton, 1985), J. L. Dillard observes that English was not originally dominant in the American colonies: "Dutch was the official language up to 1664" (91). In both this text and the more recent *A History of American English* (London: Longman, 1992), Dillard attributes the differences between American and British English largely to the formative influence on American English of various ethnic groups.

23. Gene Fowler (*Schnozzola* [New York: Viking Press, 1951], 4-6) compares Durante to the nineteenth-century Italian clown Grimaldi.

24. Elaborated in J. Gumperz, "The Speech Community," in *Language and Social Context*, ed. Pier Paolo Giglioli (Harmondsworth, UK: Penguin, 1972), 219-

31. Ethnic humor tends to be first and foremost dialect humor: "There is considerable variation in the qualities eventually associated with the nineteenth century comic Irishman, but one feature remained constant: he spoke with a brogue" (Maureen Waters, *The Comic Irishman* [Albany: State University of New York Press, 1984], 1).

25. Kaufman and Ryskind, 32.

26. The 1930s gangsters differ from the Marx Brothers largely in the amount of faith they invest in the society they are attempting to subvert. Gangsters become a version of the authorities they resent; they come to own the cars and clothes they believe to be the signs of empowerment. Alternatively, the Marx Brothers do not attempt to rise in a hierarchy to which they give only a grudging belief. Such ambition is, for instance, obviated by having Groucho already in a position of power. More significantly, several films—*Monkey Business*, *A Day at the Races* (1937), *At the Circus* (1939)—employ gangsters and/or swindlers as *ficelles* and foils, as if the films require gangsters in order to exorcise the latent gangsterism in the Brothers by showing them actively repudiating that world, as when the Brothers throw their guns into the mop bucket in *Animal Crackers*.

27. Jonathan Culler, ed., *On Puns: The Foundation of Letters* (New York: Basil Blackwell, 1988), 2. While this volume does in some places treat gender, it treats race and language not at all, despite the fact that the connections should be self-evident.

28. Referring to Hollywood's tendency toward nepotism, Ogden Nash asserted about one mogul that "Uncle Carl Laemmle / Had a very large faemmle."

29. S. J. Perelman, *Dawn Ginsbergh's Revenge* (New York: H. Liveright, 1929).

30. Perelman, 11.

31. Perelman, 13.

32. Quoted in Kyle Crichton, *The Marx Brothers* (Garden City, NJ: Doubleday, 1950), 272.

33. Mikhail Bakhtin, *Rabelais and His World*, trans. Helene Iswolsky (Bloomington: Indiana University Press, 1984).

34. Crichton, 114.

35. Ibid., 287.

36. Ronald Sanders, *The Downtown Jews: Portraits of an Immigrant Generation* (New York: Harper & Row, 1969), 306.

37. Ibid., 306.

38. Ibid., 102.

39. Richard Dyer, *Stars* (London: BFI, 1979), 102.

40. Joey Adams, *Here's to the Friars: The Heart of Show Business* (New York: Crown, 1976), 6. The founding date is about the time of the founding of American

landsmannschaft. Though the Friars Club was rather Anglo at first, several of its formative members were ethnic: Irish (George M. Cohan), Jewish (Eddie Cantor), and so on. To Dyer's possible assertion that the Club was founded by press agents as a sort of publicity stunt and so was a purely economic phenomenon, one could as easily respond that, as with film itself, ethnics subsequently manipulated the Club to mean whatever they wanted (Adams, 6).

41. The roasts are referred to as "vivisections," "murders," and so on (Adams, 51-52).

42. Crichton, 226.

43. Ibid., 286-87.

44. Even much later, after the dissolution of the Marx Brothers, Groucho stars in a film—*Copacabana*—that contains a *Comedy of Errors* plot: Carmen Miranda must play two different kinds of exotic singers (Brazilian bombshell and "Madame Fifi") in order to help her boyfriend/agent Groucho live up to a contract he has made.

45. Crichton, 250.

46. Hector Arce, *Groucho* (New York: Putnam, 1979), 150.

47. Groucho Marx, *The Groucho Letters: Letters to and from Groucho Marx* (New York: Signet, 1967), 12.

48. The skit, and some commentary on its performance, appear in Mark Slobins, "From Vilna to Vaudeville: Minikes and *Among the Indians*," *The Drama Review* 24, no. 3 (September 1980): 17-26. (The quotation cited is on page 18.) The joke is of course repeated in Mel Brooks's *Blazing Saddles* (1974).

49. In fact, one may argue that Mark Twain's and Will Rogers's versions of *A Connecticut Yankee in King Arthur's Court* (1889 and 1932, respectively) are historical bookends, containing the beginning and end of new immigration in a safe narrative of an Anglo ancestry safely controlled by a representative descendant. But, at least in the Rogers version, the obsessive images of an Old-World peasantry comically engaged in modern work-time activities— punching timeclocks, manufacturing steel and iron products, and so on— look much more like cartoons of the new-immigrant presence in America. That this story of ethnics in "magic kingdoms" derives elsewhere than from *A Connecticut Yankee* can be seen in some instances of early American films containing the Jewish theme of diaspora: *Bleeding Hearts of Jewish Freedom under King Casimir of Poland* and *The Sorrow of Israel* (both 1913).

50. Mark Winokur, "Black Is White/White Is Black: 'Passing' as a Strategy of Racial Compatibility in Contemporary Hollywood Comedy," in *Unspeakable Images: Ethnicity and the American Cinema*, ed. Lester Friedman (Urbana: University of Illinois Press, 1991), 190-214.

51. Kaufman and Ryskind, 17.

52. Sanders, 310. In Woody Allen's *Zelig* (1983) the father of the protagonist is a new immigrant who played Puck in the Orthodox production of *A Midsummer Night's Dream.*

53. Sanders, 311.

54. On American eugenics, see, for example, Gerald N. Grob, *Mental Illness and American Society: 1875-1940* (Princeton, NJ: Princeton University Press, 1983), 82, 167-78, 363.

55. For an account of the similarities between Lacan and Bakhtin, see Robert Stam, *Subversive Pleasures: Bakhtin, Cultural Criticism, and Film* (Baltimore: Johns Hopkins University Press, 1989), esp. 4-6.

56. Jacques Lacan, "The mirror stage as formative of the function of the I," *Ecrits: A Selection*, trans. Alan Sheridan (1966; trans. New York: W. W. Norton, 1977), 1-7. The article was originally published in 1937 as "The Looking-Glass Phase."

57. I shall use this description from the Classic Film Scripts version of *Monkey Business and Duck Soup* (Letchworth, Hertfordshire, UK: Lorrimer, 1972):

> (1) Camera pans with [Groucho/Firefly] as he runs across to the gap left by the smashed mirror (the alcove beyond is furnished in a mirror image of the drawing room). As he searches to and fro, Pinky peeps round the corner. They start simultaneously across the gap, but half way across Firefly notices Pinky [Harpo], and they stop.
>
> Shot of the two of them as they stare at one another. Firefly leans forward suspiciously; Pinky mirrors his actions.
>
> (2) Shot of the scene. Firefly walks away from the "mirror" pondering; Pinky does likewise. Firefly turns suddenly, trying to catch him out; bends down and wiggles his behind; comes up to the mirror again. Pinky mirrors his every move. Camera pans as they walk to the edge of the alcove. Firefly nods: "You can't fool me." Pinky does likewise, and disappears round the corner. (3) Firefly has an idea; he peers forward round the edge of the alcove, and meets Pinky doing the same.
>
> Close-up of Firefly. He has another idea. He gets down on all fours and peers round the corner again—and meets Pinky doing the same. He gets up again.
>
> Firefly ponders. He has a better idea. He trots across the gap, high-stepping; so does Pinky. He hops back sideways facing the "mirror"; so does Pinky. . . .

In a longer shot, Firefly walks slowly to the centre and does a
wild charleston, facing the mirror; Pinky does likewise, grin-
ning. Firefly spins round; (4) Pinky doesn't but strikes the right
pose when Firefly ends up facing him again. . . .

(5) Back to the previous shot as Firefly enters slowly with a
panama hat behind his back; Pinky does likewise, but we see
that he has his black top hat. Convinced that he's caught him
out this time, Firefly laughs and steps up to the "mirror"; so
does Pinky. (6) They circle round through the "mirror," reversing their position. Firefly spots the black hat and heaves with
silent laughter—now he's got him—and Pinky does the same.
They circle back through the "mirror", and suddenly Firefly
puts on his hat.

(7) Seen in a closer shot, Pinky does likewise— producing a
Panama hat he has been hiding. Firefly points—"Haha, I caught
you"; Pinky mirrors him—"haha I caught you". (8) Pinky is so
pleased with himself that he points out of turn, then pulls a
face as he realizes. . . .

(9) Chicolini enters on Pinky's side of the "mirror". Pinky gazes
in horror at his night-shirted figure and hurriedly pushes him
out of sight. . . . Firefly grabs Chicolini by the tail of his
nightshirt and holds him fast. (153-55)

58. Andre Bazin, "The Myth of Total Cinema," *What Is Cinema?* vol. 1, trans. Hugh
    Gray (1958-1965; Berkeley: University of California Press, 1967), 17-22.
59. Sydney Stahl Weinberg, *The World of Our Mothers: The Lives of Jewish Immi-
    grant Women* (Chapel Hill: University of North Carolina Press, 1988), 279.
60. Weisser briefly discusses the way in which "*landsmannschaften* were utilized
    by Jewish employers as a means of exploiting workers and breaking or
    retarding the growth of class consciousness" (20).
61. Annie Phizacklea, "Entrepreneurship, Ethnicity, and Gender," in *Enterprising
    Women: Ethnicity, Economy, and Gender Relations*, ed. Sallie Westwood and
    Parminder Bhachu (London: Routledge, 1988), asserts, "What is usually glossed
    over . . . is the extent to which this 'family' and 'community' labour is female
    and subordinated to very similar patriarchal control mechanisms" (31).
62. Richard Sennett and Jonathan Cobb, *The Hidden Injuries of Class* (1972; rpt.
    New York: Vintage Books, 1973), 108.
63. "[F]or the son to own up to shame for the parent, rather than to his parent's
    guilt, is to admit to parental inferiority rather than to his own wrongdoing.

The latter is an admission about his own person; to admit the former is to 'consent' to parental inferiority in the eyes of others (in this case, the general Gentile culture)" (John Murray Cuddihy, *The Ordeal of Civility: Freud, Marx, Levi-Strauss, and the Jewish Struggle with Modernity* [New York: Basic Books, 1974], 60). Cuddihy is generally discussing the ascent into bourgeois culture of the Freud family. But in the self-critical America of the 1910s and 1920s, it was possible to turn this self-abnegation into a critique of an inhospitable culture, as did the Marx Brothers et al.

64. As Weinberg describes it, "In America, early in the century, even working class Jewish married women seldom took jobs outside the home" (105).

65. Herbert J. Gans, *The Urban Villagers: Group and Class in the Life of Italian Americans* (London: Macmillan, 1982), contends: "By virtue of the woman's greater receptivity to education, and their premarital employment in the white-collar world, they are likely to take the lead in the process of change. The husbands . . . will probably be more reluctant to give up the old ways" (216). Of course, the discrepancy between the ideally passive woman and practical realities of peasant behavior existed even in the old country for at least economic reasons: "To buy and sell in the market, to devise ways to 'help out' often required assertiveness, shrewdness, and the ability to get by in several languages" (Weinberg, 16). Maxine Schwartz Seller, "Beyond the Stereotype: A New Look at the Immigrant Woman, 1880-1924" *Journal of Ethnic Studies* 4, no. 3 (Spring 1975): 59-70, makes the same point by using three archetypal successes, oddly reproducing under the rubric of feminism the same rhetorical strategy as capitalism itself in using these successful women to stand also for the alienated and dispossessed. Of course, women's studies was uninterested in immigrant women until relatively recently, as Donna Gabaccia avers in *Seeking Common Ground: Multidisciplinary Studies of Immigrant Women in the United States* (Westport, CT: Greenwood Press, 1992), xiv.

66. Doris Weatherford, *Foreign and Female: Immigrant Women in America, 1840-1930* (New York: Schocken Books, 1986), asserts that "[l]arge numbers of women from every immigrant group were employed decades before American observers began to take note of the phenomenon of working women" (112).

67. Weatherford argues that "if the figures lie in any way, it is probably in overestimating the fathers' contribution, for [immigrant] men sometimes saved their pride by reporting larger earnings than they received" (105).

68. This was true of both the European and Asian migrations. Weinberg asserts that "fully half the prostitutes in Buenos Aires in 1909 were Jewish" (78). Ichioka claims that "[p]rostitutes were also among the pioneers of Japanese immigrant society" (36).

69. See, for example, Ichioka, 36-38.

70. Weatherford, 69-70.

71. Gans, 61-63.

72. Jill Dolan, "'What, No Beans?' Images of Women and Sexuality in Burlesque Comedy," *Journal of Popular Culture* 18, no. 3 (Winter 1984): 37-47, discusses the relationship between insult and inaccessibility (39-40).

73. Briefly described in Sigmund Freud, *Civilization and Its Discontents*, trans. James Strachey (New York: Norton, 1961), 51-53.

74. Crichton, 93.

75. Ibid., 92.

76. Arce, 136.

77. Ibid., 165-67.

78. Ibid., 168.

79. This is especially evident when considering how the Brothers—or at least Groucho—speaks about women offstage: "Chico was a character. . . . By the time any show opened he'd fucked half the chorus. Women were crazy about him. He'd walk up to a girl and say, 'Do you fuck?' And many times they said yes" (Ibid., 80).

80. Leigh Woods, "'The Golden Calf': Noted English Actresses in American Vaudeville, 1904-1916," *Journal of American Culture* 15, no. 3 (Fall 1992): 61-71.

81. Woods, 65.

82. Burlesque was also a rhetorical equalizer: "Women were also treated democratically. . . in that their denigrating images cut across race and class lines" (Dolan, 38).

CHAPTER 4

1. David Thomson, *A Biographical Dictionary of the Cinema* (London: Secker & Warburg, 1975), 108.

2. Werner Sollors, *Beyond Ethnicity: Consent and Descent in American Culture* (New York: Oxford University Press, 1986). At moments, Sollors seems almost to be directly and practically addressing the problem of an unrepresentability of history posed by Fredric Jameson (see my introduction): "Can one say that there is an original configuration of white and Indian relations which, even if it existed only in dreams and folklore, inspired the American imagination? If so, this original tale would be one of red-white fusion, of the newcomers becoming one with the continent, of gaining legitimacy through love and in defiance of the greed for gold and the white

fathers. Residual evidence of a covered-up love story is omnipresent in American Folklore" (127).

3. This failure to distinguish between Anglophile and Anglo accounts in part for Stanley Cavell's ability, in his very insightful *Pursuits of Happiness: The Hollywood Comedy of Remarriage* (Cambridge, MA: Harvard University Press, 1981), to see the screwball comedy as deriving from American transcendentalism and Shakespeare, and why, more generally, criticism stops with the observation that screwball comedies are Anglophilic. Except to members, beneficiaries, or students of Anglo culture, Anglophilia is not always self-justifying or self-explanatory.

4. *Current Biography, 1941* (New York: H. W. Wilson, 1941), 483.

5. Charles Francisco, *Gentleman: The William Powell Story* (New York: St. Martin's Press, 1985), 157.

6. Ibid., 31-36.

7. Ibid., 49.

8. Ibid., 63.

9. Ibid., 64-65.

10. Ibid., 82.

11. Ibid., 83.

12. The connection between ethnicity, poverty, and neighborhood affiliations is a time-honored truism of sociology: "Indeed, throughout American history ethnicity has been preserved most authentically by those groups who, for one reason or another, have remained economically marginal. Even among groups that have experienced wide-scale mobility, the lower-class strata continue to function as a cultural anchor for their more affluent relatives" (Stephen Steinberg, *The Ethnic Myth: Race, Ethnicity, and Class in America* [1981; rpt. Boston: Beacon Press, 1989], 53).

13. *Another Thin Man* (1939), *The Thin Man Goes Home* (1944), *Song of the Thin Man* (1947), and *Shadow of the Thin Man* (1941), respectively.

14. As Lester Friedman has pointed out to me in correspondence, other detective films of the 1930s, notably the Sherlock Holmes and Philo Vance films, also make this inversion, though their stories tend to take place in a more homogeneously aristocratic world. Still, some of the 1930s and 1940s Holmes films are rather interesting footnotes on the subject of ethnic identity. In *Sherlock Holmes and the Voice of Terror* (1942), the villain is a German spy who has been masquerading as a member of the English gentry since World War I. More generally, the surprise ending in which the patrician is the guilty party has been a literary staple at least since *Bleak House*.

15. Identifying against the character actor may be political as well; in the cases of Blore and Horton it is obviously homophobic.

16. Dashiell Hammett, *The Thin Man* (New York: Grossett & Dunlap, 1934), 22.

17. At least one seminal ethnologist articulates the suspicion of the films that crime is a part of more than the immigrant's economic being. In a chapter on "Murder," William I. Thomas and Florian Znaniecki assert that

> there is a wide field for the second type of murder, the murder without internal conflict and tragedy committed outside of the criminal's group. The immigrant gets into contact with outsiders, with people not belonging to his family, community. . . more than he ever did. . . .His usual attitude toward this social environment is not that of mere indifference. It is essentially defensive, full of mistrust, of a vague feeling of danger, of a continual expectation of wrong or offense.

   (*The Polish Peasant in Europe and America,* ed. and abr. Eli Zaretsky [1918-20; abridged ed. Urbana: University of Illinois Press, 1984], 282).

18. There are a number of rather delightful digs, much before *Singin' in the Rain* (1952), at Hollywood's discomfiture with visual historical accuracy. In *Boy Meets Girl* (1938) a British ex-army officer, now a film extra, remarks on the inaccuracy of his chocolate-soldier uniform for a film called "Young England." The film's producer responds: "I was in London two weeks, my man . . . and I watched them change the guards personally." The extra is, of course, fired.

19. Diana de Marly, *The History of Haute Couture: 1850-1950* (New York: Holmes and Meier, 1980), 83.

20. Jean-Paul Bouillon, *Art Deco: 1903-1940* (Geneva: Skira; New York: Rizzoli, 1989), 87.

21. De Marly, 90.

22. My observations about advertising derive especially from John Berger, *Ways of Seeing* (Harmondsworth, UK: Penguin, 1972), especially chapter 7, 129-54.

23. Roland Barthes, "Myth Today," *Mythologies,* trans. Annette Lavers (1957; New York: Hill and Wang, 1972), 109-59.

24. "Cubism, Futurism, Fauvism, and the oriental opulence of the Ballets Russes, all helped give the poster artist a wider range of potential colours and images. And in their turn posters using colours and images derived from these movements, in however debased a form, enabled the public to become used to the *look* of the avant garde" (Jean Delhaye, *Art Deco: Posters and Graphics* [New York: Rizzoli, 1977], 5).

25. What is perhaps confusing is that in its public guise Art Deco painting became identified with both left and right. . . . The Nazi takeover in Germany in 1933, and the purge of so-called "degenerate art" which followed, replaced the hated Expressionists . . . with not one, but several varieties of National

Socialist art. One of these, much favoured by Hitler, strove to
return to the world of the nineteenth-century German
Nazarenes but in fact came close to the conservative form of
Art Deco Classicism as represented by French painters such as
Robert Pougheon.

(Edward Lucie-Smith, *Art Deco Painting* [New York: Clarkson Potter, 1990], 36).

26. De Marly, 86.
27. There are several ironies in the fact that the liberated dance style of the Ballets Russes should have been translated into large, unwieldy, and confining costume jewelry, or that the clothing of the Ballets should have suggested an Asian motif, given the relatively recent antagonisms of the Sino-Russian War.
28. *What Price Beauty* (Pathe, 1928), screenplay by Rambova. One critic even notices a certain affinity between the two actresses: "This Myrna Loy is an exotic looking girl, a real looker for such parts as Nazimova would revel in, but hardly for an unbridled malo [sic]" (*Variety* review of *Bitter Apples,* August 4, 1926).
29. Caroline Rennolds Milbank, *New York Fashion: The Evolution of American Style* (New York: Abrams, 1989), 115.
30. Lucie-Smith, 92.
31. Alastair Duncan, ed., *The Encyclopedia of Art Deco* (New York: E.P. Dutton, 1988), 6.
32. De Marly, 88. One is reminded of today's body parts business, in which the poor and dispossessed of Argentina, Brazil, and other countries are relieved, sans volition, of corneas, kidneys, and other organs, for assimilation by the wealthy ill of Western Europe and the United States (*The Body Parts Business* [CPB and BBC, dir. Judy Jackson, 1993]).
33. Marianna Torgovnick, *Gone Primitive: Savage Intellects, Modern Lives* (Chicago: University of Chicago Press, 1990), fully explores the use of non-Western European cultures as the screen on which we project our voyeuristic fantasies. She is especially interested in the twentieth-century origins of primitivism in anthropology (she critiques Bronislaw Malinowski's *The Sexual Life of Savages* [1929]) and in the avant-garde (in, for example, Man Ray's *Kiki* [1926]).
34. Lucie-Smith, 23.
35. De Marly, 147.
36. After the 1920s, when such extremities in style were no longer in style, Poiret helped eke out a living by playing bit parts in French films (De Marly, 93).
37. James Kotsilibas-Davis and Myrna Loy, *Myrna Loy: Being and Becoming* (New York: Knopf, 1987), 37.
38. Ibid., 119.

39. In fact, no one really liked Loy's acting in the early years. Critics often objected especially to the miscasting of Loy as exotic, making her continued presence in such roles a mystery unless one understands that the white woman is *supposed* to be visible behind the exotic: "[Walter Pidgeon] is nearly lost at sea, but is rescued by Tiza, a Spanish girl living with her father on a South Sea isle. This role is played by Myrna Loy, who is miscast" (First *Variety* review of *Turn Back the Hours*, May 2, 1928); "Myrna Loy with an affected Mexican accent and manner, hasn't much of a part and makes the least of it" (*Variety* review of *The Great Divide*, February 19, 1930); "At the same time the hopeless effort to make the theme 'original' results in Shakespear's [sic] Juliet reversing positions with Romeo and after climbing the trelis [sic], exclaiming: 'I'll do it. I always wanted to shave someone'" (Review of *Turn Back the Hours*, *Variety*, May 9, 1928).

40. Kotsilibas-Davis and Loy, 33.

41. Ibid., 36 and 37, respectively.

42. Ian C. Jarvie, "Stars and Ethnicity: Hollywood and the United States, 1932-51," in *Unspeakable Images: Ethnicity and the American Cinema,* ed. Lester Friedman (Urbana: University of Illinois Press, 1991), 99. A sometimes insightful writer, Jarvie has the problem endemic to the best statisticians of defining arbitrary parameters as norms. He arbitrarily assigns WASP ethnicity to second- or third-generation ethnics, or to extremely heterogeneous screen personae, as a way to negotiate extrastatistical complexity. Conundrums like the Loy persona are solved by referring to her as a WASP (Table 3.1, p. 99). As a result, Jarvie finds little evidence of "real" ethnicity in front of or behind the cameras, all of which suggests, not an absence of ethnicity in film culture, but a certain masochism in the desire to uncover it.

43. Maryann Oshana, *Women of Color: A Filmography of Minority and Third World Women* (New York: Garland, 1985).

44. Again, Oshana's *Women of Color* is an instructive map in this regard.

45. Sigmund Freud, principally in "A Child Is Being Beaten," *Collected Papers,* vol. 2 (London: Hogarth Press, 1946), 172-201; Gilles Deleuze, *Masochism: An Interpretation of Coldness and Cruelty* (1971; rpt. New York: Zone Books, 1989).

46. Jean-Louis Baudry, "The Apparatus: Metapsychological Approaches to the Impressions of Reality in Cinema," in *Narrative, Apparatus, Ideology: A Film Theory Reader,* ed. Philip Rosen (1975; New York: Columbia University Press, 1986), 299-318; André Bazin, "The Myth of Total Cinema," in *What Is Cinema,* vol. 1 (Berkeley: University of California Press, 1971), 17-22.

47. I will subscribe, at least at this point in the history of gender roles, to the sense that masochism is primarily a construct of masculinity. As nearly everyone

from Krafft-Ebing to Kaja Silverman asserts, it is difficult to reconcile the role-playing and directorial sensibility of the masochist with the woman who is treated badly. If one were to construct an argument for women as masochistic, then, in some sense, all women would have to be so defined.

48. A more extended version of this argument appears in Gaylyn Studlar, *In the Realm of Pleasure: Von Sternberg, Dietrich, and the Masochistic Aesthetic* (Urbana: University of Illinois Press, 1988), 177-78.

49. Theodor Reik, *Masochism in Modern Man*, trans. Margaret H. Beigel and Gertrud M. Kurth (New York: Farrar, Strauss and Co., 1941), 43.

50. "[O]f the three factors [pertaining to the masochist scenario] phantasy is the most important" (Ibid., 44).

51. Ibid., 41.

52. Ibid., 42.

53. Ibid., 41.

54. Studlar, op. cit., and Reik, 41-44.

55. Hollywood also uses most of these sources, but not often classical mythology, as if rejecting one overdetermined source of self-definition by hegemonic Western cultures.

56. Duncan, 6.

57. Leopold Sacher-Masoch, *Venus in Furs* (1870), reprinted in its entirety in Gilles Deleuze, *Masochism* (New York: Zone Books, 1989), 143-271. The question the novel poses is whether that adoption suggests an innate cruelty in her and in all women or rather a construct built by this man and all men. Deleuze opts for the former in his construction of the cold mother, while Wanda von Sacher-Masoch, wife of the author, opts for the latter in her autobiography, *The Confessions of Wanda von Sacher-Masoch*, trans. Marian Phillips, Caroline Hebert, and V. Vale (San Francisco: Re/Search Publications, 1990).

58. And, as a result, Studlar cannot adequately account for much that goes on in the von Sternberg/Dietrich collaborations: exotic settings, the presence of ethnic women such as Anna Mae Wong, and so on.

59. Kotsilibas-Davis and Loy, 71.

60. *Satan in Sables,* an unnamed Russian Lady; *Don Juan,* Maia; *Across the Pacific* (1926), Roma; *The Heart of Maryland* (1927), a mulatto; *The Jazz Singer,* a chorus girl (in blackface), *Ham and Eggs at the Front,* Fifi (a black waitress), *A Girl in Every Port* (1928), an "oriental"; *Turn Back the Hours,* Tiza; *Crimson City* (1928), Onoto; *Noah's Ark,* a slave girl. This is an abbreviated list.

61. Leopold von Sacher-Masoch, *Venus and Adonis* (New York: Windsor, 1933).

62. Though Severin does not destroy Wanda, he ends, in the frame narrative to *Venus in Furs,* by treating all women badly. He has become, in his own expression, the "hammer" rather than the "anvil."

63. Wanda von Sacher-Masoch, 85. Wanda also speaks of staying with Jewish friends who are evidently amused by Leopold's activities (85-93).
64. Reik, 258-59, 322.
65. Gilles Deleuze, in the best work on Sacher-Masoch to date, describes the novelist as "born in Lemberg, Galicia. He was of Slav, Spanish and Bohemian descent. . . . His work is deeply influenced by the problems of nationalities, minority groups and revolutionary movements in the Empire, hence his Galician, jewish, Hungarian, Prussian tales, etc. . . . He became involved in the Panslavic movement" (*Masochism: An Interpretation of Coldness and Cruelty,* trans. Jean McNeil [1967; New York: George Braziller, 1971], 9). Another, much more racist, pop-psychology account of Sacher-Masoch, translated into English in 1934, the release date of *The Thin Man,* is worth quoting at length:

> From [his Ruthanian nurse's] mouth he learned of the sad racial mannerisms of the Ruthanians, he listened to her eagerly, and he later maintained that he had her to thank not only for the maintenance of his physical existence, but in a characteristic sense for "his soul" as well. In the colorful excursions of that mixture of races in which the orient and the occident crossed, the perceptive youth soon found manifold stimuli.

(Albert Eulenberg, *Sadism and Masochism* [*Algolagnia: The Psychology, Neurology and Physiology of Sadistic Love and Masochism*], trans. Harold Kent [1902; trans. New York: The New Era Press, 1934], 90). Eulenberg elsewhere asserts that "[Sacher-Masoch's] own solution of the erotic problem might have arisen from a peculiar conception of the sexual relationship at one time rooted in Slavic folk lore; a conception of which—not without a certain deep truth—sees in love a battle of the sexes and in this battle woman as the stronger more victorious part,—as is doubtless the case in a certain sense especially among individual Slavic tribes as a result of the rich endowment and stronger will power of their women" (99).

The same text, in describing sadism around the world, uses the example of a Black man murdering white women as his representation of America. An irony similar to the one that leaves Silverman dependent on an argument by Janine Chasseguet-Smirgel that she calls "hateful" (Kaja Silverman, "Masochism and Male Subjectivity," *Male Trouble,* ed. Constance Penley [Minneapolis: University of Minnesota Press, 1993], 33), leaves the topic of race in the discourse on masochism to a racist (not to mention sexist) writer, so that a valid connection between psychology and socialization is obscured by the insistence on stereotyped gender and race roles. While nearly every writer, from Freud and Krafft-Ebing to Deleuze and Silverman, correctly notices the use of the exotic, almost no one (with the oblique exception of Reik) theorizes about it. Silverman perhaps leaves a space for such theory at the end of her essay when she asserts that "male subjectivity is far more divided than our theoretical models would suggest; it cannot be adequately summarized by invoking either the phallus, or the more flexible concept of bisexuality" (62-63). Her interest in the transgression of gender boundaries, which she shares with Deleuze and Studlar, indicates the possibility of other, that is, ethnic, boundaries to be transgressed.

66. Sacher-Masoch, *Venus in Furs*, 194-95. The characters in the novel become more exotic as well, until, in the second half of the novel, Severin is trussed up by a bevy of black servants in preparation for a beating and is at the end of the novel finally beaten by a man known to him as "the Greek."

67. Neal Gabler, *An Empire of Their Own: How the Jews Invented Hollywood* (New York: Crown, 1988), 15, 19.

68. Studlar, 35.

69. Bram Dijkstra, *Idols of Perversity: Fantasies of Feminine Evil in Fin-de-Siecle Culture* (1986; rpt. New York: Oxford University Press, 1988), 220.

70. Edward Said, *Orientalism* (New York: Pantheon, 1978).

71. The pattern of legislative discrimination aimed especially at Asian women continued at least until the Immigration Act of May 26, 1924, whose provisions included "(1) the inadmissibility of the wives and children of Chinese merchants; (2) the inadmissibility of the Chinese wives of American citizens of Chinese descent" (Shih-shan Henry Tsai, *The Chinese Experience in America* [Bloomington: Indiana University Press, 1986], 104).

72. Eugene Franklin Wong discusses both the desire and the punishment in the context of the degraded image of the Asian woman: "Whites generally accepted the idea, for instance, that Chinese women in the United States were 'of the vilest and most degraded class of abandoned women.' The strumpets, it was believed, were so debased as to offer their services, at discounted rates, to white schoolboys, imparting in the process a foreign and a presumably exotic strain of venereal disease" (*On Visual Media Racism: Asians in the American Motion Pictures* [New York: Arno Press, 1978],vii).

73. According to Eulenberg (90), Sacher-Masoch's sexually pivotal childhood experience was his Ruthanian nursemaid, Hanscha.

74. Theodor Reik even discusses the humor latent in the situation of the masoch-ist, and wrote major works not only on masochism but also on Jewish humor (*Jewish Wit* [New York: Gamut Press, 1962]).

75. Kotsilibas-Davis and Loy, 74.

76. This is the problem with David Shumway's argument against Cavell's. He accuses Cavell of what Cavell already asserts, that the screen images are

idealizations, not an attempt to transcribe reality onto the screen ("Screwball Comedies: Constructing Romance, Mystifying Marriage," *Cinema Journal* 30, no. 4 [Summer 1991]: 7-23).

77. Gayatri Chakravorty Spivak, "Can the Subaltern Speak?" *Marxism and the Interpretation of Culture*, ed. Cary Nelson and Lawrence Grossberg (Urbana: University of Illinois Press, 1988), 271-313.

78. She is in or near Paris for *So This Is Paris, Love Me Tonight, Topaze,* and *New Morals for Old*, and a French exile for *When a Man Loves* (1927).

CONCLUSION

1. Judith Mayne, "Feminist Film Theory and Criticism," in *Multiple Voices in Feminist Film Criticism*, ed. Diane Carson, Linda Dittmar, and Janice R. Welsch (Minneapolis: University of Minnesota Press, 1994), 50.

2. Gilles Deleuze and Félix Guattari, "What Is a Minor Literature?" *Mississippi Review* 11, no. 3 (Spring 1983): 13-33. They go on to argue that minor/minority literature, of necessity aesthetically inferior, is nonetheless "great and revolutionary" (26). Both assertions are probably standard assessments about film by most academics except film scholars.

3. Mark Winokur, "Marginal Marginalia: The African-American Voice in the Nouvelle Gangster Film," *The Velvet Light Trap* 35 (Spring 1995):19-32, and "Black Is White/White Is Black: 'Passing' as a Strategy of Racial Compatibility in Contemporary Hollywood Comedy," in *Unspeakable Images: Ethnicity and the American Cinema*, ed. Lester Friedman (Urbana: University of Illinois Press, 1991), 190-214.

4. Mark Winokur, "Eating Children Is Wrong," *Sight and Sound* n.s. 1, no. 7 (Nov. 1991): 10-13.

5. Jane Feuer, "The Self-Reflexive Musical and the Myth of Entertainment," in *Film Theory and Criticism: Introductory Readings*, 4th ed., ed. Gerald Mast, Marshall Cohen, and Leo Braudy (New York: Oxford University Press, 1992) 486-97; Rick Altman, *The American Film Musical* (Bloomington: Indiana University Press, 1987).

6. For example, Jonathan Munby, "The Ghetto Goes National: Aural Border Wars and the Vernacular Challenge to the Lingua Franca in the Early 1930s Talking Gangster Film," paper delivered at the American Studies Association Annual Meeting, Nashville, Tennessee, October 29, 1994.

7. Winokur, "Eating Children Is Wrong," 10-11 and passim.

8. Robert C. Christopher, *Crashing the Gates: The De-WASPing of America's Power Elite* (New York: Simon and Schuster, 1989).

9. Andrea Topper, "The Rise and Rise of Christy T," *Mirabella*, August 1993, 114.

10. Robert Stam, *Subversive Pleasures: Bakhtin, Cultural Criticism, and Film* (Baltimore: Johns Hopkins University Press, 1989), 6.

11. Ibid., 14.

12. Ibid., 79-84.

INDEX

Abbott and Costello, 136
   See also names of individual films
Abbott and Costello go to Mars, 136
Abbott and Costello in Alaska, 136
Abbott and Costello in Hollywood, 136
Abbott and Costello in the Foreign Legion,
   136
Abbott, Bud, 19
Absalom, Absalom, 44
ad lib, 143-145
Adam's Rib, 167
Adamson, Joe, 126
Addams Family, The, 126
Adler, Jacob P., 146
Adventurer, The, 48, 100, 104
African Americans, 49-50, 64, 130, 171,
   221
   orientalizing the culture of, 201-202,
      267-268n.127
   representations of in film, 7, 8, 22,
      236-237, 245n.47
After the Thin Man, 228
Agee, James, 75
alazons, 108, 130, 131, 168, 249n.77
Albee, E. F., 67
Ali Baba Goes to Town, 153
Alien Nation, 235, 236
Allen, Gracie, 15
Allen, Robert C., 12, 15-16, 65, 68, 70
Allen, Woody, 13, 138, 141

Althusser, Louis, 3, 4, 5, 240-241n.11
Altschuler, Glenn C., 40
Ambassador Bill, 154, 155 fig. 3.5, 157
America Learns to Play, 1, 16
American myths, 42
   See also tall tales, trickster tales, Puritan
      culture, Native American culture
American Vaudeville as Ritual, 75
Among the Indians, 153
Andersen, Benedict, 23
Anglophilia, 181
Anglo-Saxon immigrants, 40
Animal Crackers, 127, 128-129, 132,
   138, 145, 157, 176
animated films,
   ethnicity in, 154, 157
Another Thin Man, 228, 231
antic comedy, 18-19
   See also team comedy
Arbuckle, Fatty, 45, 46 fig. 1.4, 48, 83,
   272n.27, 273n.30, 277n.61
   See also transformative comedy
Armstrong, John, 9
Arrowsmith, 228
Arsenic and Old Lace, 191
Art Deco, 196-212, 226, 289n.24, 289-
   290n.25
   and advertising, 198-199
   and ethnicity, 201-203
   and the feminine, 197-200

Deco Chinoiserie, 204-206
Deco Exotic, 204, 209, 212, 218
Deco orientalism, 210
in Hollywood, 196-197, 201, 203 fig. 4.4, 204-212
Art Nouveau, 198, 198 fig. 4.2
As I Lay Dying, 44
Asian Americans, 130, 261n.73
    See also names of individual ethnic groups
assimilation, 16, 38, 60, 61, 62, 70, 126, 179, 180, 221, 225-226, 230, 231-234, 275n.50
Astaire, Fred, 190

Babes in Toyland, 154
Bachelor and the Bobby Soxer, The, 191
Bailyn, Bernard, 40
Baker, Josephine, 199, 200 fig. 4.3b. 202
Bakhtin, Mikhail, 15, 113, 137, 142, 160, 237
Balazs, Bela, 45, 47
Ball of Fire, 190, 232
Ballets Russes, 199, 201, 202, 206, 289n.24, 290n.27
Bara, Theda, 209, 215
Barbarian, The, 220, 222, 225, 228
Barker, Adam, 12
Baroness and the Butler, The, 187
Barrymore, John, 52
Barthes, Roland, 8, 15, 199
Baudry, Jean-Louis, 22, 212-213
Bazin, Andre, 22, 166
Beau Geste, 183
Beautiful City, The, 183
Beck, Martin, 67
Beckett, Samuel, 91
Bellamy, Ralph, 56
Ben Hur, 206
Bergman, Henry, 117

Bergson, Henri, 14, 18, 57, 99, 100, 101, 102 fig. 2.5, 104, 106, 165, 168, 247n. 60, 277n.65
Berkeley, Busby, 159
Berlin, Irving, 179
Bernhardt, Sarah, 73
Best Years of Our Lives, The, 230
Bier, Jesse, 28
Bird of Paradise, 210
Birth of a Nation, 40, 72
Bitter Tea of General Yen, The, 204
Black Watch, The, 210, 214, 215-218, 220, 222, 223
Blade Runner, 235
Blair, Walter, 32, 45
Blue Bird, The, 157
body, the,
    as used in comedy, 104, 105, 106, 107-108, 110, 111
    criticism of, 106-107, 108, 109, 110, 111
Bogart, Humphrey, 181
Bohemian Girl, The, 154, 156 fig. 3.6
Boone, Daniel, 31, 35, 97
Boorstin, Daniel, 44-45
Bordwell, David, 14-15
Boucicault, Dion, 91
Boulet, Denise, 197
Boy Meets Girl, 56
Bread Givers, 39, 80
Brennan, Walter, 190
Bright Shawl, The, 183
British music hall tradition. *See* England
Buffon, Comte de, 32
Bunyan, Paul, 36
burlesque, 15-16, 287n.82
Burne-Jones, Edward, 198
Burns, George, 15
Bush, Clive, 23, 37, 38
Byrd, William, 28

Cagney, James, 181

Cahan, Abraham, 80

Calhern, Louis, 130

Cameo Kirby, 220

Camonte, Tony, 139, 140

Campbell, Patrick, 178

Cantor, Eddie, 15, 126, 153-154
    See also names of individual films

Carnegie, Andrew, 42

Casablanca, 151

Cates, Phoebe, 209

Cavell, Stanley, 5, 8, 10, 14, 19, 58, 230

Champion, The, 96

chapbooks. *See* England

Chaplin, 89

Chaplin, Charles, 4-5, 13, 17, 18, 20, 21,
    42, 44, 48, 51 fig. 1.6, 75-91, 78 fig.
    2.1, 84 fig. 2.2, 85 fig. 2.3, 95 fig.
    2.4, 124 fig. 2.9, 127, 152, 273n.30,
    276n.56
    American success story, 79-80
    and technology, 99, 101-105, 111,
        102 fig. 2.5
    and the body, 104, 105, 110
    as creator of immigrant myth, 98
    as English, 78, 79, 80-81, 272n.23
    audience's relation to, 88-90
    childhood of, 77-78, 80, 82, 86, 88,
        273n.31
    deportation of, 77, 79
    ethnicity of, 77, 80, 90, 271n.12
    national status of, 79
    persona of, 76, 82, 86-87, 88
    sound and, 123-124
    technique of transformation, 101-102,
        104
    the tramp persona of, 82, 83, 86, 88,
        89, 90, 93-94, 97, 109-110
        and body criticism, 107-108
        and technology, 101-105

and torture, 109, 110, 111

and transformation of institutions,
    122-123

and transformative ability of, 75,
    76, 278n.73

and work, 96, 115-116, 117, 118

immigrant status of, 76, 80, 81-82,

incarceration of, 118

rootlessness of, 96-97, 98

similarities to the stage Irishman,
    90-91, 92, 93

use of objects by, 98-100, 101,
    102, 104, 105, 116, 277n.72,
    278n.73

See also names of individual films

Chaplin, Reginald R., 77

character actors. *See* Hollywood

Charles, Nick. *See* The Thin Man films,
    Powell, William

Charles, Nora. *See* The Thin Man films,
    Loy, Myrna

Charlie Chaplin's Own Story, 79, 83, 86-88

Chevalier, Albert, 67

Chevalier, Maurice, 150

Chinese Americans,
    depictions of in American film, 221
    discrimination against, 202, 212
        Chinese women, 212, 221, 294nn.
            71, 72
    huigans of, 129
    Six Companies, 129

Chinese Immigration Exclusion Act, 212,
    294n.71

Christian, Barbara, 3

Christopher, Robert C., 7, 8, 237

Circus, The, 87, 96

City Lights, 48, 104, 127

Cixous, Helène, 107

Clockmaker, The, 31

Cocoanuts, The, 127, 141, 145

Cohan, George M., 15

Cohn, Harry, 5, 43, 55, 67, 180

comedy,

and misogyny, 172-173, 176-178

and technology, 99, 100, 101

and the body, 104, 105, 106, 107-108, 110, 111

and torture, 107-109, 110-111

antic comedy, 17, 136-137. *See also* team comedy

early sound comedy, 15, 136-140

ethnic humor, 70-71, 281n.22

screwball comedy, 17, 179

silent comedy, 100

slapstick comedy, 99, 106

team comedy, 136-137

transformative comedy, 17, 18, 99, 104, 107, 106

See also names of individual comedians and comedy teams

Comic Mind, The, 13

Connecticut Yankee, A, 157, 206, 215, 217 fig. 4.10, 221, 283n.49

Cooke, Ebenezer, 26, 27, 28, 29, 41, 256n.32

Cooper, James Fennimore, 32

Cooper, Gary, 138, 190

Copacabana, 125

Coppola, Francis Ford, 236

Corbett, Jim, 69

Count, The, 94, 98

Country Peddler, 153

Coyote, 130

Crawford, Joan, 205 fig. 4.5

Crèvecoeur, J. Hector St. John, 26, 30, 33

Crichton, Kyle, 173

Cripps, Thomas, 7-8

Crockett, Davy, 31, 32, 34 fig. 1.2, 35 fig. 1.3, 35, 36, 54, 56, 97, 98, 102, 259n.47

Crosby, Bing, 136, 145

Cuddihy, John Murray, 4, 172

Culler, Jonathan, 140

"Dance of the Oceania Rolls," 48

Dangerous Money, 183

Dash, Julie, 236

Dawn Ginsbergh's Revenge, 141

Dawn Patrol, The, 181

Day of the Locusts, 158

Day, Clarence, 141

Deleuze, Gilles, 18, 52, 212, 215, 218, 228, 235, 293-294n.65

De Palma, Brian, 236

Der Yiddisher Kenig Lear, 158

Desert Song, The, 206, 220, 221, 223, 228

Deslys, Gaby, 66

Dietrich, Marlene, 209, 210, 214, 215

Dijkstra, Bram, 220

Dimeglio, John, 65

Dinnerstein, Leonard, 57, 64, 91-92, 105-106

Diplomaniacs, The, 154

Disney Studios, 154, 157

Doane, Mary Anne, 15

Dog's Life, A, 86

Domestic Manners of Americans, 30

dominatrix. *See* masochism

Don Juan, 49, 206

Double Wedding, 187, 229

doubling. *See* Marx Brothers, the

Duck Soup, 14, 20, 26, 49-50, 125, 127, 130, 133, 147 fig. 3.1, 148 fig. 3.2, 148 fig. 3.3, 150, 154, 157, 158, 162 figs. 3.7-3.9, 175 fig. 3.11, 176

the mirror scene in, 159-161, 163, 164, 165, 166, 168, 169-171, 284-285n.57

Dulles, Foster Rhea, 1, 2, 11, 13, 15, 16

Dumont, Margaret, 128-129, 135, 151, 158, 172, 173, 174, 176-177, 178

Dunajew, Wanda von. See Sacher-Masoch, Wanda von

Durante, Jimmy, 15, 136

Durgnat, Raymond, 13

Dyer, Richard, 20-21, 146

Eagleton, Terry, 3, 4

early sound comedy, 15
    and ethnicity, 137-140

Edison, Thomas, 12, 53, 55

Egypt,
    representations of in Hollywood, 202, 203 fig. 4.4, 206, 209

eirons, 19, 131, 168, 249n.77

Eisenstein, Sergei, 38, 159

El Dorado, 24, 25, 41

Elsaesser, Thomas, 12

England,
    immigrants from, 272n.20
    Irish immigrants in, 91
    jest books and chapbooks, 30
    music hall tradition in, 64

Enemy Mine, 236

ethnic theater, 64-65, 130, 144, 146
    See also vaudeville, Yiddish theater, stage Irishman

"exotic masochism." See masochism

Family Jewels, The, 127

Faulkner, William, 44

Fenian Brotherhood. See Irish Americans

Fields, W. C., 18, 67, 127

film moguls, 53-57, 179-180, 185
    and ethnicity, 53-57, 180, 245n.46
    and Leopold von Sacher-Masoch, 218-219
    See also names of individual moguls

Fink, Mike, 29, 31, 32, 36

Finnish Socialist Federation, 130

Fireman, The, 93, 96

Fleisher Studio, 137, 150, 154

Floorwalker, The, 96

Flying Deuces, The, 136

Flying Down to Rio, 210

Flynn, Errol, 81

Fool There Was, 209

Foolish Wives, 99

Footlight Parade, 209

Foucault, Michel, 4, 17, 106-107, 109, 110
    See also body

Fox, William, 67

Franchot, Jenny, 25

Francisco, Charles, 185

Frankfurt School, 1

Franklin, Wayne, 2-3, 11, 30, 242n.21, 253n.19, 256n.33

Freud, Sigmund, 13, 14

Friar's Club, the, 146, 280-281n.40
    sexism and, 171

Friedman, Lester, 12

Frye, Northrop, 14

Gable, Clark, 181, 185, 229, 232

Gabler, Neal, 5

Gallagher, Skeets, 15

Gamin, the. See Modern Times

gangsters. See Hollywood

Gans, Herbert, 172

Gardiner, William H., 32

Garland, Judy, 157

Gay Divorcee, The, 190

Geduld, Harry M., 79

Gellner, Ernest, 8, 9, 243n.34

General, The, 48, 99, 100

General Died at Dawn, The, 204

Gentlemen Prefer Blondes, 28

German-Americans, 65
    in vaudeville, 71

ghetto/fourth wall, 145-146, 150

Gilbert, Douglas, 65, 67, 70

Gilbreth, Frank, 49

Gilliatt, Penelope, 13

Go West, 132

God, Man and Devil, 158

Godard, Paulette, 115

Godfather, The, 236

Gold Diggers of 1933, 195

Gold Rush, The, 42, 48, 99

Goldfish, Samuel. *See* Goldwyn, Samuel

Goldwyn Follies, 56

Goldwyn, Samuel, 15, 180, 182, 184-185

Goodwins, Leslie, 79

Gordin, Jacob, 158

Gospel Societies. *See* Japanese immigrants

Grant, Cary, 21, 61, 138, 152, 181, 191, 232, 233

Gravity's Rainbow, 28

Great Depression, the, 126

Great Dictator, The, 81, 93

Great Escape, The, 118

Great Gatsby, The, 183

Great Ziegfeld, The, 187

Greed, 180

Greenblatt, Stephen, 17

Griffith, D. W., 38, 55, 72, 77

Guattari, Félix, 52, 235

Gunga Din, 214

Haliburton, T. C., 31

Hall, Joseph, 26

Hammett, Dashiell, 191, 196

Hams and Eggs at the Front, 208 fig. 4.7

Handel, Leo, 11

Handlin, Oscar, 6

Hardy, Oliver, 19

Hart, Moss, 141

Hart, William S., 153

Haven, C. K. Dexter, 19

Hawks, Howard, 236

Hayes Production Code, 65, 114

"Head of a Bull," 48, 50 fig. 1.5

Hellzapoppin, 145

Hemingway, Ernest, 49

Hepburn, Katharine, 21, 61, 138, 232

Higham, Charles, 14

High-Class Moving Pictures, 12

His Musical Career, 96

His New Profession, 96

Hitchcock, Alfred, 77, 189

hobble skirt, 197

Holiday, 61

Hollywood,

accents in, 137-138

African-American depictions in, 7, 8, 22, 236-237, 245n.47

and its "English colony," 81

and the oriental femme fatale, 206

Anglophilia in, 181

Art Deco in, 196-197, 201, 203 fig. 4.4, 204-212

character actors in, 234

classical era of, 179-180

contemporary depictions of race in, 235-237

depiction of gangsters in, 139, 140, 236, 282n.26

dominatrix in, 215, 220, 222, 223 *See also* masochism

ethnic filmakers in, 53-57, 180, 245n.46, 262n.77

miscegenation in, 230-234

representations of Egypt in, 202, 203 fig 4.4, 206, 209

white woman as exotic in, 209-210

Hollywood Pinafore, 56

homosexuality, 107

Hoodlum Saint, The, 187

Hope, Bob, 136, 145

Horatio Alger myth, 42
Horse Feathers, 132, 150, 157, 177
Horton, Andrew S., 15
Horton, Edward Everett, 191
Howe, Lyman H., 13
Huckleberry Finn, 44, 138
huigans. *See* Chinese Americans

I Love You Again, 187, 192, 229
Iago, 130
Icart, Louis, 196, 197
Idle Class, The, 86
Immigrant, The, 83, 93
immigrants, 264n.98, 265n.109
    women, 172, 286n.65, 286n.66
    See also individual names of immigrant
      groups
"An Invitation to Lubberland," 26, 27
Irish,
    in England, 91
    See also Irish Americans
Irish Americans,
    and *landsmannschaft,* 129
    Fenian Brotherhood of, 129
    in vaudeville, 70-71
    See also stage Irishman
Isle of Escape, 220
It Happened One Night, 58, 232, 234
Italian Americans, 130, 171
    and *landsmannschaft,* 129
    paisani, 129
    representations of in contemporary
      film, 236
Izod, John, 11, 44

Jacobs, Lewis, 42
Jameson, Frederic, 3, 4, 5, 6, 241nn.12,
    19
JanMohamed, Abdul, 5
Japanese Americans,

and *landsmannschaft,* 129
Gospel Societies of, 129
Nihonjin Kutsuko Domekai of, 129
Jazz Singer, The, 49, 206
Jefferson, Thomas, 26, 30, 33
Jenkins, Henry, 15, 16, 17, 21, 65, 68,
    126, 127, 247-248n.65
jestbooks. *See* England
Jewish Americans, 49-50, 67, 130, 171
    as filmakers, 49-57, 245n.46
    See also individual names of filmakers
Jewish Tales, 218
Jolson, Al, 51-52
Jowett, Garth, 12

Katzenjammer Kids, The, 173
Kaufman, George S., 135, 141, 146, 172
Kaye, Danny, 67
Keaton, Buster, 18, 48, 82, 83, 136
    See also transformative comedy
Keeler, Ruby, 209
Keillor, Garrison, 138
Keith, B. F., 63, 67, 68, 70, 72
    See also vaudeville
Kellerman, Annette, 69
Kennedy, Edgar, 49, 130
Keystone Kops, The, 18, 130
Kid, The, 86
Kid from Spain, The, 153
Kid Millions, 153
Kindem, Gorham, 11
King in New York, A, 87, 94
King of the Khyber Rifles, 214, 223
Kismet, 209
Knight, Sarah Kemble, 28
Kolodny, Annette, 25
Krutnick, Frank, 15

L'Inhumaine, 204
La Cava, Gregory, 183

Lacan, Jacques, 18, 20, 160
Lady from Shanghai, The, 163
Laemmle, Carl, 183, 282n.28
land speculation, 41
landscape, 26, 33, 35, 38, 39, 44,
   255n.26
   and vaudeville, 69
landsmannschaft, 127, 129, 130, 135,
   146, 151, 237, 280n.7, 285n.59
   and its repression of the feminine,
     171, 178
   as a psychoanalytic dynamic, 159-161
Langdon, Harry, 18, 45, 82
   See also transformative comedy
Langtry, Lillie, 73, 178
Lasky Famous Players, 112
Lasky, Jesse, 43, 67, 182-183
Last Command, The, 184
Lauder, Harry, 67
Laurel and Hardy, 18, 20, 136, 154, 156
   fig. 3.6
   See also names of individual films
Laurel, Stan, 19
Lawrence of Arabia, 210
"Le Cocktail," 196 fig. 4.1
le vague. See hobble skirt
Lee, Spike, 236
Lewis, Jerry, 15, 127, 136, 153
Libeled Lady, 182, 193
Life on the Mississippi, 36
Limelight, 86, 89
Linder, Max, 47
Little Caesar, 139
Living It Up, 136
Lizzies of the Field, 100
Lloyd, David, 5, 48
Lloyd, Harold, 82
   See also tranformative comedy
Loew, Marcus, 67, 219
Lolita, 28

Lombard, Carole, 232, 233
Lopokova, Lydia, 66
Lord, Tracy, 19
Lourdeaux, Lee, 5, 243n.27
Love Crazy, 229
Love Happy, 125
Love Me Tonight, 206, 209, 226
Lovingood, Sut, 32, 71, 102, 138,
   259n.45
Loy, Myrna, 20, 49, 61, 138, 185, 187,
   193, 224 fig. 4.11
   and doppelgängers, 228
   as Art Deco woman, 196, 197, 201,
     206, 207 fig.4.6, 209, 210, 211
     fig. 4.8
   as assimilated Anglo, 222-230
   as disguised ethnic, 180-181, 222
   as dominatrix, 215-218, 220, 222,
     223, 225, 226
   as exotic, 212, 215-218, 219-220,
     221, 222, 225, 291n.39
Lubitsch, Ernest, 13
Lucie-Smith, Edward, 201-202, 204
Lucky Night, 229
Lysistrata, 114

Macherey, Pierre, 4
Maclaine, Shirley, 209
Magyar Egylet for Hungarian Americans,
   130
Making a Living, 96
Making Movies Black, 7-8
Maland, Charles J., 75
Maltby, Richard, 56-57
Man Who Would be King, The, 210
Manhattan Melodrama, 182, 184, 185-
   187, 190, 192, 193, 228, 230
   ethnics in, 186
Mann, Horace, 91-92
Marc, David, 15

Marey, Edward, 45
Martin, Dean, 136
Marx Brothers, the, 15, 17, 18, 20, 21,
    61, 125, 131-132, 179, 180, 212, 219
    accents of, 137-38
    ad lib in the works of, 143-145, 146
    alien photography in the works of,
        153-159
    and degeneration of ethnic presence in
        the films of, 125-126
    and landsmanshaft, 127, 129, 131, 132,
        133-134, 135, 138, 151, 159,
        171, 237
    and screwball comedy, 126
    and sexuality, 65-66
    doppelgänger in films of, 127-128
    doubling in the works of, 150-153
    ethnic identity of, 130, 137-138
    ghetto/fourth wall in the works of,
        145-150
    MGM films of the, 126, 127
    mirror scene of, 159-161, 162, 163,
        164-165, 166, 168, 169-171
    Paramount films of the, 128
    psychoanalysis offered by, 161
    puns and digression in works of,
        140-143
    satire of the wealthy by, 128, 158
    writers for the, 141
    See also names of individual films and
        performers
Marx, Chico, 132, 133, 134, 142, 169-
    170, 287n.79
    accent of, 138, 139
Marx, Groucho, 19, 132-134, 142, 151-
    152, 167-170, 172
    accent of, 138-139
Marx, Harpo, 19, 134, 142, 146, 151,
    152, 163-164, 167-169
    silence of, 139, 164

Marx, Leo, 23
Marx, Minnie. See Minnie Palmer
Marx, Zeppo, 133, 151
marxism, 15, 20, 23
Mask of Fu Man Chu, 215, 216 fig. 4.9,
    220, 221, 225
masochism, 212-215, 291-292n.47
    dominatrix role in Hollywood, 215
    role of the exotic in, 212-215, 219-220
    three characteristics of, 213-214
Masquerader, The, 94, 98
Mast, Gerald, 13, 17, 75, 99, 114
May, Lary, 3, 42
Mayer, Louis B., 5, 6, 54 fig. 1.7, 55-56,
    179, 180, 185
Mayne, Judith, 235
Mclean, Albert, 65, 68, 69, 73, 75
Meet John Doe, 190
Meller, Raquel, 66
Men in White, 228
Menjou, Adoph, 56 fig. 1.8, 56
Meredith, George, 14
Merman, Ethel, 157
MGM, 125, 126, 127, 184-185, 204, 230
Millward, Jessie, 178
minstrelsy, 38, 65, 66, 70, 81
    and vaudeville, 66
mirror scene. See Duck Soup
mirror stage, 160
    See also mirror scene
Mobsters, 236
Modern Times, 20, 48, 76, 86, 87, 88, 103
    fig. 2.6, 104, 110, 112-113, 114, 115,
    120 fig. 2.7, 121 fig. 2.8, 124, 136
    incarceration in, 118, 119
    role of the Gamin in, 114-115, 117
    transformation of institutions in,
        122-23
    transformation of workplace in,
        115-116, 117, 119, 122-123

See also Chaplin, Charlie
moguls. See film moguls, vaudeville
Monkey Business, 132, 142, 143, 177
Monsieur Verdoux, 81, 94
Moreau, Gustave, 198
Morgan, Helen, 66
Morton, Thomas, 26
Mr. Peabody and the Mermaid, 187
Mrs. Trollope, 30, 37, 45
Mundus Alter et Idem, 26
Murder by Death, 231
Musser, Charles, 12, 13, 16, 17
Mutual Aid Society, 281n.13
Muybridge, Eadweard, 45, 49
My Geisha, 209
My Man Godfrey, 58, 181-182, 183, 184,
    187-188, 234
    and the immigrant myth, 188
My Trip Abroad, 79
My Wonderful Visit, 79

Nation, Carrie, 69
Native American culture, 24, 27, 35, 37
    folklore of, 251nn.7, 8
    and humor, 256n.30
Nazimova, Alla, 201
Neale, Stephen, 15
Nesbit, Evelyn, 66
Nethersole, Olga, 178
Neve, Brian, 11
Never Give a Sucker an Even Break, 127,
    157
Neverending Story, The, 235
New English Canaan, 26
New Jack City, 236
New Janitor, The, 96
New Morals for Old, 209, 226
New York, 183-184
Nichols, Roger L., 57
Night at the Opera, A, 126, 127, 132, 176

Night at the Show, A, 94
Night Flight, 228
Night in Casablanca, A, 127, 132, 177
Nihonjin Kutsuko Domekai. See Japanese
    Americans
Niven, David, 81
Noah's Ark, 206
Normand, Mabel, 82, 83, 273n.30
    See also transformative comedy
Nothing Sacred, 136
Nutty Professor, The, 127

O'Casey, Sean, 91
Odyssey, The, 14, 150
Olivier, Laurence, 81
Olsen and Johnson, 136, 145
omadhawn, 91, 92, 98
One AM, 94, 104
One Night of Love, 154
Ordeal of Civility, The, 4
orient, the, 138
    See also orientalism
orientalism, 197, 206, 220, 225
    and Hollywood's femme fatale, 206
    Deco orientalism, 210-212
Oshana, Mariann, 209-210
Our Gang, 18, 48

paisani. See Italian Americans
Palmer, Minnie, 172-176, 177-178
Panofsky, Irwin, 22
Paramount Studios, 125, 145, 146, 182-
    183, 185
Paramount-Famous Pictures-Lasky, 183,
    184
Pardners, 136
Parker, Dorothy, 141
Parks, Robert, 2
Pastor, Tony, 67, 68, 70
Patterson, Orlando, 3

Pawn Shop, The, 88, 96, 100, 102, 104, 127
Pay Day, 96
Pendleton, Nat, 185
Penthouse, 228
Perelman, S. J., 141, 172
Persona, 169
"The Petrified Man," 36
Philadelphia Story, The, 19
Pitts, Zasu, 19
Plato, 14, 22
Poiret, Paul, 197, 199, 201, 206, 290n.36
Polish Americans, 129
Porter, Edwin S., 12, 13, 55
Porter, Joseph, 56
Powell, William, 20, 21, 61, 181-195,
    224 fig. 4.1
    and his transition to sound film,
        184-185
    as disguised ethnic, 180-181
    divided loyalties in the films of,
        192-195
    ethnic dichotomies in the films of,
        187-188
Powers, Tommy, 139, 140
Princess Caraboo, 209
Prisoner of Zenda, The, 167
Prizefighter and the Lady, The, 228
Proctor, F. F., 67, 68
    See also vaudeville
Property Man, The, 96
Public Enemy, 139
puns. *See* Marx Brothers, the
Puritan culture, 1, 2, 3, 9, 10, 24, 25-26,
    244n.39, 250-251n.6, 252-253n.17,
    253n.20, 256n.30
Pursuits of Happiness, 10

Rabasa, Jose, 23, 252n.12
Ragtime, 236

Rambova, Natacha, 201, 206
Ramsaye, Terry, 42
Rapf, Harry, 15
rapparee, 91, 92, 98
Rear Window, 169
Rebecca, 167
Reflexivity in Film and Literature, 16
Reik, Theodor, 213-214, 218, 219, 225
Reimers, David M., 57
Renoir, Jean, 159
Rhodes, Chip, 39
Rico, 139, 140
Riefenstahl, Leni, 159
Rink, The, 98
Rise of David Levinsky, The, 80
Ritz Brothers, 21, 136
RKO, 204
Rogers, Ginger, 190
Rogers, Will, 157
Roman Scandals, 153
Romantic Melodies, 154, 157
Romola, 183
Rounders, The, 94
Rourke, Constance, 28
Rousseau, 33
Ruby, Harry, 150
Rumann, Sig, 130
Ryskind, Morrie, 141

Sacher-Masoch, Leopold von, 18, 214-
    215, 218-219, 292n.57, 293n.65
    and Hollywood moguls, 218-219
Sacher-Masoch, Wanda von, 215-216,
    218, 292n.54
sadism, 135, 172, 293n.65
Said, Edward, 221
"Salome," 199, 200 fig. 4.3a
Salome, 201
Satan in Sables, 215
Saxton, Alexander, 38

Scarface, (1932), 139, 236

Scarface, (1983), 139, 236

Scarlet Letter, The, (Hawthorne) 32

Scarlet Pimpernel, The, 181

Scarry, Elaine, 18, 107-108, 109, 110-
    111, 279n.85

Schatz, Thomas, 14

Scheff, Fritzi, 66

Schiaparelli, Elsa, 202

Screening out the Past, 3

screwball comedy, 14, 18, 19, 21, 126,
    179, 195, 288n.3

Sedgwick, Eve Kosofsky, 107

Seidman, Steve, 13, 14

Seller, Maxine Schwartz, 64, 172

Selznick, David O., 183, 185

Selznick, Lewis J., 183

Selznick, Myron, 183

Semon, Larry, 48

Sennett, Mack, 47, 48, 49, 55, 82

Sennett, Richard, 60, 171-172

Sennett, Ted, 13, 45

Shadow of a Doubt, 189

Shadow of the Thin Man, 228

Shanghai Express, 204, 209

Shaw, Bernard, 91

She, 214

Shearer, Norma, 138, 180

Sherlock Holmes, 183

Sherlock, Junior, 169

silent comedy. *See* transformative comedy

silent film, 111-112

Silverman, Kaja, 219, 292, 293-294n.65

Singleton, John, 236

Six Companies. *See* Chinese Americans

Sklar, Robert, 96

slapstick comedy, 47-48, 63, 64, 99-100,
    119, 279n.85
    and the body, 104, 106, 107-108, 110,
        111

and torture, 110
    See also transformative comedy

Slavs, 218

Slick, Sam, 31, 32, 258n.41

Slotkin, Richard, 23, 24

Sly, Christopher, 113, 114

Smith, Anthony, 9

Snyder, Frederick, 68

So This is Paris, 209

"The Sotweed Factor," 26-27, 28

Sollors, Werner, 10, 11, 52, 181,
    244n.39, 287-288n.2

Solomon, Barbara Miller, 60-61

Sons of the Desert, 136

Spellbound, 167

Spirit of the Times, 32

Spivak, Gayatri Chakravorty, 226

Spy, The, 32

Squall, The, 215, 218, 222

Stage Door, 146

stage Irishman, 91, 92, 93, 257n.35

Staiger, Janet, 15

Stam, Robert, 16, 237, 248n.67

Stanwyck, Barbara, 191

Staples, Shirley, 65, 72

Star is Born, A, 42, 56, 126

Stein, Gertrude, 49

Stewart, Jimmy, 152, 169

Street of Chance, 183, 184, 185, 228

Student of Prague, The, 167, 194

Studlar, Gaylyn, 214, 215, 219

Suggs, Simon, 32, 36

Sunnyside, 86, 98, 105

Sweet Sweetback's Baadasssss Song,
    237

Swiss Miss, 154

Synge, J. M., 91

Take the Money and Run, 118

tall-tales, 31, 32, 33, 36, 38, 44

Taming of the Shrew, The, (Shakespeare) 113, 177

Taylor, John Russell, 5

team comedy, 18-19, 136-137
    See also names of comedy teams

technology as an emblem in film comedy, 47-49, 99-103, 104

Temple, Shirley, 157, 191

Ten Commandments, The, 209

Test Pilot, 229

Thalberg, Irving, 5, 6, 125, 180

Thief of Bagdad, The, 206, 209

Thin Man, The, 20, 21, 182, 190, 191-196, 223-225, 224 fig. 4.11
    assimilation in, 225
    character actors in, 190-191
    See also The Thin Man films

Thin Man films, The, 184, 189-190, 193, 228, 229-230, 233
    and assimilation, 225-234
    class in, 189-190, 194-195, 225-226, 231-232
    criminals in, 193, 194
    miscegenation in, 230-234
    sexuality in, 194
    See also names of individual films

Thirteen Women, 215, 222, 223

Thompson, Kristen, 14

Three Amigos, 153

Thurber, James, 141

Tilley, Vesta, 66

Tillie's Punctured Romance, 44

Tin Pan Alley, 50

Todd, Thelma, 19, 172, 177

Toland, Greg, 153

Too Many Kisses, 183

Topaze, 209, 222, 225, 226

Torgovnick, Marianna, 26

Torres, Raquel, 177

torture, 107-109, 110-111

    See also Scarry, Elaine

Totheroh, Rollie, 163

Touch of Evil, 209

Trachtenberg, Alan, 8-9, 11, 97

Tracy, Arthur, 157

tramp, the. *See* Chaplin, Charlie

Tramp, The, 20, 86, 93, 94, 97

transcendentalism, 9, 10, 58

transformative comedy, 17, 18, 99
    and the body, 104, 106, 107
    See also slapstick comedy, *and names of individual comedians*

transvestitism, 272n.21, 276n.55

trickster tale, 32, 33, 36
    See also tall tales

Trollope, Mrs., 30, 37, 45

Turner, Frederick Jackson, 23

Turpin, Ben, 45, 48, 99

Twain, Mark, 20, 36, 37

Two Tars, 100

U.S. Steel, 42

Under the Red Robe, 183

Universal Studios, 183

Utopia, 136

Valentino, Rudolph, 201

Van Dyke, William S., 185

variety hall, 65, 72, 266-267n.122
    and sexuality, 65-66

vaudeville, 1, 15, 43, 62, 265-266n.110, 268n.135
    and anxiety about inclusion, 69
    and assimilation, 70
    and comedy genres, 70-71
    and ethnicity, 63, 64, 66-67, 69-70, 70-71
    and gentility, 71-73
    and its moguls, 67, 68, 73, 268n.132
    and its similarities to film, 67-68

and landscape, 69
and sexuality, 65-66
Chinese forms of, 266n.117
high form of, 66-67
Irish acts in, 70-71
orientalization of, 66
the origins of, 63-65
the star system of, 67-68
Venus and Adonis, 215, 218
Venus in Furs, 214-215, 218, 292n.62,
   294n.66
Vesta, Victoria, 67
Von Stroheim, Erich, 99, 180
Von Stuck, Franz, 199

Warner Brothers, The, 151, 154, 157,
   230
Weales, Gerald, 13, 14
Welles, Orson, 77
West, Mae, 67
When Knighthood Was in Flower, 183
White, Stanford, 66
Who Framed Roger Rabbit?, 157
Whoopee, 153, 154
Wife vs. Secretary, 229
Williams, Roger, 25
Williams, Warren, 138
Wilson, Woodrow, 40
Winchell, Walter, 151
Windsor Theatre, 153
Witke, Carl, 105-106
Wizard of Oz, The, 42
Woman in Room 13, The, 220
Woman of the Year, 232
Wong, Anna Mae, 210, 211 fig. 4.8, 212,
   215
Wood, Michael, 11
Work, 96

Yezierska, Anna, 39, 80

Yiddish King Lear, The, 146
Yiddish theater, 64, 144, 146, 153
You Bet Your Life, 151
You Can't Take It With You, 58, 234
You Try Somebody Else, 157

Zeleznick. *See* Selznick
Zukor, Adolph, 183, 219